Shades of Green

The North's Civil War
Andrew L. Slap, series editor

# Shades of Green

## *Irish Regiments, American Soldiers, and Local Communities in the Civil War Era*

Ryan W. Keating

Fordham University Press
New York 2017

Visit us online at www.fordhampress.com.

Library of Congress Cataloging-in-Publication Data

Names: Keating, Ryan W., author.
Title: Shades of green : Irish regiments, American soldiers, and local communities in the Civil War era / Ryan W. Keating.
Description: First edition. | New York : Fordham University Press, 2017. | Series: The North's Civil War | Includes bibliographical references and index.
Identifiers: LCCN 2017003965 | ISBN 9780823276592 (cloth : alkaline paper) | ISBN 9780823276608 (paper : alkaline paper)
Subjects: LCSH: United States—History—Civil War, 1861–1865—Participation, Irish American. | Irish American soldiers—History—19th century. | United States—History—Civil War, 1861–1865—Regimental histories. | Connecticut—History—Civil War, 1861–1865—Regimental histories. | Illinois—History—Civil War, 1861–1865—Regimental histories. | Wisconsin—History—Civil War, 1861–1865—Regimental histories. | United States—History—Civil War, 1861–1865—Social aspects. | Community life—Connecticut—History—19th century. | Community life—Illinois—History—19th century. | Community life—Wisconsin—History—19th century. | BISAC: HISTORY / United States / Civil War Period (1850-1877).
Classification: LCC E540.I6 K43 2017 | DDC 973.7/473—dc23
LC record available at https://lccn.loc.gov/2017003965

Printed in the United States of America

19 18 17 5 4 3 2 1

First edition

For My Parents

# *Contents*


Introduction | 1

1. Illinois and Mulligan's Irish Brigade | 19

2. An Irish Regiment in the Nutmeg State | 43

3. The Formation of the 17th Wisconsin | 68

4. Ethnicity and Combat | 94

5. Disorder and Discipline | 112

6. Connecticut, Illinois, and Wisconsin React to the New York City Draft Riots | 132

7. Patriotism and Sacrifice on the Home Front | 155

8. Wounded Warriors, Public Wards: The Consequences of Military Service | 174

Conclusion. Irish Americans in the Civil War: Myth and Memory | 203

Appendices

A. Nationality of Volunteers by Company | 215

B. Counties of Birth of Irish Volunteers | 223

C. General Courts Martial | 227

*Acknowledgments* *239*

*Notes* *243*

*Bibliography* *287*

*Index* *305*

*Photographs follow page 154*

Shades of Green

# Introduction

In April 1861, newly elected president Abraham Lincoln found himself in a precarious situation. Although he had won the presidency in the November elections, his victory was by no means a mandate from the people for the Republican Party platform. The nation was perilously divided. Winning less than half the popular vote in 1860, the tall, gaunt lawyer from Illinois looked on as his nation teetered on the brink of civil war. To keep the nation together, the new commander in chief drew support from a rather tenuous alliance of political rivals openly divided in their opinions about the actions of their southern brethren. The attack on Fort Sumter in Charleston, South Carolina, however, galvanized public opinion throughout the north and fostered, at least momentarily, a powerful wartime alliance between Republicans and Democrats that allowed Lincoln to carry out a war to preserve the Union. As Federal troops lowered the Stars and Stripes in surrender from the ramparts of the bastion in Charleston Harbor, banners were hoisted in towns and cities across the North as men of all ages, ethnicities, classes, and backgrounds rushed to the defense of their flag and their nation.

The Irish in America, both foreign and native born, joined in a vocal chorus of support for the Lincoln administration and backed their words with physical displays of fealty, as thousands of volunteers came forward to defend the Union. Many of these men, representatives of both their homeland and their local communities, sacrificed themselves in defense of the Union. Their gallantry on the battlefield, furthermore, reinforced perceptions of the patriotism and loyalty of these adopted citizens of the United States. Although visible Irish enclaves in cities such as New York, Boston, and Philadelphia have traditionally dominated the story of Irish participation in the Civil War, the experiences of soldiers and civilians living in those cities provide only one part of the nuanced tale of immigrant soldiers and their communities who supported the Union during the four years of bloody sectional conflict. Individually and in groups, ethnic recruits flocked to the Federal ranks from towns and cities across the North. For the Irish from Connecticut, Illinois, and Wisconsin who formed ethnic units and marched to war to defend their adopted nation, their service and sacrifice helped define the ethnic experience, both locally and nationally, in the Civil War. Furthermore, they stand as examples of the similarities and differences within the experiences of immigrants in the United States during the nineteenth century in terms of settlement patterns, assimilation, and access to opportunity and advancement within the regions in which they settled.

So great was the response of Irish Americans to Lincoln's call for troops in 1861 and afterwards that most Northern states fielded at least one self-professed "Irish regiment" whose volunteers marched to war proudly displaying banners that attested to both their Irish and American loyalties. Nationally, the most prominent Irish regiment that organized in 1861 was the 69th New York commanded by immigrant and Irish nationalist Michael Corcoran. The volunteers from New York, representatives of America's largest ethnic enclave, captivated a Northern public already enamored by war. After the First Battle of Bull Run, with Corcoran held as a prisoner of war in Richmond, another outspoken Irish nationalist, Thomas Francis Meagher, assumed command of the 69th New York and undertook the organization of the "Irish Brigade," which was composed of three Irish regiments (though ultimately five were rotated through this unit over the course of the war) and was attached to the Army of the Potomac.

The Irish Brigade has assumed an unmatched place within the memory of Irish service in the Civil War, and the men who fought under Meagher earned fame for their tenacity under fire in some of the fiercest fighting in the war. These Irishmen held the Federal line at Malvern Hill in July 1862 and charged, time and again, the Confederate position in the Sunken Road at Antietam on that bloody autumn day two months later. At Fredericksburg they surged across a mile of open field, their lines finally cresting as withering fire broke their charge; their ranks were decimated. They stood strong at the Wheatfield on the second day of the fight at Gettysburg and fought ferociously with Grant on the Overland Campaign. Over the course of the war only three Federal units sustained higher causality rates than did the Irish Brigade, and the sacrifice of the men in this unit played a vital role in the legacy and memorialization of ethnic participation in the Civil War. The high visibility of the service of these immigrant soldiers reaffirmed—if only momentarily, for the postwar era was marked by the revival of nativism—the loyalty of these men to the Union and carved out a place for these adopted citizens within American society.[1]

In 1863 a newspaper editor in Dublin, Ireland claimed that "the Civil War, has given us back our military reputation in its pristine luster. . . . The valour and the self sacrifice of the Irishmen who strove and fell so heroically before the batteries of Fredericksburg, and in a hundred other fights of the war, have scattered to the winds the malignant calumnies of traitors and open foes, and made manifest to the world the might of Irish prowess." No truer words were spoken, and notable here is the broader view of the war as seen from across the Atlantic, for although the Irish Brigade became the symbol of the Irish contribution, those in Ireland recognized that this unit was only one part of the ethnic war effort. This book looks at some of those other Irishmen and their comrades: volunteers from Connecticut, Illinois, and Wisconsin who organized Irish regiments and marched to war in defense of their adopted homeland. The Civil War affected these men and their families in vital ways, defining and reaffirming their place within their communities while simultaneously serving as the platform upon which their dual loyalties to Ireland and American could be expressed. Their stories illustrate the many shades of green through which these men and their families saw their place within American society during the Civil War era.[2]

Nineteenth-century Irish Americans were bound, by varying degrees, to a shared diasporic identity that was merely reinforced by military service between 1861 and 1865. Constructed around common themes of exile and exclusion, this identity was, in part, reinforced by shared religion, national fraternal and military organizations, a strong sentimental attachment to Ireland, and an American public that all too often cast immigrants in broad ethnic and stereotypical terms. The result was the creation of a multigenerational, distinctive group of hyphenated-American men and women capable of professing both their American and their Irish identity when necessary, and especially on important holidays such as St. Patrick's Day. Present during these occasions is an inclusive sense of ethnic pride and heritage that draws together disparate groups connected only by the fact that someone in their family fled Ireland for the relative safety of America's shores at some point in time. The Irish have been an integral part of the American experience; in 2012, the U.S. Census Bureau released the statistic that over 10 percent of the total population, or more than 34 million Americans, claimed Irish heritage, an astounding number considering that Ireland itself has a population of just slightly more than 4.5 million.

The experiences of Irish immigrants and their children in the nineteenth century have an intrinsic emotional appeal. Fleeing tyrannical rule and the social and economic devastation of the Potato Famine, exiled Irish men and women crowded into America's cities, where they struggled for survival in the nearly impossible conditions found in the nation's urban slums. Compounding the economic crisis that many of these desperately poor Irish immigrants faced was the social stigma and xenophobia that seemed to follow them wherever they settled. Their Catholicism (in particular, their alleged allegiance to the Pope), a cultural predilection for alcohol, their seemingly blind commitment to the political machines of the Democratic Party, and the general instability of nineteenth-century urban centers (often attributed to the Irish presence) combined to arouse the open animosity of American nativists. In the late twentieth century, study of this nineteenth-century nativist view of the immigrant Irish gave rise to the controversial argument that within a racially divided antebellum society, the Irish were not viewed as "white." The emergence of the discipline of whiteness studies has further contributed to the already compelling narrative of the rise of Irish America and has served to better explain the marginalization of Irish immigrants in the United States during this period. The narrative of alienation indicates just how bad the situation was for some immigrants during the nineteenth century and, consequently, just how far these men and women have come in their assimilation as Americans.[3]

Alienated by their religion, socioeconomic condition, politics, and cultural proclivities from Americans who considered themselves "native," Irish Catholics held a tenuous place within American society throughout this period. Tensions grew in the 1840s as the Potato Famine in Ireland forced hundreds of thousands to flee their homeland for refuge in the United States, though they often ended up in notorious slums in Eastern cities such as New York, Boston, and Philadelphia. Native-born Americans viewed these Irish Catholic refugees with apprehension. Crowded into urban slums, they personified the social and economic destabilization and chaos that came with the rapid industrialization occurring at mid-century. The Irish, because of their cultural proclivities and their allegiance to the Pope, made true assimilation and loyalty to the United States virtually impossible, it was said. For men who were termed "voting cattle" by their critics, the Civil War offered an opportunity to prove their worth to their adopted nation.[4]

Despite these tensions and animosities, the United States was the preferred destination for Irish emigrants, who were drawn in not only by the political and social freedoms guaranteed by the Constitution but also by the availability of work. America's laissez-faire attitude toward immigration yielded an open-door policy for most of the century, and the Famine helped to create a strong emotional attachment between the sons and daughters of Erin and the United States. As an adopted homeland for the fleeing masses of starving Irishmen and

Irishwomen, America offered salvation of the "Irish race." Some, such as Irish nationalist Daniel W. Cahill, championed the sanctuary the United States offered. America, he claimed, was "the country where the broken heart of Ireland is bound for, her daughters protected, her sons adopted: where conscience is free, where religion is not hypocrisy, where liberty is a reality, and where the Gospel is a holy profession of Divine love, and not a profligate trade of national vengeance." In one of a number of "Letters from America" addressed to his countrymen, he further encouraged them leave Ireland with the claim that "no man of any trade or class can want employment in the United States of America if he be a good workman and have good conduct."[5]

Not all felt this way. For many, the realities of immigrant life contradicted Cahill's romanticized views of the land of plenty. The Irish American newspaper *Phoenix* that reprinted Cahill's letter ran in the same issue an editorial reflecting on the recent collapse and burning of a cloth mill in Lawrence, Massachusetts and the many Irish names on the lists of those killed and wounded. "Thus do the exiled Irish suffer," noted its writer. "Scattered over the earth, they are the victims of accident, the slaves of capital, the bondsmen of adverse circumstances, mated with poverty and hardship, and toil to make wealth for the heedless stranger." Another letter to the editor from "An Irishman" openly responded to the piece by Cahill; "could my feeble words be heard in Ireland," he wrote, "I would advise all Irishmen to stay in the land of their birth, and try to earn an honest living, no matter what capacity, rather than come to America where they are in many places looked upon with contempt." Such opposing perspectives defined the Irish experience at mid-century and made the Irish response to the outbreak of war all the more compelling. Widespread acceptance, Daniel Cahill suggested, could intimate that these ethnic soldiers saw a vested interest in the preservation of their adopted homeland and enlisted to keep it safe. A disconnect might indicate, perhaps, that these men had something far greater to prove through their willing defense of their adopted homeland—trading blood sacrifice for broad acceptance into American society.[6]

But arrival in the United States did not necessarily mean that recent immigrants eagerly sought to assimilate. Perhaps the most visible evidence of the continued bonds connecting immigrants to Ireland was the growth of Irish nationalist organizations in America's cities. Most vocal in their loyalties to Ireland were the Fenians. These men were radical nationalists who attempted to cultivate followers willing to sacrifice their lives for an independent Ireland. They recognized that Ireland, in desperate need of salvation, had nowhere to turn save to her exiled sons in the United States. By "dying for Ireland," the

Dublin Fenian newspaper *Irish People* claimed, "each falling generation bequeaths to its successor the same sacred cause and heroic spirit, and the fresh generation does battle for the hallowed trust with the souls of men who nobly love their land."[7]

From a national political perspective, Irish Americans came under attack during the decades before the war as nativists groups, led by the American Party, sought to limit the political influence of the poverty-ridden Catholic masses who flooded into the North during the 1840s and 1850s. So prominent was the anti-Irish rhetoric that it created a shared memory of exclusion that this ethnic group was unable to overcome until the mid-twentieth century. The extent to which nativists were successful in enforcing the physical alienation of recent immigrants is unclear, but the public discourse in Connecticut, Wisconsin, and Illinois is striking for its passionate attacks on Irish immigrants; it mirrored sentiment directed at larger and more visible ethnic enclaves in cities such as New York, Philadelphia, and Boston.[8]

Nativism reflected fears of foreign influence, in particular that of the Pope in Rome, as well as evangelical Protestant perceptions of growing instability within American society, and concern over the radicalism of foreigners and their influence on American politics. The massive influx of Irish immigrants coincided with the religious revivals known as the Second Great Awakening, which created a sense of urgency among many Protestant Americans. The revivalism of the mid-nineteenth-century stressed, among other things, "the moral content of education, liquor licensing and prohibition, Sabbath closing and the suppression of popular 'lewd and tumultuous' conduct," and reform was "urgently needed by the new industrialists, to be sure, for it promised them a disciplined labor force, pacing its toil and its very life cycle to the requirements of the machine and the clock, respectful of property and orderly in its demeanor." The platform of the American Party, more commonly known as the Know-Nothings, reinforced fears of foreign influence as it sought to limit government positions to "those only who do not hold civil allegiance, directly or indirectly, to any foreign power, whether civil or ecclesiastical." In many regards, then, the outbreak of war and the rapid organization of ethnic regiments in April 1861 forced Northerners to directly confront questions of loyalty that had undercut social relationships between immigrants and their American neighbors for some time.[9]

Irish Catholics were always a part of the immigrant population in the United States, and animosity between Catholics and Protestants occasionally boiled over, most notably in Philadelphia in 1844 when riots broke out in the neighborhood of Kensington over the use of the Bible in public schools. By mid-century, the Catholic Church, led by Archbishop John Hughes, "began to assert itself with unprecedented militancy," and became an important social and political force in the North while also serving as the major support network for recent immigrants. Ultimately, though, it was a fungus that had the greatest impact on the visibility of this ethnic group within American society. Its arrival in 1845 must have been terrifying. One can imagine a young child, waking early to feed their family's livestock, only to find the potatoes—the food source for millions of Irishmen and women and their livestock—had turned black. Screams must have sounded out across the Irish countryside. Or perhaps it was a more subtle collective moan as countless men and women, toiling on small plots of land, realized the true implications of the potato blight—their primary source of sustenance, their one connection to the English market economy, their hopes of survival, rotting before their very eyes. The blight, brought to Ireland, ironically, in the holds of ships from North America and able to flourish in the damp clime of that island nation, wreaked havoc on Ireland's already shaky economy. Subsequent crop failures in1846, 1847, and 1848 left the Irish people reeling. It is estimated that as many as two million men, women, and children died and another two million fled their homeland for destinations abroad. Ireland's population, which stood at nearly 8 million in 1845, was reduced by nearly half by mid-century.[10]

The failure of the potato crop marked the culmination of nearly thirty years of deindustrialization and the transition of a large part of the Irish population to subsistence farming. This ultimately cast most Irishmen and women apart from the English market economy and isolated them economically. The decline of British demand for Irish agricultural products in the wake of the Napoleonic Wars and the removal of custom barriers between Ireland and England in 1825 marked the start of economic turmoil that was only compounded and intensified by the Famine. Population growth, a consequence of the economic prosperity of the late eighteenth century, spurred an increased reliance on the potato, a crop that could sustain large families on small plots of land. Subdivision of estate lands under notorious "middlemen" or middling tenants, and the growing practice of tenancy at will, which allowed a landlord to break a lease at any time, created a tenuous social and economic situation in Ireland by the middle of the 1830s. The situation was so dire that nearly 30 percent of the population of Ireland, approximately 2,385,000 people, were in need of some form of public assistance for thirty weeks of the year during that decade. These numbers, which illustrate the dire economic circumstances many Irish faced even before the potato crop failed in 1845, increased exponentially at the height of the famine.[11]

In Ireland Catholics also faced widespread legal persecution due to their religion. Restrictions on land and property ownership as well as limitations on basic freedoms of religion and political participation, legalized through Penal Codes first passed in 1691 and established to "prevent the further growth of popery," resulted in the decline of Catholic land ownership, so that by 1750 a mere 5 percent of all Irish land was owned by Catholics. Despite the emergence of a small merchant class, the vast majority of the Irish were "segregated from the rest of society and the normal process of law," relegating these men and women to a subclass, unable, among other things, to own land, to vote, or to own weapons. Thus began a form of English quasi-control over the Irish nation, which was formalized in 1801 when the Irish Parliament was absorbed into the English Parliament under the Act of Union, which legally and politically incorporated Ireland into Great Britain.[12]

The impact of this long economic decline on the Irish population could be seen in the nineteenth century in the streets of America's cities, as poor and unskilled men and women crowded by the thousands into dirty tenements, eking out a living in unimaginable squalor. When they arrived in North America, these exiled Irishmen had hope of escaping not only the desperate economic conditions in their homeland but the political inequities there as well. The future of Ireland, some Irish American nationalists believed, rested in the continued health of the American republic, an attitude that created an immediate and strong bond between these immigrants and their adopted nation. This outlook would also become a significant component of the rhetoric of ethnic recruiting during the Civil War. But for many, sheer survival was their first concern. The numbers, at least for New York City, which held the largest ethnic enclave, speak to the destitution of recent arrivals. The Irish made up nearly one quarter of the population of that city of approximately 800,000 in 1860, and nearly 70 percent of Irish men were employed as unskilled laborers. Of the generation that arrived in New York during the famine (1845–1852), three-quarters were classified as laborers or servants. The remainder identified as artisans (12 percent), farmers (9.5 percent) and businessmen (2 percent). Between 1851 and 1855 the proportion of unskilled workers rose. Men and women who identified themselves as laborers or servants constituted between 79 percent and 90 percent of all arriving passengers, while there was a simultaneous decline of those working in other professions. Furthermore, approximately 90 percent of the 1.5 million men and women who arrived in the United States during this period were Roman Catholic, adding considerably to the strength and visibility of this already embattled religious group, and contributing to the growing concern among nativists.[13]

Poverty prevented many of these men and women from undertaking a journey away from their ports of arrival, and a majority ultimately settled in urban areas where they were "concentrated in the lowest-paid, least-skilled, and most dangerous and insecure employment; [and] with few exceptions, they also displayed the highest rates of transience, residential density and segregation, inadequate housing and sanitation, commitments to prisons and charity institutions, and excess mortality." Rising land prices in the West and declining opportunities for artisans only compounded the Irish plight by limiting opportunity elsewhere. In neighborhoods such as Five Points in Manhattan, immigrants clustered in wooden tenements "far less comfortable than buildings used as *barns* or cattle-stalls," with an "atmosphere productive of the most offensive and malignant diseases." Press reports, such as those appearing in *Harpers Weekly,* called these buildings the "crazy pigeon-holes of the Five Points," and described how "every inch . . . is covered by structures of various kinds and degrees of discomfort, into which is crowded the reeking, seething mass of poverty, vice, sickness, and wretchedness." The focus of significant public attention, this neighborhood appeared to many as conclusive proof of the Irish propensity for violence, alcoholism, and disorder—issues that would only be compounded during the Civil War.[14]

But the New York Irish were not alone in their struggles. In Boston, in 1847 alone, some 37,000 Irish arrived, leading one observer to note that "Suffolk County had become a 'New England County Cork,' and the city of Boston . . . turned into 'the Dublin of America.'" Although cities such as New York and Philadelphia offered immigrants an opportunity to settle among diverse ethnic groups, the Massachusetts tradition of social and cultural exclusivity, which dated back to the colonial period and could be felt particularly in Boston, "meant that the social antagonisms were not easily diverted, diffused, and blurred. It was all too easy to keep one's hostilities in focus on a single target." Bostonians, in the wake of this massive influx of foreigners, "were appalled at the unsanitary living conditions . . . and complained they were turning Massachusetts into a 'moral cesspool.'" Men and women, fond of alcohol and "living in 'filth and wretchedness,' all crowded together in 'foul and confined apartments,'" created considerable tension and led to the rise of xenophobia, which reached a head in 1855 when nativists succeeded in wresting control of local and state governments.[15]

These issues made the immigrant question a significant concern during the years leading up to the Civil War. Democrats and Whigs debated the threat of the immigrant influx throughout the 1840s and 1850s, and their newspapers provide insight into broad opinions on the topic. "THE CHILDREN OF BIGGOTTED, CATHOLIC IRELAND, like the FROGS which were sent out as a plague against the Pharaoh have come into our houses, bed-chambers, and ovens and kneading-troughs," the *Ohio Statesmen* lamented in 1843. The "IRISH, when they arrive among us, TOO IDLE AND VICIOUS to clear and cultivate the land and earn a comfortable home, DUMP THEMSELVES DOWN in our large villages and towns, crowding the meaner sort of tenements and filling them with WRETCHEDNESS, FILTH and DISEASE. In a political point of view, WHAT ARE THEY BUT MERE MARKEATABLE CATTLE!" Although time and again Democrats rose to defend their Irish constituencies, the attitudes of Whigs and Know-Nothings—whose parties were both absorbed into the Republican Party—illustrate the challenges that faced the Irish when the Civil War broke out in 1861.[16]

In the 1860 election, Irish America largely supported the Democratic Party, and although politicians, newspapermen, and civic leaders hotly debated the role of immigrants in the potential sectional conflict in the months leading up to the outbreak of hostilities, by mid-April "the ambivalence of many Irish Americans in the North melted, and sympathy for the South crumbled." Any concerns surrounding Irish disloyalty were quickly put to rest as Irish Americans across the North rushed to answer the president's call for troops. For these men, like most other northerners in the months following the fall of Fort Sumter, the sanctity of the Union was the primary concern and motivation for enlistment. The zeal with which the Irish flocked to the defense of the flag reflected their commitment to the Union, the Constitution, and the republic.[17]

Despite the fact that their patriotism momentarily quelled questions of loyalty, these immigrants remained conscious of their tenuous place in the United States and continually sought to display their patriotism and loyalty to the Federal government over the course of the war. Though often at odds over policy, the men who volunteered to serve in the Irish units that were organized in Connecticut, Illinois, and Wisconsin and the communities that supported them did not openly waiver in the outward support of the broader war effort that they first displayed in April 1861. They became increasingly outspoken in their support as their ethnic regiments proved themselves on the battlefield early in the war, and the willingness of Irish Americans to sacrifice themselves in defense of their adopted nation spurred on ethnic recruiting in all three states.

For all of the debate that surrounded Irish Catholic loyalty during the antebellum period, these adopted citizens did not shy from the fight. Irish Americans flocked to the defense of the Union with enthusiasm equal to that of their native-born friends and neighbors. Over 150,000 Irish-born men volunteered to serve in Union armies, representing approximately 10 percent of the total number of Irish immigrants living in the North when the war broke out in 1861. Although most of these men served in ethnically mixed regiments, an overwhelming proportion of the attention, both during the war and after, has focused upon the distinctly Irish units that were organized in many cities throughout the North. Led by notable Irishmen such as Michael Corcoran, James Mulligan, and Thomas Francis Meagher, these units marched to war behind emerald green banners displaying Irish national symbols and accompanied by bands playing traditional Irish melodies. It must have been an awesome sight as thousands of exiled Irishmen, many of whom had retained strong attachments, sentimental and otherwise, to the land of their birth, marched to war in the blue uniforms of their adopted homeland. As casualties cut apart the Irish Brigade in the Army of the Potomac, however, Irish support for the war seemingly shifted; antiwar sentiment ostensibly reached its zenith in July of 1863, when draft riots rocked New York City. Despite the fact that this event was hardly emblematic of the sentiments of Irish Americans, broadly, the New York City Draft Riots nevertheless became symbolic of lingering questions surrounding Irish loyalty to the United States.[18]

Almost immediately after the war, Irish Americans fought to preserve their place within the historical narrative. The revival of nativism in the postwar period made such efforts vital to ethnic interests, as a renewed focus on Irish American disloyalty and support for the antiwar Copperhead movement overshadowed the loyalty and sacrifice of the men who had fought and died in defense of the Union. Regimental histories published in the years after the war, both those focused on ethnic and on non-ethnic units, provide useful accounts of the war resulting from the juxtaposition of the author's personal views and agendas with a broader narrative of historical events, even if at times such accounts may overemphasize the unit's heroism. Beginning with Daniel Conyngham's early history of the Irish Brigade (1867), all such accounts of Irish American service sought to preserve within the historical record the patriotism—American patriotism *and* Irish patriotism—of these Union volunteers. Steeped in ethnic language, these accounts nevertheless stress the notions of patriotic sacrifice for the Union and appear as overt attempts to both preserve the war record of these units and to counter the growing power of postwar nativism. As historian Craig

Warren suggests, these unit histories represent a refusal by Irish American leaders "to let history dismiss as meaningless the Irish blood spilled at Fredericksburg," and the resulting literature was "remarkable for its propensity to mythologize Irish participation in the Civil War, North and South."[19]

The legacy of the Irish in the Civil War has persisted and become an important component of Civil War history, myth, and legend. One need only look at representations of Irish soldiers in American cinema—in films such as *Glory* and *Gettysburg*, with their characterizations of gruff Irish drill sergeants, and *Gods and Generals*, which portrays the Irish Brigade's famous charge at Fredericksburg—to see how the public has remembered and revered these men and their contribution to the war effort. The strength of the Irish American community in the United States has reinforced and cultivated this memory. Irish American service was, however, much more complex than is widely realized.

For all the attention that Irish regiments received during and after the war, the first major analysis of the Civil War soldier, Bell Wiley's *The Life of Billy Yank* (1952), does not contain any in-depth analysis of the impact or experiences of ethnic soldiers. While Wiley notes an Irish presence among the ranks of Union soldiers, ethnicity typically appears as a descriptive tool—a methodological decision that continues to appear time and again in current literature as a means of identifying soldiers, without any significant commentary on what that ethnic background denotes. In 1954 the first full-length study of ethnic participation in the Civil War was published. Ella Lonn's *Foreigners in the Union Army and Navy* is an impressive attempt to identify both the experiences of ethnic soldiers and their motivations as part of the larger war effort. As a narrative of ethnic service, Lonn's work provides an excellent overview of the role of immigrants in the war, and her historiographical statistics are still cited in studies of ethnic soldiers. Nevertheless, her work leaves many important historical questions unanswered, especially those regarding the motivations and experiences of Irish soldiers and civilians during the war.

No major studies of the Irish in the Civil War were published for more than forty years after the appearance of *Foreigners in the Union Army and Navy*. In 1998 William Burton's *Melting Pot Soldiers: The Union's Ethnic Regiments* offered the first comprehensive historical analysis of the motivations behind ethnic enlistments during the war. Burton's argument for the assimilatory nature of military service ignited an important debate surrounding minority military service. In particular, the suggestion that immigrants experienced the war in unique ways—tied to both their place within nineteenth-century American society and their understanding of what loyal sacrifice could do for the broader immigrant community—marked a vital contribution to our understanding of the social impact of the Civil War and military service. Since the publication of Burton's work, historians such as Susannah Ural Bruce, Christian Samito, Martin Öfele, and David Gleeson have continued and expanded the debate surrounding Irish motivations and the consequences of military service. Considering their work as a whole, these scholars have done an excellent job of explaining the nuances of the Irish experience within the broader themes of loyalty, patriotism, and the place of immigrants and their communities in nineteenth-century America. Their contributions have defined the contemporary field of ethnic Civil War studies, and without their work this project would have been impossible, for they have laid an impressive groundwork.[20]

This book continues and broadens the discussion of Irish American service in the Civil War. William Burton notes in his prologue to *Melting Pot Soldiers* that at the outbreak of the Civil War, "the ethnic scene in America was extraordinarily complex"—a rather simple statement at first glance, but more recent work on the Irish has shown just how perceptive Burton was.[21] The deeper historians dig into the lives of Irish Americans at mid-century, the clearer it becomes that a conclusive narrative of ethnic service is difficult, if not impossible, to reach. The multifaceted and often contradictory nature of ethnic motivations—in particular, the fact that soldiers' identities were fluid, often changing or adapting to different situations and different environments—is evident in the historiography. Consequently, there is a need for further analysis of Irish soldiers and their communities during this period.

*Shades of Green* moves the historical debate away from the motivations and sentiment of "Irish America"—the idea of a cohesive national entity with common experiences and attitudes—and toward "Irish Americas," a view of men and women connected to both local and national communities. Such an approach allows us to better understand how these adopted citizens, their comrades in arms, and their friends and neighbors experienced the Civil War era. I attempt to illustrate their worlds from three perspectives. First, I discuss the experiences of three regiments, the Ninth Connecticut, 23rd Illinois, and 17th Wisconsin. As self-proclaimed Irish units, these regiments claimed to represent the immigrant communities in each state. They were, however, not totally Irish. Thus a further point of analysis involves the study of the individual soldiers of these regiments, both Irish-born and not; and while this work focuses primarily on Irish volunteers, it is vital to understand the ethnic composition of these regiments in order to see the similarities and differences among soldiers' experiences. Finally, this study traces experiences on the home front, analyzing Irish Americans as part of, rather than disconnected from, their local communities in Connecticut, Illinois, and Wisconsin, as a means of understanding the intersection of military and civilian life during the war.

Ultimately, although there were similarities in experiences across the North, there is no one simple narrative with which to describe ethnic service in the Civil War. Motivations, loyalties, expressions of patriotism, and political identity were nuanced and shifting. Irish recruiters in Connecticut, Illinois, and Wisconsin made clear the broader goals that minority military service represented: staunch commitment to the Union and the republican experiment that simultaneously helped subvert nativism. First and foremost these regiments represented immigrant loyalty to and inclusion within the United States, but for many soldiers they also stood as a reflection of a transatlantic republican identity that bound the men to both their home nation and their host nation—for the preservation of republicanism in America was vital to the spread of this ideology abroad. Yet in the formation of these regiments we find a collision of ethnic and American nationalism. The men who joined them did so for innumerable, and often unrecorded, reasons. Men and women on the home front professed an array of loyalties and expectations that in some instances matched the broader political rhetoric of the time, ethnic and national, and in other instances reflected unique local experiences.

Certainly these local communities were not isolated. They were, in fact, intimately connected to other Irish communities scattered throughout the United States at mid-century. Men and women in New England, the central Midwest, and the upper Midwest were aware of broader issues concerning their countrymen throughout the nation. Irish affairs, broadly, were discussed on the pages of ethnic newspapers such as the *Irish American* and the *Phoenix*, and issues confronting immigrants were discussed on the pages of local and national nonethnic newspapers. When war broke out, these communities were engaged in both local and national discussions regarding the crisis of the Union and looked to the successes of their comrades as justification for their own service and commitment to their adopted nation. Although national politics and the nationwide war ran as an undercurrent of experience for soldiers and civilians from Connecticut, Illinois, and Wisconsin, these men and women were also intimately attuned to and involved in their local communities. These communities were, in fact, as important or more important to daily life for these immigrants than the broader national issues confronting their immigrant group. This is most notable in the discussions surrounding regimental organization, in which leaders professed strong attachments to local, national, and ethnic communities as a means of justifying the creation of Irish regiments in their respective states. This shift in perspective does, however, make it difficult to fit Irish regiments, ethnic soldiers, and local communities into a specific and singular "ethnic" narrative. Rather, close analysis reveals just how complex motivations, identities, loyalties, patriotism, and military service were during the nineteenth century.

The reframing of the Irish experience at war is by no means unique; it is part of a vibrant movement within the broader field of Civil War history to better understand the impacts of the war on local communities and individual soldiers. Recent studies focusing on soldiers and communities expound upon the intersection of national issues and local communities, soldiers, and civilians. Creating a sense of balance within the historiography of the Civil War, this scholarship helps identify the ways in which individuals experienced the war and contributes significantly to our understanding of, among other things, patriotism, loyalty, identity, manhood, and nationalism in nineteenth-century America.[22] In line with this focus, *Shades of Green* argues that comparative analysis of Irish regiments and their communities will begin a conversation that focuses on diverse ethnic experiences in the Civil War and allows us to better contextualize the various ways that Irish-born and American-born men and women of Irish descent understood their place in nineteenth-century America.

I began this study with a simple set of questions: What did it actually mean to be an "Irish" regiment? What, if any, were the similarities between Irish regiments that organized in different Northern states? How did individual communities, whose men served in these regiments, experience the war? Who were the men who fought and how did their service reflect the immigrant experience, locally and nationally? And, finally, how did the soldiers, civilians, and veterans experience and understand their place in American society before, during, and after the war? The regiments in this study, the Ninth Connecticut, 17th Wisconsin, and 23rd Illinois, were chosen because, first and foremost, all three openly identified themselves as ethnically Irish units. The men who organized these regiments made very public their ethnic affiliations and, seemingly, the volunteers chose to join the unit in part because of this shared identity. All three marched to war surrounded by visible displays of ethnonationalism and throughout the conflict were referred to at home in ethnic terms (though ethnicity became less and less important as the war progressed). Furthermore, none were part of the Irish Brigade or the Army of the Potomac, meaning that the experiences of soldiers in these regiments will complement and expand our existing knowledge of the ways that immigrants negotiated wartime and postwar America. Geography was also a factor when it came to choosing regiments for, like their countrymen in larger East Coast cities, Irish and Irish Americans in Connecticut, Illinois, and Wisconsin joined both ethnic and mixed regiments and dedicated the next four years of their lives to the salvation of the Union. Expanding the analysis of ethnic service to include men from outlying states and smaller cities broadens the discussion and provides insight into the lives of Irish men and women who lived outside of the major cities on the East Coast.

The most important component of the research for this book, and what distinguishes this project from others in the field, was my systematic attempt to identify the soldiers—all the soldiers—who served in these three regiments. Containing 5,029 men, the database of soldiers from these regiments that I developed for this project is the most accurate compilation possible. This statistical work represents the first systematic analysis of men who served in Irish regiments, and it opened a host of problems that subsequently affected and complicated the project. Foremost among these was the ethnic diversity within these regiments. Irish-born men comprised the majority in the Ninth Connecticut alone. The men who joined Irish regiments in Illinois and Wisconsin were mostly native-born, at least when one looks simply at the place of birth provided by these volunteers. But these regiments also contained men of many other ethnic backgrounds. While the regiments chosen for study labeled themselves Irish, the evidence of ethnic diversity at company and regimental level complicates the narrative. While we can begin to describe the experiences of Irishmen who joined in defense of the Union, these experiences were often intertwined with, and indistinguishable from, those of soldiers born in other places. While ethnic ties were often vital to regimental formation and public identity, the ethnic diversity within these units points to the importance of local American communities and local interactions. Thus, while this is, first and foremost, a study of Irish regiments and Irish soldiers in the Civil War era, one must keep in mind that Irish units were unique manifestations of their local communities, and the organization of Irish units in Connecticut, Illinois, and Wisconsin illuminates the duality of immigrant life at mid-century. Influenced to a degree by ethnic solidarity, soldiers in these regiments were also bound, politically, socially, and economically, to their local communities, and they adapted their identities to meet the constantly changing wartime environment.[23]

*Shades of Green* is a study of three Irish regiments and the men who filled their ranks. The stories of these volunteers, who were driven to war to fight under the dual auspices of Irish and American identity, unfold within the pages of muster and descriptive rolls, census sheets, courts martial files, pension records, and in local newspapers. As a social history the book seeks to uncover the lives and experiences of men and women who have been all but lost to the larger historical narrative of the Civil War, for most of these soldiers left no written account of their years at war, and their contributions as Union volunteers have been largely forgotten, memorialized only indirectly in more general postwar accounts of Irish American service and sacrifice. Despite the fact that for the past 150 years the records of these regiments lay in relative obscurity, the sacrifice of the men who made up the ranks nevertheless provides important insight into the array of experiences those Irish soldiers and their communities faced during the war and broadens our understanding of the roles, ideologies, and experiences of ethnic soldiers in America's greatest conflict. Their stories show that the lens of ethnicity through which the service of Irish regiments and Irish communities has typically been viewed shrouded the lives of these men in shades of green that must be stripped bare in order to understand more fully their roles in this pivotal period in American history.

# 1 Illinois and Mulligan's Irish Brigade

The Irish American experience—a least, the ways in which men and women navigated socioeconomic spaces in America's towns and cities—was incredibly diverse, much more so than the stereotypical portrait so often sketched by mid-century nativists. Although a greater proportion of Irish men from communities in this study were employed as unskilled than as skilled laborers, neither the depressing statistics concerning the New York City labor force nor the oppressive ghettoization that occurred there and in cities such as Boston and Philadelphia appears to have been replicated in towns in Connecticut, Illinois, and Wisconsin. When the Irish went to war in 1861 they did so with the hope that military service would help to dispel once and for all the negative stereotypes of Irish Americans. But more importantly, when these men volunteered to defend the Union, they did so as men not cast apart from mainstream American society, but as full economic participants in a vibrant Northern society.

On the eve of the Civil War, Illinois was home to a large and vibrant Irish immigrant population who found, in the Midwest, a liberal society that provided greater social, political, and economic opportunities than were available to their countrymen in large eastern cities. Although the influx of famine immigrants to Chicago, the state's largest city, sparked some concern among nativist circles, in smaller cities throughout the state Irishmen and women found homes within burgeoning communities that appeared to welcome, or at least to tolerate, their arrival. The outbreak of war, however, brought with it questions about Irish loyalty, as men and women in Illinois wondered whether this largely Democratic voting bloc would support Lincoln's war to preserve the Union. Bucking those concerns, these immigrants raised their voices in a resounding chorus of patriotism as they rushed to join military units organizing throughout the state. For a time their acts dispelled lingering questions regarding the Irish commitment to the Union cause. The sacrifice they made in defense of the nation served, at least momentarily, as proof of the fealty of these men to the United States and solidified their place in their adopted homeland.

Although Irish volunteers joined a number of regiments that formed during the first months of the war, it was the organization of the 23rd Illinois, James Mulligan's "Irish Brigade," that symbolized ethnic service both in Illinois and nationally. Pieced together from recruits from towns and cities throughout Illinois and neighboring states, the unit reflected the determination of the area's Irish to field an ethnic regiment that would project their own sense of loyalty to the Union. Ultimately, the service and sacrifice of Mulligan's Irish Brigade in the autumn of 1861 personified the pluck and spirit of Irish troops which, in turn, came to reflect, nationally, the virtues that true and loyal American soldiers should exhibit. On the battlefield, these immigrants became, in essence, American. Organized as an Irish regiment, the men who served under James Mulligan thus transformed themselves, using military service as a means of gaining acceptance as full-fledged citizens of the American republic.

The federal census taken the year before the war began shows that 87,000 Irish claimed Illinois as their home. In 1860 some 19,889 of them were living in the city of Chicago, where they composed nearly 20 percent of the city's population. Although the Illinois Irish were outspoken in their support of the Union in 1861, the years leading up to the war had seen a rather contentious relationship between immigrant and native born, especially in that city. Propelled by the completion of the Erie Canal in 1825, Chicago would emerge, over the course of the nineteenth century, as the preeminent midwestern port city. Already by the early 1830s her citizens had begun to realize the implications of their place in the economic growth of the midwestern states. "Chicago must eventually become the greatest place for business in all the Northwest," noted an observer in a letter to the *Chicago Democrat* in February 1834. "Schooners," it continued, "are the principal vessels that now navigate Lake Michigan. In 1831 the number of arrivals was seven; in 1832, about forty-five; during 1833, about one hundred and twenty. More than one hundred dwelling houses, stores and shops were erected during the summer of 1833. There are about thirty stores, some of which do extensive businesses. Three houses for public worship were built in 1833. A respectable academy is taught by a gentleman and lady." In April 1834 an article in the same paper noted that with the arrival of spring, "emigration to this place has commenced in earnest. Within the last ten days over one hundred persons have arrived by boat and otherwise." By the end of May the editors estimated that over a thousand immigrants had arrived in that month alone. In 1835 Chicago had a population of 3,279. Twenty-five years later that number had skyrocketed to 108,305.[1]

By 1839 Irish immigrants had become so involved in the city's affairs that one local newspaper, the *Chicago American*, warned its constituents of the growing threat of Irish political dominance: "American Citizens! Stop! Think! Reflect! To what pass are we fast approaching? Already an Irish representative and an Irish sheriff, with entire foreign deputies; two Irish candidates for recorder and five Irish candidates for the offices of county clerk, county surveyor and constables. In the name of all we love most, our country and our liberty, shall we submit to such dictation?" The 1840 election illustrated the political divisions within the city; the *American* was of the opinion "that the Democratic or Loco-foco triumphs were confined to the neighborhood of the canal—that the party was supported not by the farming community of the state, but by the transient laborers and scalawags who congregated along the canal."[2]

Tensions increased after the passage of the Kansas-Nebraska Act in 1854, leading one observer to sarcastically note that Democrats were not above influencing the vote in whatever way possible. It was "unceasing [political] warfare" with the platform, described as "Plank first, Niggers; Plank second, Whiskey; Plank third, Niggers; Plank forth, Whiskey." The rallying cry of those who supported the Democratic platform, concluded the observer, was "'principles *never*—power *ever*.'" Despite the growth of Irish power, though, nativism still played an important role in mid-century politics, especially during the elections of 1855, and continued to define relationships between immigrants and native born as the nation descended into war.[3]

In 1855 the Republican *Chicago Tribune*, echoing the sentiment of the *Chicago American* fifteen years earlier, came out in support of the Know-Nothing candidate Levi D. Boone. "Who does not know that the most depraved, debased, worthless and irredeemable drunkards and sots which curse the community, are Irish Catholics?" a *Tribune* article noted. "Who does not know," its author continued, "that five-eighths of cases brought up every day before the Mayor for crime, are Irish Catholics?" The *Chicago Democratic Press* reported sourly that the election was "the old story. Demagogism has triumphed over public interests and excited people have become willing instruments of corrupt and scheming men." The attempts by nativists to limit foreign political participation, noted an editor of the *Daily Illinois State Register*, "goes beyond the alien and sedition law policy of Federalism under the elder Adams." In 1855 the *Chicago Times* championed the political defeats across the nation of "sectarian zealots

[who] under the veil of secrecy and humbug of danger to America . . . formed to break down the Democratic party," and pointed out that the same immigrants whom the nativists had so vehemently attacked were the ones who ultimately decided the fate of the party at the polls. "Is not this base Know Nothing slander on the American Catholics falsified by every page of our history?" the *Times* asked some months later. The debates smoldered for the rest of the decade, and questions surrounding immigrants' place in America reemerged during the secession crisis.[4]

The rise of nativism in Illinois coincided with the growth of the Irish population in the state, but the Know-Nothings could do little to physically prevent the Irish from securing a foothold in Illinois. In Chicago in 1860, Irish could be found living in all ten of the city's wards and there was no neighborhood in which they made up less than 14 percent of the ward's population. Their presence was greatest in wards 4 and 10, where Irish-born men and women accounted for approximately one-quarter of the total population. Irish immigrants began arriving en masse in the late 1840s and had settled along the Chicago River, in neighborhoods they named for towns and cities in Ireland, and the concomitant growth of Irish power in Chicago could be seen by the religious and social organizations that arose in that city. On the eve of the Potato Famine, in 1844, for example, a single Catholic church served all of the Catholic residents of Chicago. Two years later, in 1846, there were three. By 1848, the diocese contained thirty churches. Equally important to public displays of Irish presence within the city was the growth of social organizations, in particular ethnic military regiments. By the mid-1850s, there were three Irish militia units, the Jackson Guards, the Emmet Guards, and the Shields Guards. The men who served in their ranks would ultimately play a significant role in the organization of the 23rd Illinois in April 1861.[5]

Perhaps the most telling evidence of the position and security of the Irish in Illinois, however, is employment statistics for Irish-born residents living there when the war broke out. More than 70 percent of the Irish in New York City worked in low-paying, unskilled positions, and their high visibility likely contributed to the nativist backlash there. The experiences of the Irish in Illinois were subtly different. The occupations of Irish-born men in Illinois suggest a vibrant and socially mobile immigrant community within the state. In Chicago, for example, less than 50 percent of the Irish men sampled were employed as unskilled workers. Although nearly 84 percent of these workers listed their occupation as simply "laborer," the remainder were employed in various jobs in and around the city as bartenders, draymen, servants, movers, or on the railroad. Of these unskilled workers as a whole, 60 percent owned no property, and property ownership was lowest among the common laborers. Among men who listed their occupation as "day laborer," however, a seemingly unreliable form of employment, more than three-quarters were property owners. Among draymen, the third largest group of unskilled workers in this sample, the proportion of property owners stood at slightly more than two thirds. Furthermore, of this group, most, nearly 70 percent, were married and had, on average, two children, suggesting a degree of stability.

Artisans—skilled workers and tradesmen—made up slightly more than one quarter of the Irish working class in Chicago, a greater proportion than within the whole of the immigrants who arrived in the United States in the years before the war. "Carpenter" was the most common occupation among skilled workers, accounting for nearly 20 percent of this group—perhaps a reflection of the massive growth of the city during this period and the need for skilled builders. Masons, plumbers, plasterers, painters, teamsters, machinists, and blacksmiths all found employment as well, and these occupations represent only some of the wide array open to skilled Irish workers in Chicago. Around half of these men owned property, real and personal, meaning that skilled workers appeared to have moderately better security than unskilled workers in Chicago; but among those who were able to accumulate property there was an incredible socioeconomic cross section. One-eighth of the men identified as part of this class owned property worth more than $1,000 in 1860, a considerable amount. More than half of these men were married, and those that were had, on average, two children. Finally, nearly 10 percent of Irish men were employed in white-collar professions. Clerks made up the largest single group within this class. Most of them were unmarried and had yet to acquire any significant property. Nevertheless, some forty other professions were identified among this group, which included merchants, teachers, engineers, and grocers. More than 60 percent of these men were property owners and more than half were married.

Although Chicago was the preeminent urban center in the Midwest and home to the largest number of Irish immigrants of any city in this study, Irishmen settled throughout Illinois and were instrumental to the war effort after the secession of the Southern states. One hundred miles west of Chicago, nestled on the right bank of the Illinois River, the town of LaSalle also attracted immigrants and cultivated a similarly vibrant ethnic enclave. The town emerged as the terminus of the Illinois and Michigan Canal, and during the twenty years before the Civil War the town grew steadily as railroads, steamboats, and industry made it, according to one history of the area, seem "destined and fitted, both by nature and art, to become one of the most important commercial points in the West." Rich soil and the pacification of the frontier further encouraged urban growth, and LaSalle became a town where "work was plenty; men were plenty; money was plenty," though the population, "save a few trades-people, was entirely composed of laborers on the canal and railroad." It is unsurprising, then, that numbers of Irish, who often during the middle of the nineteenth century found work building America's transportation infrastructure, would have ended up living in a town such as this.[6]

In 1860, only nine years after LaSalle's incorporation, some 1,418 Irish immigrants, making up nearly 30 percent of the total population, could call that town their home. These men and women likely played a visible part in day-to-day life in the town. As one county historian recounted, many Irishmen and women remained in LaSalle after the completion of the canal, and "numbers of these, and others who came from the favorable representation of their friends here, have settled on farms and become wealthy." Demographics of Irish men conform to what one might expect based on the town's origins. Slightly more than half of Irish workers labored in unskilled jobs, and most of these men were common laborers. Railroad laborers and coalminers made up the second- and third-largest occupations. Nearly one-fifth of the military-aged men worked as artisans, and while these occupations were underrepresented among the Irish in LaSalle in comparison with the Irish in Chicago, perhaps the numbers speak to the fact that the town was only beginning to establish itself. Furthermore, the lower number of artisans and white-collar workers was offset by the fact that nearly 10 percent of LaSalle Irishmen worked in agriculture, and a majority of them owned their own farms. Unskilled workers in LaSalle were less likely to own property, but artisans and white-collar workers were more likely to be property owners, both in terms of real estate and personal property, than were artisans and white-collar workers in Chicago; and, on the whole, it was more common for the Irish of LaSalle of all classes to be married than unmarried. The average couple had three children—again suggesting a degree of stability within this community.[7]

Twenty-two miles east of LaSalle, and eighty-six miles from Chicago, also straddling the Illinois River, stood Ottawa, a city with "an appearance of permanence, a 'well-to-do look,' that were it the creation of a railroad it would not wear." Although "the flashing shuttle of the iron loom found it and wove it into the chain of towns and cities" scattered throughout the Illinois countryside, Ottawa had emerged before the railroads arrived. Its location at the intersection of the Fox and Illinois rivers gave farmers and traders access to the Mississippi

River and, thus, to the Gulf of Mexico. Work on the Illinois and Michigan canal, which connected that city to Chicago, brought laborers "composed mostly of emigrants from New York and the New England States." By 1840 the town had grown considerably and hosted an array of stores, merchants, and professionals.[8]

By 1860 some 1,300 Irish-born residents lived in the town of Ottawa. Well over half of these men worked in unskilled positions, most simply as laborers. Artisans made up 20 percent of the immigrant workers and were employed as blacksmiths, carpenters, masons, moulders, and stonecutters, a cross section that helps complete a portrait of a family-oriented working-class immigrant community (less than 3 percent of the Irish-born in Ottawa were white-collar workers) with some access to social and economic mobility. In all three cities, the proportion of Irishmen working as unskilled laborers was significantly greater than the proportion of unskilled laborers among the general population of military-aged men in the state—some 11 percent of the total number of Illinois men in this age bracket listed their occupation as "laborer" in the 1860 census. Nevertheless, vibrant immigrant communities did exist in the towns and cities of Illinois. Undercutting nativist fears of a large immigrant population that was poverty ridden, dissolute, and disloyal, many of these men reinforced their commitment to their adopted country by their decision to enlist in Illinois's Irish Brigade.

When in April 1861 Abraham Lincoln called for troops to put down the rebellion in the South, many awaited, with some degree of trepidation, the reaction of the Irish in the North. Would these adopted citizens join in a war against the South launched by a Republican president, a war underpinned by abolitionist rhetoric, or would they and other Democrats withhold their support in an act of protest, which might have crippled Lincoln's ability to put down the rebellion? For these exiled sons and daughters of Ireland, though, loyalty was unquestionable. "For us—the adopted children of this glorious nation—our duty in the premises is clear and well defined," noted the editors of the New York *Irish-American*, the most influential ethnic news outlet in the country in 1861. "Our standing in this community, the freedom and equality we proudly claim, are due to no local or sectional concession, but comes to us directly from the whole Union, to which our first allegiance is due, under the guarantees of the Constitution which we have sworn to uphold. . . . Irish Americans, we call on you . . . to be true to the land of your adoption in this crisis of her fate." And they were. In public forums, from the pulpit, in newspapers, mass meetings, and through volunteering for service, Irish men and women loudly proclaimed their allegiance to the Union and Lincoln's war effort.[9]

For all of the debate that surrounded Irish loyalty during the antebellum period, these adopted citizens did not shy from the fight. Irish Americans flocked to the defense of the Union with enthusiasm equal to that of their native-born friends and neighbors. Over the course of the war more than 150,000 Irish-born men, approximately 10 percent of the entire Irish population in the Northern states, likely enlisted in Union armies, a rate nearly identical to the overall percentage of white men who served in relation to the total Northern population. While national focus centered on the Irish of New York, led by Archbishop John Hughes, Michael Corcoran, and Thomas Francis Meagher, these men were not unique in their militant enthusiasm. In fact, the zeal with which the Irish flocked to the flag was noted and encouraged in all Northern states.[10]

The onset of war ended the political bickering and, momentarily, unified, the state. In Chicago, reported Springfield's *Daily Illinois State Journal*, "partisan disconnections . . . faded out of sight. Democrats and Republican have locked shields and stand shoulder to shoulder in behalf of their country and its flag. As an evidence of the feeling of loyalty animating the Democracy, it is reported that a committee of leading Democrats . . . called upon . . . [the] editor of the Chicago *Times*, a rank secession shoot, and notified him that unless his paper ceased to preach treason, the Democracy would put it and its editor into the Chicago river." As early as April 17, the *Chicago Tribune* reported that "several of our Irish Companies [are] zealously brushing up their tactics, and with a good zeal and loyalty that have given to Irish soldiers a name to live in all military annals. From two to three hundred of these will be in readiness to be offered to the Government on call." These few hundred swelled quickly, and the *Daily Illinois State Journal* soon noted enthusiastically that "a regiment of Irish citizens is organizing in Chicago to be tendered for the service of the government . . . the name of the 'Irish Brigade' is a natural title significant of deeds of glory, bravery and hard fighting. The secession rebels should say their prayers before they encounter a charge from the Irish Brigade of Chicago."[11]

The support of the Irish for the Union was on display in other towns throughout the state as well. Rockford's *Rock River Democrat* reported that a meeting held in the town to organize an Irish volunteer company "was largely attended, and a number of names were enrolled. The sons of the Green Isle are not wanting in patriotism, and the fire of freedom ever burns bright in their hearts—they appreciate its untold blessings." The *Chicago Tribune* described how in Aurora, Illinois, some forty miles west of Chicago, Irish recruiting was accompanied by "a number of eloquent speeches . . . among others by the Rev. Mr. Powers, a Catholic Priest":

> He said when a boy, upon his native hills in Ireland, he looked forward hopefully to the time when he should look to the Stars and Stripes for protection [Applause.] He had never advised his countrymen in political affairs, but he would say to Irishmen now, *Come up to the rescue of the flag of your adopted country.* [Loud Applause] He hoped to find them in the front rank, fighting nobly for liberty and Union. *Liberty must not die.* [Applause]

For the men who were volunteering, defending the Union reflected the broader duality of an ethnic identity that stressed the necessity of American liberty and the continued health of the republican experiment for the eventual triumph of Irish nationalism and an independent Ireland. America not only served as the adopted homeland for these men and women, but the survival of the Union—the physical manifestation of the ideals of liberty—was paramount for this group of exiles, who had so long been denied those ideals in their country of birth.[12]

In Springfield, the editors of the *Daily Illinois State Journal* spoke highly of the long tradition of Irish military service to the United States. "In every war that America has waged for Independence, to repel invasion, or to sustain national honor, our fellow citizens of Irish birth have been found fighting beneath the stars and stripes," they wrote, "and there is scarce a battlefield from Bunker Hill to Chapultepec that has not drank in the maligned life-tide of Irish and American hearts. . . . Our glorious flag waved from many a cathedral spire, and at the first call to arms thousands of strong-armed, brave hearted sons of Erin pressed forward to swell the ranks of the grand army of the Union." A day later, the same paper reprinted an editorial from the Philadelphia *Press* aimed at discounting nativist fears of the Papacy; it noted that Catholicism holds "its devotees with singular tenacity to its teachings, and always submissive to the laws of the country in which it is located. In such an age as this, however, and especially in such a crisis in the affairs of the United States of America, many favorite theories are repudiated, and that which has been regarded as established and inexorable has been changed . . . There is not today, in all the free States, a distinguished member of the Catholic Church that has not warmly enlisted on the side of his country."[13] By reinforcing the role of these immigrant volunteers as part of a broader history of Irish Catholic patriotism and loyalty to the United States, this rhetoric served both as a recruiting tool and as a means of combating any lingering nativist concerns. The bodies of Irishmen of Illinois who fell defending their adopted homeland would soon back up the claims of these editors.

In the fall of 1861 the editors of the *Rock River Democrat* reflected back on the first six months of war. They noted that although it was a war to save the Union, "few of our citizens are aware that between fifty and one hundred of the Irish citizens of this city and county have been fighting the battles of our country under the Stars and Stripes. . . . In view of the fact that our foreign born citizens are so freely offering their services to the country, does it seem possible that such an organization as Know Nothings could ever rear its head again in the land and have followers?" The question was intriguing, made more so by the apparent dichotomy of Irish service. Immigrants who were alienated in the antebellum period by men who believed there was no place for Irish Catholics in American society were some of the first to volunteer their services to defend that nation. The rousing response of these adopted citizens played an important role in the early war rhetoric in Illinois, Wisconsin, Connecticut, and elsewhere, and was revived time and again through the war to refute periodic charges of ethnic disloyalty. There stood no greater example of Irish American support for the war effort than the formation of self-proclaimed Irish regiments, which served as physical manifestations of ethnic loyalty and patriotism. As the war dragged on, the success of these immigrant soldiers on the battlefield helped alleviate, for a time, the antagonism over shifting war measures that appeared in larger communities on the East Coast.[14]

The formation of an Irish regiment in Illinois began almost immediately after the first shots were fired in Charleston. The effort was led by an outspoken proponent of Irish organization, James A. Mulligan. Mulligan was the natural choice for such a task. Born in New York to Irish parents, he had slowly worked his way upward within the social and political circles of Chicago, becoming increasingly involved with local and state affairs, first as the editor of the Catholic newspaper *Western Tablet*. A lawyer and staunch Democrat, he spent 1857 in Washington, D.C. as a clerk in the Department of the Interior. In the years before the war Mulligan was nominated to lead a number of important Irish committees in Chicago while also serving as a lieutenant in the Shields Guards. That unit was openly affiliated with the Fenian movement, a transatlantic Irish nationalist movement intent on overthrowing English rule in Ireland. By the outbreak of the Civil War, Fenian circles had organized in nearly every Northern state and had committed themselves to the liberation of their homeland. By 1861, Mulligan would have been an excellent choice for Governor Yates, a Republican, to select for a political commission, simultaneously consolidating control over the state and creating a strong alliance between political opponents.[15]

In undertaking the organization of an Irish Brigade in Illinois, Mulligan parlayed the same public enthusiasm that his compatriot Michael Corcoran used to raise his regiment, the 69th New York, and by the end of April 1861, both men found themselves at the center of a highly publicized recruiting frenzy. The similarities ended there. The formation of the 69th New York was, by all accounts, a spontaneous and overwhelming event, with Corcoran forced to turn away hundreds of men who flocked to the regiment's recruiting office in lower Manhattan in the days following Lincoln's call for 75,000 volunteers. Accepted as part of New York's initial quota of volunteers, the Irishmen marched south to Washington, D.C., where one soldier reported amusingly in early July, "[W]e have been hunting secessionists. . . . All I saw done was the first families of Virginia running away from the first families of Ireland."[16]

Fighting heroically at Bull Run later that month, the New York Irish have come to symbolize ethnic service and sacrifice during the war. While the memory of their extemporaneous organization and service has remained as evidence of the broad public support lent by the ethnic community in the spring of 1861, the experience of the 69th New York did not reflect the realities of ethnic organization in other Northern states. By that spring, Colonel Corcoran was already an internationally renowned figure; he had been released from state custody in New York City—where he was being held awaiting court martial for his refusal to present the 69th New York Militia for the parade in honor of the visit to Manhattan of Edward Albert, Prince of Wales, in October 1860—because authorities believed him invaluable to ethnic recruiting. By contrast, James Mulligan, though a prominent member of Chicago's Irish community, did not possess the same national political clout as Corcoran, and as he rushed to organize an Irish regiment in Illinois, he and his supporters faced an arduous task.[17]

Although he would become the public face of the regiment, Mulligan was not alone in conceptualizing Chicago's "Irish Brigade." During the spring and early summer of 1861 he operated in concert with a group of prominent Irish Americans who sought to bring an Irish unit into existence. The 23rd Illinois may very well not have come to exist without the oversight and financial backing of these men. At the same time, however, their attempts to bring Irishmen from across the state into the regimental fold illuminate the struggles that Mulligan and his supporters faced in striving to unite men of common ethnic backgrounds in a regiment that might not even take the field. Men wanted to fight, and Mulligan's unit organized too late to be accepted as part of the initial ten regiments authorized by the state of Illinois in late April.

Mulligan began to envision his own small militia unit, the Shields Guards, as the nucleus for a larger ethnic brigade almost immediately after war was declared. A committee of fifty Irish Americans from Chicago, men who met for the first time two weeks after Fort Sumter fell, supported him in this endeavor. These men united "for the purpose of procuring funds to Aid in the Equipment of the Irish Regiment now being organized in Chicago; and also for the support of the Families of those volunteering in the same." Furthermore, they closely oversaw Mulligan's movements. On April 25 they sent him to Springfield, Illinois, the state's capital, to petition the governor to accept the Irish Brigade for state service. By May, however, it was clear that this was a futile effort, and the committee vetoed sending Mulligan more funds to support his stay there. They wanted to incur "no more liabilities" in dealing with the state government. Funds were appropriated instead "to defray Major Mulligan's Expenses to and from Washington," and on May 8 he left Springfield for Washington, D.C. with a letter of introduction to Vice President Hannibal Hamlin and the hope of securing Federal authorization for the organization of an Irish regiment in Illinois.[18]

While Mulligan was away, the executive committee continued fundraising in Chicago for their regiment, despite what must have been lingering uncertainty over whether the unit would ever take the field. When word of Federal authorization finally reached Illinois, though, the committee disbanded and left the recruiting to Mulligan and his lieutenants. Short-lived though it was, the existence of this executive committee hints at the complexities of ethnic recruiting and the important behind-the-scenes role that the Irish community of Chicago played in the initial phases of organizing the 23rd Illinois. Their support was important because it bridged the gap between the initial frenzy of volunteering in late April and the eventual acceptance of Chicago's Irish Brigade into Federal service in May. They sustained enthusiasm for Mulligan's regiment in spite of growing doubt among others in the state as to whether an Illinois Irish regiment would ever materialize.

Mulligan wanted his regiment to unify the Irish diaspora in Illinois, and in late April he wrote to Patrick Dunne, a fellow Fenian and captain of the Emmet Guards of Peoria, Illinois, to see if they would join the Shields Guards in an Irish Brigade. The request illustrates the importance for Mulligan of the link that bound members of the Fenian movement. Such connections developed long before the outbreak of war and bound together professed Irish nationalists across the North. Beginning in 1858, John O'Mahony had begun organizing a militant nationalist organization in America dedicated to the overthrow of English rule in Ireland. He did this, in part, by bringing together disparate Irish militia scattered throughout the North and uniting them under the common bond of Fenianism. O'Mahony wrote in the first issue of his republican newspaper the *Phoenix* of Irishmen's "grand national purpose of ridding themselves of foreign tyranny," and declared that "the course which my friends have selected me to represent must be advanced, if at all, by self-sacrifice, by labor and continual vigilance and care"; those "friends" were men who "have pledged to [that course] their lives and energies." In spite of lingering xenophobic questions surrounding Irish loyalty, the Fenians did not see their commitment to Irish nationalism as a contradiction of their place in American society. Rather than undermine the democratic experiment of the United States, Fenians stressed the potential support that the government and people of the United States could offer the movement. For O'Mahony, all Irish republicans had "a direct interest" in upholding the health of their adopted nation. The *Phoenix*, as mouthpiece for the movement, would "inculcate upon all its Irish American readers the duty of allegiance to the constitution and laws of the United States." While the *Phoenix* would not ignore the "sectional questions" inflaming American politics by 1859, the paper would remain neutral—but only to the point at which such questions threatened "to destroy the integrity of the American Republic and thereby endanger the success and grand experiment of self-government."[19]

Irish organization relied primarily on the local militia units. By 1861, Irish militia companies from across the North had pledged their allegiance to O'Mahony and the Fenian agenda. Beginning in late 1859, the *Phoenix* published a growing list of Irish militia companies and social organizations that had committed themselves to the nationalist agenda. Links between the 23rd Illinois and Fenian militia units were evident. James Mulligan was a member of the movement, as were future officers Daniel Quirk, James Lane, James Quirk, and John McDermott. Similar transitions from Fenian member to Union Army officer can be seen in the 69th New York, Ninth Massachusetts, and Ninth Connecticut. Mulligan's early attempt to unite the Illinois Fenian militias appears to have been a logical extension of Fenian organization, but it was a failure. In his reply to Mulligan's letter, Patrick Dunne explained that the Emmet Guards had "tendered their service to the Governor some days back and may be called in before your regiment is: in which case they could not with honour await the call on you." "But," Dunne continued, "if it could be arranged that the Regiment got the prior call there is nothing would give our Company so much pleasure as to unite their fortunes with their fellow countrymen of the 'Irish Brigade.'" Despite shared Irish heritage, the men from Peoria wanted to fight and would go with whatever regiment first offered them that opportunity.[20]

This attitude was not unique. "My object in writing to you," Michigan resident R. F. Farrell wrote to Mulligan on April 26, "is to know what the Shields are about. Are they going to the 'tented field?' if they are please let me know. There is any quantity of fifing and speech-making here, but no action. . . . Michigan is drowsy." His inquiry was conditional: His Irish Wolverines would join Mulligan *if* Mulligan's regiment would take the field in short order. "On receiving our daily paper this morning," wrote another Irishman, P. Flynn, in late May, "the first thing under the telegraphic head is the acceptance through your noble exertions of the Chicago Irish Brigade all hail to you." "There are several young Irishmen," he continued, "who would like very much to join an Irish regiment in preference to any others." Although Flynn himself could not go, "placed as I am with a business on my back and a family to take care of," he was confident that he could raise thirty or forty men for Mulligan if called upon. Charles Coffee and the Ottawa (Illinois) Guards joined with Mulligan's command less because of their ethnic affiliation than because they had missed the first round of enlistments and longed for an opportunity to join in the fight. For such men, the federal government's acceptance of Mulligan's regiment proved an opportunity to bypass state quotas. As a result, the dashing colonel was inundated with volunteers from across the Midwest.[21]

When federal recruiters arrived in Chicago in June 1861 to muster these volunteers into service, their first trip was to a brewery on West Polk Street, where Mulligan had established camp for his Irish Brigade. There, "several companies of stalwart fellows who only need uniforms to give them an excellent appearance as soldiers were put through their facings and formed in lines as visitors passed down." When finally clothed in "a gray shirt and gray pantaloons trimmed with green cord, blue jacket with green collar and blue army regulation cap," these soldiers paid fitting tribute to Ireland and the Union. Cobbled together from throughout the region, the men in the regiment represented twenty-seven different towns and five different states. For the most part, though, the companies within the regiment had organized locally in towns scattered throughout Illinois and neighboring states.[22]

Of the initial group of men who volunteered for Mulligan's regiment in the summer of 1861, the largest single identifiable contingent, 255 men, called Chicago their home. The presence of this large cohort of men combined with the leadership's base in Chicago and the fact that the regiment mustered there has given that city prominence in the historical record, despite the fact that other cities and towns sent proportionally greater numbers of their citizens to serve in the 23rd Illinois. Local reports stressed the significance of the regiment to the Irish citizens of Chicago and alluded to the growing excitement there in June and July as the men came together at Camp Chase. On June 15, for example, the *Chicago Times* reported that Captain Francis McMurray of Company C was "presented with a brace of revolvers by a number of his friends. . . . [T]he gift was an appropriate acknowledgement of the Captain's arduous services in the military cause, and was well merited." The men themselves "seem to have strong ambition to excel each other in quickly acquiring a knowledge of various drills," and "would soon be in soldierly trim." The ladies of Chicago were quick to organize and "aid in fitting the Brigade with some many things necessary to put it into service," claiming "it would be a shame to the citizens of Chicago to have [the 23rd Illinois] depart more meanly provided for than other regiments from other sections. The men who compose the Brigade have nearly all been poor, hard-working men, and they are not able to provide themselves with the thousand and one little necessities which conduce to the comfort of the soldiers." On July 10, Company K received the first of these efforts, one hundred havelocks. Captain Daniel Quirk wrote that he could assure those at home "that the men will often recall to mind and be cheered and strengthened by the recollection that pure and brave hearts have put aside for a time the comfort of their own homes to remember and provide for the true men willing to risk life and home for their country. It will always cheer us, however toilsome and dangerous the march, to know that toil and danger is preserving the homes of the ladies" of Chicago.[23]

Despite the preeminence of Chicago, other communities were well represented in the regiment, and their presence illustrated the broader appeal of Mulligan's unit. Nearly fifty men travelled from Ottawa, a town of some 6,500, to join the 23rd Illinois. Although this company eventually filled their ranks with men from Chicago, Detroit, and Milwaukee, Ottawa residents Charles Coffee, Thomas Hickey, and James Hume retained command of the unit. Second lieutenants Daniel Crowley and Thomas Rae represented the Chicago contingent, and it is possible that their commissions were a concession made by the men from Ottawa to appeal to the interests of the men from Chicago. Patriotism abounded at home in Ottawa as the volunteers marched north to Chicago. "I must tell you why I did not write you for several days last week," Ann Wallace wrote to her husband Will on July 1:

> It was necessary for the sake of the 'example' aside from the wish to hasten the work that I should devote my heart [and] time to the work. Tilly took my sewing machine to Judge Hollisters, where Emma [and] [and] Mrs H. gathered in the neighbors [and] did a big share of the work. Mr Butler let me use his machine at Mrs. Buchannans. I sewed there from early morning till late at night from Tuesday morning until Friday noon. There was a room full of ladies. . . . Every Lady came to me to see how to do this that [and] the other. . . . The work was for you.[24]

Hearing of these efforts, Charles Coffee wrote home that "the Havelocks which you propose to send us will be a welcome gift our company now numbers ninety men, out of which sixty four are from LaSalle County." Furthermore, he noted, "the ladies of Chicago are now preparing the same article for all the Companys of the Brigade that were organized in this City—and I do assure you sir, and through you the Ladies of Ottawa, that it is with no small pride that we know that the 'Ottawa City Guards' are not forgotten by the fair daughters of the City from which we proudly take our name."[25]

From Earlville, Illinois, Captain Samuel Simison marched to Chicago at the head of his company, the Earl Rifles. When finally mustered, the company retained a strong connection to Earl, as all but one of the officers, Second Lieutenant Patrick Pillion, lived in that town before the war. Like their counterparts in Ottawa, the ladies of Earlville were caught up in the frenzy of recruiting. They sent their men a flag "pronounced to be of fine material and as handsome in design as any flag carried by any company through this city. May our loyalty to this flag," one volunteer wrote, "be as great as their act was generous." The women also sent one hundred sixty linen towels, a symbolic gesture to inspire the company to "effectually wipe out from existence the secessionists, as those towels will wipe the perspiration from our brows." Finally, one hundred havelocks were forwarded, along with a note asking what more the soldiers needed. "God bless the women," one soldier wrote after receiving these gifts. "If we had not a single spark of patriotism for our country, we could endure all the privations and hardships of the war—could give our life in their defense and call it pleasure."[26]

From Detroit came a group led by Irishman John McDermott. Like Mulligan, McDermott was a prominent member of his community before the war; during that time he had built a large shipbuilding business that employed upwards of five hundred men. When war broke out in 1861, he organized two and a half companies for service, but was unsuccessful in getting those men

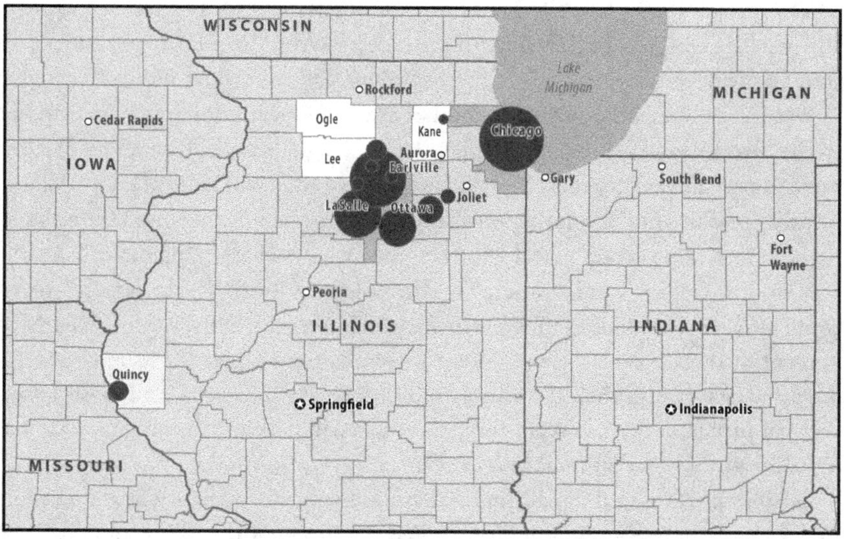


Figure 1 Enlistment patterns of 23rd Illinois volunteers by county (darker shading reflects higher enlistment numbers) and by city (circles reflect numbers of volunteers from each city).

accepted for service by the state of Michigan. When McDermott heard that Mulligan's regiment was officially organizing, he and his men journeyed to Chicago and joined the 23rd Illinois as Company A.[27] Ties to Detroit were clear in the organizational structure of the company. All but two of the sixteen commissioned and noncommissioned officers, Lieutenant James Cosgrove and Corporal Matthew Sharp, were from Detroit. In a series of resolutions, these Irish Wolverines publicly justified their decision to join an Illinois regiment instead of one from their home state. "Having been proscribed by know-nothing fanaticism and deprived the privilege of drawing our swords in behalf of our adopted country in our own state and whereas, our fellow countrymen, comprising the Irish Brigade, having opened their golden ranks and extended to us the hand of fellowship," they chose to march to war with the boys from Chicago. In language that reflected the enthusiasm of the early months of war, the men from Michigan concluded "that we stand by the noble and gallant Colonel James A. Mulligan and his command until death, in defense of the Union, the Stars and Stripes, and the Constitution, so that by our acts we may be enabled to aid and assist in adding another link to the golden chain which has ever bound the hearts of the Irish Brigade."[28]

On July 16, behind a kelly green flag, "the gallant Irish Brigade left Quincy [Illinois] . . . anxious for a clash with the rebels," wrote the *Chicago Tribune*.[29] In spite of the popular portrayals of this regiment, the men who followed Mulligan to war were not all Irish. Out of a total of 832 volunteers known to have enlisted in the 23rd Illinois before the regiment left Chicago, information about place of birth is available on 559 men; among this 559, just over half were born in Ireland. Nearly one-third of the volunteers were born in the United States, and the remaining soldiers came from a host of other countries including England, Canada, Scotland, Germany, and France. Of the American-born volunteers, however, some sense can be made of their enlistment in Mulligan's Irish Brigade. Nearly 70 percent of these American volunteers can be loosely identified as having Irish ancestry by virtue of their last names and immigration records, and these volunteers of probable Irish descent must have contributed to internal and external perceptions of this regiment as Irish.[30]

Also important to delineating the Irish identity of the regiment was the fact that a number of its companies took on ethnic designations. Two companies, A and C, referred to themselves as the Jackson Guards, likely a reference to the United Irishman William Jackson, who was arrested and tried for his revolutionary acts and ultimately committed suicide in jail. The men of Company B called themselves the Montgomery Guards, likely referring to Irish-born general Richard Montgomery, who was "killed during the American siege of Quebec in 1775 . . . [and] . . . became a cult figure second only to Washington" among Irish radicals in America. The Shields Guards (Companies I and K) harkened for inspiration to Irish-born General James B. Shields, a hero of the Mexican War and a U.S. senator from Illinois from 1840 to 1855, while the men of the Mahoney Guards (Company G) were likely expressing their commitment to Fenian leader John O'Mahony.[31]

Men such as James Barnes were representative of the Irishmen who filled Mulligan's ranks, though. Before enlisting in June 1861, Barnes, a County Armagh native, worked as a laborer in Archibald Ingram's blacksmith shop in the town of Lemont, on the Michigan-Illinois Canal, just southwest of Chicago. He volunteered with John, George, and Henry Lovekin, three brothers from County Cork. The four men enlisted with Mulligan in the early summer of 1861 and then returned together that winter to reenlist in the 23rd Illinois as three-years men in Company B. Jason Cosgrove arrived from Ireland a year before the war broke out and moved in with his sister in Detroit. He enlisted with another Irishman, Corporal Daniel Hogan, who recalled that the two were acquainted and travelled to Chicago together in the spring of 1861 to enlist. Despite the fact that Cosgrove had been in Detroit only a short while, enough men knew him and thought highly enough of him to elect him first lieutenant of Company A. Cosgrove later served as the adjutant of the regiment. Another Irishman, John Ward, a native of Galway, joined the Irish Brigade in June 1861, only months after the outbreak of war. A twenty-five-year-old corporal, Ward immigrated to the United States in 1854 and eventually settled in Earlville, some eighty miles west of Chicago. Ward joined Company D, where he served with twenty-one-year-old fellow Irishman William Scully. In December 1861, Scully was admitted to Columbia General Hospital in Washington, D.C. with a fractured skull; he succumbed to his injuries later that week. Two years later, after his discharge, Ward married Scully's widow, Mary, in a ceremony in Mendota, Illinois.[32]

Although the stories of most Illinois 23rd volunteers remain unavailable, certain characteristics can be identified. The average Irishman who enlisted in 1861 was thirty years old, seven years older than the average American-born volunteer. Born sometime in the early 1830s, many of these men may well have emigrated as a result of the Potato Famine (80 percent of the Irish immigrants who arrived in the United States between 1820 and 1860 arrived after 1845) and thus may have had a shared memory of this tragedy, which might have had an impact on their collective decision to enlist in an ethnically affiliated regiment. Less than half of the total number of Irish-born volunteers in the 23rd Illinois (40 percent) lived in Chicago, and just under half of the volunteers (47 percent) who enlisted from that city were born in the Emerald Isle. While this still represents a considerable Irish presence, it is nevertheless surprising given the number of Irish men of military age living in Chicago in 1861.

Mulligan's regiment, as intimately linked as it was to Irish identity, in fact attracted to its ranks only 1 percent of Irishmen of military age living in Chicago. The Irishness of the regiment becomes more pronounced, however, when one looks at enlistments from other cities. Of the 47 men who enlisted from Ottawa, for example, 31 (66 percent) were Irish. From the town of LaSalle, 53 men joined, 41 of whom (77 percent) had been born in Ireland. These numbers represent 5 and 6 percent, respectively, of the total Irish male population of military age of each town. While not all Illinois 23rd soldiers were Irish, the Irish presence was undeniable and certainly must have contributed to the outward sense of ethnic identity that the regiment espoused. This Irishness was likely reinforced by the ethnic background of many of the American-born men. There is a high probability, for example, that 10 of the 14 American-born recruits from LaSalle were of Irish descent, and it is likely that 33 of the 52 American-born volunteers from Ottawa were of Irish heritage.

The demographics of the Irish soldiers also illuminate a rather diverse cross section among those who enlisted in the summer of 1861. Of the volunteers, 144 (69 percent) were staunch members of the working class. Exactly half of this group (72 men) were unskilled workers, with a vast majority listing their occupation as simply "laborer." The other half of these working-class men were artisans, employed in an array of occupations. Approximately one-quarter of the Irish men listed their occupation as "farmer," while white-collar workers made up some 6 percent of the Irish volunteers. In comparison, there were far fewer unskilled workers among those men born in the United States. Just 56 percent of the 73 American-born soldiers in the 23rd Illinois in 1861 were members of the working class, and of this group more than two-thirds were artisans or skilled workers. Farmers made up 33 percent of the American-born, and white-collar workers nearly 10 percent of the total.

By city, however, the numbers reveal slightly different patterns. Among Irish-born men of military age in Chicago, unskilled workers made up slightly less than 50 percent of the population. In the 23rd Illinois, however, unskilled Irish workers from Chicago made up only 35 percent of the volunteers. Skilled workers, only 25 percent of Chicago's Irish population, made up 44 percent of the regiment's Irish-born volunteers; thus there was a significant deviation in terms of the type of Irish men who chose to enlist with Mulligan as compared to Chicago's Irish-born population as a whole. In Ottawa, where Irish farmers made up a mere 5 percent of the total Irish-born population, nearly 70 percent of Irish volunteers worked in agriculture. On the whole, while American-born soldiers were occupationally better off than their Irish counterparts, it is nevertheless clear that the Irish soldiers in the 23rd Illinois were a rather diverse group of men and generally better off (at least occupationally) than their countrymen as a whole in Illinois.

Mid-July found the regiment on the move, headed toward Missouri, where they were tasked with protecting the loyal Union government then in session at Jefferson City, the state's capital. Missouri—a vital border state—remained in the balance throughout the war, but never was Federal control of it tested more than during the spring and summer of 1861, when the Confederates launched their only successful military campaign into the state, under the command of General Sterling Price. After the Union defeat at Bull Run, Lincoln appointed John C. Frémont commander of the Western Department with the hope that his leadership would tip the balance in the West in favor of the Union. Despite this increased Federal presence, Missouri's fate was still very much in question as July turned into August. During this time, Union forces under Nathaniel Lyon were initially successful in pushing Price's Confederates back to the southwest corner of the state, but this hold was tenuous, based on a two-hundred-mile-long supply line that stretched from St. Louis to Springfield, Missouri. The Confederates focused on disrupting that line in a renewed campaign that fall.[33]

As Mulligan and his regiment moved southwest from Chicago, they unknowingly became part of the target of a Confederate campaign that eventually culminated in the trenches outside of Lexington, Missouri. The 13,000 Missouri militia and Confederate troops under General Price and General Ben McCulloch posed a considerable threat to General Lyon, whose 5,000 troops were nearing the end of their initial ninety-days enlistment. Simultaneously, Confederate feints in the southeast portion of the state threatened Cairo, Illinois, the major base of Union operations on the Mississippi River, and forced Northern attention away from Price's militia, bleeding much-needed reinforcements away from Lyon. Recognizing the immediate threat posed by Price's army, the Federal commanders moved to intercept, and on August 10, 1861 the two forces met at Wilson's Creek, ten miles south of the town of Springfield. Despite being outnumbered nearly two to one, Federal forces achieved some degree of success early in the battle. Dividing their force, General Franz Sigel, in command of six cannon and two regiments, had marched fifteen miles around the southern portion of Price's force on the evening of August 9. At eight the next morning, Lyon, with the larger body of the Union army, advanced on the Confederate lines. The commencement of artillery fire to the north signaled for Sigel to launch his attack on the Confederate rear. Though well coordinated, the joint Federal assaults met stiff resistance from their foe. A correspondent for the *St Louis Democrat* reported that the battle "raged with a fierceness seldom if ever equalled, for over three hours," when Lyon was killed by Confederate fire. "The smoke hung like a storm-cloud over the valley," he wrote, "a fit emblem of mourning for the departed hero." Fighting continued for two more hours when, low on ammunition, Union forces withdrew from the field. Their retreat opened the western portion of Missouri to a Confederate invasion that ultimately led to a showdown between General Price's men and Mulligan's 23rd Illinois on the fields outside of Lexington.[34]

Buoyed by the victory, Price moved north, and a concerned Frémont ordered Mulligan from Jefferson City to garrison Lexington. The Irish Brigade covered the one hundred fifty miles in nine days, arriving at Lexington on September 9, just outpacing Price's army. Men and women throughout the nation watched the events unfolding in Missouri with anticipation, and misinformation was rampant as Northerners anxiously awaited news of the fate of the Union forces in the West. On September 20, reports from Lexington verified that Mulligan, though vastly outnumbered, had withstood Price's initial assault on the city's defenses. The *New York Tribune* reported that Price, "desirous of achieving an easy victory . . . sent Col. Mulligan a formal summons to surrender, but received a defiance couched in terms more forcible than elegant." Mulligan kindly told the Confederate general, "Go to hell."[35]

The Irish Brigade concentrated their line of defense along a bluff outside of town. The works were "of earth, 7 feet high and 12 feet thick, with a ditch of 6 feet deep and 12 feet broad surrounding them. Another smaller work [was] erected inside, defended by a ditch—the whole capable of holding 10,000 troops." According to reports, nearly a hundred of Price's men were killed and from two to four hundred were wounded during the initial assault on this formidable position. Mulligan's losses were reportedly a mere five men killed and several wounded. It was a "brave defense" by Mulligan and his Irishmen. By September 23, news reached the East that Mulligan had surrendered his post. Optimistic reports of the regiment's tenacity appearing in the early edition of the *New York Daily Tribune* that day were refuted that evening, when news arrived that "Mulligan was compelled, at last, to yield to superior numbers after four days of hard fighting." He surrendered the city only after his men had been without water for two days and there was little hope of relief.[36]

This marked the second time in three months than an Irish regiment had played a key role in a major battle. It was also the second time that Irish Americans had displayed their courage and loyalty in the face of overwhelming odds. Yet, despite their tenacity under fire, both units were forced to surrender. On July 21, in a heroic rearguard action, the 69th New York had made it possible for a large portion of the defeated Union army to escape the disaster at First Bull Run. Their steadfastness "proved to many native-born Americans that Irish soldiers could serve loyally and bravely . . . and behave well under fire, which could not be said of many Union forces on that July day." Many saw Mulligan's defense of Lexington in a similar light. Outnumbered, without water, and with no hope of being reinforced, Mulligan and his men became symbols of American loyalty and perseverance. Also interesting was that while Mulligan, a first-generation Irish American, was portrayed in the press as the personification of American heroism, John C. Frémont, a staunch Republican and antebellum hero, was highly criticized for his failures during the Missouri campaign—illustrating the ways that military service influenced public perceptions of loyalty and social inclusion.[37]

Mulligan became wildly famous in the wake of the surrender of Lexington. A biographical sketch of the thirty-one-year-old "brave defender of Lexington" published in an Albany, New York paper days after the battle provides some insight into this acclaim. "Col. Mulligan is worthy of all praise. A purer, a better man does not live in the state of Illinois," the author noted. "Six feet three inches in height, with a wiry, elastic frame—a large, lustrous, hazel eye—an open, frank, Celtic face, stamped with courage, pluck and independence," Mulligan was "honorable in all relations—respected by all." Noting that he had been a promising lawyer when the war commenced, the sketch declared that "now he is—long may he continue so—one of the brave defenders of the Union." The article concluded by noting that Mulligan, in one of his last correspondences before his surrender, wrote that "if I die, if I fall in defense of our laws and Constitution, let my example be followed by all—by every man who loved the fame and renown of the fathers who made us a great and honored people." "Chicago has every reason to be proud of her brave Irish officer," proclaimed editors in Wisconsin a month later.[38]

The surrender of Lexington, Missouri was, by all accounts, a consequence of forces far beyond the control of the men in the regiment. They were defeated not by any weaknesses of their own, but because of ineptitude in the chain of command and the "cowardliness" of their rebel foe, who allegedly chose a siege rather than fight Mulligan's men on open ground. The actions of Mulligan's Irish Brigade became, in that instance, reflective of the collective notion of Northern military prowess. More important, however, was the fact that "Mulligan's Irish Brigade" was adopted by, and into, the nation at large. Furthermore, the language that accompanied the news of Mulligan's surrender illustrates that, more often than not, the public viewed these men as American soldiers first, despite their eclectic ethnic backgrounds and avowed loyalty to Ireland. Irishness took on favorable meaning in the eyes of the public, becoming fused with a sense of Americanness that embodied notions of honor, loyalty, and military prowess.

While the Irish response to the war eased anxieties over the devotion to the Union of these adopted citizens, the service of the 23rd Illinois helped reinforce positive ethnic stereotypes by casting Irish service and sacrifice within the broader themes of American nationalism, patriotism, and loyalty. It was the willing sacrifice and tenacity in the face of overwhelming odds of soldiers like those of the 23rd Illinois that gained the approval of the Northern public, and the regiment's reputation set high standards for other units in the Union Army, both ethnic and otherwise. Irish Americans throughout the nation took great pride in the action of the 23rd Illinois and used this regiment as an example to motivate Irish enlistment in other states. The actions of the 23rd Illinois at Lexington, combined with the stand of the 69th New York at Bull Run, emboldened Irish Americans in their recruiting efforts in Connecticut and Wisconsin, as men in these communities pushed for the creation of their own Irish regiments. In the fall of 1861, ethnic recruiting was transformed into ethnic competition, as communities clamored to put together their own regiments that might win similar honors on the field of battle. Irishmen who had watched the 69th New York and 23rd Illinois march off to war in the spring and summer of 1861 saw them return that fall as national heroes, and desperately sought to imitate this success.

# 2 An Irish Regiment in the Nutmeg State

In Connecticut, only a short train ride from New York City, Irish communities were flourishing. By no means immune to the xenophobia that materialized in the antebellum period, Connecticut's Irish were, nevertheless, able to carve a place for themselves within the state's burgeoning industrial cities. In April 1861, they, like their countrymen in Illinois, rushed to the defense of their state and nation. Inundated with volunteers, however, the state had no immediate room for an all-Irish regiment. Instead, these immigrants and their sons watched from the sidelines as units such as the 69th New York and the 23rd Illinois marched to glory on the battlefield. But as it became clear that no single decisive battle would end the war, Connecticut's adopted citizens were given the chance to prove their military worth to the Union. In language that reflected dual patriotism to Ireland and the United States, they organized into the Ninth Connecticut (Irish) Volunteer Infantry under the command of Thomas Cahill, an Irish American and leader of the Irish community of New Haven. Although the public supported the formation of this regiment, there was still some lingering apprehension surrounding ethnic service in the state, and this grew as the stereotypical Irish behavior of some of the recruits—drinking and carousing—tested the patience of local residents. A unique manifestation of the Irish communities dispersed throughout the Nutmeg State, the men of the Ninth Connecticut struggled for acceptance in the early months of the war, illustrating that the act of volunteering was not always sufficient to dispel lingering questions about the place of immigrants. Sometimes, approval came only with the onslaught of enemy shot and shell.

The Irish in Connecticut had long played a prominent and honorable role in the military affairs of the state, fighting in early wars against Native Americans and later enlisting in both the Revolutionary War and the War of 1812. Histories of New Haven and Hartford, rich with biographies of the cities' most important men, openly celebrated the Irish heritage of some of their most prominent citizens.[1] The early history of the Irish in New Haven was not always so worthy of celebration. A history of the city published some thirty years after the Civil War quotes the reminiscences of a New Haven resident concerning the start of the nineteenth century: "It is believed that the first Irish family was brought to the city in a vessel owned by Messrs. Prescott & Sherman; and these gentlemen were threatened with prosecution, for fear the emigrants might become an expense to the town; but the man being a mechanic, he and his family were provided for by charitable persons." The details were inaccurate, for in 1764 the *Connecticut Gazette* of New Haven reported the arrival of a number of Irishmen from Dublin, "Irish Servants, both Men and Women, to be sold cheap."[2] But nevertheless the sentiment the account alludes to reflects the way that residents of New Haven viewed the arrival of immigrants to their city: as potentially burdensome. The Irish population of Connecticut exploded in the 1830s and grew rapidly in the years prior to the Civil War, drawn in by employment opportunities in the carriage industry, the New Haven Clock Company, the Sargent hardware factory, and on the New Haven railroad.[3]

Rarely has Connecticut been portrayed as an epicenter of nativism. While the local press was sympathetic, to a point, to the Irish men and women who began arriving in the latter 1840s in the wake of the Potato Famine, by the 1850s these refugees became the focus of negative attention. Observers did recognize the plight of the poverty-ridden immigrants and the struggles of life in America's urban centers. "If a plan could be devised and carried out by which immigrants, as soon as they arrive in New York, could be sent into the country and into the far West," wrote the editors of Middletown's *Constitution*, "immigration might then be a good thing for all parties considered. So long as they huddle together in the large cities of the seaboard they are only burdens to themselves and to the communities where they live."[4] The nativism that emerged appeared to be steeped as much in xenophobia as in realistic fears of the ever-worsening socioeconomic conditions in eastern cities. The Middletown editors' observations were prescient, however, for westward migration actually did yield considerable advantages for immigrants who could afford the journey, and these men and women made important contributions to the vibrant growth of the Midwest.

The rise of nativist power came as a result of political platforms that focused on fear mongering that was often in clear contrast to the very real examples of Irish assimilation. Patriotic Irishmen, who had defended the flag in America's past wars, became "Americans by adoption, by feeling, and by principle," the editors of New Haven's *Columbian Register* wrote in March 1855 in support of their foreign-born constituents. Loyal Americans (foreign born or native born), they argued, would truly suffer if the Know-Nothings were to gain control of the state's government. Two months later, the same editors cited Henry Clay, who in an 1832 speech to the Senate had proclaimed that "of all foreigners, none amalgamate themselves so quickly with our people as the NATIVES OF THE EMERALD ISLE." Such language, they noted in an attempt to shore up political support, "is in bold contrast with Know Nothing rant, and the absurd attacks made upon the class of persons to whom Mr. Clay refers—it should be read, with edification, by all whigs who revere the memory and profess to adhere to the political principles of Henry Clay."[5]

In spite of these arguments, nativists succeeded in wresting control of the Connecticut's government in 1855 and began to implement policies aimed at the political and social disenfranchisement of immigrants there. Fearing the growth of foreign influence and following in Massachusetts' lead, Governor William T. Minor disbanded Irish militias, on the grounds that "Military Companies organized as foreign Companies, and composed entirely of foreign born, are believed to be detrimental to the military interests of our State." The Middletown *Constitution* quoted current opinion: some believed that foreigners "are subjects of foreign governments and are under the protection of, and owe their obedience to, foreign powers. Such men ought not to be in our military companies." This sentiment was not unique to Connecticut and Massachusetts; an Albany newspaper reported a New York politician arguing that "it was in bad taste to have military companies where a majority were foreign born. Just now, men seem to have wonderfully fallen in love with foreigners—now when 'fusion' seems to be the order of the day. . . . Patriotism which objects to this bill is not skin deep." Another politician commented on "the practice now prevalent in the larger cities, of organizing volunteer companies and battalions composed wholly of foreigners, bearing foreign names, wearing foreign uniforms, and parading under foreign colors. . . . Now sir, this is all wrong, and would be tolerated by no other Government on the face of the earth."[6]

The men of the disbanded units were, the supportive *Columbian Register* of New Haven argued, "industrious and skillful mechanics and . . . as a company, and as individuals, they have discharged promptly and faithfully, all the duties that are required by law. . . . We have no doubt, they would shed their blood and sacrifice their lives as heroically, in defense of American liberty, as any other company in this state." Despite these claims, a vocal majority supported the bill that disbanded the state's ethnic militia. Governor Minor, argued an opinion piece in the nativist-leaning *Connecticut Courant*, was well within his rights; the act was a "sound policy, for the foreign-born population to be organized into distinctive military companies, with the arms of the state of Connecticut in their hands and her money in their pockets, [were] ready at all times to foster a clannish spirit and prevent that absorption into the general mass." "When military companies are thus formed under a *distinct national* organization, they cease to be American, and are upheld and spoken of as 'Irish' or 'German,'" the writer continued. "Why is it not better for 'citizens' of Irish or German extraction to mingle in the ranks of the ordinary military companies with native American citizens?" The editors of the *Columbian Register* retorted, "We hardly know which [aspect of the militia law] is the most despicable, the injustice of the act, or the hypocrisy which attempts to excuse it." Although reversed in 1856 following victories by the Democrats in the state, the law nevertheless stood as a reminder of lingering questions surrounding Irish American loyalty that reemerged time and again during the Civil War.[7]

The demographics of Irishmen in Connecticut's major cities hint at the differences among immigrant populations in different geographical areas—even areas in relatively close proximity to each other, such as New Haven and New York. New Haven presents an interesting example for, only ninety miles from New York City, it was easily accessible by train. Irish immigrants made up nearly 20 percent of New Haven's population in 1860, numbering 7,759 out of 38,989 residents of that city. Although they settled in all of the city's eight wards, the most heavily Irish neighborhoods were wards 3 and 5, where Irish-born residents made up 26 percent and 37 percent of the residents, respectively. The first Catholic church in New Haven was constructed in 1834, and by 1861 two others, along with an orphan asylum, served the growing Roman Catholic community.[8] At the time of the nativist purges in 1855, two Irish militia units had organized in New Haven, the Washington-Erina Guards and the Jackson Guards, further illustrating the strength of the immigrant group living there. In 1857, after Governor Minor was voted out of office, these units reformed and reorganized as the Emmet and Montgomery Guards.[9] The Emmet Guards was so named in honor of nationalist Robert Emmet, an Irish republican who had led a failed uprising in Ireland in 1803. Emmet secured a place in history as a result of his "Speech from the Dock" on the eve of his execution, in which he asked to "rest in obscurity and peace, my memory be left in oblivion and my tomb remain uninscribed, until other times and other men, can do justice to my character. When my country takes her place among the nations of the earth, then, and not till then, let my epitaph be written."[10] The Montgomery Guards were named for the Irish-born General Richard Montgomery, who served in the Continental Army during the Revolutionary War. The men in these units led the charge when it came to organizing Connecticut's Irish regiment.

The Irish community in New Haven proves interesting when compared to communities in other eastern cities in proximity to it. Whereas the journey to Illinois or Wisconsin would have been a considerable expense for those arriving in New York or Boston, New Haven was relatively accessible (in terms of cost of travel) to poorer immigrants. Yet less than half—40 percent—of men working in New Haven in 1860 reported working in occupations that are considered unskilled labor, though nearly 80 percent of this group listed their occupation as, ambiguously, "laborer." Almost half of the unskilled workers owned some kind of real or personal property, meaning that compared to Irish residents of Chicago, New Haven Irish residents actually may have been better off; and, compared to life in the ethnic enclaves of New York City, life in New Haven seems to have offered significantly better opportunities for recent arrivals.

Nearly 45 percent of Irish men in New Haven were skilled workers or artisans, many of them working in the carriage-making industry, though ultimately eighty-five different professions were identified among the sample, illustrating the broad array of job opportunities available to the skilled workers. Property ownership among this group was actually less common than among the unskilled workers; a substantial minority (8 percent) of these men, though, were apprentices who owned no property, but may have had access to diverse economic opportunities in the future. By contrast, only 1.5 percent of the skilled Irish workers in Chicago claimed to be apprentices in their chosen occupation, suggesting, perhaps, the existence of a more structured and established Irish working-class community in New Haven. Conversely, though, a mere 5 percent of the Irishmen of military age in Connecticut's largest city were white-collar, low nonmanual workers, and a majority of these men worked as clerks, grocers, police officers, and teachers. Among this group, however, all were property owners to varying degrees. Among all three groups in New Haven, artisans were the least likely to be married; 49 percent of them were married in 1860, while marriage rates stood at 59 percent among laborers and 73 percent among white-collar workers. As a whole, this group averaged 2.5 children, more than their counterparts in Illinois.

Hartford's 6,457 Irish-born residents were spread throughout the city's three wards, making up approximately 22 percent of the city's total population. Industrial growth, and then the Famine, led to a rapid increase in the foreign-born population, from fewer than five hundred in 1844, to over two thousand in 1850, and to over six thousand by the time the Civil War broke out. Construction on the Enfield Canal, which began in 1827, brought nearly four hundred Irish workers to the city, and railroad construction, which began in the 1830s, created even more opportunity for immigrant laborers. Urban and industrial growth, dependent upon both skilled and unskilled laborer, provided stable employment for the growing immigrant population. In 1860 unskilled workers composed 42 percent of the Irish workforce in Hartford, among whom 80 percent called themselves, simply, laborers. Of this group, nearly 60 percent owned varying amounts of real or personal property; a majority claimed personal property worth between $25 and $100, but no real estate.[11]

Artisans made up some 40 percent of the Irish working class in Hartford and they worked in sixty-six different professions, with cordwainers, blacksmiths, joiners, teamsters, tailors, and stone masons the most heavily represented, in that order. Gunsmiths and machinists were also found among the ranks and reflected Hartford's industrial growth and the presence of a major firearms company there. Among this group just over 50 percent owned property, a significantly higher proportion than among the artisans in New Haven, just 35 percent of whom were property owners. As in New Haven, a majority of the Irish artisans claimed property worth between $25 and $100, though one in every ten of these men claimed more than $500 in real and personal property—a sizable amount. Among the working class, both skilled and unskilled workers, marriage rates stood at 53 percent and 62 percent respectively, and on average these men had two children.

As in New Haven, men employed in white-collar professions made up a relatively small proportion, only 5 percent, of the Irish male population, and there appears to have been less diversity within those professions than in New Haven or Chicago. The numbers of grocers, boardinghouse owners, liquor dealers, and engineers were the highest. Nearly 80 percent of these men were property owners, most claimed to own property worth between $100 and $500, though nearly 40 percent claimed ownership of total property—personal, real, or combined—worth over $1,000. Among these men there was a clear correlation between property ownership and marriage, for all married men (70 percent of this group) owned property, while three-quarters of the unmarried men owned none. In Connecticut's two largest and most important cities, similar trends existed among the Irish working-class population and, importantly, like those immigrants living in Illinois, they show a vibrant socioeconomic cross section and reflect what appears to have been relatively stable and engaged immigrant population.

Irishmen living in Waterbury, a city in northern New Haven County, showed the most significantly skewed employment statistics. Nearly 80 percent of the Irishmen in this city were employed as unskilled laborers. However, three-quarters of those workers were specific in identifying themselves as "factory worker" rather than the using the general term "laborer," reflecting, perhaps, the fact that sixty-seven corporations, many engaged in manufacturing, were organized in Waterbury between 1846 and 1860. The authors of one early history of the town note the clear links between industrial and urban growth in the region. For Bridgeport, a relatively "new" town, incorporated in 1836 and selected as one of the hubs for the Housatonic Railroad connecting Connecticut and Massachusetts, the statistics are equally skewed, though in the opposite way. In 1860 less than 30 percent of the Irish in that town worked as unskilled laborers, while nearly 55 percent were employed as artisans. More than 70 percent of the artisans and laborers were also property owners. Occupational statistics from Connecticut as a whole show that approximately 24 percent of the workers in 1860 were engaged in unskilled trades, and thus, as in Illinois, the Irish in the major cities were disproportionally represented in these types of jobs. Nevertheless, occupational diversity within these communities is an important indicator of immigrant place in that state in the years immediately before the war.[12]

After war was declared, the Irish in Connecticut came out in vocal support of the Union. On April 23, 1861, reports came from Hartford that two Irish companies had formed. Observers from Middletown reported that Irish residents "have shown a great readiness to volunteer, and several are enrolled in the company which has just been formed." "The Irish population," noted the Middletown *Constitution*, "are unanimous in their wish and determination to support the Government. In spite of the prophecies of many to the contrary," the paper noted, "we have not heard of a single Irishman who has shown a disposition to prove false to the stars and stripes."[13] In New Haven, Captain Thomas Cahill received word from Governor William Buckingham that "officers chosen by that company [the Emmet Guards] shall be fully commissioned immediately upon being reported by the Adjutant-General, without the usual formalities attending the organization of military companies," a procedure that gave preference to the already organized Irish company over others that were just beginning to form in that city at the time.[14]

On May 11, the *Columbian Weekly Register* of New Haven reported that the Irishmen in Waterbury were organizing a company as well. When the Emmet Guards of New Haven volunteered their services to the state in late April 1861, some residents saw the irony in the act, recalling that "the arms of such companies as are composed of Catholic adopted citizens, were taken from them, under a boldly imputed doubt of their loyalty. . . . Let justice be done them, by a generous acknowledgement of their loyalty and the restoration of their character. Such Soldiers cannot be spared." Another editorial the same day repeated that claim, noting that "in the days of Know Nothingism, when adopted citizens were under the ban, and Gov. Minor revoked the charters of military companies on the plea that people of the Catholic persuasion owed a political allegiance to the Pope of Rome, above their oath to support the Constitution of the United States, we remonstrated against the ostracism, and contended that they were as loyal as native born citizens—We had no doubt of it then—we have none now." As the Union stood in the balance, the reaction of these Irishmen in Connecticut stood as a staunch rebuttal of the antebellum accusations of immigrant disloyalty that had been espoused by local nativists.[15]

Newspapers in Connecticut and other states reported that a Catholic priest in Auburn, New York had called for "every man who can leave his family to enlist. This is the first country the Irishman ever had that he could call his own country. The flag of the Stars and Stripes is the only flag he can fight under and defend as his own flag. . . . There are two classes whom I most despise—cowards and traitors;—and those who can enlist, and do not, are either one or the other." The *Irish-American*, based in New York, reported that none in Connecticut so "hastens to don the armor of his country and to strike in her defense as the much-maligned and proscribed Irish Catholic." The writer further declared, "I will not say that all other classes do not arm for conflict in defense of the Union, but none . . . fight more bravely than this very class, which has been so often pronounced by these falsehearted politicians as faithless to freedom and insensible to its many blessings. Let Irishmen . . . demand the respect their devotion to truth and to freedom and Union deserves." "Look in our Army," the editors of the *Connecticut Courant* encouraged readers; "in the front ranks we find Irish, Germans, Scotch, all clinging to this government as to the horns of the altar for protection." In the midst of the sectional crisis, Connecticut's Irish appeared as worthy defenders of the republic. Yet no ethnic regiment from the state came into being during the first months of the war.[16]

When Michael Corcoran led the 69th New York to war, the *Hartford Daily Courant* reported that "the departure for the war of the sixty-ninth regiment . . . [of] New York, is an indication that the Irishmen who have always been famed as soldiers, are not the boys to flinch at this time of trial." In late June, there were reports that the 69th's chaplain, a Catholic priest, had blessed a cannon at Fort

Corcoran—one of the fortifications guarding Washington, D.C. constructed by the 69th New York during the early summer of 1861—and gave an eloquent sermon which concluded, "I shall guarantee to you that this promising boy [the cannon being blessed] will speak for the first time in loud, clear accents . . . and, in name as in effect, he will hunt traitors from this fort, while the echo of his voice will be as sweet music, inviting the children of Columbia to share the comforts of his father's home: and thus may he soon speak, to the glory of the Stars and Stripes, honor to the name that he bears, and lasting credit to the Sixty-ninth New York." Such sentiment and language, which placed the New York Irish at the forefront of the defense of the Union, literally blocking the path the Confederates would have to traverse to reach Washington, must have struck a deep chord among the Irish in Connecticut, and only further encouraged them to push for their own ethnic unit. Driven by competition between communities, the organization of the Ninth Connecticut took on the unique flare of the immigrant communities of the Nutmeg State when war broke out. Unlike their countrymen in the 69th New York, however, the men who enlisted in Connecticut's Irish regiment struggled for acceptance in the face of popular stereotypes of Irish disorder.[17]

Close ties existed between the Irish of New Haven and those of New York. Before the war the Emmet Guards and the 69th New York had paraded together in New Haven, and after the attack on Fort Sumter, Thomas Cahill invited the leader of the 69th, Thomas Francis Meagher, to lecture the Irishmen of the Elm City on their duty to the Union. Reports on the First Battle of Bull Run that appeared in Connecticut's papers often mentioned the tenacity of the New York Irish on the battlefield, while reinforcing the ethnic bonds that existed between immigrant communities in the two states. The *Hartford Daily Courant* ran dispatches on the battle written by special correspondents for a New York paper. "Our men fought with determined vigor, and accomplished results worthy of veterans," one of these reporters wrote; "[t]he Seventy-first, the Zouaves, the Sixty-ninth, and the Fourteenth Militia, are most frequently mentioned as among the New-York regiments that most resolutely contested the field." Another battlefield reporter wrote that despite the defeat, "I cannot see that the spirits of our men have been destroyed. . . . [T]he Sixty-ninth, and Seventy-ninth, and Seventy-first declare their determination to have two lives for every man of their regiments that are killed or wounded." Readers of New Haven's *Columbian Weekly Register* were told that Lincoln "sent his grateful acknowledgements to the New York Sixty ninth regiment, for their splendid bearing in the fight. Foremost in a gallant army, the Irishmen are gathering in the laurels of the war." As these Irishmen rose to fame, back in Connecticut Irish recruiting began to gather steam, reinforced by both the close personal ties that existed between the Irish there and in New York, and the larger views of the role this group could play as part of the Union war effort.[18]

As the Union army retreated in disorder from Manassas, Virginia, after First Bull Run, 500,000 three-year volunteers were organizing in Northern states. Northerners, for the most part, showed a renewed commitment to the war, and volunteers came out in droves, responding with enthusiasm to the president's call. Connecticut's Irish citizens finally had the opportunity to prove their loyalty, and their efforts were justified by the press, who pointed not only to the early success of Irish units in battle but also the rich military tradition of Irish soldiers in foreign armies. Prominent Irish Americans reciprocated by stressing the continued patriotism of immigrants in the fight to preserve the American republic. Furthermore, as Irish soldiers proved themselves time and again, nativist presses began "revising their image of Irish Americans, and this revision was based largely on that groups' dedicated battlefield service."[19]

Less attention was paid in Connecticut to the organization of the 23rd Illinois, perhaps because of the physical distance between the two states. Nevertheless, the fight at Lexington, Missouri propelled the Illinois Irish regiment onto the front pages of Connecticut's newspapers. "Colonel Mulligan is spoken of in the highest terms," the editors of the *Hartford Daily Courant* recounted. "He displayed great bravery during the action, and when asked to surrender he refused. His sword was taken away by force." Surrendering the city, Mulligan "wept like a child" and made the decision only after he "offered to take a position on a level spot of ground" and fight Price's Confederates, giving the rebels "odds of four to one in a fair and open fight," an offer the enemy declined. "The gallant defense of Col. Mulligan is the theme of admiration among distinguished military men," the *Columbian Weekly Register* in New Haven reported three days after the regiment's surrender. A brief biography of Mulligan that appeared in the Middletown *Constitution* painted the colonel as the embodiment of the true American hero. Since the war began, the writer concluded, Mulligan "has labored unweariedly in the cause of the American Union. His gallant defense of Lexington against overwhelming numbers, proves that he is a brave, skillful and determined commander." Through these stories he came to embody the true and good American, "said to be a rigid temperance man, in height six feet three inches, a fine scholar, a good speaker, and a brilliant writer." Heroic in the face of overwhelming odds, Mulligan became a gauge by which other Irishmen could judge their service.[20]

In Connecticut, a state with strong and visible ethnic communities with close connections to national organizations and, in particular, to the Fenian movement, the Ninth Connecticut came together rather easily as men flocked to volunteer for a regiment organized by local community leaders. Responding to accusations that the some Irish were hesitant patriots that autumn, the editors of the Middletown *Constitution* wrote emphatically that, "like the gallant Sixty-Ninth of New York, the Irishmen of this section are among the foremost defenders of a constitutional government." In May, soon after the departure of the 69th New York for Washington, recruiting posters displaying the words "Forward the 9th!" below a "woodcut of an American eagle defending the American shield" began appearing throughout the state. In Meriden, organization began under a local Catholic priest, Father Walsh. "All in his charge are thoroughly loyal," reported the *Hartford Daily Courant*, and the company "will soon be ready to go into rendezvous." In one day, according to the *Middletown Constitution*, an Irish company in Hartford gained nearly forty volunteers.[21]

The Ninth Connecticut began to take shape in August, and Thomas Cahill, a native of Boston who had been "born within a stone's throw of Bunker Hill" (as his supporters ironically noted at the height of the nativist purges of the mid-1850s), received his appointment as colonel in early September.[22] On September 5, the New Haven *Palladium* reported the enlistment of Irishmen from that city. "The Emmet Guard Going," ran one headline, under which appeared an account of "a large and enthusiastic meeting of the Emmet Guard" during which the company "voted to enlist for the war. The meeting was addressed by Col (late Capt.) Cahill in a feeling and eloquent manner. They will meet in their armory tomorrow night to receive such members as may wish to join their war organization." On September 10, the former militia unit paraded through New Haven, making a "very fine show" in a display that was "very admirable . . . which did a credit to those engaged in it." Enthusiasm was high among the Irish throughout the state. When William Wright, a veteran of the Second Connecticut (a ninety-days enlistment regiment) opened a recruiting office in Hartford, the *Daily Courant* noted that "there is no reason why Hartford should not be represented by a full company of Irishmen in the 9th, under Col. Cahill; They *can* be raised and Lieut. Wright will do it." His recruiting campaign was capped by an "eloquent appeal to the patriotism" of the Catholic community there, who presented the newly appointed captain with a massive bible donated by the congregation of Saint Peter's Church.[23]

While statewide recruiting efforts yielded volunteers, most of the recruiting was done by the members of the Emmet Guards themselves. Avowed Fenians, these men played a vital role in bringing the regiment together. Fifteen members of the Emmet Guards were commissioned as officers and were instrumental in regimental recruiting. Their presence imbued Connecticut's Irish regiment with a degree of radicalism, for these officers were very open in their allegiances to the Irish nationalist movement. Perhaps equally important, however, the transition of these men from militia officer to regimental officer illustrates the role that individuals played in mobilizing support for the Irish regiment, as local leaders, both civic and military, successfully overcame antebellum animosity to unite the Irish in the Nutmeg State.

For most of the companies in the 23rd Illinois the nucleus had been a local community, but few of the Illinois towns sent complete or nearly complete companies to join Mulligan in Chicago. Organization of the Ninth Connecticut was different, relying heavily on countywide recruiting efforts and local militia leaders to bring volunteers to the ranks. New Haven served as the most important recruiting center for Connecticut's Irish regiment, but eight of the ten companies within it were organized in a single town or county, reflecting the strength of these communities when it came to unit organization and the importance of strong leadership in the recruitment process.

Table 2-1 Residency of Volunteers to the Ninth Connecticut

| Company | Number of Volunteers in Company | Volunteers Providing Residency | Percentage from Same Town | Town | Percentage from Same County | County |
|---|---|---|---|---|---|---|
| A | 109 | 87 | 64 | New Haven | 68 | New Haven |
| B | 96 | 83 | 38 | Meriden | 82 | New Haven |
| C | 102 | 79 | 69 | New Haven | 90 | New Haven |
| D | 106 | 67 | 47 | Bridgeport | 79 | Fairfield |
| E | 105 | 64 | 43 | New Haven | 91 | New Haven |
| F | 54 | 36 | 63 | Waterbury | 97 | New Haven |
| G | 96 | 67 | 50 | Hartford | 87 | Hartford |
| H | 111 | 85 | 48 | Norwich | 68 | New London |
| I | 95 | 88 | 21 | Bridgeport | 34 | Fairfield |
| J | 89 | 62 | 15 | Bridgeport | 47 | Fairfield |

Before the war, for example, Patrick Garvey of Meriden served as captain of Company D, the Jackson Guards of New Haven, a unit that fell victim to the Know-Nothing militia purges in 1855, as Thomas Murray recounted in his history of the regiment. Garvey was responsible for recruiting 90 of the 96 original volunteers in Company B. Michael McCarten served under Thomas Cahill in the Washington-Erina Guards of the Second Regiment Connecticut Militia in the 1850s, and then again as Cahill's second lieutenant in the Emmet Guards before war broke out. McCarten recruited 78 men for Company C and was elected the unit's captain.[24]

Although less than half of the volunteers in Company D were from Bridgeport, their captain, Thomas Coates, brought 99 men with him when he reported to Cahill for duty. In 1852, Coates had led the organization of the Montgomery Guards, a group of naturalized Irish who were Bridgeport citizens, and who, Murray remarked, had spent "a considerable amount of money to equip themselves with uniforms, etc., and devoted much time to the study and practice of infantry tactics. . . . [A]t regimental muster [they] made as fine an appearance . . . as any company in the field."[25] They too had been disbanded in 1855. Fenian James P. Hennessey of the Emmet Guards was responsible for 76 men in Company E, and Hartford resident William Wright, a graduate of Trinity College, Dublin, a former regular in the British Army, and a veteran of First Bull Run, raised 90 men for Company G. Company I was largely recruited by Bridgeport resident Frederick Frye. Frye was the great-grandson of Colonel James Frye who died at the battle of Bunker Hill, and the "last of a race of citizen soldiers who had taken active and honorable part in the wars of the last century and a half in this country." A veteran of the Third Connecticut, a ninety-days regiment, after his initial mustering-out he travelled throughout the state to recruit men into his new company.[26]

Irish volunteers who enlisted in the Ninth Connecticut that autumn made up some 65 percent of the total number of soldiers in the regiment, making it the most ethnically Irish of the three regiments examined in this study. The 165 American-born soldiers in the regiment made up less than one-quarter of the volunteers, and among them some 115 (77 percent) were likely to have been of Irish descent. The remainder of the unit consisted of men from England, Canada, Denmark, Germany, Holland, and Scotland. More importantly, Irish recruits made up a significant majority in nine of the ten companies that composed the regiment. James McCarty, who enlisted as a private in Company E on September 9, 1861, was one such recruit. McCarty had been born in Ireland, in County Cork, in 1828. The son of a farmer, he likely emigrated from Ireland with thousands of his fellow countrymen to escape the devastation of the Famine. Arriving in New Haven in 1847, McCarty found work as a boot crimper. His future comrades-in-arms, brothers James and Michael Doolan, along with their

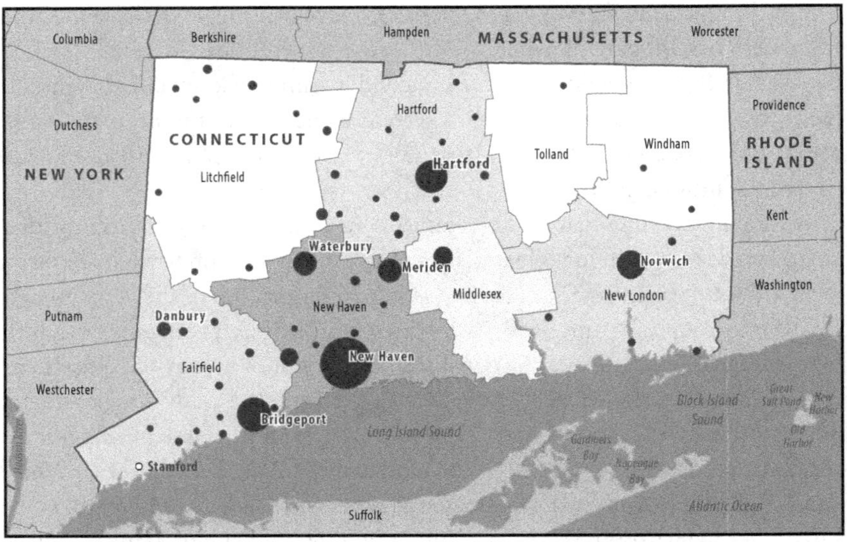


Figure 2 Enlistment patterns of Ninth Connecticut volunteers by county (darker shading reflects higher enlistment numbers) and by city (circles reflect numbers of volunteers from each city).

father and sister, also natives of County Cork, arrived in the United States in 1850. They all made their home in the town of Derby, before the young men enlisted in Company E in the fall of 1861.[27]

Men enlisted for a multitude of reasons, including ethnic ties as well as more personal considerations. Civic ties as well as military organizations, often emerging organically from ethnic communities, encouraged the growth of friendships. Before Francis McKeon enlisted in the Ninth Connecticut he "was one of the strongest men you could wish to see. he was a foreman and belonged to a Military Co," the Emmet Guards of New Haven. He was also a member of a local fire department and was often seen running to fires throughout the city with the rest of the men in this volunteer company. Lieutenant Terrence Sheridan, another member of the Emmet Guards and a local firefighter, swore that McKeon was "one of the toughest you could find." When war broke out in April 1861, the first man to sign Company E's rolls was thirty-four-year-old Charles Doty. Born in New York, Doty left his wife and three children to serve under McKeon, a decision likely influenced by the fact that the two had served together as firemen in the same company before war broke out.[28]

Edward Murray and James Callahan knew each other in Bridgeport before the war and enlisted together in October 1861, though they served in different companies. After the war, when John Hanlon sought proof of his war-related rheumatism, he received support from men he met in the service as well as from friends and comrades with whom he enlisted, such as James Glancey and Charles Dinon. Captain Michael McCarten and Private John Reilly were acquainted in New Haven before the war, and it is possible that McCarten's high standing within the community played some role in Reilly's decision to enlist. Recruiting trends suggest that there were men within individual companies who were connected at some level to those they served with. Sometimes this was simply a matter of knowing someone before the war, then choosing to enlist with that person, or in a company under that person's command, when the regiment began to organize.[29]

The demographics of the Irish volunteers in the Ninth Connecticut differ significantly from those of the recruits who joined the 23rd Illinois. Nearly all of the men (92 percent) were members of the working class, and unskilled workers made up just over half of the total number of volunteers who enlisted in 1861. Artisans composed approximately 40 percent of the volunteers, and worked in 75 different professions, among which painters, moulders, and blacksmiths were the most heavily represented. By comparison, in the major cities of Connecticut, approximately 80 percent of Irish men of military age were members of the working class, and thus the men of the Ninth Connecticut were, as whole, more solidly blue collar than the communities from which they were recruited. Volunteers who enlisted in Mulligan's Irish Brigade, on the other hand, represented a much more diverse socioeconomic cross section of Illinois society.

Why such disproportionate demographics between the volunteers from Connecticut and Illinois? It is possible that the recruiting tactics of the winter of 1861 drew a different sort of volunteer to the ranks. In particular, the introduction of a cash bounty for volunteers in Connecticut may have encouraged men from the laboring classes to leave their jobs and join the army. It is also probable that these numbers are exaggerated because the Ninth Connecticut was raised primarily in Connecticut's large industrial cities, whereas James Mulligan drew many recruits from smaller, more rural towns in central and southern Illinois. Though the Irish working class in Illinois was proportionally smaller than that in Connecticut, the difference was not significant enough to account for the variances between these two regiments. Similar socioeconomic trends can be seen when comparing the American-born volunteers in the two regiments as well. In the Connecticut regiment over 70 percent of these volunteers were members of the working class, a proportion nearly 20 percent higher than that seen among the American-born recruits in Mulligan's Irish Brigade. As one recruiting advertisement claimed, enlisting in the Ninth Connecticut was "an excellent opportunity for Irishmen. Good and prompt pay." A report linking the act of volunteering to the incentive of pay recounted that a "wealthy gentleman of New Haven, finding four stalwart fellows 'lying about loose' on the Green with no employment, proposed to them to enlist and promised each $5 bounty if they would do so." Two days later the "Hibernian quartette marched into his store and demanded a settlement of their little bill . . . it was satisfactorily ascertained that they had enlisted in the 9th Regiment."[30]

By city, economic trends among recruits become clearer. Of the 157 Irish men who enlisted from New Haven, for example, nearly all were members of the working class, and they enlisted in proportionally greater numbers than the overall working-class Irish presence in that city. Nearly 60 percent of all volunteers from New Haven were unskilled workers, nearly every one a laborer, while only 40 percent of the total number of working-class Irish in New Haven claimed membership in that class. Approximately 94 percent of the Irish recruits from Hartford can be identified by their occupations as part of the working class, whereas approximately 80 percent of the Irish in that city worked in those types of jobs. Of these Hartford men, slightly more than half were unskilled labors, a much larger proportion than among the general immigrant population, which perhaps suggests that military service had financial appeal for men from this group. In the city of Bridgeport, 85 percent of the men born in Ireland could be identified as members of the working class, but every one of the Irish volunteers from Bridgeport who enlisted in the Ninth Connecticut was employed in a working-class job. More importantly, although less than 30 percent of the general Irish population of Bridgeport toiled as unskilled workers, more than 55 percent of the soldiers claimed to be, simply, laborers. Statistics were similar for the other major towns in the state. Thus, as Thomas Cahill's Irish regiment began to form in the fall of 1861, it was overwhelmingly composed of men from the lower ranks of Connecticut's Irish communities. While there is no evidence that the soldiers themselves were mired in poverty, it is interesting to see the type of men who were drawn to enlist in the fall of 1861, after the initial war fervor had settled and with the state had begun to offer enlistment bounties.

As these volunteers were mustered into service, observers were pleased with the way the Irish regiment was shaping up. Passing through Camp Welch, the Ninth camp in New Haven, witnesses were met "with the neat and tidy appearance of the grounds and equipage," reported the *New Haven Register*. "The men appeared cheerful and contented. They appear to be an excellent body of men."[31] By October, however, with recruiting for the Ninth Connecticut well underway, Thomas Cahill received a letter from one disenchanted volunteer, who accused some of his comrades of disloyalty. "I would terriably hate to have our Gallent 9th go away with the slightest taint of dishonner," the unnamed soldier wrote, recounting the story of a wayward patriot who had enlisted in Cahill's regiment and then, reconsidering his decision, sought to purchase his way out of the ranks. While optimism abounded among the community and in the pages of the Democratic press, cracks were beginning to surface, for despite enthusiasm over the unit's organization, a vocal group of critics, both within and outside of the regiment, began to single out many of the new recruits for their dishonorable behavior.[32]

Supply issues plagued the regiment, which compounded interpersonal conflicts. One report claimed that "there has been a delay in providing the men with uniforms, because the men were so much larger than the common run of soldiers that the garments wouldn't go on." The Irish regiment remained undersupplied through the winter months, and this became a constant frustration for the officers and reflected poorly on both the Ninth and the state. Lacking even a soldierly appearance, the "exuberant, ragged, roistering volunteers [of the Ninth ] taxed the best efforts of New Haven's inadequate police force," and Governor William Buckingham began to receive complaints from residents of New Haven regarding the conduct of the Irishmen. A picture thus begins to emerge of the regiment in the fall of 1861 that differs considerably from that of other units who marched to war in the early months of the conflict. As members of an Irish regiment, the volunteers were lauded by the press and by their local communities for their patriotism and loyalty to their adopted state, and they were portrayed, time and again, as Connecticut's own version of the 69th New York and the 23rd Illinois. Yet lacking uniforms, and refusing to submit to the authority of their commanding officers, these volunteers failed to live up to the gallant image that their countrymen had earned during the first months of the war. The prospect of a drawn-out conflict and the realities of the lengthy process of organization (at least when compared to the formation of the initial ninety-days regiments) perhaps dulled the willingness of the general public to tolerate the rowdy behavior of these green recruits.[33]

So bad was the behavior of the men that Governor Buckingham sought desperately to send them away from New Haven as quickly as possible. By happenstance, General Benjamin Butler was in New England raising regiments for a New England Brigade that he hoped to bring to the front with haste, and he was looking for Connecticut regiments. Buckingham was much relieved when General Benjamin Butler offered to take the Ninth off his hands.[34] As Butler—who was himself not Irish—noted in a report, he took command of a regiment that "owing to the somewhat exuberantly turbulent character of its recruits, could not be readily reduced to discipline at the hour of its recruitment, and was not in a condition to be properly sent away except under a fostering care."[35] This decision had far-reaching consequences for the men of Connecticut's Irish regiment. The close antebellum relationship between the New Haven and New York Irish militias could very well have led to the inclusion of this regiment in Meagher's Irish Brigade. Instead, they were spared the carnage of the battlefields in northern Virginia. But the regiment also missed out on the national prominence that came with service along the Potomac River and in that prominent unit. Instead of being remembered for heroic service at Antietam and Fredericksburg, the Ninth Connecticut spent most of their war service in New Orleans and along the Mississippi River, and despite their sacrifice, they received few public accolades.[36]

On November 4, 1861, approximately eight hundred volunteers left New Haven. A disorderly group, they made their way to Camp Chase in Lowell, Massachusetts, where the regiment continued to recruit and drill. The trip to Massachusetts was not without incident. The men of the Ninth Connecticut continued their rowdy behavior on the journey east. The move from home came with mixed emotions. Negative perceptions aside, the volunteers of the Ninth, recalled regimental historian Thomas Murray years after the war, "were united, like a band of brothers, to defend the Flag," and no regiment went to war with a "more intense *American* spirit or more loyal devotion to the cause of the Union" than those Irishmen. "*They* will be the men to meet our southern brethren in the field," reported the editors of the *Hartford Daily Courant* optimistically.[37]

The spirit of the men was overshadowed by commentary on their "New Haven behavior," which seemed to follow them wherever they went. Newspapers in Connecticut printed accounts of rowdiness among the troops, which were of such a concern to some in the regiment that a number of officers travelled home to refute allegations that the volunteers had destroyed property along the route. "They were so full of fight," the *Hartford Daily Courant* noted in defense of the men, that "the broken windows of the cars" stood as symbols of the men's enthusiasm. Not everyone saw this destruction of property in such a positive light. Responding to accusations of disorderly conduct that appeared in newspapers such as the *New Haven Register* and the *Hartford Courier*, the *Courant* further assured its readers that the regiment had "some good officers, and a body of men, that under such discipline as they will have to submit [to] under Butler, will fight well, and we trust will prove an honor to our state." Speaking to dissenting voices, these editors further stressed that it was "in exceedingly bad taste to represent these men" in such a manner, for they acted with "lamb like gentleness" during their trip to Lowell. "Beyond the breaking of a few window lights," the *Courant* concluded, "the injury to the car was very slight, and a majority of the men conducted themselves with propriety."[38]

The accusations levied against the regiment, however, were of such a concern to some of its members that some of the officers travelled from Lowell back to Hartford to meet with the press to address the issue of the conduct of their troops. "We yesterday received a visit from several gentlemanly officers of the 9th regiment," wrote the editors of the *Daily Courant*. "They called for the purpose of vindicating the regiment from the statements made in the Connecticut papers. . . . Since the arrival of the regiment at Lowell, the regiment has commended itself by its good conduct and the improvement of drill. . . . The officers with whom we conversed professed a strong desire and belief that the future of the regiment should cause the State to be proud of it." The unit, they claimed, had "some first rate officers and some first rate men . . . but many of them will have to be taught by B. Butler . . . that there is a vast difference between a sojer and a soldier."[39]

When the men of Ninth Connecticut arrived in Lowell they joined nearly seven hundred other volunteers at the newly constructed Camp Chase, located on the city's fairground. Although the number of troops in Lowell eventually swelled to over twenty-five hundred, public anxiety focused on the Irish regiment from Connecticut. Upon hearing the news that Irishmen were destined for Camp Chase, the residents of Lowell panicked and organized a special police force to keep order. Although this proved unnecessary—for ultimately, historian Murray noted, "the people of Lowell laughed at the fears they had entertained"—their initial reaction was telling with regard to public sentiment toward the men under Cahill's command and the reputation that followed them. Although specific references to ethnicity do not seem to have been made, the focus of the press and local communities on the behavior of the soldiers of Connecticut's only Irish regiment suggests that perhaps nativist animosity lingered in Connecticut and Massachusetts, despite the visible displays of patriotism by the Irish in those states.[40]

Disorder reigned as troops poured into Lowell. Sergeant Daniel O'Sullivan, a Kerryman, wrote to a friend that during the regiment's time there the men "had to drill very Hard but . . . were well provided for with every necesary in the line of food but the dicipline was very argreouss. . . . I went out of camp twice while in Lowell and that was enough." "It was a hard place," he lamented. "Once I went out in command of a squad of men to Hunt up deserters and were it not for my men being armed I would fare worse than in the hands of secech."[41] Supporting these assertions, the *Lowell Daily Citizen* recorded the round-up of sixty-two such wayward volunteers from numerous units as Butler's troop prepared to leave the Bay State.[42] Despite the fact that deserters came from all of the regiments stationed in Lowell, the public focus remained on the men from Connecticut. A *New York Times* correspondent reported that while encamped at Camp Chase,

> these unruly spirits from the land of steady habits won an unenviable notoriety by their unruly conduct. A high board fence inclosed the camp, but when the humor seized them the cry would be heard, "Connecticut over the fence." And away they went like so many catamounts, in defiance of all restraint. They roamed through the town at will, pulling the timid in fear, and considerably augmenting the labors of the police. When factory girls saw them coming, they too would cry out "Connecticut over the fence," and beat a double-quick to get out of their way.

It was not until the regiment embarked for the South that attitudes began to change. A strong easterly wind followed their ship, the *Constitution*, from port, and "the experience of the rough passage from Boston [to Portland, Maine, where a Maine regiment was supposedly waiting to join Butler's force] had evidently chastened the rampant spirits of the Ninth," the *Times* correspondent continued. "The sober realities of their condition now stared them in the face." "It will be gratifying," the writer concluded, "to learn that the conduct of these sons of the Emerald Isle is greatly improved. The evil spirit has been exorcised by the power of old ocean; we hear no more of 'Connecticut over the fence,' and they are now as docile as lambs." But the reporter's optimism was short lived.[43]

According to Sergeant Daniel O'Sullivan, the first leg of the journey passed with little incident. The ship arrived at Union-held Fortress Monroe on Virginia's Yorktown Peninsula; "after a week's sail the weather was cold after we left Portland untill we came on the deleware shore when it gradualy became warm and at Fort Monroe it was delightfull." The *Constitution* stayed one night before heading south for Ship Island, Mississippi, a route that took them around Key West and into the Gulf of Mexico. The journey was incredibly difficult. The weather was stifling, O'Sullivan wrote; "a dead calm prevailing not a ruffle on the water. We fared hard on ship board so many men huddled together in one ship, such bad water, such a scarcety of food, such confusion." Their troubles, though, vanished when the New England troops saw the southern shoreline for the first time. There was "such wild cheering when we came in view of secesh soil [that it] was enough to make any sane man crazy," O'Sullivan concluded. On December 4, 1861 the *Constitution* came within sight of Ship Island, set to be the base of operations for Union forces in the Gulf of Mexico. The New England Brigade was destined to spend at least the foreseeable future in the Gulf of Mexico and in particular on Ship Island, which would become the staging ground for the eventual invasion of New Orleans. "On the 4th of Dec we came in view of Ship Island South of the mouth of the Mississippi River," Sergeant O'Sullivan wrote home on Christmas Day, 1861. Their new home was "a spot more desolate than Robinson Crueso's." Yet in some ways the isolation was good for Cahill's men, for in the Gulf of Mexico they had no access to the vices that had so encouraged their rowdy behavior before they left New England.[44]

Connecticut's Irish Brigade disembarked on what was literally, a spit of sand in the midst of the Gulf of Mexico. Ship Island was "an island 10 miles long by 2 wide all loose sand, a few trees and some rushes. it was once an inhabited place but three months ago it was destroyed by the rebels when they saw they could hold it no longer on the west and there is a small fort which they tryed to destroy but did not succeed," wrote O'Sullivan. Confederate forces under General David E. Twiggs evacuated the island on September 16, 1861, and sailors from the *USS Massachusetts* immediately moved in to occupy the position. The island commanded the waterways that connected the Southern gulf ports and was invaluable to the Union blockade during 1861–62. For the men from Connecticut, notions of the glory of military service may have vanished when they laid eyes on this barrier island, for the enemy was nowhere in sight.[45]

During the winter of 1861–62, Ship Island served as the staging point for the invasion and occupation of New Orleans, and over the course of the early spring of 1862 the Ninth Connecticut spent a majority of its time drilling in preparation for that campaign. By March 1862, twelve regiments and parts of four artillery and two cavalry companies were garrisoned on the island, and command anticipated the arrival of another 6,000 men by April. For the men of the Ninth, the daily routine revolved around drill. "We dont drill any here but 4 hours a day," Daniel O'Sullivan wrote to his father-in-law; "we have to get up at the first day break then call the role and get breakfast and go to drill at 7 oclock and Drill until 8 then we rest until 1/2 past 9 oclock then drill till 1/2 10 and rest until 4 then we drill until 6." For his part, Thomas Cahill bragged to his wife that "the men are in Excellent Conduct and spirits and improving rapidly in their drill they do not look or act much like the men of Camp Welch."[46]

Although the men were increasingly military in appearance, internal dissent, supply issues, and the general difficulties that accompanied military life still plagued the regiment. Many of Cahill's soldiers were without either uniforms or arms until March 1862—sad commentary on the provisions set aside for Connecticut's Irishmen. While the once motley-looking Irish regiment drilled in the bright white sand, though, their appearance began to change. Thomas Cahill was optimistic about the changes that had occurred among the men in the regiment during the time since they had disembarked at Ship Island, but nevertheless army life was still dangerous. Soldiers in the Ninth Connecticut suffered from a variety of diseases and injuries during their first year in the South. In the years after the war, many men viewed their service in the Gulf as the primary reason for their physical deterioration as they grew older. Their accounts provide some insight into the day-to-day experiences of these soldiers during their first year in the South and attest to the daily difficulties of military life. On Ship Island, it was, according to Captain Michael McCarten, the "heavy drilling which was very bad on account of the sand . . . [that caused the men to become] . . . strained and weakened by the drill and working in the sand." McCarten further stated in a postwar account that "while on Ship Island drilling 8 hours a day for 5 months in that loose white sand besides morning inspection Dress Parade the severity of long hours of drill Reduced some of our best men to living skeletons." Cahill and his officers were intent on whipping their regiment into shape, and their isolation in the Gulf of Mexico provided them with the first real chance to drill their men regularly since the unit's inception. While McCarten's account is disturbing, and while a number of men attributed their postwar physical decline to these months on Ship Island, only one man, Private John Anderson of Company D, was discharged for disability while the regiment was stationed there.[47]

At the same time, Cahill and his men became embroiled in early political debates surrounding the issue of the emancipation of slaves. When Brigadier General John W. Phelps, a Republican from Vermont, landed on Ship Island, he issued a proclamation "to the loyal citizens of the Southwest." Attacking the institution of chattel slavery, in this declaration Phelps stated that "we believe that every State that has been admitted as a slave State into the Union since the adoption of the Constitution has been admitted in direct violation of that Constitution." Slavery, he continued, "as a social evil, might for a time be tolerated and endured, but as a political institution, it becomes imperious and exacting, controlling, like a dread necessity, all whom circumstances have compelled to live under its sway, hampering their action, and thus impeding our national progress." In conclusion, he stated, "It is the conviction of my command as a part of the national forces of the United States, that labor—manual labor—is inherently noble . . . [O]ur motto and our standard shall be, here and everywhere, and on all occasions, 'Free Labor and Workingmen's Rights.'"[48]

The *Hartford Daily Courant* noted a "good deal of indignation" that the general "should have so far forgotten his military duties as to issue a political proclamation." It was an "absurd document . . . from an absurd general." The *Columbian Weekly Register* of New Haven claimed that "Phelps is in 'personal appearance a regular John Brown.' It is evident from his proclamation that he does not bely his eminent prototype in other respects." "The re-establishment of the Union on its Constitutional basis," the same editors noted, "depends very much now, on the firmness and practical good sense, as well as the gallant bearing, of our officers."[49] Echoing other emancipation orders issued by General John Frémont and General David Hunter, the issues Phelps brought to light struck at the heart of the political debate raging across the nation during this time, as well as the broader confusion surrounding the intent of the war. With regard to General Phelps's emancipation proclamation in the Gulf of Mexico, Thomas Cahill wrote home that he was afraid that such a declaration would "make trouble here." Many were against it, including the regimental chaplain, Father Daniel Mullen who was "bitter against it and says he will denounce it as Containing Sentiments anti Catholic." Cahill made no mention of the reaction of soldiers in his command, but did note that one of the Massachusetts regiments was on the verge of resigning their service in reaction to Phelps's order. As a personal policy, the Irish colonel vowed to "be Cautious in my movements but certainly shall not Endorse Either Abolition or Infidelity or sectarianism."[50]

The impact of Phelps's proclamation still lingered as winter turned to spring. "I do not know when anything has occurred which has caused me more annoyance that the issuing of that proclamation and it came near getting us into difficulty too," Cahill wrote to his wife. Mullen wrote a scathing letter to Phelps, who had responded by threatening to court-martial the priest. Many officers on Ship Island, however, concurred with Mullen's opinion pronouncing Phelps's document "a most senseless and bigotted production." "I am sorry that he issued the 'Proclamation,'" Cahill wrote at the end of February. In March, Sergeant Daniel O'Sullivan also made note of Phelps's political maneuverings. "I expect you recd his Proclamation in some of the papers," he wrote home, "I seen it here in some of the boston Papers stating that it was condemed By all politicians of the North he is in the feaver of niggers a little but I tell you he is a good old fellow his name is J T Phelps." The broader impact of this proclamation on the mostly Democrat volunteers of the Irish regiment is unclear, though such a statement must certainly have appeared to make the war a crusade for the end of slavery—something taboo for many Connecticut Democrats in late 1861 and early 1862.[51]

The Northern public enthusiastically followed the exploits of the 23rd Illinois and 69th New York as they won acclaim on the battlefield in the summer and fall of 1861. Not all ethnic units were so fortunate. In Connecticut, ethnic organization was stymied because the state was inundated with volunteers, and there did not seem to be a need for an ethnic unit that first summer of the war. With Lincoln's call for troops after First Bull Run, however, Connecticut's Irishmen were finally given the opportunity to prove their loyalty to their adopted nation through the formation of an ethnic unit—for Irish volunteers from Connecticut did enlist and serve patriotically in mixed regiments early in the war. Justifying their service in patriotic terms, these men pointed to the success of other Irish regiments as proof of ethnic military prowess and sought to replicate those successes with their own outspoken acts in defense of the Union. Nearly 60 percent of the men in the Ninth Connecticut were born in Ireland, and Irishmen made up the majority in all but one of the companies, illustrating the broad-based appeal that service in this unit had among the immigrant population in that state. Organized after Connecticut authorized state bounties, however, the socioeconomic demographics of these men were different than those of their counterparts in Illinois, and they largely represented the working-class communities of Connecticut's cities.

In spite of the excitement surrounding the organization of Connecticut's only Irish regiment, the men were not spared criticism at home. The new volunteers were disorderly, and their acts more often than not were a poor reflection of a state nicknamed the "Land of Steady Habits." Perhaps, too, animosity at home reflected lingering nativism, an echo of the Know-Nothing purges of the mid-1850s that had succeeded in disbanding the state's ethnic militia units amid fears of immigrant loyalty. As the regiment moved south as part of Butler's New England Expeditionary Force, optimism nevertheless remained high, and both Cahill and his officers were certain of their ability to whip their raw unit into shape. In a sense, though, the Connecticut men were lucky, for their early conduct in New England spared them from the slaughter that decimated the Irish Brigade in battles along the Potomac. They faced what ultimately became three years of occupational duty in the Deep South, where disease and alcohol emerged as their primary enemies.

The experiences of the regiment and the reactions of those in New Haven and Hartford, Connecticut and in Lowell, Massachusetts did not reflect a universal disdain for Irish volunteers but, rather, illustrated local responses to local situations—a prudent observation to keep in mind when contextualizing the Civil War service of immigrants. As 1862 progressed, the Ninth Connecticut would be tested for the first time on the battlefield, where they performed heroically and lived up to every expectation placed upon them. Reports of the regiment's gallant service flooded home, and the animosity that had cast the Ninth from New Haven was soon forgotten, replaced by the same excitement that had driven the unit's creation seven months earlier. As the Irishmen of the Ninth Connecticut drilled on the blinding white sands of Ship Island, however, awaiting their first test under fire, their countrymen to the north in Wisconsin found themselves in their own battle, fighting for their rights as citizen-soldiers in a mutiny championed by many at home.

# 3 The Formation of the 17th Wisconsin

As Cahill herded his "hard sort" onto train cars for the move to Camp Chase in Lowell, Massachusetts, the Irish in Wisconsin were only just organizing into a coherent unit. Hardly a reflection of the general support of Wisconsin's Irish American population for war, the lethargy with which the 17th Wisconsin organized spoke largely to more general trends in volunteering seen throughout the North during this time. As in Illinois, Irishmen in Wisconsin were eager to serve, and during the early months of the war that desire trumped ethnic organization. In the late summer of 1861, however, immigrants in Wisconsin, like their countrymen in Connecticut, began to conceptualize their own brigade. Recruiting rhetoric in Wisconsin mirrored that of organizers in Connecticut, but the regiment that ultimately materialized in Wisconsin was a unique reflection of the state and of the settlement patterns of the immigrant population living there. This "Irish" regiment was more diverse than those of Illinois and Connecticut, had no strong connections to the state's major urban center, Milwaukee, and the men of the 17th Wisconsin also had a much different relationship with their state and their communities than their comrades to the south and east. Their regiment, though, made a powerful statement. Though the Irish were scattered throughout the Badger State, they played important and visible roles in their communities, and Irish volunteers (though proportionally fewer than in other Irish regiments) bestowed upon the 17th Wisconsin a strong sense of ethnicity that was championed at home and within the ranks. The voluntary enlistment of the immigrants in an Irish regiment appeared to solidify the relationship between these adopted citizens and the state. In signing the muster rolls they became citizen-soldiers, reaffirming their relationship to the state even before they fired their rifles for the first time on the field of battle.

By 1860 nearly 50,000 Irish immigrants called the Badger State their home, though their arrival and settlement patterns differed substantially from those of their countrymen to the south and east. On average, these men and women had spent some seven years in other states prior to their move west, meaning that many immigrants undertook that move only after they had achieved some degree of economic stability. Wisconsin's Irish do not appear to have conformed to the stereotype of Irish immigrants as "urban pioneers," but, rather, seemingly settled haphazardly, scattered in small communities throughout the state. The land for the city of Milwaukee, approximately ninety miles from Chicago and bordering Lake Michigan, was purchased between 1835 and 1840 in a flurry of buying, in transactions that were, according to the U.S. Commissioner of Public Lands, the "the largest and most remarkable sales known to the department." Milwaukee was incorporated as a city in 1846, and by the turn of the decade it was a bustling port with a burgeoning industrial base. In 1850 alone, 55,774 passengers disembarked on the city's wharfs, and 2,800 Irish settled in Milwaukee itself. That number grew over the decade, but not substantially. While Milwaukee's population soared past 45,000 in 1860, the Irish numbered only 4,277, less than 10 percent of the total population, a proportionally smaller presence by half compared to major cities such as New Haven, Hartford, and Chicago. Despite its small size, this Milwaukee community was the largest single Irish enclave in the state. The Irish working class in Milwaukee, however, bore some similarities to those in other cities. Less than half of the working-age Irish-born men were unskilled laborers. Approximately 72 percent of these unskilled laborers identified themselves simply as "laborers" or "day-laborers," but they made up just 33 percent of the total number of Irish workers in the city, meaning that Irishmen in Milwaukee were less likely to be employed in unstable or insecure jobs than those in Chicago, New Haven, and especially New York City. More than half of the unskilled workers in Milwaukee were property owners, and more than one quarter of these men owned personal property and real estate worth more than $200, making this group the most financially stable across the major cities in this study.[1]

Artisans represented just over 35 percent of the sample of Irish workers in Milwaukee and just under half of the blue-collar working class. They were employed in forty-two discrete occupations. Shoemaking, carpentry, and blacksmithing attracted the highest numbers of men, but opportunity abounded for brick makers, masons, express men, painters, plasterers, printers, and teamsters, to name just some of the many occupations pursued by skilled workers among Milwaukee's Irish. Approximately 65 percent of these men were property owners and nearly 20 percent of this group claimed ownership of $500 or more in personal property and real estate. Nearly three-quarters of the skilled and unskilled workers were married, and families averaged two children. White-collar workers made up approximately 11 percent of the Irish workers, and a majority of these men were employed in low nonmanual positions, working as clerks, grocers, and police officers. Property ownership among this class stood at nearly 70 percent, and among those men, 75 percent held assets worth at least $500. Nearly 60 percent of this class were married—a lower percentage than found among the laboring class—and family size was nearly identical.

The birthplaces of some of these men's children provides insight into immigrant mobility within the United States prior to the Civil War. The oldest son of thirty-five-year-old Irish laborer John Sullivan, for example, was born in New York in 1847. He and his wife had other children, one born in New Jersey in 1850, one in New York in 1856, one in Illinois in 1858, and one in Wisconsin, two months before the 1860 census was taken. Thomas Mahan's eldest son was born in Canada in 1848 before he and his family crossed the border to Maine, where two more sons were born, in 1850 and 1857. The family moved to Wisconsin at some point thereafter, as his youngest son—nine months old when the census was taken—was born in Milwaukee. Similar trends existed among at least one-third of this sample of Irishmen in Milwaukee, illustrating the diverse paths that some immigrant men and their families took from Ireland to the East Coast of North America, and then west, in the years before the Civil War.

Madison, Wisconsin, centered around four lakes, lay in an "agricultural country of unsurpassed fertility," according to a local historian in the nineteenth century. The site remained largely unsettled until the nineteenth century, but when the territorial government was organized in July 1836, and Madison was established as the capital. Although at the time "only three white men resided in what is now Dane county," Madison's central location was appealing to state lawmakers, who pursued its transition into the state's capital. In 1840 the population stood at just 146. According to one early settler, Madison in 1845 was "an insignificant hamlet standing in a dense forest thicket, without streets, avenues, walks or improvements of any kind. . . . Population had but barely discovered it. . . . There was but one German settler . . . and three Irish."[2]

By 1851, however, over 1,500 residents called Madison home, a number that grew to over 7,500 by 1860. By 1857, enough Irish had arrived to warrant the formation of an ethnic militia unit, and by 1860, Madison was home to 835 Irish men and women, who made up 11 percent of the total population—a proportion similar to that of the Irish in Milwaukee. Among Irish residents of Madison of military age, in 1860 blue-collar workers made up 81 percent of the working class.

Nearly 80 percent of these men were employed as unskilled workers, and almost all of this group worked as "laborers" or "day laborers" in the city. Artisans made up approximately 18 percent of the working class, and represented a mere ten different professions, among them printers, plasters, tailors, molders, and shoemakers. Property ownership for both unskilled workers and artisans hovered around 60 percent, and nearly 80 percent of these men were married.

As in Milwaukee, Irish men employed as white-collar workers—so identified for their work as surveyors, railroad agents, fruit dealers, and the like—represented 11 percent of the total sample. Nearly two-thirds of these men claimed some property, but a majority owned no real estate and their personal property was worth less than $50. Nevertheless, three-quarters of these men were married and had, on average, three children. The birthplaces of children of Madison's Irish immigrants reveal the same trend in antebellum movement evident among Milwaukee Irish, namely, the slow progression west from initial port of entry in the decade before the Civil War.

Fond du Lac, north of Milwaukee on the southern tip of Lake Winnebago, also attracted a number of immigrant settlers, who began arriving in the late 1840s. Fond du Lac was first linked to the city of Sheboygan on Lake Michigan by a plank road, but the Rock Valley Union Railroad was completed in 1854, and construction on the Chicago and North Western Railway, begun in 1851, was completed in 1859, further connecting Fond du Lac to points east. Writing home to Ireland after his arrival in the village, one recent immigrant noted that Fond du Lac "calls to me mind the state of Carthage when Aeneas entered it All persons bussy about building Some in this street some in that street All cluttering about business and buildings." Opportunity abounded. As in Madison, a great many of the Irishmen in Fond du Lac belonged to the working class, and a majority of these workers classified themselves simply as laborers. Artisans made up nearly one-fifth of this group of working class Irishmen. White-collar workers made up less than one-tenth of the total number of employed Irishmen. Nearly 60 percent of the blue-collar workers were property owners, and among this group all but one man claimed a net worth of more than $100. Men employed in the business professions showed even greater security; all were property owners with real estate and personal property worth more than $500, suggesting a level of stability among men of all classes not found in towns or cities in Connecticut or Illinois.[3]

In Beloit, a town on the Rock River that straddled the southern border of Wisconsin along the Illinois state line, Irish employment was the most skewed of any town or city in the three states this book examines. In 1860, 461 Irish lived in Beloit, making up just under 10 percent of the total population. Among the sample of Irish men in the town, none were professionals. Just over three-fourths of the men worked at manual jobs, and nearly 80 percent were unskilled workers, almost all "laborers." Beloit was home to the largest agrarian population of any city in this study—one fifth of the men were in farming, though most worked as farm hands rather than owning their own farms. Of the total Irish population of Beloit, 70 percent of the men were employed in nonspecific jobs as "laborers," whether that meant on local farms or in the town itself. A majority of these men owned no property. Such numbers seem to confirm an observation made by the Emigration Commissioner of the State of Wisconsin in 1853, that "if it be true that the Irish emigration is near as extensive as the German, the reason why comparatively so few of them appeared at the office is . . . that the greater portion arrive with but limited means, and are therefore induced to seize upon the first work offered them for subsistence."[4]

In Wisconsin as a whole, unskilled workers made up less than 20 percent of the total workforce. Nevertheless, these statistics should not be misconstrued to suggest an overwhelming mass of unskilled immigrants clustering in western urban centers. The reality was that these towns were comparatively small. Only 262 Irish men lived in Fond du Lac in 1860, and Beloit was home to 180 more. Milwaukee and Madison contained total populations of Irish-born men of military age of 1,661 and 365 respectively. Furthermore, that nearly 80 percent of unskilled workers were married suggests some degree of stability among these men. Spread throughout the state in small communities, by 1860 the Irish in Wisconsin were, seemingly, thriving, and when war broke out, many of these men would choose to take up arms in defense of their adopted homeland.

In spite of the relative socioeconomic stability of the Irish population of Wisconsin, public concerns emerged, as in Connecticut and Illinois, surrounding the presence and potential impact of this immigrant group within the state. The Irish held undue political influence in Wisconsin in the decades before the war, and their Democratic allies succeeded, in 1844, in passing a law granting limited suffrage to "all white male inhabitants over twenty-one years of age who had resided for three months in the territory." Reflecting the realization by Democrats that the party "could not have retained control in the first state and national elections but for this enfranchisement of non-naturalized citizens," voter qualifications became an important issue in state politics thereafter. For their part, nativists fought to limit the impact of the immigrant vote by calling for a law that "would force the foreigner to reside in the country twenty-one years previous to exercising political suffrage." These men believed that full participation in American politics took "study—and a term of years is necessary to elapse before it is supposed that a sufficient quality of political knowledge is gained to make the elector vote intelligently."[5]

For some, though, fear lay simply in the ever-narrowing gap between numbers of immigrants and numbers of native born, which might "leave the natives of the soil in a minority in their own land." Others, such as the editors of the *Wisconsin Daily Patriot* in 1854, feared that the Know-Nothings would "deprive our adopted citizens of all political rights. This shows a case of clear, premeditated, hypocrisy." The rise of the Republican Party, "tainted with that Know-Nothingism," the *Weekly Wisconsin Patriot* commented two years later, "constitute a party favorable to the worst species of Slavery propagandism—they are determined to *enslave* the religious sentiments of a large portion of our people." It is important to note that in Wisconsin, as in the other states examined in this study, expressions of nativism appeared hand-in-hand with public support of the immigrant population that was, arguably, as powerful as nativist propaganda, and perhaps reflected the very real connections that existed between adopted citizens and their states in the years before the outbreak of the Civil War. Furthermore, the impact of nativism was limited in Wisconsin in large part precisely because of the significant size of the state's immigrant population. Nativist candidate Millard Fillmore received less than one percent of the state's vote in his failed bid for the presidency in 1856. The rhetoric of support for these immigrants, first exhibited in the antebellum period, appeared time and again throughout the war as the press, politicians, and public figures came to the defense of the patriotism of the state's adopted citizens.[6]

As the nation moved towards war, questions about Irish loyalty reemerged, and public assertions of fealty quickly put these fears to rest. Democrats throughout the state openly disavowed secession in the winter of 1861–62. "Our Republic," the editors of the *Weekly Wisconsin Patriot* cried, "would cease to be a refuge for the oppressed of all nations if broken in twain, and under no circumstances would their condition be tolerable in a Sothern slave Confederacy. . . . Under such circumstances of peril, it behooves every good citizen to stand firmly by the Union." Even before the first shots were fired in Charleston, observers in Milwaukee enthusiastically noted the outspoken patriotism displayed by the Irish during their annual St. Patrick's Day celebration. "Never before has it been our good fortune to be present at a gathering of the Sons of Old Erin," wrote the *Daily Milwaukee Press and News*, "where so much true Irish heart and feeling was manifested, so genuine and unselfish a love of native land exhibited, so much loyalty to this, their adopted land displayed." After hearing the news of Fort Sumter's fall, Milwaukee's Catholic citizens hoisted an American flag above their cathedral. "We happen to know the bishop," reported the editors of the *Milwaukee Sentinel*, and he, "like all other good Catholics, is a Union man." In Fond du Lac, following the declaration of war "strong resolutions passed without reference to party to sustain the Union at all hazards," and the Irish Hibernian Guards reported for duty.[7]

Although the unionism that emerged in April 1861—accompanied by the outspoken proclamations of loyalty made by Irish Americans in the state—played an important component in momentarily uniting the state, it ultimately reflected more a rejection of secession than an abandonment of party principles. "Revolutions do not go backward," Wisconsin Governor Alexander Randall admonished in January. "We want no compromise. We ask none. We will submit to none." Pressure from Northern Democrats for compromise with their Southern brethren was eased, for a time, by the winds of war. "The Madison *Patriot* is [now] the most enthusiastic of union sheets as it was the most persistent of Democrats," the *Milwaukee Sentinel* announced in late April. "The North," the editors of the *Wisconsin Daily Patriot* wrote, responding to the outcry over Fort Sumter, "was slow to anger—slow to start—patient, enduring, and even forgiving of the most wanton insults, for the sake of peace; but since her very toleration has been treated as an evidence of weakness and cowardice, she has now risen in the majesty of her might, and woe to the provokers of her wrath." In their support for the Union, Wisconsin's Democrats, Irish and native-born alike, helped to momentarily ease lingering doubts about loyalty and questions about patriotism. Despite this support, however, suspicions still lingered under the surface as antebellum political and social animosities continued to define relationships in Northern states.[8]

Wisconsin editors cited the eager enlistment of immigrant volunteers in the eastern states as encouraging proof that "this class of citizens would be true to their allegiance." An "appeal to Irishmen" that first appeared in the Boston press and was reprinted in Wisconsin asked that "every adopted citizen remember the oath which he has taken to support the constitution, and no people pay greater reverence to the sanctity of an oath than those of Irish birth." Wisconsin's Irish took up the call. Disloyal Irish were "a few designing, traitorous demagogues," for "the Irish people on this continent are loyal to the Union, the constitution and the government, and will support them by every means in their power." As spring turned to summer, enthusiasm for the war remained high. In Janesville, the Irish came together in an enthusiastic meeting to organize a volunteer company. "The Irishmen of this city are responding cheerfully to the call of their adopted country," wrote the editor of the *Janesville Daily Gazette*, "and have issued a notice for a meeting this evening to organize a volunteer company. We predict that this company will be filled with an alacrity and a class of able-bodied, true men worthy of Irish patriotism and the active citizens who have initiated the movement." "The natives of Ireland in this country can get up one of the best companies in Wisconsin and we have no doubt they will do so," observers noted a week later. By June, reports came in from Milwaukee that an Irish brigade had begun to organize there.[9]

As in Connecticut, though, no Irish regiment formed in the Badger State. In part, these men lacked leadership. In 1860 Wisconsin's preeminent Irish militia unit, the Union Guards of Milwaukee, had their arms confiscated by the governor as a result of a political scuffle over the Fugitive Slave Act, an event that created some animosity between the Irish and their adopted state. Then, in September of that year, the Irish community was struck a serious blow when the steamship *Lady Elgin* sank on her return voyage from the Democratic convention in Chicago, taking with her a large number of Wisconsin's prominent Irish politicians and military leaders, including the commanding officers of Milwaukee's militia units. This event seriously hindered Irish power in the state and seems to have had repercussions on ethnic organization in 1861.[10]

For those volunteers who wanted to fight alongside other Irishmen, options did exist. "Irish patriots of Wisconsin, who wish to fight for your country, you can still do so; go to Chicago and join the Irish brigade, or go to some other State where you will be called into active service," noted one editorial in the *Daily Milwaukee News* in June 1861, "so that you can show to the world your devotion to your country's flag and cause, where you will be respected as men, and prove your valor by spilling your blood, and fighting under the star spangled banner of your adopted country." A year later the editors of the *Wisconsin Daily Patriot* noted with satisfaction that

> a few years ago the greater part of the political party now styled Republican, and professing to be *par excellence* the guardians of the government, were the *know-nothing party*, and were carrying on a crusade against the Roman Catholic people of the country on the alleged score that they were not loyal to the government and should not be trusted in any of its offices. . . . We can speak for this section, that the Catholics have shown their loyalty to our Government, without flinching. They are ready to fight for the Government and its institutions and laws, as established by our forefathers—He who

seeks for toryism among the Catholics will seek in vain, for a more chivalrous, patriotic class cannot be found on this or any other continent.

Yet during the enlistment frenzy of the spring of 1861, when the Irish American community in Wisconsin needed powerful advocates to push for the creation and acceptance of ethnic units, no leaders emerged.[11]

In a manner similar to that of the Irish in Connecticut, Wisconsin's Irish understood the organization and service of the 69th New York and 23rd Illinois to reflect the potential of their race and sought to mirror those displays at home. "I saw the Sixty-ninth (N.Y.) Regiment, Col. Corcoran, march down Broadway," a correspondent for the *Milwaukee Daily Sentinel* wrote. "It is mostly, if not entirely, composed of Irishmen; and, with the 'Stars and Stripes' they carried the green flag of Erin. It seemed as though all countrymen and countrywomen, for many miles around, had thronged into Broadway to bid them good-bye and God-speed! Their parting was a most enthusiastic one," he concluded. "Every nationality is represented in the grand army of defense now being called into the field," the *Weekly Wisconsin Patriot* reported in another article on the famous New York regiment. "Probably no Company can be found in which are not more or less of our patriotic adopted fellow citizens," another commentator reported enthusiastically. "This is perhaps best exemplified in New York city, where the fires of patriotism [among the Irish] are burning with unwonted effulgence." Readers were given detailed accounts of Thomas Francis Meagher's departure from New York for Washington that summer. Meagher's men "represented the Irish element in the full sense of the term. The men are strong, active and wiry, and when they get a fair chance, judging from appearance, they will 'clear the track before them,' and pioneer themselves into the front rank of military men." "Until the hour of departure," this *Weekly Wisconsin Patriot* article reported, "the headquarters . . . was crowded by the relatives and friends of the brave lads who were about being drafted off to a field of glory and death. It was pleasing to observe the spirit which actuated and filled the bosoms of those fair ones of the Emerald Isle, who were present to bid their adieux to their relatives and friends."[12]

Accounts of Irish heroics at Bull Run flooded the midwestern papers. The New Yorkers "performed prodigies of valor. . . . They stripped themselves, and dashed into the enemy with the utmost fury," reported the *Weekly Wisconsin Patriot*. As the enemy retreated, the "Sixty-ninth, by a flanking movement, took them in the rear, and pouring a deadly fire into their ranks, afterwards charged them with the bayonet. The slaughter was terrible, and the defeat complete."

"The 69th (N.Y. Irish) fought with splendid and tenacious courage," the *Wisconsin Daily Patriot* recounted. "They charged batteries two or three times and would have held them but for the reinforcements which were constantly and steadily poured in"—a subtle comment on broader sentiment surrounding Irish action in the early months of the war, that defeats were not due to the inadequacy of the ethnic soldiers but, rather, to circumstances far beyond their control. The charge of the 69th, which drove a regiment of Louisiana Zouaves from the field, led to praise from General Irwin McDowell, who doffed his hat to the 69th and said, "[Y]ou have just gained the victory." The *Daily Patriot* printed verses penned by a passionate Irish American lyricist who spoke to the heroics of Corcoran's Men: "On! Sixty-Ninth, where glory leads the standard of the brave, /And guard the land our father's blood unto their children gave." In this eulogy to the embattled defenders of the Federal retreat at First Bull Run, the poet emphasized the importance of the 69th New York Irish Regiment to the larger diasporic community, who were drawn to, and encouraged by, the action of their countrymen in Virginia.[13]

Similar narratives appeared after the stand of the 23rd Illinois at Lexington. When Mulligan's Brigade mustered into service in June 1861, the citizens of Milwaukee were assured that "this body of men is highly spoken of and will do good service if the opportunity is afforded them." Excitement grew when, in September, Chicago's Irish Brigade was finally cast into battle. As in Connecticut, Mulligan was mythologized in early reports from Missouri. When he told Sterling Price to "go to hell," Mulligan became a national hero. The editor of the *Janesville Daily Gazette* applauded the move, bluntly noting, "we ADMIRE his curt and daring answer. And saucy, rough, pointed, earnest, and unmannerly as it is, it speaks volumes" of the colonel's commitment to his nation's cause.[14]

An account of battle in the *Weekly Wisconsin Patriot* found Mulligan leading a charge against rebels who "scattered like a flock of sheep," and described the colonel in the aftermath as uninjured save for a "buck shot through the leg" and a coat riddled with bullet holes, where "six or seven balls and buck shot [had passed] through the green blouse he wore." In another account, Mulligan, wounded, "would not give up his sword until taken from him by main force." The Irish Brigade, the *Wisconsin Daily Patriot* applauded, "fought for 59 hours without water and had only 2 barrels of vinegar to quench their thirst all that time," and their surrender came only after "Mulligan was compelled to yield to a foe more terrible than the 27,000 rebels who surrounded him." To the *Daily Patriot*, the stand of the Irish at Lexington was proof that these men, who newspapers of Chicago "used civilly to style 'voting cattle' have covered themselves with glory in the cause of the Union. Mulligan's Irish Brigade justify the reputation which their native countrymen have won in every civilized nation for loyalty and higher military courage . . . [and] . . . deserve to be ranked [in gallantry] with the gallant New York Sixty-ninth. . . . *The naturalized citizens of this country have been as patriotic and self sacrificing in war as the native born*" [emphasis in original].[15]

News of Mulligan's service drew envy in Wisconsin. In a recruiting advertisement that appeared in Watertown, Wisconsin under the bold heading of "Irishmen! Rally to the Rescue!" the author noted that "Illinois has won for herself fame by the heroic conduct of her brave Col. Mulligan and his Brigade on the bloody field of Lexington; let the Irishmen of Watertown and surrounding country not be the hindhand"! "Hurrah for the GALLANT 69th," the author stated further, "Cannot the Irishmen of Wisconsin do as well as her sister state?" "Our gallant countrymen of the gallant Sixty-Ninth have covered themselves with imperishable glory" and must be revenged, noted the *Appleton Crescent*; "Let there be ten thousand Irishmen on the south bank of the Potomac in twenty days, their battle cry being—Corcoran, Rescued if Living, Avenged, if Dead!" The Meagher Guards soon began organizing in Madison, and the city's *Daily Patriot* confidently assured its readers, "It is well known that Irishmen are quite at home and never behind on the battle field, and it is certain that a regiment of such, will 'clear the way' every time." "Let Us Fill Up the Ranks," read another headline in the Janesville paper; "what could the little handful of men with the brave Col. Mulligan be expected to do with so overwhelming a force as was known to be concentrating against them?" In the darkest hours of the first year of the war it fell upon these Irish volunteers to sacrifice themselves to save the Union. National support for these Irish regiments spurred on the creation of the 17th Wisconsin, the state's first and only Irish regiment, which began recruiting that fall.[16]

The task of bringing the Irish together fell to forty-seven-year-old Irish immigrant and lawyer John Doran. Doran was well known in Milwaukee. Captain of the local militia unit the Montgomery Guards, he had served as a representative to the state's constitutional convention and, in 1860, had led the committee to search and identify bodies of victims of the *Lady Elgin* disaster, a grim task but one that nevertheless reflected his standing in the community. Commissioned colonel of Wisconsin's "Irish Brigade" in October, Doran began the arduous task of building his regiment. The lack of a large ethnic enclave in the state meant that Doran, who sought "to fill a regiment that will be a credit to the state and to its Celtic residents" and lead "as fine a body of patriotic Irishmen as ever marched to victory," traveled throughout the state speaking on the "organization and duties of Irishmen, and citizens generally, in connection with the war."[17]

Both James Mulligan and Thomas Cahill benefitted from statewide pressure to organize an Irish unit early in the war. In Wisconsin, however, the impetus for organization was muted until the late fall of 1861, in particular because many Irish soldiers chose to enlist in ethnically mixed regiments. Recruiters in smaller communities pushed for volunteers, broadly, and in each state there were public forums where men debated the duties of Irishmen, but generally the adopted citizens in Connecticut and Illinois seemed open to, and supportive of, these units from the first days of the conflict. Doran, however, found himself travelling from town to town across Wisconsin speaking at war meetings, urging ethnic support for his Irish regiment. From Madison he travelled south to Janesville, where he addressed a meeting of Irish citizens meeting to discuss "their opinions as to the present war and the position they ought to hold as guardians of their adopted country." Doran made "an eloquent speech, setting forth the duty of Irishmen as citizens of America, incumbent upon them to support, sustain, and defend the flag that affords them, their children, and their wives, its proud protection." The meeting "adjourned with that warmth and patriotism that promises a full contingent of the Celtic element in this neighborhood to wield the arms of our country in the defense of our families, our altars, and our firesides."[18]

Father Napoleon Mignault, chaplain of the newly forming Irish Brigade, expressed similar views when he lectured before a large crowd in Watertown. In a speech designed to boost recruiting efforts, the priest

> closed with an earnest and patriotic appeal to the Irish citizens of Wisconsin to do as the Germans, French and Norwegians had done in this and other States—fill up the ranks of the Irish Brigade, take their fortunes on the field of battle, in defense of the starry flag that had always protected them—in support of the constitution that secured them equal rights—in the maintenance of that Union they had hoped would be perpetual—and against the traitors who were trying to dismember a Republic that had brought to all nothing but blessings, prosperity and honor.

This appeal to ethnic and civic loyalty was successful, and by December 5, a full company was raised in Watertown under the command of Donald D. Scott, a thirty-four-year-old railroad conductor. The local paper warned that "those intending to join this company will find it for their advantage to do so now.... [T]he present opportunity for the display of patriotism and valor may soon pass away and its like will not probably return in this generation." In Janesville the regiment was seen as "a very favorable opportunity for our Irish citizens to enlist under officers and a chaplain of their own nationality." If ethnic allegiances were not enough, recruiting advertisements in Milwaukee promised "Pay to Privates, $13 per month for single men and $18 for married men, $100 *Bounty and* 150 *Acres of Land!*" Broadly, then, the rhetoric in Wisconsin was poignantly focused on the duties of Wisconsin's ethnic citizens to the Union, which included the formation of an Irish regiment. Open enthusiasm for an all-Irish regiment had contributed greatly to unit formation in the East. In Wisconsin, Doran and his lieutenants struggled to convince the residents and create a tangible link between patriotism and the formation of the 17th Wisconsin. Despite initial hesitation, though, attitudes changed quickly as fall turned to winter.[19]

On January 4, 1862, Doran notified the state that the 17th Regiment was full up, and requested to be ordered to camp. Some two weeks later, eighteen- year-old Ebenezer Wescott arrived at Madison's Camp Randall with his company. Led by Captain John McGowan, the Corcoran Guards of Sheboygan were eager for their chance to go to war. "We arrived here at twelve o'clock Friday night," he wrote to his mother on January 19. In the morning Wescott and the other men of Company E, an ethnically diverse group, "went to the Capitol and were mustered into the United States service, and drew our uniforms and ... [became] ... full fledged volunteer soldiers of Uncle Sam." The men's spirits were high, he wrote, and "most of the Boys think now that they could whip the whole Southern Army, if only they had a chance."[20]

The organization of the 17th Wisconsin was successful, to a degree. The optimistic colonel initially received state authorization to organized twenty ethnic companies—two full regiments. Though his goal was to form a brigade of Irishmen, he ultimately fell well short of his initial plan. Thirteen companies presented themselves in Madison that winter and became, after the consolidation, the 17th Wisconsin "Irish" regiment. Unlike the strong connection that existed between the 9th Connecticut and New Haven's militia units, the organization of the Wisconsin's "Irish Brigade" reflected geographic, ethnic, and political diversity within the regiment.

The names of the first three companies that formed the regiment are understandable. The Mulligan and Corcoran Guards were named, of course, for the commanding officers of the 69th New York and 23rd Illinois and reflect both

Table 3-1 Companies that Volunteered to Fight in the 17th Wisconsin

| Company Name | Geographic Origin | Commanding Officer |
|---|---|---|
| Mulligan Guards | Kenosha | Hugh McDermott |
| Corcoran Guards | Sheboygan | John McGowen |
| Emmet Guards | Dodge County | Patrick McCauley |
| Doran Guards | Outagamie | Welcome Hyde |
| French Mountaineers | Brown County | William Southworth |
| Watertown Infantry | Jefferson County | Donald D. Scott |
| Sauk County Union Guards | Sauk County | Charles Armstrong |
| Jackson Guards | Juneau County | John Crane |
| Fond du Lac Guards | Fond du Lac | Patrick O'Connor |
| Harvey Guards | Dane County | William Wheeler |
| Oconto Rifles | Oconto County | McAfee |
| Peep o' Day Boys | Racine | Patrick Geraughty |
| Milwaukee Badgers | Milwaukee | Richard Rooney |

the urgency of the ethnic organization in the fall and winter of 1861 and the prominence of these officers. The Emmet Guards, like their counterparts in New Haven, derived their name from Irish nationalist Robert Emmet. The Jackson Guards, like comrades from Connecticut, Illinois, and Michigan, again likely drew inspiration from the United Irishman William Jackson. The origins of the name French Mountaineers is unclear, though it could suggest a relationship between the Irish of Wisconsin and the "Wild Geese," Irish exiles who fought for France and won renown for their service in Europe. Two company names, though, stand out. The name Harvey Guards is most likely a reference to Beauchamp Bagenal Harvey, a Protestant who led the forces of the nonsectarian Irish nationalist movement the United Irishmen at the Battle of New Ross (County Wexford, Ireland) during the 1798 Rebellion. He was, historian Robert Kee has remarked, one of the men responsible for "founding the separatist republican movement" in Ireland. The strangest name here, within the context of the Irish references, is that of the Peep O' Day Boys from Racine, whose name refers to an agrarian Irish Protestant movement that emerged in the eighteenth century. Referencing defenders of the Orange Order and perpetrators of anti-Catholic violence in Ulster during the last two decades of the eighteenth century, a company so named seems very out of place in a regiment that was so closely connected to Irish nationalism and the Catholic Church, but its presence is, perhaps, reflective of the inclusive nature of Wisconsin society during the nineteenth century.[21]

Furthermore, the degree of geographic diversity within the regiment served as a testament to Doran's recruiting efforts and the lack of a central recruiting base in Wisconsin. Irishmen enlisted from towns and cities across the state, a pattern reflecting the diverse settlement patterns of these immigrant men and women in the Midwest. The composition and organization of the 17th Wisconsin bore little resemblance to those of sister regiments in Connecticut and Illinois, and even contemporary observers struggled to determine where exactly the regiment was from. Newspapers throughout Wisconsin referred to the 17th as "Wisconsin's Irish Brigade," but some reporters, including Sylvans Cadwallader, a journalist for the *Chicago Times* attached to Ulysses S. Grant's headquarters, were under the impression that Wisconsin's Irishmen were came mainly from Milwaukee, a misconception likely driven by the prominence of the Irish enclave in that city and Milwaukee resident John Doran's role in organizing the unit.[22]

The most notable difference between the 17th Wisconsin and the regiments from Illinois and Connecticut examined in this book was the lack of identifiable recruiting centers, such as New Haven County, Cook County, and LaSalle County. Companies in the regiment contained men from across the state and were geographically diverse. Only in Company C were a majority of men from the same town, Fond du Lac, and even there volunteers from that town represented only slightly more than half of the total number of recruits. But recruiting numbers are telling of the appeal of Doran's message in communities outside of Milwaukee. When the war broke out, there were only 262 Irishmen of military age in LaSalle, compared to 1,661 who lived in Milwaukee. Yet Milwaukee residents who enlisted in the 17th Wisconsin did so individually and in small groups, and most importantly, there were very few Irishmen among those recruits. Of the 64 men from Milwaukee who enlisted in the winter of 1862, only 16 were Irish. Most of them were, in fact, of German descent. Thus, unlike with the regiments from Illinois and Connecticut, it is difficult to draw any firm conclusions about the types of men from the major towns in Wisconsin who enlisted in the Irish Brigade.

Although enlistment patterns in Wisconsin suggest that ethnic neighborhoods or wards were rather unimportant when it came to unit organization, company-level recruiting nevertheless displayed some similarities with the Ninth Connecticut and 23rd Illinois. This was especially true when it came to the relationship between an individual's place in an antebellum community and his receiving a commission, both at company and regimental level. In 1861, for example, Martin Curran found himself an officer in the Hibernian Guards

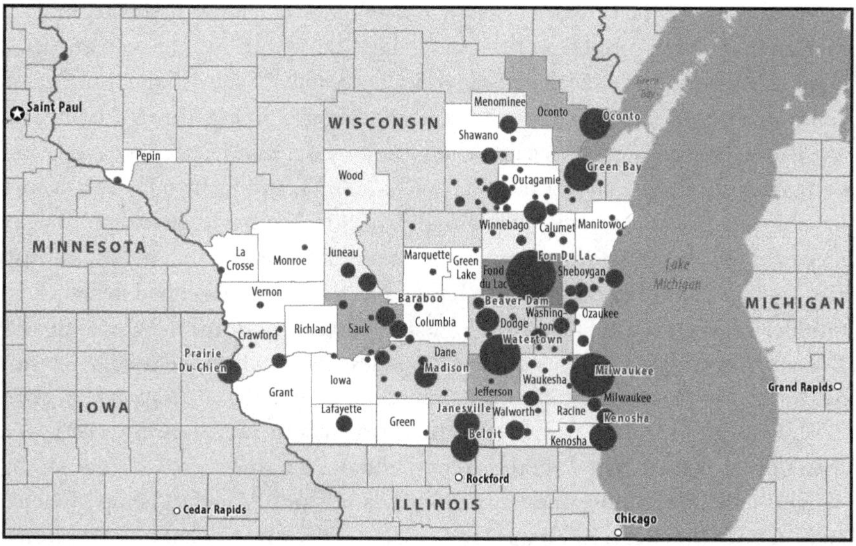


Figure 3 Enlistment patterns of 17th Wisconsin volunteers by county (darker shading reflects higher enlistment numbers) and by city (circles reflect numbers of volunteers from each city).

of Fond du Lac. According to a local historian, it was "composed of ninety-three of the active young Irishmen living there. . . . When news came of the firing on Fort Sumter and the excitement was great, the young men in the ranks of the Hibernians partook of the feeling that prevailed and expressed themselves as ready to enter the army." At a recruiting rally at the city court, though, the Hibernian Guards were told by the quartermaster general of the state that "there are enough young Americans to put down this trouble inside of ninety days and we do not want any red faced foreigners." Such outspoken nativism undercut the enthusiasm of these men, who promptly put down their arms and disbanded their company. Denied the opportunity to enlist in the spring of 1861, Curran led members of his former command to Madison that winter, where they became part of Company C.[23]

Patrick McCauley and John Crane were both commissioned as second lieutenants early in the war after they enlisted in the Sixth Wisconsin. They resigned in October of 1861, purged from the ranks by their colonel, who "under the thin disguise of failure to pass examination" drove out the Irish officers and their friends. Crane, noted a comrade early in the war, was "a fine young officer . . .

[and] one of the best instructors in the manual of arms in the regiment." McCauley, born in Tipperary, lived in Dodge County prior to the war, and led a large contingent that eventually served in Company A. Crane, an Ohio native, came from Juno County, and led the second-largest cohort in that company. They were commissioned as captain and first lieutenant, respectively, in Company A. A similar trend can be seen in Company E. After the outbreak of war, Peter Feagan "put aside all business and personal considerations and began recruiting a company for active duty. John McGowery of Cascade [Wisconsin] also began recruiting a company . . . at the same time. As neither had the required number of one hundred men they joined forces and thus formed Company E." Despite unifying their forces, they still had less than half of the requisite number for an entire company. Darius Palmer, first lieutenant of Company H, born in Oneida, New York, was one of the first teachers in Sauk County. He was "a man of native growth and spotless reputation, with a sincere relish for learning which made him almost one with the pupils of study." David Bishop of Company K built the first schoolhouse in Oshkosh, Wisconsin. Charles Armstrong, captain of Company H, was a member of the state legislature, and John Doran, among other positions, had served as a representative to Wisconsin's constitutional convention. Although individual companies reflected a great degree of regional diversity, the officers, like those in the Ninth Connecticut and 23rd Illinois, were often some of most important men in their communities, reflecting broader trends found in both Union and Confederate armies.[24]

As this diverse group of volunteers began to flood into Madison to join the 17th Wisconsin, observers took notice. One group of men from the town of Whitewater stood out. "My attention was arrested by one of their number, well advanced in years, full of life and energy," S. Hanson wrote to a local paper. When asked about himself, the recruit, Rufus Brockway, provided a stirring patriotic narrative. "I am now in the seventieth year," the old volunteer noted. "I was a volunteer in the last war with England [the War of 1812] for nearly three years. . . . I am now a farmer in the town of Beaver Dam, Dodge County. . . . My son was a volunteer in the Federal army at the battle of Bull Run, had his nose badly barked and his hips broken in and disabled for life by a charge of the rebel cavalry, and now I am going to see if the rebels can bark the old man's nose." A "Yankee from the State of New Hampshire," the elderly Brockway claimed that "if England pitches in you will see a great many old men like me." Perhaps drawn to enlist in his state's Irish regiment by a shared hatred of England, Brockway's age and story attracted the attention of the press, and his presence helped legitimize the volunteers as true citizen-soldiers.[25]

Hugh Dorsey joined Brockway, enlisting in Company C on December 18, 1861. A resident of Fond du Lac, he had emigrated from Ireland in the 1850s and took his naturalization papers on February 29, 1858, at the age of twenty-three. Forty-one-year-old Dennis Harkins of Chilton, Wisconsin, enlisted in the same company. A farmer by trade, Harkins was born in Donegal, Ireland. He came to the United States with his wife Bridget sometime before the war, and the two eventually made their way to Wisconsin. Unlike Harkins, James Connelly, a private in Company F, immigrated to Wisconsin in the early 1850s, before he was married—likely arriving with his parents. His future wife, Mary, whom he had known in Ireland, followed him to America in 1853, making her home in New York until 1862, when she moved to Janesville, Wisconsin. The two reunited when he was home on furlough, and they were married about two months after his discharge in 1865.[26]

Nicholas Gille and Victor Melin enlisted together in Oconto, Wisconsin. They were Belgian immigrants who had met in 1855 or 1856, and they were well acquainted by the time they joined Company G. John Looze (Loos), another recruit from Belgium, knew Melin for two years before the war and served as sergeant of their company, and their captain, William Beaupre, also "knew Victor before the war, though not very well." Welcome Hyde owned a lumber mill in Bear Creek, Wisconsin, and the Vermont native employed a number of men from the area, including Nathan Phillips and David Bishop, who joined Company I and served with their old boss, who, in service, became their new boss when he was commissioned captain of the company.[27]

August Sechoapke and Gotleib Raisler joined this group of men, likely because they had known Phillips for some time before the war began. Edward Riley, James Madigan, and Martin Kehoe were childhood friends before they enlisted in Company F. The Irish-born Kehoe may have regaled his friends with the rich history of Irish soldiers, stories that, along with the early-war renown of other Irish regiments, may have struck a chord with Riley, whose parents were themselves Irish immigrants. William L. Copeland, known as Lervy, and his stepfather, William C. Copeland, enlisted in Company D from Watertown, Wisconsin. The "old man claimed to be French, but it was supposed in the community that he was part negro." One resident of Watertown recalled, in rather distasteful language, that William "could drink more whiskey and do as much cradling as any man I ever saw. He was a mixed breed between nigger, indian and french—a tough lot." Men in town and in his company called Lervy "half nigger," and such insight into Lervy's ethnic and racial background illustrates the diversity of this regiment and, perhaps, the fairly liberal stance on race that some had in this community. Lervy joined the regiment with his close friends George and William Doust, men "of a roving deposition," who "appeared like a low class of gypseys—quite a low class of people." These three men had been close since they were young, and had earned a degree of ill-repute among their neighbors for stealing chickens. While many other volunteers from Watertown knew the Copelands and Dousts, few had good things to say about those families. As in the Ninth Connecticut, not all recruits were upstanding citizens—and bad behavior often accompanied the men into the ranks.[28]

The range of experiences of volunteers before the war mirrored the diversity of the regiment itself. Irish soldiers made up just one-third of the total number of recruits who volunteered to serve under Doran in his "Irish Brigade" in the fall and winter of 1861–62. More American-born men enlisted in the 17th Wisconsin (317 of the total of 864 men who recorded their place of birth in the muster rolls) than Irish-born men, though it is possible that as many as 64 percent of these American-born were of Irish descent. German-born men made up a substantial minority of the volunteers, composing nearly 10 percent of the regiment, a significantly higher proportion than in the other two regiments in this study, which speaks to the strong presence of that ethnic group in Wisconsin.

Furthermore, Irish-born soldiers constituted the majority in only four of the ten companies. Despite this, the ethnic identification of the regiment is understandable, as the Irish presence was undeniable. Following trends found in the 23rd Illinois and Ninth Connecticut, Irish-born men clearly made up larger proportions of the units identified as "Irish" than the proportion of Irishmen in the state's population, and the overrepresentation of these immigrants likely contributed to the perception that this was a predominately Irish regiment, despite the fact that its soldiers were rather ethnically diverse. Take, for example, Janesville, Wisconsin: of the 40 Irish-born men of military age living in the town in 1860, 19, or nearly half, enlisted in the 17th Wisconsin. The Irishness of the regiment must have been etched, then, in the minds of men and women of the town as they watched these Irishmen march off to war.

The average Irish recruit who enlisted in 17th Wisconsin was, at the age of thirty, slightly older than his Irish counterparts in other regiments, while the average age of American-born soldiers, at twenty-four, appears consistent with American-born volunteers in both the Ninth Connecticut and 23rd Illinois. The demographics of the Irish-born soldiers from Wisconsin tell the story of unique ethnic fighting corps. Working-class volunteers made up more than half of the total volunteers in the regiment, and among that group, 70 percent were unskilled laborers. Fewer than half of the Irish volunteers, though, were laborers. While unskilled workers made up a greater proportion of the Irish volunteers in the Wisconsin regiment as compared to the 23rd Illinois, they were a significantly smaller presence compared to the proportion of unskilled Irish workers who enlisted in the Ninth Connecticut. As in Connecticut, though, it is possible that these men were drawn by the state bounties that were offered that fall and winter. The citizens of Fond du Lac, for example, "raised $3,500 to fit out volunteers and support their families." On February 20, Governor Louis Harvey addressed the state legislature on the matter of support on the home front. Ordering the 14th, 15th, and 16th regiments to St. Louis, Harvey scolded state lawmakers for refusing to provide for the families of these soldiers and suggested the sale of $200,000 worth of war bonds for the support of those left at home. It's likely that the families of the 17th benefitted from these measures as well. With regard to the socioeconomic cross section of the regiment, what stands out is that nearly 40 percent of the Irish-born soldiers who enlisted in it described themselves as farmers, significantly more than in the other two regiments and a much higher proportion than that of Irish farmers living in the state in 1860. Compared to the American-born soldiers in the regiment, however, the numbers were disproportionate. Only 30 percent of the men born in the United State claimed membership in the working class, while 65 percent listed their occupation as farmer. Nevertheless, the Irish-born soldiers who did join Doran that winter appear to have benefitted from opportunities available in Wisconsin that were less available to their comrades in other states.[29]

Following the zealous recruiting efforts, many were optimistic about the Irish Regiment, predicting that it "will be as brave and gallant a body of men as any sent from Wisconsin, and, if occssion is presented, will maintain the character for heroism and daring for which their countrymen are renowned." Though Doran was confident in the abilities of his men, by the spring, rumblings of discontent began to spill from the ranks. On March 18, 1862, a fire broke out in the regiment's quarters at Camp Randall in Madison, consuming nearly 200 feet of barracks. "The men," one newspaper noted, "turned out in a hurry, but many of them left their equipments behind, and some secured only part of their clothing. About two dozen guns were destroyed." Thomas Davis, a private in Company C, recalled that the "Barracks Caught on fire which caused me to run out in order to save my life." He stood and watched the blaze for nearly half an hour in "about 18 inches of snow . . . with nothing by my shirt drawers and stocking." Davis was lucky. "One member of the company, was unable to escape, and fell a victim to the raging flames. Half of his head was completely burnt to a cinder as well as half of his arms. . . . [H]e was aged about

18 years. Four or five other members of the company are also dangerously burnt, and we learn that one has since died," the *Wisconsin Daily Patriot* reported the day after the fire.[30]

The fire forced to the surface a lingering sense of animosity that many volunteers in the 17th Wisconsin had begun to feel. In fact, rumors persisted that the fire was not an accident, but, rather, an act of protest designed to keep the regiment from moving south to St. Louis and then on to join Grant's Army. The new volunteers were upset. In the days leading up to their departure, rumors circulated among the ranks that the 16th Wisconsin had been paid before the regiment headed south, and that the men of Irish 17th would be the first volunteer unit to leave the state without receiving their back pay. Although untrue, these rumors left many a man "cursing in the tongue wherein he was born," and on March 19, the day after the fire, "in a rather demoralized state, a large number of men declared they would not go [to St. Louis] without pay."[31]

The protestors did not fade quietly into the night, and their outcry over their alleged mistreatment caused serious rifts among the volunteers. Company A voted to leave Camp Randall, a decision that was "said to have drawn threats on the company from others of the regiment, who were averse to starting without pay." On March 22, approximately one hundred men boarded train cars for St. Louis, but four companies, Companies B, E, G, and H, unanimously voted to stay in Madison and began to arm themselves to resist any forced attempt to make them leave the city. Meanwhile, citizens there, believing the "presence of such a number of unrestrained and incensed soldiery" would lead to chaos, also began to arm and organize their own independent police force to help quell the mutinous soldiers.[32]

Springing into action, some officers of the newly formed regiment earned public accolades for the hard line they took with the men under their command. Captain Patrick McCauley, the *Wisconsin Daily Patriot* recounted, stood before his company and said "'now boy's, order arms. Those who wish to stay will remain at "order," but those in favor will "present." But to make your action as unanimous as possible, I have only to tell you,['] showing his revolver as he spoke, [']that the man remaining at "order" gets his brains blowed out.'" At that, the "gallant company (who had previously been on the verge of mutiny) marched gaily on board the cars." In another instance, Walter Hutchens, "a jaunty, wiry, soldierly-looking fellow," recently promoted to second lieutenant of Company I, took command of a squad of loyal men, "marched to the barracks, got the guns away from those who were hanging back, and then told them they were bound to go with the Company dead or alive."[33]

Despite these efforts, the mutiny persisted, causing considerable disorder in town. Unable to convince the most dedicated mutineers to peacefully end their demonstration, Governor Louis P. Harvey dispatched a telegraph to Camp Douglas in Chicago seeking military assistance. "The Seventeenth Wisconsin Irish Regiment are in Mutiny in this city and refuse to leave without pay," he wrote on March 20; "send two companies here . . . by special train." Two days later he followed up his initial correspondence: "[S]pecial train left Madison half past ten," he wrote, "takes two hundred men of the seventeenth Wisconsin (those whose attitudes had changed when threatened by their officers) about seventy five very turbulent will need a guard of at least two Cos to St. Louis." James Mulligan and a detachment of the 23rd Illinois responded to the governor's plea for assistance and quickly boarded trains for Madison.[34]

Undeterred by news of the Mulligan's arrival, the hardest of the mutineers, led by Company G, the French Mountaineers, began to purchase ammunition and "declared their intention to resist to the death any attempt to compel them to leave without pay." The press eagerly anticipated the impending arrival the detachment of the 23rd Illinois, and some hoped the "gallant defenders of Lexington" would put a quick end to the mischief of their countrymen. Talk of resistance was short-lived. Mulligan's men, Private Richard Curran wrote, "came in the next night when they were a sleep and captured them and took there guns from them and made them march of with them some of them didnt want to go but they used there bayonets and forst them off they had to go there was a couple of them stabed with the bayonets." Another eyewitness wrote, in a letter to a newspaper, "Col. Mulligan's men, of Lexington notoriety, with several officers, arrived well armed; and every soldier remaining in camp, about two hundred, suddenly awoke, at early dawn, with a bayonet, not his own, at his breast. Such a surprise party you never saw."[35]

These dissenting acts were directly related to the issue of pay and the expectation that the state should provide back pay for soldiers before they went to war. Joining the army, these men entered into a contract with the government, becoming citizen-soldiers. While the citizen-soldiers of all three regiments examined in this study professed a clear understanding of the relationship between their service and inclusion within the broader nation, in their protest over pay, the men of the 17th Wisconsin illustrated what Riccardo Herrera has called an "ethos of republicanism," in which, as American soldiers, they "believed themselves to be citizens first and foremost." When the state did not live up to its end of the contract, this had an impact not only on the soldiers but on their families; and fearing for the welfare of their loved ones, these men of the 17th

Wisconsin believed that it was their right to resist any attempt to force them away without the pay that was owed them. The crisis over pay provided these men with the opportunity to publicly express the ways that they personally understood the relationship between their service and the nation. While volunteers from the Ninth Connecticut and 23rd Illinois were equally cognizant of this relationship and often expressed it during more private interactions, the public nature of this event in Madison, Wisconsin speaks volumes about the actual relationship between these men and their adopted nation. Irish and German immigrants (and there were a significant number of Germans in Wisconsin's Irish Brigade) placed great value on the American republican experiment; this is clear in their public rhetoric and their private correspondence, and was one of the major motivating factors behind ethnic enlistment in 1861 and 1862. That these men of the 17th Wisconsin protested in such a manner illustrates how pervasive this ideology was.[36]

Equally important is the way the public viewed these acts. Sociologist Warren Young has remarked that "minority-military service can take the theme of 'quid pro quo,' that is, full support of the war effort on the part of the minority and its leadership in return for full citizenship rights or other benefits for minority-group members." Such a relationship between service and citizenship was recognized in Wisconsin, and in a number of instances the press came out in support of the protest of members of the 17th Wisconsin. Publicly, the mutiny became symbolic of the rights of citizens. "We do not regard these men as Napoleonic conscripts, but freemen, who leave their homes and families so that . . . [we] may live in peace and quietness," noted one Wisconsin editor. The *Wisconsin Daily Patriot* encouraged the mutiny, claiming that "the 17th Regiment is the first that has left the State without pay," an argument that another press outlet took up, stressing that with "the knowledge that the families of some were suffering for want of the pay due to them, it is not strange that they were firmly impressed with the ideas that there was something wrong some where, and that the surest way to right it was to stubbornly refuse to leave their quarters." Even Governor Harvey—before seeking reinforcements from Chicago—had supported the troops, promising the men that they would receive their pay as soon as they reached St. Louis. When Harvey was finally forced to request support, he did so in order "to give the authorities [in Madison] power to compel obedience," not to punish offenders.[37]

The protest ultimately failed, according to Richard Curran, because of divisions within the regiment, not because the men were wrong. "If the whole Regiment had to stauck to gether," he wrote, "they couldnt take them but half of them went off and the other haf stuck out and wouldent go without there pay." One Madison editor concurred. "If the Companies of the 17th Regiment had been organized a little longer," he observed, "and some of the field and line officers had been a little better acquainted with their men, and manifested a little more pluck and spirit, there would have been much less trouble." Although internal divisions among the troops themselves over the means of protest ultimately limited the power of collective action, those who stood up in defense of their contractual right to be paid nevertheless made their grievances public in a very compelling, very American manner. Hardly the act of disloyal or reluctant men compelled into service against their will, the "mutiny" of members of the 17th Wisconsin at Camp Randall, and how it was handled, illustrates the ways in which soldiers, regardless of ethnic background, understood their relationship with the state, and the way the state understood its contractual obligations to the volunteers.[38]

When finally compelled, at the point of bayonets, to the front, the mutineers were, interestingly, left to their own accord, without punishment for their participation in the mutiny. As time and distance were placed between the 17th Wisconsin and their mutinous behavior, there were accounts of loyalty within the regiment, and the event was downplayed in the press. Morale increased as the men moved from Camp Randall to a warmer region. Furthermore, the trip through Illinois gave the regiment a sense of the strong nationalism that existed among Northerners, as they witnessed first hand what one volunteer called the "strong Union feeling existing among the people—cheers from the men waving of handkerchiefs from the ladies, greeting us at every station." Unlike soldiers of the Ninth Connecticut, who were largely isolated from the Southern population during their journey south aboard the *USS Constitution*, the volunteers from Wisconsin experienced a Southern welcome first hand. When they arrived in St. Louis on March 24, they were pleasantly surprised at the welcome reception thrown by the citizens of that city. Crossing over from East St. Louis, the regiment marched five miles to Camp Benton. Along this route, "quite gratifying Union demonstrations from the ladies flanked both sides," the unnamed volunteer wrote, "which made me think that the hard stories told of Southern ladies being such dreadful rebels was what might be termed unqualified humbug." His letter continues, "[I]t was as much as I could do to keep some of the good looking girls I passed from kissing me." Ever cautious, however, and perhaps with stories of Southern misdeeds still in the back of his mind, the soldier refused the advances, fearing that some of the women might have poison on their lips and he would be "picked up a lifeless but beautiful corpse."[39]

The 17th Wisconsin left St. Louis on March 26 aboard the steamer *Imperial*, bound for Pittsburg Landing, Tennessee, and arrived as the battle at Shiloh was reaching its climax. The scene that greeted them was described by Captain D. D. Scott as "truly awful and sublime." The landing on the Tennessee River was "surrounded by barren cliffs and inaccessible rocks, separated occasionally by ravines. . . . Along the landing for miles, nothing presents itself but the unceasing coming and going of Steamboats." The men then moved to what Scott called "a city of canvas," eight miles long and four miles across, where they awaited Grant's next move. "It begins to look more like business than it did while we were in camp up North," Private Ebenezer Wescott wrote to his mother. Although the excitement of Pittsburg Landing was a welcome relief from the monotony of camp life, the young private looked upon the upcoming campaign with trepidation. "Sometimes I wish I was up North now instead of here, but here I am and here I will stay, I suppose," he concluded, a sentiment likely compounded as news of Shiloh, what Captain Scott called "all its horrors, carnage, and desolation," spread among the regiments encamped at Pittsburg Landing.[40]

A year after the opening salvos of the war, Irishmen from Wisconsin were organized, armed, and poised to enter the fray. The men had not fired a shot in anger against the enemy but, instead, were perpetrators of a major mutiny. Yet there are no records of men court martialed for their behavior and no evidence of any internal disciplinary action. In fact, the arrival of Mulligan's men from Chicago was met with relief, the citizen police force disbanded, and for the rest of the war the only negative commentary dealing with the 17th Wisconsin focused on the internal discord that arose between Colonel John Doran and his officers. That conflict, which eventually led to Doran's arrest and resignation, in fact dealt with issues regarding pay and abuse of power that were similar to those that had motivated the original mutiny in March 1862.

Evidence of disorderly conduct or disloyalty often stuck fast to regiments—especially, as historian Christian Keller has illustrated, to ethnic regiments, once burdened with perceptions and accusations of cowardliness or ineptitude on the battlefield. Yet such animosity failed to take root when men in Wisconsin's Irish Brigade mutinied, and that absence mirrored broader attitudes surrounding the rights and responsibilities of citizen-soldiers and those of their state and nation. At no point in the wake of the departure of the volunteers from Madison was that event referenced, and, as the war progressed, the loyal service of these volunteers was honored time and again by observers at home. These soldiers from Wisconsin, many of them Irish Catholic immigrants whose loyalty to the United States was often questioned in the antebellum period, were given immense leeway as volunteers in the defense of the Union, when their "disloyal" behavior was seen through the lens of republican ideology. The reactions of the Wisconsin public, contextualized against those of the rather hostile community in Connecticut, provide considerable insight into the regional variances and ideologies at play within the United States during this period, and the ways in which different communities understood and responded to the initial impulses of ethnic service.[41]

# 4 Ethnicity and Combat

Wartime and postwar accounts often glorified and romanticized Irish American service in the Civil War. While the casualty rates among regiments in the Irish Brigade in the Army of the Potomac attest to the fact that this unit was involved in some of the heaviest fighting of the war, no empirical evidence exists to prove that soldiers in these regiments were, in fact, better fighters than their comrades in other regiments. There was, however, something profoundly captivating about Irish regiments, both to their local communities and to the nation at large. Perhaps it was the pomp and circumstance that followed those early regiments to war—immigrant soldiers, dressed in blue, marching behind both the star-spangled banner of America and the emerald-green silk flag of Ireland, prepared to sacrifice themselves for their new home—that initially drew observers to single out the Irish among the initial excitement of the summer of 1861. Perhaps, too, it was the actual tenacity of Irish soldiers on the battlefield that garnered attention, for time and again these men held their lines in the face of withering fire and overwhelming odds. Ethnicity and ethnic identity, in this case, became important descriptive tools used to bestow a certain gravitas upon the men from Connecticut, Illinois, and Wisconsin.

The courage of these volunteers under fire reinforced a sense of inclusion and solidified the commitment of those at home to the Union war. Their commitment to the Union was further secured with the remuster and reenlistment of soldiers in all three units over the course of the war. Glory on the battlefield did provide a means of overcoming antebellum animosities, earning these men and their units a fierce reputation in their hometowns. Yet ethnicity also shrouded these volunteers' service in hues of green, linking them invariably to the other Irish units and communities and, consequently, to the rise and fall of Irish American support for the Union that came as a consequence of the devastating casualties among the Irish Brigade. For the soldiers from Connecticut, Illinois, and Wisconsin, however, the war was different from that of their countrymen serving in the Army of the Potomac. The successes of the Ninth Connecticut, 23rd Illinois, and 17th Wisconsin on the battlefield preserved morale on the home front, ultimately reinforcing a sense of ethnic loyalty within these states, attitudes that diverged from the reemergence, nationally, of nativism as events in the summer of 1863 unfolded in America's largest ethnic enclaves.

After the siege of Lexington, the soldiers of the 23rd Illinois, briefly prisoners of Sterling Price, were paroled and sent home. James Mulligan was held captive by Sterling Price and brought south with the retreating rebels. When released, he returned to Chicago, welcomed as a national hero. Letters poured forth inviting the colonel to speak to communities throughout the North. Interestingly, the invitations were sent from diverse groups; some were Irish, but many others represented a variety of interests and agendas. Requesting Mulligan's presence before the Adelphi Society of Knox College in Galesburg, Illinois, James Tompkins recalled that "the brave and heroic manner in which you defended the liberties of the nation and sustained the honor [of] our glorious flag has made your name familiar throughout the land, and caused it to be spoken everywhere with pride and gratitude." George Hamilton wrote, "I can confidently claim the benefit of a lecture from you as the distinguished hero of Lexington. . . . Your friend here Catholics and Protestants would be happy to see you." Another sponsor from Albany, New York, offered $1,000 plus all expenses if the colonel would travel east for a two-week speaking tour. Although it is unclear the degree to which Mulligan benefitted financially from these engagements, during the winter of 1861–62 he did speak in cities throughout the North as he made his way from Chicago to Washington, D.C. to petition the Federal government to reinstate the 23rd Illinois as a three-year unit. The impact that Mulligan's service had on the strengthening of bonds between Irish immigrants and their adopted nation cannot be understated. As Mulligan stood on the balcony of his hotel in Springfield, Illinois to address the crowd that had gathered to cheer the news of his return and the reorganization of the 23rd Illinois, he must have felt a degree of excitement driven not only by the energy of the men and women standing before him, but by his own meteoric rise to prominence.[1]

"After repeated calls," the colonel "made his appearance at one of the parlor windows and was received with an enthusiasm which not even the chilling atmosphere could allay," wrote the *Daily Illinois State Register.* In an impromptu speech which "breathed the fervid patriotism which has characterized his every act in public life," Mulligan presented "a flag saved from the hand of the rebels. . . . [I]ts folds, riddled by the shots of the felon foe, brought vividly to mind the risks that its defenders have undergone. . . . Let the riddled flag," the editors of the *Register* proclaimed, "be preserved as a memento of the gallant conduct of the gallant men who stood by it so nobly in an hour when their patriotism was shrouded in despair." In Rockford, Illinois, the citizens were exuberant over Mulligan's visit, hoping to have the "opportunity to pay their respects to the gallant soldier and scholar." A poem about the stand of the 23rd Illinois at Lexington, published in the local Republican newspaper that February, proclaimed that "*'Twas ammunition failed: not God nor Right / Surrender was of hand,* not hearts or might! / Hurrah for Mulligan! Brave Ireland's Son! / *The battle-field of Lexington's not lost but nobly won!*" The appearance of the poem in a Republican paper was an interesting statement of support from the avid political opponents of Irish Americans, and one that illustrates the ways in which views of ethnic soldiers shifted in the wake of battlefield bravery. Mulligan's ethnicity and Irish identity was undeniable, as was that of his regiment. Yet his men, "gallant" defenders of the flag, were transformed into patriots—American patriots—with their sacrifice in defense of the United States. Because Mulligan's surrender was not due to a lack of "will," it could, thus, not be considered a loss. Similar themes, of course, drove ethnic recruiting throughout the North and formed an important component of the inclusive language of military service.[2]

That fall the War Department authorized Mulligan to reorganize the 23rd Illinois as a three-year regiment, with the original muster date set back to June 1861. While this news was met with great excitement, reorganization was problematic, because many of the original volunteers had returned home after their parole, and had either obeyed the conditions of their release—not to again take up arms against the Confederacy—or joined other regiments. Private Adam Blaul, for example, was paroled after Lexington and traveled around Illinois and Wisconsin in search of work before he reenlisted, joining the First Wisconsin Heavy Artillery in 1864. George Winfrey fought at Lexington as a member of A Company of the Illinois 23rd. A "good stout man" though "not very bright," he returned to his hometown of Dowagiac, Michigan and reenlisted, becoming a member of the 12th Michigan. After the war, when William Crowell applied for his pension, he was told, to his dismay, that he was listed in regimental muster rolls as a deserter, despite the fact that he had actually reenlisted in a New York regiment and served loyally throughout the war. This act, though later labeled by the army as desertion, appears to have been an innocent misunderstanding more than anything more sinister. In another instance, Captain John McDermott wrote to Mulligan in early January 1862 to tender his resignation because he had received an appointment as Lieutenant Colonel in the 15th

Michigan Volunteers. In sum, with the expiration of the 23rd Illinois's original ninety-days service, some were, justifiably, confused about their obligations to the newly remustered Irish Brigade.[3]

During the winter and spring, however, new recruits poured into Chicago to fill the gaping ranks of Mulligan's regiment. According to muster rolls, some 225 men failed to report to the reorganization of the regiment after their parole from Lexington. At the same time, approximately 681 new volunteers joined Mulligan, and they more than made up for the loss. Among these volunteers was twenty-year-old farmer Albert Phillips from Earlville, Illinois. Phillips was born in Earlville, and neither of his parents was an immigrant. While it is impossible to determine his family's lineage from the available sources, there is a possibility that it was Irish. Some 15 percent of all immigrants with the surname Phillips entering the United States between 1820 and 1957 came from Ireland. Phillips's postwar diary contains a number of songs about his regiment, including one titled "The Irish Brigade," whose lyrics exude a strong sense of ethnic pride and, perhaps, reflect Phillips's personal connection to the Emerald Isle, though it is possible that this sense of connection could have also have simply been a consequence of his service in the 23rd Illinois. His family was fairly well off, and though Albert lived at home with his mother and father, according to the 1860 census he personally owned some $800 worth of land in the town of Earlville. Well educated and, perhaps, an aspiring intellectual, Phillips served as the secretary for a literary group called the Farm Boys Association, a prewar debate club and private library organized by local teenagers. Members included his brothers, Melville and Walter, his neighbors, Eliza, Lavinia, and John Imel, and a number of others from the town and surrounding areas.[4]

In early January 1862, Phillips arrived at Camp Douglas in Chicago, where he enlisted in Company D of the 23rd Illinois. There were not many Irishmen of military age living in Earlville in 1861, and only eight enlisted in the 23rd Illinois. Most of the volunteers from that town were American-born, so Phillips's choice to join the Earlville men in Company D is neither surprising nor unique. But his decision, like that of many who enlisted in these regiments, was also personal. Enlisting, he joined his friends John Ward, a corporal in the 23rd Illinois, and John Carter. Both fought with Mulligan in the summer of 1861 and had counted themselves members of the Farm Boys Association prior to enlisting. John Phillips, Albert's brother, and two other members of the short-lived literary society, Frank Ross and Eugene Larkins, had also enlisted with Ward and Carter in June 1861 and served with the 23rd Illinois at Lexington. Phillips's neighbor John Iman enlisted in December 1861. The following September, Melville Phillips joined his brother and friends in the ranks of Company D. Of these men, only Ward was Irish-born.[5]

In early March another group of young men left home to join a party organizing in White Pigeon, Michigan, some one hundred miles from Chicago on the Michigan-Indiana border. None of the seventeen men from that town who eventually joined Company C were Irish, though twelve were likely of Irish descent. There were, however, ties among this group. Martin Simmons, John Bisby, and the Dickey brothers, Samuel and Stuart, were boyhood friends. Bisby was a near neighbor to Henry and John Morris, sons of one of the town's blacksmiths. Simmons and another volunteer, Robert Foster, worked together before the war. Although the connections that linked the other volunteers to this group are ambiguous, the Simmons and Bisby families were grocers in White Pigeon, and it is quite possible that these men knew each other, as well as many others in the community, simply as a result of daily interactions.[6]

As a group, however, a majority of the new volunteers (62 percent) called Chicago home, and this represented a significant geographical shift in the make-up of the regiment, for only slightly more than one quarter of the men who volunteered in the summer of 1861 resided in Chicago. Nearly half of the total group of new volunteers were Irish, but Irish made up the majority (66 percent) of the Chicago recruits, and the Chicago Irish represented 90 percent of the total number of Irish recruits in the reorganized 23rd Illinois, meaning that service in Mulligan's regiment was more appealing among Chicago's immigrant population in 1862 than it was in 1861.

The employment demographics of these new recruits were markedly different from those of the volunteers who enlisted in Mulligan's Irish Brigade in the summer of 1861. Nearly all of the 1862 volunteers were members of the working class and most were unskilled laborers. There was a significant shift among American-born volunteers as well. Fewer working class and business class volunteers joined Mulligan, while the number of farmers in the ranks increased noticeably. Such statistics reflect, perhaps, the growing financial appeal of military service. In July 1861 the Federal government authorized a bounty, an act that the editors of the *Chicago Tribune* hoped would provide sufficient motivation for those wavering in their patriotism. Perhaps, then, it was this monetary boon that explains in part the significant shift in the type of men (in terms of ethnicity, geography, and socioeconomic position) who joined the 23rd Illinois, as this financial perk, along with the sudden fame of the regiment and the national renown so recently bestowed on Irish soldiers, may have encouraged men who had held back from volunteering in the summer of 1861. As a whole, the make-up of the ranks of the 23rd Illinois fundamentally changed in 1862, and the Irish volunteers largely reflected the ethnic stereotype—unskilled workers from the lower class. The characteristics of this new group of volunteers, however, had little impact on either public perceptions of the regiment or the unit's effectiveness, despite some rowdy behavior in Chicago.[7]

During this same period, the Ninth Connecticut and 17th Wisconsin took the field for the first time as part of larger Federal moves along the Mississippi River. Though the Connecticut men had struggled through their drills on the loose white sands of Ship Island, the onset of spring brought the opportunity to finally prove their merits on the battlefield. There they lived up to the standards set by the 69th New York and 23rd Illinois, though on a much smaller stage. "The rough ninth have been trooping around the Splendid summer residences of the southern aristocracy built upon the meanest of all foundations: the unwilling labor of the Black," Thomas Cahill wrote of the regiment's expeditions on the mainland that spring. Their presence struck fear into the rebels. Upon landing in Biloxi, private George Hill recalled, the Southern civilians "all run away . . . for [fear] we was going to take all their property and burn the town but they found when we left we was not as bad as they had been told we were the town was ransacked from one end to the other for firearms and contraband of war but no private property was touched." Hill also reported, ominously, the early impact of the war on the Southern home front, for Biloxi was "a very pretty town with nice houses . . . [but] the most of the people that remain are poorly clad and half starved."[8]

On April 4, 1862 the soldiers of the Ninth finally met the enemy at Pass Christian in Mississippi. There, charging the rebel line "with an Irish 'Y-a-a-a-a-ah!'" they routed the Third Mississippi and distinguished themselves by becoming, allegedly, the first Union regiment to capture a Confederate battle flag. "Ship Island letters speak in high terms of the conduct of the 9th Connecticut," the *Hartford Daily Courant* reported in the aftermath of the battle. "It is hardly necessary for me to say that the conduct of your men meets my cordial approval," Governor Buckingham wrote to Thomas Cahill, adding, "I am proud of both officers and their command." Benjamin Butler congratulated Cahill and his men for their "gallant courage and good conduct" during the expedition. More importantly, Butler wrote:

> After having been for months subjected to the privations necessarily incident to camp life upon this island, these well-disciplined soldiers, although

> for many hours in full possession of two rebel villages, filled with what to them were most desirable luxuries, abstained from the least unauthorized interference with private property and all molestation of peaceful citizens.
>
> This behavior is worthy of all praise. It robs war of half its horrors. It teaches our enemies how much they have been misinformed by their designing leaders as to the character of our soldiers and the intention of our Government. It gives them a lesson and an example in humanity and civilized warfare.

Connecticut's Irishmen faced battle with honor and courage, a fact not lost on those at home. Furthermore, after their behavior in New Haven and Lowell, their conduct under fire marked an important change in both the regiment's demeanor and the way they were viewed on the home front. In battle, these volunteers lived up to the expectations that the state had placed upon her Irish soldiers. Returning to Ship Island, they awaited their next opportunity to fight.[9]

It would be a while. A majority of the men's time after Pass Christian was spent preparing for the invasion of New Orleans. On paper, this was a formidable task. Union forces faced the intimidating fortifications at a turn in the Mississippi River known as English Bend, some seventy miles southeast of the city. Fort Jackson and Fort St. Philip were "verry heavy Forts said to mount near two hundred heavy guns," the colonel wrote home to his wife, "of which 50 are trained to Cover one spot in the channel of the size of a ship, which would oblige a ship passing to stand the concussion of from 50 to 300 shots before passing it scarsely seems possible to reduce such forts with wooden vessels." But on April 24, 1862, the Federal fleet under David Farragut succeeded in silencing the Confederate batteries by, simply, running past them. As the Federal fleet steamed upriver, Butler's men, including the Ninth Connecticut, were left to secure the fortifications. This task was made significantly easier when the conscripts manning the forts mutinied. Many of these men were Irish, and it is very likely that some later volunteered for Federal service in the Ninth Connecticut.[10]

Anticipating a chilly arrival on the docks of New Orleans, where accounts of pro-Union sentiment were hard to come by, the men of the Ninth Connecticut were surprised by the friendly reception given them by the Irish population of the city. As Private Franklin Terrell recalled, "the morning we arrived in New Orleans Gen Butler ordered our regiment to land, which was the first regiment to land on the soil of New Orleans. After our regiment had cleared the dock we marched to Jackson Sqr in New Orleans. The regiment was put on police duty." After a grand review of Butler's troops, there was "not a word of noise or insolence and the people dance to the music on the side walks." The welcome reception given the Ninth by the Irish population of New Orleans suggests that lingering bonds between immigrants could, at times, trump sectional loyalties. Certainly such ties were found in the relationships between antebellum Irish militia and within the political rhetoric that emerged soon after the war broke out. Although the Irish in the South typically rose to the defense of their states, the response of the ethnic community in New Orleans illustrates the connections that bound this diaspora in the United States during this period. Furthermore, Union occupation also brought a reprieve for the much-maligned immigrant group in the South's largest city, which may have also played a role in their enthusiastic reception of Cahill and his men.[11]

New Orleans was home to a large contingent of immigrants, many of whom were skilled workers or employed in the city's manufacturing or on the docks. The onset of the war alienated many of these immigrants, who were not paid during the early war push for manufacturing of war materiel, and, in particular, ironclads to defend the city. This led to growing animosity between laborers and the Confederate government, which only worsened with the implementation of conscription in order to raise troops to man Fort Jackson and Fort St. Philip. The growing discontent contributed to the garrison's mutiny and surrender in late April. "Our men find lots of Old acquaintances here," Cahill wrote soon after he arrived in New Orleans, "[and] I think if we were to stay here another week we would have the biggest half of the Irish here with us."[12]

His words were prophetic, for recruits flocked to join the Ninth soon after the regiment landed in New Orleans, swelling its ranks. Of the 197 men who joined the Ninth Connecticut in Louisiana between April and July 1862, only 56 claimed residency in the North, all but one of them volunteering from the state of Connecticut. No antebellum residence was recorded for the remaining 141 volunteers, but Cahill reported that "I am taking a large number of recruits and they are very stalwart men much larger than the overage of our men," suggesting that many of these men could have been from Louisiana or the surrounding areas. "They are natives of Ireland Germany and some of the Northern and Western States," the colonel wrote of these new recruits, and "they represent themselves as having suffered terribly during the last year and seem glad to come among us." The men who joined the regiment during those first months in Louisiana brought the Ninth nearly to full strength for the first time in the war and were assigned primarily to companies C, D, and G. Outfitted like their Northern comrades in a uniform similar to that of Thomas Francis Meagher's

Irish Brigade, "sky-blue overcoats, dark blue or black dress coats, blue trousers with a green stripe, high black hats with a pair of green tassels [and] a green scarf of silk," many of these men served their adopted state with distinction. These new recruits were nearly all immigrants, with Irish and Germans making up the largest contingent (42 percent and 30 percent respectively). Nineteen-year-old Charles Michalk joined the Ninth Connecticut on May 27. Born in Germany, the young farmer immigrated to Bastrop County, Texas before the war, but fled his adopted home for Mexico after the war broke out, "because I did not want to serve under the Confederate government [after] the old people explained to me what the war was about." Although he and a number of other New Orleans volunteers ultimately transferred to the First Texas Cavalry (Union) in November 1862, his experiences nevertheless provide some insight into the type of recruit Cahill's troop attracted.[13]

Moving from New Orleans, Cahill and his men settled into the old Confederate fortifications at Camp Parapet, part of a defensive line that stretched from the Mississippi River to Lake Pontchartrain, securing the western approaches to the city. They stayed in that position until midsummer. Like Ship Island, Camp Parapet lacked adequate shelter and clean water, and numerous soldiers cited their time there as the cause of malarial fever and rheumatism, attributing these lingering diseases to the dampness of the campgrounds. While these conditions only worsened as the spring dragged on, the men from Connecticut were not alone in their suffering. Some four hundred miles north, the volunteers of the 17th Wisconsin battled similar conditions, though in Tennessee the mosquitos were compounded by hoards of angry Confederates defending their homes against Union invasion.[14]

Although they avoided the slaughter at Shiloh, the Wisconsin men were soon on the move, albeit slowly. After Shiloh, General Henry Halleck assumed command from Grant and turned his army towards Corinth, Mississippi, some twenty miles south of Pittsburg Landing. There, General P. G. T. Beauregard and the remnants of the Army of the Mississippi, along with forces under the command of General Earl Van Dorn, lay in a defensive position astride the vital western rail hub. Though both sides expected a bloody battle over the city, Beauregard evacuated Corinth, leaving it to Halleck's encroaching forces.[15]

As the men from Wisconsin settled into occupational duty, both the Ninth Connecticut and the 23rd Illinois were again on the move. On May 9 the Connecticut regiment boarded transports for Baton Rouge, where they stayed for a month before moving further north to Vicksburg. Opposite that city, known as the "Gibraltar of the West," Cahill and his men were charged with digging a canal to reroute the Mississippi River "and leave her [Vicksburg] alone on her Bluffs which she has so impudently attempted to use to ban our progress up the Mississippi," he remarked. And in early June, Mulligan and the 23rd Illinois embarked by rail for the Shenandoah Valley. Emotions ran high in Chicago, and Camp Douglas was alive with activity as the men of the 23rd Illinois prepared to leave the state. Rumors ran rampant. "The report is now that we leave here Saturday after noon," new recruit Amaziah Hadden wrote; "whether we shall go then or not I cant say but it is probably that we shall go soon for we have commenced packing up our duds. I hope that we shall meet before long but how long it will be god only knows I don't the will of god be done not mine." On Saturday, June 14, the regiment marched out of Chicago. "At nine oclock . . . Cannon fired once. . . . [We] fell in [and] the 65 Illinois escorted us out in the city," Albert Phillips noted in his diary. The *Chicago Times* reported "a large number of the friends of the Irish boys assembled at the depot to witness their departure." It was an enthusiastic crowd that assembled to cheer the men on their way to defend the nation's capitol and reflected the continued excitement that surrounded Chicago's Irish Brigade.[16]

For the soldiers of the Ninth, the reality of life in the swamps opposite Vicksburg was much different from the way reports on the home front portrayed it. Despite the imposing logistics, Cahill believed the task of digging a canal "a great scheme if it will work as it promises and it may be another Evidence that we Cannot be stopped when we want to go ahead." While optimism abounded at home, the hot summer months decimated the ranks of the Irish regiment as malarial fever ravaged the troops. According to Lieutenant Colonel Richard Fitzgibbon, "Nearly 3/4 of the whole brigade under the command of Genl [Thomas] Williams, was stricken down with malarial fever and diarehia" during their time there. Captain Lawrence O'Brien reported that "we could not give a funeral escort to the dead; the few who were able to do guard and picket duty could not attend to any extra duty. . . . I saw men drop of out line exhausted, and when we returned many of them would be dead." Thomas Knablin described the situation bluntly to his wife in a letter of July 28. "I have been sick with the Fevour and Ague but thanks be to the Almighty Gods I am much better," he wrote; "we lay in the swamps opsite Vicksburge for nearly a month until one Regiment the 7 Vermont lost over 50 men and all of 200 sick the 30 Massachutts were in the same predickment also a Western Regt suffered the same war We lost about 24 men but none out of our company If we had staid there a week longer half of the 4 Regiments would be burried there."[17]

A year later the memory of Vicksburg still haunted Knablin, who wrote home that "[w]hen leaving Camp Parapet 12 Months ago for Vicksburge, Our Company numbered 100 and 4 effective men. it is now about half that number. . . . there has been but one or 2 died by the hands of the Enemy, the worst Enemy we have to contend against is the Swamps and the Malaria that arises from them there is none of our men but has had the Fevor and Ague." In total, 153 men died, a rate of nearly five per day, and an untold number more were rendered permanently disabled during the two months the regiment was engaged in operations around Vicksburg. Such numbers, though similar to casualty rates sustained by Irish regiments in the East, came as a result of relatively unheroic work and gave the men of the Ninth little to hang their hats on.[18]

After struggling for weeks, Cahill was exasperated. "The Enemy is pretty strong here," he wrote, "too strong for the weak detachments sent up from New Orleans we have not yet got the ditch cut through that is to turn the Missippi River out of its Course don't know when we shall." They never did. At the end of July the regiment boarded transports and limped south to rest and recover. Their recuperation was cut short by rebel advances in Mississippi when General John C. Breckenridge moved to retake Baton Rouge, part of General Earl Van Dorn's broader attempt to relieve Vicksburg and secure control of the Red River, protecting Confederate access to vital western supply points. The Confederate march was stymied by the intense southern heat, and by the time Breckenridge finally brought his forces into action, on August 5, Federal commanders were well aware of his campaign. Battle seemed to motivate the weary troops of the Ninth Connecticut, and "as if by a miracle, many of the men in the hospitals found themselves recovering and rejoining their outfits. The powerful and magic tonic was the prospect of a fight," historian John Winters has remarked. Although the Confederates made considerable progress during their initial assault, Federal gunboats eventually turned the tide, and their withering fire drove the rebels from the town. In the midst of the battle, though, the Irishmen from Connecticut rose to the challenge and led Union forces to victory.[19]

"Victory at Baton Rouge," the *Hartford Daily Courant* announced on August 19, 1862, in an exaggerated account of the relatively minor engagement—at least when compared to the fighting around Richmond that summer. Thomas Cahill assumed command of Union forces after Brigadier General Thomas Williams was killed by a musket ball to the chest, and helped the rout of the Confederates, despite his troops being outnumbered nearly two to one. The rebels "got their fill of it there though sick as we were," wrote Thomas Knablin, only one day removed from the hospital himself when the battle broke out. "There was onley

2 Sergents out of 5 out that morning [in Company D] that was Laurie and Myself," he wrote of the unit's strength; "The Remander was sick and out of a Company of 90 men all we could muster was about 40, It was so with every Regiment and Company that was at Vicksburge In fact the whole of them were little better than sick men." The *Courant* reported, "The Irish soldiers of the United States army at Baton Rouge have been highly complimented for their bravery," adding with satisfaction that many Irishmen living in New Orleans had taken an oath of allegiance to the Union. "We have always been in the advance," Cahill wrote after the battle, "but I rather expected that as it seems to be expected by the people of every thing that has the name of being Irish in the fighting line; well we have not suffered more than Others and we have a good name, wherever we are known at home or here." "Wherever Irish regiments have snuffed the smoke of battle they have done well," those at home read in the *Courant*. Ethnicity appeared in both public and private correspondence as a means of bestowing a specific narrative on battle and a certain gravitas on the Irish troops. In particular, the "Irishness" of the soldiers of the Ninth Connecticut was cited as evidence of their effective soldiering. They rose to the occasion, ignoring disease and injury to rally to the fight—just as their countrymen had, time and again, in the other battles of the war. Their success in battle also served to overshadow the darker experiences during their months across from Vicksburg.[20]

As the Ninth Connecticut struggled in the swamps in Louisiana, Mulligan and his men were in the Shenandoah Valley chasing Confederate forces that always seemed one step ahead of them. At Clarksburg, Virginia, they set up a camp they named "The O'Donoghue" after the Irish nationalist Patrick O'Donoghue, a leader of the Young Ireland movement that led the failed 1848 Irish rebellion against England. "The spirit of Young Ireland is still alive, and may it ever be thus," Captain Daniel Quirk wrote, linking the soldiers under his command to their Irish revolutionary heritage. Forming lines at Parkersburg to ward off a suspected attack, the men were "cheered as the brave Irish regiment who know no danger." Reports filtered into camp that nearly 7,000 Confederates had massed to fight Mulligan. "Just think of it," Quirk wrote, "7,000 men to attack one Irish regiment!" Though the attack never materialized, ethnicity was utilized to reinforce to the public at home the prowess of the men in the 23rd Illinois. Nationalism and courage went hand-in-hand, becoming celebrated "ethnic" traits used to reinforce the notoriety of the regiment. As time wore on, men of the regiment grew weary of their service in the Valley. After one forced march of some forty miles, Private Albert Phillips reported that "at roll call every man was greatly crippled," and the following day, "All the men was w[e]akened." Failure to meet the enemy in battle and shifting political moves in Washington caused Mulligan to write in disgust in his diary that "the administration is feeble. The Army is desponding." But, he concluded with gusto, "the Irish yet remain." This interesting comment, like many of the other ethnic references regarding these three regiments, served to connect these men to the broader nation, instilling within the troops and those at home notions of the loyalty and fortitude that bound them intrinsically to their adopted nation.[21]

At Corinth in Mississippi the men of the 17th Wisconsin sat, still awaiting a chance to finally spar with the enemy. Their first opportunity came on September 17, 1862, when guerillas, who believed that "the seemingly amicable terms the 17th was on with the surrounding farmers and planters" had lessened their vigilance, assaulted four companies of Irishmen defending a rail line east of Corinth. Amid heavy firing from pickets, "the four companies in camp, to a man, sprang to their arms, and before the drummer had time to beat the 'long roll' they were drawn up in line of battle." Colonel Doran "came down the line laughing, as is his wont when there [was] a chance to take the boys into action." Asked whether they were prepared to move to the front, the soldiers leapt to their feet and, to the rousing cries of their commander, they answered in unison: "Yes, Colonel, all ready, lead us on." Not a man shrank from his duty, the *Wisconsin Daily Patriot* reported, and, as in the accounts from the soldiers of the Ninth Connecticut at Baton Rouge, the "sick and wounded who had not done duty for two months turned out and shouldered their guns to a man." It was "a striking instance of the good effects of discipline and 'pluck,'" in spite of the regiment's fondness for "whiskey and fresh secesh pork." Though subtle, assumptions about ethnicity nevertheless appeared in the *Patriot's* article, couched in stereotypical references to alcohol consumption and disorderly conduct. Battlefield success, though, underscored the broader notion that these stereotypical traits, which had caused some animosity before the war, had little impact on the men's combat readiness or enthusiasm to defend their country. In reality, the 17th Wisconsin's first "battle" was merely a skirmish, and it was another two weeks before the regiment was truly tested against Confederate regulars.[22]

North of Baton Rouge, General Braxton Bragg attempted to break Union momentum by moving back into Tennessee to relieve Chattanooga and threaten the Federal position at Nashville. In support of this campaign, Confederates under Sterling Price moved from Tupelo, Mississippi into the southwestern corner of Tennessee, where they united with Bragg. Grant left the defenses at

Corinth to meet the threat, and at Iuka, Mississippi, on September 19, he checked Price's move and forced the Confederates under Price to retreat south to Ripley, Mississippi, where they joined troops under Earl Van Doran. On September 28 this reorganized Confederate army, numbering nearly 22,000, left Ripley bound for Corinth, where they hoped that a victory would help drive the Union forces there back into Tennessee. There, on the bloody fields of Mississippi, the men of the 17th Wisconsin finally proved their true merit under fire.[23]

At 7:30 on the morning of October 3, 1862, the Confederates advanced in force against the Union line north of Corinth. By 11:00 a.m., amid the "rapid discharge of musketry and artillery," it had become "pretty evident [to the men of the 17th Wisconsin that] our right was falling back. [General Thomas] Davies' division did not come on our right so as to reach the Memphis road, and the rebels took advantage and easily gained the camps of our regiment and the 21st Missouri," a participant wrote in an account, dated October 19, 1862, that he sent to a Wisconsin newspaper. The Confederate advance separated the Union left from the main force, and the men of Wisconsin's Irish Brigade found themselves defending the far right of that isolated Union position. As Confederates tried to flank their position Doran countered, ordering "Charge bayonets! Forward march!" Advancing rapidly across the field, the 17th drove four Mississippi regiments back and regained the overrun forward positions. This "Irish charge, with its accompaniments, rather astonished the enemy, I think," remarked the writer of this account. "The soldiers of the Seventeenth distinguished themselves all through the fight," another outlet wrote, "particularly in a bayonet charge which was led by Col. Doran." Such language, which couched the fight in terms of ethnic bravery, tied these men to popular conceptions of the ferocity of the Irish soldiers and their willingness to undertake daunting assaults in the face of the enemy and in defense of the Union.[24]

The regiment suffered forty men killed, wounded, and missing as a result of their actions that day, and that night as they marched through Corinth to their new position on the far right of the Federal line, the men were "loudly cheered by the other regiments in the division" for their decisive role in single-handedly driving the Mississippi Brigade from the field. The response by their comrades was a further testament to the heroic conduct of the Irish Brigade, and their actions were further evidence, for those at home, of the loyalty and patriotism of their men-in-arms. The bravery and sacrifice of the 17th Wisconsin was reminiscent of the service of other Irish regiments in larger battles in the East and stood as a testament to the tenacity of these men on the battlefield.[25]

The second year of the war dawned brightly for the Irishmen from these units. As winter gave way to spring and summer, all three regiments again took to the field. There was little news to report from New Orleans and Virginia, though. May 1863 found the Ninth Connecticut still operating by company, with units stationed at Pass Manchac, Proctorville, Algiers, and in Lafayette Square in New Orleans. The regiment saw limited action during the spring and early summer, responding mostly to Confederate feints north and west of New Orleans. They were at Thibodaux in June when Confederate forces under General Richard Tyler advanced on New Orleans in a feeble attempt to recapture the city. Events to the east and north, though, captivated attention in Louisiana. "Grant has Crossed the Mississippi to the East side and taken into the Country after Capturing Grand Gulf to cut off the Rebel Rail Roads and destroy their connections," Cahill wrote home in May. "Everything is looking splendidly I do not see what can save vicksburg now." Unbeknownst to him, of course, this grand move cast his countrymen from Wisconsin into the thick of battle yet again.[26]

Mulligan's regiment too, was spread out in the Shenandoah Valley and saw light action at Phillipi, Altamont, Rowlesburg, and Fairmont, Virginia. "The boys," Mulligan noted contently in his diary during this time, "are well and in spirits." At Greenland Gap in April 1863, Captain Martin Wallace of the 23rd Illinois and a small detachment of men from his regiment and from 14th West Virginia were surprised by a larger Confederate force. They retreated to a log church at the mouth of Greenland Gap and were surrounded, whereupon Confederate General William Jones produced a flag of truce and demanded that the Federal troops surrender. "I told the bearer," Wallace wrote in his after-action report, "'Go back with your rag; I don't care if he has a million [men]; I will not surrender until compelled.'" The fighting resumed for a brief period of time until, again, Wallace was told to surrender before cannon were brought up to force the men from the church. "Tell him he has got none," Wallace responded; "if he has, bring them on. We are Mulligan's men, and we will fight to the last crust and cartridge." Ultimately, with the roof ablaze, the men from Mulligan's Brigade were compelled to surrender. "Bravely they fought—long and well," reported the *Chicago Tribune*. Even against overwhelming numbers, "the Irish boys refused to give up, and it was not until the roof fell that they surrendered. Glory to the fallen braves." The tenacity of these Irishmen and their refusal to surrender to overwhelming odds was becoming commonplace, and continued the theme of battlefield courage that would follow these men throughout the war.[27]

Back west, in the spring of 1863 the men from Wisconsin found themselves a part of the larger Federal campaign to capture Vicksburg. Outside of that city, on May 16, 1863, the 17th was "in the hottest of the fight" at Champion Hill, and the regiment "distinguished itself for its fidelity and bravery during the fiery trial." Losing nearly one quarter of their men, the volunteers from Wisconsin's Irish Brigade continued the precedent of hard fighting that they had set the previous year at Corinth. Ebenezer Wescott, in the vivid imagery typical of his correspondence, wrote of the battle: "[A]bout 1 o'clock in the afternoon [we] came up to Pemberton's army at Champion Hill and before four o'clock had whipped him besides taking thirty piece of artillery and about four thousand prisoners." The next day the regiment "marched straight for Vicksburg; came up to the Rebel works about ten o'clock in the forenoon of the 19th and about two o'clock made a charge, but had run against a snag and were driven back. Made another charge the 22nd with no better success." Selected to lead the advance on the morning of May 20, the men from Wisconsin moved forward with fixed bayonets and "charged through an abattis of felled trees, which severed our ranks much . . . [and] . . . exposed [the men] to a crossfire of shot and shell" from the Confederate positions on their right and left. "No regiment could stand such a tempest of lead and iron," wrote one soldier, defending the stalled assault. After the failed assault, Wescott believed that the Union's only chance of defeating the Confederates at Vicksburg lay in their ability "to starve them out."[28]

Time and again the soldiers of the 17th Wisconsin advanced without support as the soldiers in the regiments on their left and right faltered under enemy fire. Despite "the withering fire of the enemy," the boys from Wisconsin charged lines "so thick [with enemy soldiers] that all the front rank of them had to do, was to fire and throw back his gun for a comrade to reload while he was firing others." When the attack stalled on the afternoon of May 22, General Thomas Ransom allegedly lamented, after ordering a retreat, that "if I had put the 17th ahead, we should have been inside now." Such performances under fire were commonplace for Irish regiments, especially in the East, where men of the Irish Brigade earned international renown for their charges at Antietam and Fredericksburg. The men from Wisconsin exhibited a similar steadfastness under fire and won renown at home for their deeds, first at Corinth and then at Vicksburg. Although their service received little attention in circles outside of their home state and failed to cement their place in the broader historical memory of ethnic service to the Union, such deeds of heroism played an important role in reinforcing the strong ties between these Irishmen and their adopted state.[29]

The rest of 1863 played out without major incident for any of the regiments. After the surrender of Vicksburg, the 17th Wisconsin became a mounted infantry unit, patrolling south into Louisiana, where they participated in battles around Trinity and Natchez in a campaign that culminated in the capture of Fort Beauregard, part of the Confederate river defenses. During this same time the 23rd Illinois continued their service in the Shenandoah Valley—long periods of drudgery interspersed with moments of terror under fire. Rarely was the regiment engaged as a whole, for companies were widely dispersed in the region to protect Federal assets. Largely, though, the 23rd Illinois played little part in the bloody spring and summer of 1863, an ignominious role for a regiment that had earned such notoriety during the first months of the war. The Ninth Connecticut remained on provost duty in New Orleans, and had almost no contact with the enemy save light skirmishing at Brashear and Bayou Teche, where Cahill and his men did little save retreat in the face of what was supposed an overwhelming enemy force commanded by General Richard Taylor. In all, though, during the tumultuous first two years of war, as the ranks of the Irish Brigade were thinned and disillusionment grew among Irishmen and women in the home communities of those regiments, the men from Connecticut, Illinois, and Wisconsin experienced an altogether different war. They experienced success and earned fame for themselves, their regiments, and their states, and their service fostered a unique blend of patriotism and loyalty in the ranks and among those at home.

Irish regiments marched to war in 1861 and 1862 hailed by observers for their fighting pluck—an identity they assumed before they fired a shot and one that was prescribed as a result of their open ethnic affiliations. Time and again soldiers in all three regiments lived up to their reputations as Irishmen and proved themselves heroically under fire. At home, newspapers reported these fights in glowing terms, using ethnicity as a means of connecting readers with the exploits of their sons and husbands on far-away battlefields. "Irishness" meant something tangible, for it referred to an array of qualities; it called to mind tenacity and courage, qualities that were appealing to both Irish *and* American readers, for they were the characteristics of true, loyal soldiers. Certainly these soldiers, and in particular their officers, made bold references to ethnicity in published accounts of combat and camp life. Irish songs were sung and Irish blessings given at dinners and dances in honor of these regiments. Irish battle cries rang from the ranks as these men rushed into battle, and they fought with a ferocity few other regiments could match—because of their heritage. But these references shrouded the service of the soldiers themselves, who rarely appeared to think of their time in the army and, in particular in battle, through ethnic lenses. This does not mean these men did not identify ethnically—for their heritage, combined with their decision to enlist in an Irish regiment, was an affirmation of their individual identities. In a broader sense, however, it is clear that the public use of ethnicity was vital to the Americanization of these regiments, and their service reaffirmed individual conceptions of republicanism and the place of these men within their adopted nation. Meanwhile, the continued support of the war effort on the home fronts in Connecticut, Illinois, and Wisconsin defined the nature of immigrant loyalty for years to come, and stood in stark contrast to the public rejection of Federal policies of emancipation and the draft that emerged from ethnic communities in New York in the summer of 1863.

# 5 Disorder and Discipline

In January 1862, when the 17th Wisconsin was in Memphis, Tennessee, Corporal Samuel McClement and his uncle received permission from their captain, Peter Feagan, to travel to town to have their pictures taken. Soon after, the regiment broke camp and boarded a steamer headed south down the Mississippi River. It would be a day and a half before anyone realized that McClement had deserted. On August 23, 1863, Private Ebenezer Wescott happily reported to his parents that after a nearly eighteen-month absence, his friend had returned to the ranks of his own accord. Though Sam provided no reason for his desertion, he told Wescott that between January and August of 1863 he had "been in Tennessee about twenty-five miles from Memphis . . . working on a plantation." Pressured by Confederate cavalry to enlist, Sam escaped to Memphis, where he "took the oath of allegiance, went to the Capitol of the state and said he wanted to enlist and go to our regiment." Voluntarily returning to service, Sam somehow managed to avoid charges of desertion. He served loyally for the remainder of the war, reenlisting as a veteran volunteer in February 1864 and mustering out with his regiment in June 1865.[1]

All three regiments examined here suffered a degree of disorderly conduct over the course of the war, though the number of general courts martial trials varied considerably, both when compared to one another and to the Irish regiments in the Army of the Potomac. Men deserted from the ranks, especially in situations where there were opportunities to drink, carouse, or join other regiments. But, as Sam McClement's story suggests, some of these acts were perhaps more complicated than they seem. Lauded in the public eye for heroism and courage on the battlefield and steadfast in their continued commitment to the war effort, men from the three units nevertheless acted, at times, in ways far outside the social and military norms. Furthermore, their behavior often reflected many of the negative ethnic stereotypes that had played such an important part of antebellum nativist rhetoric. Civil War regiments were, of course, rife with disorder. National rhetoric during this period, however, stressed the loyalty, patriotism, and virtuousness of the citizen soldiers. Similarly, religious beliefs emphasized the notion of "the good death" and often portrayed soldiers as virtuous men on a noble crusade to save the Union. The public portrayal of citizen-soldiers in these ways is understandable, reflecting as it does a conscious effort to focus on positive aspects of the war. This was particularly important to the Irish, who believed their military service would debunk the incendiary accusations of the more xenophobic portion of the Northern populace. Yet the realities of life for volunteers often contradicted the imagined life of the wholesome, brave soldier boy embodied in these popular representations of soldiers. Although much focus was placed on maintaining these appearances, disorderly acts provide important insight into the daily activities of soldiers and the relationships (strained and otherwise) between men during war.[2]

The Ninth Connecticut, 23rd Illinois, and 17th Wisconsin marched to war in 1861 and 1862 amid lingering questions about their potential effectiveness, largely related to stereotypes surrounding the ethnicity of the volunteers. Accusations of disorderly conduct, both accurate and exaggerated, that emerged during this period hearkened back to allegations levied against Irish Americans by Know-Nothing politicians during the decade before the war. The public enthusiasm for the formation of Irish units, combined with the proclamations of loyalty and support espoused by the Irish American communities in these states, did ease tensions. While reports of disorderly behavior were commonplace during the early months of organization, once these regiments left for the South such rhetoric disappeared, and the accounts that appeared on the home front are notable for their largely positive narratives of the service of these ethnic units.

This did not mean that the men's behavior changed. In fact, officers in all three units struggled to maintain order in the ranks and among themselves. Disciplinary issues were not unique to specific regiments, and Irish units exhibited an array of transgressions. In the later years of the war, some Union officers certainly fingered ethnic soldiers (especially those who were drafted or enlisted late in the war) as the primary perpetrators behind disorderly conduct, but this was due as much to misperceptions as to reality. For the regiments in this study, the responses at home to the men's behavior, at least early in the war, were mixed. In Connecticut, the men of the Ninth were ostracized for their behavior during the first weeks of their service, while in Wisconsin, the public championed the men's disorderly behavior as the inherent expression of democratic protest. Moving to the front lines shielded the men's problematic behaviors from the scrutiny of those at home but by no means ended internal conflict between the men themselves. Analysis of the conflicts and disorderly behaviors among the men in all three of these regiments expands the narrative of ethnic military service, illustrating the ways these soldiers understood their place both within the military and as members of their nation.

Interactions among officers in the three regiments reflected a high degree of interpersonal animosity—something that many regiments in both Union and Confederate armies struggled with. Such issues played out among the ranks as well. Regiments brought together over one thousand men of different ages, ideologies, and backgrounds, and while some soldiers joined with friends and acquaintances, many others were strangers united only by their decision to join a specific unit. As evidence from the mutineers of the 17th Wisconsin in March 1862 shows, company-level harmony was often undercut simply because it was difficult to bring men from various regions together, but necessary in order to fill companies. Although cohesion developed over time, especially when the men experienced combat, such conditions often led initially to animosity within units. As regiments mustered at large camps, typically in the state capital, the volunteers became part of an ever-growing mass of men, most of whom had had little formal military training (despite the participation of some of the volunteers in antebellum militia companies), and many of whom were skeptical of the hierarchy that came with military service. In sum, then, a large number of men were thrust together, away from the watching eyes of families and friends, with some money, a fair amount of free time, and a willingness to question orders. Soldiers did not suddenly become friends as a result of shared circumstances and their military service did not somehow transform them into moral and well-behaved citizen-soldiers—in spite of social values and norms. Military life provided men with abundant potential for disorderly conduct, and men of all ranks, in all regiments, fell victim to these temptations.[3]

Conflict among the officers was, perhaps, the most visible expression of the disjointed relationships that existed in all three regiments, and animosity between officers also played out, to a degree, on the home front. Although ethnic ties were an important part of the recruiting of all three regiments, and a majority of the officers were Irish-born or of Irish heritage, common ethnic background did little to ease tensions that arose between ambitious men. Certainly in the mutiny of the 17th Wisconsin early in the war can be found evidence of these issues, as the events that unfolded at Camp Randall pitted soldiers and officers against one another. But the specific nature of that event, combined with broad popular support for the disaffected volunteers and the eventual reunification of the regiment, made those issues exceptional and momentary.

Much more problematic were rifts among officers that affected regimental efficiency while on campaign. Colonel Thomas Cahill, for example, struggled early in the war with command issues when Captain John Nelson arrived at Ship Island with a detachment of men. When the Ninth Connecticut left New Haven for Lowell, Cahill had left Nelson behind in Bridgeport to continue to recruit for Company K, which had only twenty-five recruits. Nelson joined the regiment at Lowell, but again remained behind to continue recruiting when the rest of the regiment left for the Gulf of Mexico. In October 1861, however, the *Hartford Courant* reported that Cahill refused to accept Nelson's troop into his regiment because of the Nelson's "inamiable disposition." Tensions came to a head when Nelson landed on Ship Island and informed Cahill that he and his men had enlisted with the 13th Massachusetts, and that he had resigned his Connecticut commission to accept a position in the Massachusetts regiment. In essence Nelson traded his cohort of volunteers for a higher rank in the Massachusetts regiment. "I do not want him," Cahill wrote to his wife, "but I want his men"; Cahill still needed them to fill his ranks. Nelson "played me that scurvy with regards to Company K," he wrote home a month later. "One thing is for certain, I shall not allow anny trifling with the Rights of the State of Conn." Nelson ultimately resigned and returned home in large part because of the conflict between himself and his colonel, but he was just the first of a number of officers who became disillusioned with Cahill's leadership.[4]

Over time, word filtered back to New Haven that some of the officers were worried about Cahill's leadership abilities. Margaret Cahill wrote to her husband, concerned about a report from Lawrence O'Brien from which she learned "that some of your officers are finding some fault with you because you do not tolorate their New Haven Conduct." Tensions rose to the point that seven officers resigned and returned home to Connecticut in the spring of 1862. "You do not say anything about our returned officers in your letters," Cahill wrote to his wife in July 1862. "I suppose they are giving me a fine riddling if so I can only say that I am sorry that I did not give them some occasion." Two of the officers who resigned did later write to Cahill, asking him "to take them back and expres their sorrow for having left the Regt." He was unimpressed with their pleas; "I have not heard of their having used any ill Language towards me but I have no idea of leaving men who remain and work with the Regt out in the Cold while these gentlemen are Enjoying themselves as home." But in that July letter Cahill also begged his wife to tell him, "if you think I am too severe on the New Haven Capts . . . as I have no desire to think ill of any one." While Cahill sought to preserve some degree of solidarity among the men, it was clear that he and some of his officers had different views on alcohol consumption and discipline, and those differences ultimately undermined relationships between him and these men.[5]

Colonel John Doran faced similar struggles with the officers serving under him in the 17th Wisconsin. In May 1862, Quartermaster John Gee resigned his post; according to a Sheboygan, Wisconsin newspaper, his resignation was "owing to the tyrannical conduct of Col. Doran, against whom strong charges have been preferred, signed by every officer in the regiment." In early June these tensions escalated when Doran wrote to Wisconsin's governor, Edward Salomon, requesting permission to promote a Lieutenant Edwin Moore, an aide-de-camp to General Benjamin Prentiss, to replace Major Thomas McMahon, who had recently tendered his resignation. Doran claimed there were no qualified company-grade officers in the 17th to replace McMahon. The problem, the colonel wrote, was that the "Irish military organizations in this country are different . . . beyond the officers, who got up or recruited the companies, you cannot find a man from education, appearance, temper, or judgment fit to take the place of commissioned officers." Moore, Doran claimed, was "a young gentleman of good military experience," and thus qualified to fill the vacant position. Doran's view of the soldiers under his command caused considerable animosity among the men in the ranks, and it was a view that historical evidence proves to have been certainly in error, for men of means and education appeared in all ranks and positions in all of the Irish regiments examined here.[6]

Doran's refusal to promote from within, he told the governor, "brought down upon me much of the most malignant of that turbulent disposition" among the other officers in the regiment who were determined "to promote [Patrick] McCauley [then serving as captain of Company A] or destroy me." In a postscript, the beleaguered colonel lamented to Salomon that "the mustered out officers have conspired with the friends of McCauly [*sic*] to misrepresent me to you, in some manner, so as to secure his appointment, and indirectly to assume Command of the Regiment." Refuting Doran's claim of incompetence, the commissioned and noncommissioned officers of the 17th wrote to Salomon themselves on August 29, recommending promotions to fill a number of vacancies in Companies B and I. "Unfortunately," the petitioners wrote, "in this instance we can pay no regard to the <u>order</u> of promotion as those entitled to promotion by <u>seniority</u> in those two companies have proved themselves <u>unworthy</u> of holding positions higher than that which they now occupy. We therefore recommend those who <u>have</u> proved themselves competent, and worthy, in every respect. . . . [T]hey will be the right men in the right place. . . . [Those] commissions . . . [would] be 'Merit rewarded.'" Combat in and around Mississippi momentarily eased tensions, but the animosity between the colonel and his officers lingered through the summer, coming to a head that winter and illustrating just how fleeting ethnic ties could be when it came to command decisions.[7]

On November 21, 1862, Brigadier General John McArthur placed Doran under arrest and confined him to regimental camp. Dolan was "charged with many very serious affairs against both the military and the law" and ultimately resigned his commission on November 25. The *Chicago Times* and *Milwaukee Daily Sentinel* reported that the colonel was "under arrest on a long string of charges and specifications. . . . [M]uch ill feeling has existed between himself and the officers and men of his regiment, for months past." The final straw for the men of the 17th Wisconsin came when the colonel, according to a report sent to General Grant's headquarters, "improperly retained the post fund of $93"—money arising from a tax on sutlers, meant to be sent home to aid families of soldiers in the regiment. Lieutenant Colonel Adam G. Malloy, in accusations against Doran, stated, "I do not hesitate in saying that the mustering out of service of Col. Doran will be of greatest benefit to the service. He is a man who maintains no discipline, is at constant fraud with his Officers and whose personal and moral character is such to render him entirely unworthy the position he holds." According to Sylvanus Cadwallader, an aide to Ulysses S. Grant, "Col. Doran's convivial habits unfitted him for usefulness and finally made him so obnoxious that the regiment was on the point of mutiny. Some time before this [before the post fund accusations] charges had been preferred against him for drunkenness." The only solution to the quarrels was the removal of Doran from command. A speedy resignation saved him from trial, and he was replaced by Adam Malloy, whose promotion was supported unanimously by the regiment's commissioned officers.[8]

Officers in the 23rd Illinois contended with similar internal discord. The men of Company G also struggled with conflict over promotion. In their case, concern lay in the nepotism of their colonel rather than with ineptitude. In July 1862, the soldiers of that company wrote Illinois governor Richard Yates in protest of Colonel Mulligan's decision to promote his brother, Samuel Mulligan. Sam was "only a boy of seventeen or so," and an example to many that Mulligan "does nothing but pile up all the vacancys in this regiment with his friends and Relations that never was in Service before." The men further questioned whether the governor would "allow this or do you not allow us the Right to elect our own officers." Conflict between officers also occurred over a vacancy in Company E. Michael Gleeson, captain of Company B, forwarded his support for the promotion of John Healy to the Adjutant General of Illinois. Mulligan, on the other hand, supported the promotion of Second Lieutenant Harry Pease. Healy believed that he had secured the promotion, and when word arrived that he had, in fact, been passed over in favor of Pease, Healy petitioned Governor Yates for a transfer. "You may think it rather strange," he wrote to Yates, "but as things are not working in a military form, I came to the conclusion that I can not hold my 1st Lieutenancy with honor and self respect at the same in this Irish Brigade." Shielded from civilians at home, such power struggles nevertheless illustrate some of the realities of military service in the Civil War. While ethnicity brought these men together, it did not necessarily cultivate harmony amongst them.[9]

At times, animosity between officers was more inflammatory. On July 27, 1862, for example, Captain William Wright, the same man the *Hartford Courant* had heralded in 1861 for his efforts at raising an Irish regiment in that city, was arrested at Baton Rouge for intoxication and resisting arrest. Cahill, present at the arrest, reported that Wright went into a verbal tirade against the Federal government and the war effort. Wright "wished that he . . . was in the Confederate service; that he wished the Federal Service was in hell . . . [and] that the Federal Government was a Cheat a Swindle and a humbug." On the evening of the alleged incident, Lieutenant Colonel Fitzgibbon observed Wright in the office of the provost marshal, "sporting Shakespear and making fun," after his arrest for causing a public nuisance. According to Patrick Garvey of Company B, Wright "was much enraged at being arrested by privates," leading to his outburst. Although Wright was found not guilty of public use of "treasonable and seditious language," the number of witnesses—commissioned officers and privates alike—illustrates the extent to which these sorts of acts could potentially influence the behavior of enlisted men in the regiment. In fact, the rather lenient verdict in Wright's case may have actually encouraged this type of behavior.[10]

In another instance, Captain Patrick O'Connor of Company C of the 17th Wisconsin was arrested in the trenches outside of Corinth in the spring of 1862. Intoxicated, O'Connor was "shouting and making so much noise" that the entire camp was turned out under arms, responding to what they believed to be an enemy attack. A sergeant who attempted to calm his captain down reported that O'Connor "took me by the neck and struck me three or four times and hit me." Colonel Doran was forced to intervene and pull O'Connor off the unfortunate soldier. Captain Patrick McCauley of the same regiment was arrested and charged for a similar offense when, on November 19, 1862, "being in a state of intoxication [he] did enter the chaplains tent and insult his superior officers as well as others present by cursing—swearing and shaking his clenched hand in a most furious manner—evidently intending to provoke a quarrel and causing the officers in order to avoid a personal altercation to leave the tent in disgust."[11]

After spending the evening drinking, Captain Terrence Sheridan of Company E of the Ninth Connecticut was arrested in November 1863. Aboard the steam ship *Iberville*, Sheridan, under the influence of alcohol, "did cause a disturbance by pursuing the stewardess, a Colored woman round and round the boat, and on the same evening did attempt to associate with colored women in the lower deck of the said boat and this in the presence of enlisted men." Sheridan was found guilty on three of five charges set against him, and his rank was suspended for a period of one month. In response to the verdicts, which found Sheridan at fault for conduct unbecoming an officer, the young Irishman addressed the court in an effort to clear his name. On the night of the incident, Sheridan stated, he "was not drunk," though he "had a drink with some of the officers aboard and the captain." Drunkenness, he claimed "is an act so offensive and apparent as to be susceptible of easy proof—but there is no complaint nor evidence of any neglect of duty on my part . . . nor any overt act indicative of drunkenness." Sheridan further defended his actions and downplayed the altercation with the stewardess, claiming it was a case of miscommunication, and that even if he was guilty of making inappropriate advances, it was "a whisper [and thus] confined to the recipient, and a woman can rid herself of annoyances, when confined to whispers."[12]

When the 23rd Illinois was reorganizing at Camp Douglas in the winter and spring of 1862, newspapers spoke to many of the same issues that Cahill and Doran had struggled with when mustering their regiments into service—disorderly conduct. "More Trouble at Camp Douglas," reported the *Chicago Tribune* after a group of drunken soldiers from the Irish Brigade stormed the camp's guardhouse. Yet the men of the 23rd Illinois were not singled out, for headlines spoke of innumerable incidents of rowdiness, disorder, and desertion that occurred among all regiments stationed in Chicago. Still, some 148 men deserted Mulligan's unit during the spring and summer of 1862 while stationed in Chicago, at least 100 of whom were new volunteers, perhaps fed up with their brief stint in the military and eager to explore opportunities available in Chicago. The most notable incident, however, occurred when Lieutenant Patrick Higgins of Company C was charged with aiding the escape of rebel prisoners. As the *Tribune* reported, "for a certain sum, to be paid in advance by each prisoner who desired to regain his liberty, he would assist them to pass through the guard and escape." Although Higgins was known for "his bravery and kindness to his men," his arrest and trial, which highlighted the fact that he, an Irishman, was aiding in the escape of Irish-born rebels, his countrymen, became a public spectacle, though it had no discernable impact on public support for Mulligan's Irish regiment.[13]

The conflicts among officers and incidents for which men were court martialed reflect some of the broader issues that plagued these Irish regiments. Disciplinary struggles existed in all units, though the Irishmen from the Nutmeg State suffered a considerably higher number of court martial trials (86) than did their countrymen in either the 23rd Illinois (29) or the 17th Wisconsin (18). The men who served in the Ninth Connecticut acted out significantly more often than their comrades in the other two regiments, as reflected by records of courts martial. In fact, the number of trials of members of the Ninth was higher than average for volunteer infantry regiments from Connecticut as well. The average number of court martial trials for the twenty-nine regiments from the Nutmeg State was 28, and only two units, the Fifth and Sixth Connecticut, had similarly high numbers of arrests. Compared to other Irish units serving in Federal armies, in particular the five regiments that served in the Irish Brigade (69th New York, 88th New York, 63rd New York, 28th Massachusetts, and 116th Pennsylvania), the numbers are even more interesting. General courts martial in these regiments ranged from 46 in the 116th Pennsylvania to 68 in the 69th New York. Thus, the Ninth Connecticut was considerably more disorderly than other Irish regiments, broadly, while the men from Illinois and Wisconsin were relatively subdued.[14]

Table 5-1 Number of Court Martial Trials

| Regiment | Total Soldiers | Number of Trials | Percentage of Men Tried |
|---|---|---|---|
| 9th Connecticut | 971 | 86 | 8.86% |
| 17th Wisconsin | 1,823 | 18 | 0.98% |
| 23rd Illinois | 2,235 | 29 | 1.23% |

The discrepancies likely reflect where these regiments served, as much as they indicate that the Ninth Connecticut was itself more unruly than other ethnic or state regiments, though their early months in service certainly suggest a penchant for acting out among the men. A primary difference between the Ninth Connecticut and the other two regiments, though, was the fact that the men from Connecticut spent the majority of the war in garrison duty in and around New Orleans. The 17th Wisconsin and 23rd Illinois, on the other hand, spent most of their war campaigning along the Mississippi and in the Shenandoah Valley, far removed from any major urban center and, thus, from the temptations that permeated nineteenth-century urban environments. The sheer number of trials held in New Orleans attests to the impact of location on regimental order and disorder. Of the 86 trials of men in the Ninth Connecticut, 55 were the result of misbehavior in and around New Orleans. Of these trials, 38 dealt directly with incidents involving alcohol, absence from camp, or mishaps on guard duty. More importantly, on the few occasions when the Ninth Connecticut was campaigning, the number of incidents dropped significantly, and the differences between these units appear much less drastic.[15]

When the overall representation of ethnic soldiers in the Ninth Connecticut, 23rd Illinois, and 17th Wisconsin is considered, it does become evident that a disproportionate number of the offenders in these units were Irish. Nearly three-quarters of the cases in the Ninth Connecticut dealt with men who were Irish-born, though Irishmen made up only 58 percent of the regiment as a whole. In the 17th Wisconsin and 23rd Illinois the numbers were even more drastic. Irish soldiers appeared before military courts at rates almost double those of the regiment as a whole. Yet the Irish were not overly represented on any one specific charge, and the rates of occurrence for these incidents, when compared against the total number of soldiers in the units from Illinois and Wisconsin, are so small as to make them anomalies rather than the norm.[16]

Table 5-2 Nationality of Defendants

| Nation of Origin | 9th Connecticut | 17th Wisconsin | 23rd Illinois | Total |
|---|---|---|---|---|
| Cuba | 1 | 0 | 0 | 1 |
| England | 6 | 0 | 1 | 7 |
| France | 1 | 0 | 1 | 2 |
| Germany | 0 | 2 | 0 | 2 |
| Ireland | 60 | 7 | 18 | 85 |
| United States | 9 | 5 | 7 | 21 |
| Unknown | 9 | 2 | 2 | 13 |
| Grand Total | 86 | 16 | 29 | 131 |

Because of the paucity of cases in the Illinois and Wisconsin regiments, no firm conclusions can be drawn about the relationship between ethnicity and disorderly conduct. Furthermore, although the number of incidents involving Irish soldiers in the Ninth Connecticut was relatively high, the majority of these occurred in New Orleans; thus it is possible that outside influences, including a fairly large and friendly Irish population in that city, may have had a certain degree of impact on those numbers. Regardless, though, it is clear that the men from Connecticut continued their "New Haven conduct" even after leaving the state, and, despite the optimistic reports of the *New York Times* during the journey south, neither Benjamin Butler nor the wrath of the Atlantic Ocean could calm the temperament of these volunteers.[17]

Table 5-3 Charges Levied against Irish-Born Soldiers

| Charge | 9th Connecticut | 17th Wisconsin | 23rd Illinois | Total |
|---|---|---|---|---|
| Absence without leave | 10 | 1 | 1 | 12 |
| Aiding in POW escape | 0 | 0 | 1 | 1 |
| Assault with intent to kill | 0 | 0 | 1 | 1 |
| Burglary | 0 | 0 | 1 | 1 |
| Conduct prejudicial | 8 | 0 | 1 | 9 |
| Conduct unbecoming | 3 | 0 | 0 | 3 |
| Contempt | 1 | 0 | 0 | 1 |
| Desertion | 10 | 3 | 10 | 23 |
| Disobedience | 2 | 0 | 0 | 2 |
| Disrespect | 0 | 1 | 0 | 1 |
| Drunk and disorderly | 8 | 0 | 0 | 8 |
| Drunkenness on duty | 7 | 1 | 0 | 8 |
| Drunkenness | 0 | 0 | 1 | 1 |
| Leaving guard post | 1 | 0 | 1 | 2 |
| Neglect | 1 | 0 | 0 | 1 |
| Quitting guard | 5 | 0 | 0 | 5 |
| Sleeping while on guard | 1 | 0 | 0 | 1 |
| Stealing | 1 | 0 | 1 | 2 |
| Striking commanding officer | 0 | 1 | 0 | 1 |
| Using insulting language to officer | 1 | 0 | 0 | 1 |
| Unknown | 1 | 0 | 0 | 1 |
| Grand Total | 60 | 7 | 18 | 85 |

Certainly, behavior that could be identified as stereotypically Irish—acting out as a consequence of over-indulgence—occurred among the ranks, and alcohol appears to have fueled much of the bad behavior. Colonel Thomas Cahill, for example, squabbled time and again with the officers under his command over lack of discipline. In September 1863, while the regiment was stationed in and around New Orleans, thirty-five-year-old Sergeant Thomas Knablin complained about this laxness in a letter home to his wife. The men, he wrote, "are continually drunk and it is frightful to hear the oathes of them Oh how I long to be from amongest them, the officers seem to taken no notice of them whatever." Such behavior was by no means new. "As Col[onel]," Margaret Cahill scolded her husband a year earlier, "you must be very careful they [the enlisted men] do not like you because . . . they have had such a Splendid time under their other commanders." Although no mention of alcohol abuse appeared in local papers following the mutiny of the 17th Wisconsin in March 1862, this event happened to coincide with St. Patrick's Day celebrations in Madison, which were—and still are—notorious for the liberal consumption of spirits across the nation, and one wonders how much the libations may have influenced the mutineers' decision to resist local authorities.[18]

Alcohol consumption often resulted in visibly disruptive behavior among men of all ranks. Alcohol often gave privates the courage to stand up to their superior officers and made those same officers lash out in manners unbecoming of their rank. Alcohol use was, however, viewed differently depending on rank and perspective. The temperance movement, led by Father Theobald Mathew, had infiltrated some segments of Irish American society, and there was a belief that abstinence would encourage reform within Irish society. But the men and women who took this pledge in the United States were the exception rather than the norm. Alcohol consumption was an acceptable component of American society during this period. Cahill took a temperance pledge in the 1850s, and this pledge, along with his leadership role in the Ninth Connecticut, had an impact on his perspective on drinking in his regiment—which is ironic, for the colonel often drank beer and wine, which he apparently did not consider a breech of this pledge. On the other hand, when Sergeant James Lawler was questioned whether his comrade Thomas Cummings appeared to be drunk during an altercation with his superior officer, "No Sir," Lawler responded, "for I dont think a man drunk until he is down in the gutter."[19]

Over the course of the war, alcohol use and abuse plagued Union armies and created serious discipline problems, particularly during long periods of inactivity or boredom. Between 1861 and 1865, some 3,133 Union soldiers were tried by general court martial, charged with being drunk on duty. Alcohol consumption often fueled soldiers' frustrations and at times caused them to act out against their comrades-in-arms. In some extreme cases this behavior was well beyond societal norms. For the officers, public drunkenness in the presence of enlisted men often served to subvert their authority. It is possible, too, that the actions of officers may have only further encouraged enlisted men to act out, and at times the men justified their behavior in a rudimentary language of republicanism. When Private John Foley was arrested for entering the premises of Benjamin Kelley, a resident of Algiers, Louisiana, for example, he confronted his commanding officer "using insulting and disrespectful language . . . saying to said officer, 'You are a damned fool; I dont care a damn about you; you are always drunk yourself,' and used highly indecent and obscene language." Foley, in other words, justified his own drinking because he had seen his commanding officer exhibit similar behavior. On January 9, 1863, Corporal John Burke tried to stop First Lieutenant Daniel [O] Sullivan from going out the gate of Lafayette Square. Lieutenant Terrence Sheridan ordered Burke to let Sullivan pass, as he was on the provost guard and had a pass from the provost marshall general. "'I dont give a damn,'" Burke replied, "telling 1st Lieut Sherridan to go to his quarters, it was none of his God damned business." Tasked with guard duty, Burke was reluctant to cede authority and power, even when ordered by an officer.[20]

In New Orleans, when Captain Michael Williams attempted to assist the guard in the arrest of Private John Hagarty, the private responded by "calling him a 'son of a bitch' and a 'damned fool' and saying that he would have satisfaction if he ever met the said Captain on the battle field." On another occasion, Thomas Cummings, a private, threatened his commanding officer Lieutenant John Cogan, telling Cogan that he would to "put a bullet through his head if he did not go back to his own street and let him alone." These men and thirty-eight others were all tried in front of the same court in New Orleans on March 7, 1863—eighteen from the Ninth Connecticut, eight of them for drunkenness on duty. In the other regiments, alcohol was not cited in incidents of open dissent by private soldiers, but it is clear that men did not refrain from questioning authority if and when they felt that officers overstepped their bounds, and it is possible that liquor encouraged a boldness among private soldiers that they otherwise may not have exhibited. Issues with authority, however, plagued Civil War armies, a direct consequence of the larger problems of disorder that accompanied the nineteenth-century American citizen army. Put simply, soldiers often struggled to deal with the dichotomy between American freedom and military hierarchy.[21]

Alcohol also often fueled disorderly conduct that initially emerged from personal grievances between men in the ranks. In many cases, it appeared to simply exacerbate preexisting issues, causing men to act out in manners far beyond the norm. Defending these acts in front of the court, at times these men explained their behavior in ways that reflected their rudimentary understanding of individual democratic values. In other words, men often became angry when situations appeared unjust and thus acted out to correct or regulate those issues. For example, Private Henry Reed entered the tent of his lieutenant and "used abusive and threatening language towards his superior officer in the presence of divers officers and soldiers of his regiment." Shoved out of the tent, Reed "picked up two stones one in each hand and was going to strike him [Lieutenant John Daily.]" When Daily "came out with a pistol cocked it and pointed it at him," Reed "tore his shirt off his breast and told him to shoot." When Lieutenant John Brown attempted to arrest Private John Doyle for fighting with Lieutenant Maurice Fitzgerald, the private threatened to kill the provost martial for interfering with the brawl. These men ignored their superior officers because they saw their interference as a nuisance that hindered their ability to defend their honor, and they were often willing to challenge officers who attempted to stop what soldiers believed to be justified expressions of anger.[22]

Private John Kelly of the 17th Wisconsin was put on extra duty by his first sergeant for not answering roll call the prior evening. When he arrived for duty, Kelly noticed that other soldiers who committed the same offense had been excused from the same duty. When questioned why these other men were excused, Sergeant Delany "said it was none of my damned business." Kelly responded with considerable anger, calling the sergeant "a damned fool," and "a damned stinking liar," and said "damn your soul." William Dwyer struck Sergeant John Whalen in the face, inflicting a severe bruise, when the sergeant tried to intervene in a fight between Dwyer and another soldier. Although soldiers were required by military law to obey the command structure, Kelly's response to what he saw as an unfair situation illustrates just how willing men were to speak out against that hierarchy when they saw injustice in it. In some ways these court proceedings speak to the rather spontaneous nature of interactions between men, regardless of rank. Men overstepped military regulations with regard to rank when they felt threatened or believed they were being treated unfairly. Soldiers appeared to regard rank in very liberal terms, perhaps reflecting their own skepticism of the military hierarchy. Officers, for their part, did not sit idly by as victims, though they were shielded by regulations that protected them from these types of interactions. When challenged, officers often fought back, which is understandable given the level of threats brought to bear. But when they did they used their rank to their defend acts, which may have only further alienated men under their command. Combined, these actions all served to undermine military order. Fortunately these acts were largely confined to periods of inactivity and garrison duty and had little impact on the men's performance under fire, and their success against the enemy appears to have shielded them from broad criticism on the home front.[23]

Like drunkenness and disorder, desertion was a reality of military service, and nearly one in every ten men in the Union army left service on his own accord at some point during the war. Desertions of draftees during the later part of the war, in combination with the New York City Draft Riots and draft resistance in other parts of the country, suggest that volunteers, draftees, and substitutes (many of whom were ethnic) who joined the ranks during that period were far less enthusiastic about their service than the men who volunteered during the first two years of the war. Although they served in Irish regiments, the men of the Ninth Connecticut, 23rd Illinois, and 17th Wisconsin—both those who enlisted in 1861–62 and those who volunteered later in the war or were draftees or substitutes—were no more prone to desertion than soldiers who served in other regiments in the Union Army. Despite the larger questions about Irish American political loyalties circulating in the North during this period, desertion was actually lower in these three regiments than in other "mixed" or "American" units. When looked at closely, however, incidents of desertion, like those of disorderly conduct, attest to one undeniable motivation: opportunity. Men fled service when they were in convenient places.[24]

According to muster and descriptive rolls, in the 23rd Illinois, 148 men deserted out of a total of 1,744 volunteers. In the Ninth Connecticut, 67 men deserted out of a total of 1,112. In the 17th Wisconsin, 148 men deserted from a regiment that saw nearly 2,000 men file in through its ranks over four years of war. Men in "Wisconsin's Irish Brigade" deserted half as often as soldiers in the Union Army as a whole. Perhaps of equal importance, of the 264 men who volunteered for the 17th Wisconsin between May 1862 and May 1864 (at a time when the Irish American home front was supposedly turning against the war), only 18 men deserted, and only one of these men was Irish. Similarly, of the 290 men who joined the regiment as draftees in the fall and winter of 1864, only four deserted. Of the 98 men who enlisted as substitutes for others at home, only one man fled the ranks during his period of enlistment. In the other regiments, desertion rates were also less than in the aggregate. In the case of these three Irish regiments, furthermore, there is no evidence that Irish-born soldiers deserted at a higher rate than their American-born comrades.[25]

Men left the ranks at various times during service, though it seems that proximity to home could influence the decision to desert, as could long periods in camp. While in New Orleans, for example, soldiers in the Ninth Connecticut often absented themselves for hours or days at a time, indulging in the city's "cultural" offerings. In at least two cases, when soldiers returned to camp and efforts were made to detain them, they reacted violently against their captors, which suggests that the men were intoxicated, though they were not charged specifically for drunk and disorderly conduct. For example, when Private James Costello returned to camp after two days' absence, he "acted with contempt towards his sergeant," yelling that "you may kiss my ass and go to hell." Outside of Atlanta in 1864, while the 17th Wisconsin was in the line of battle, Private James Ginnesty "appeared drunk and made disturbances in the company." Calling his sergeant "a son of a bitch," Ginnesty fled the front and was later arrested for absence without leave. Private Andre Anderson faced an altogether different fate. Considered to "not have sense enough to receive in struction or judgment enough to use a musket," his lieutenant defended him in front of the court, claiming that "he did not know better [than to not desert] because he is not a man of sound mind," and therefore should not be held accountable for his actions.[26]

Some soldiers, like Daniel McMullen, were perpetual stragglers. McMullen had been arrested twice for desertion before he was dishonorably discharged from the service. A note was attached to his file claiming that he "will never be of any benefit to the Service either in prison or out of it." Another soldier, John Harrington, of Company B of the 17th Wisconsin, was apparently so eager to leave the service of Company B that he jumped from aboard a transport as it cast off from the docks at Memphis to move south down the Mississippi. Edward Downey deserted from the division's hospital on June 1, 1864 and returned home to Ottawa, Illinois, where he was arrested by a detective and returned to his regiment that December. John Sullivan deserted the 17th Wisconsin in the spring of 1862 at Corinth and joined the 12th Illinois, where he served until his arrest in July 1864. The soldier told the court that his comrades harassed him for being sick and unable to perform his share of duties, so he joined another troop. While in New Orleans, both Jerry Daly and Garret O'Tolle donned civilian clothes and deserted the Ninth Connecticut, joining the 26th Battery New York Volunteers; they enlisted under aliases in order to receive the regimental bounty. In these cases, the men were not necessarily disloyal to the Union cause or fundamentally bad soldiers but, rather, opportunists.[27]

Desertion spiked in all three regiments when they were in camp. Desertions in the 17th Wisconsin peaked in March 1862, when the regiment was preparing to leave the state to join the war effort. Similarly, Mulligan lost the highest number of men when the 23rd Illinois moved from Chicago to New Creek, Virginia. Although a few members of the Ninth Connecticut deserted immediately after

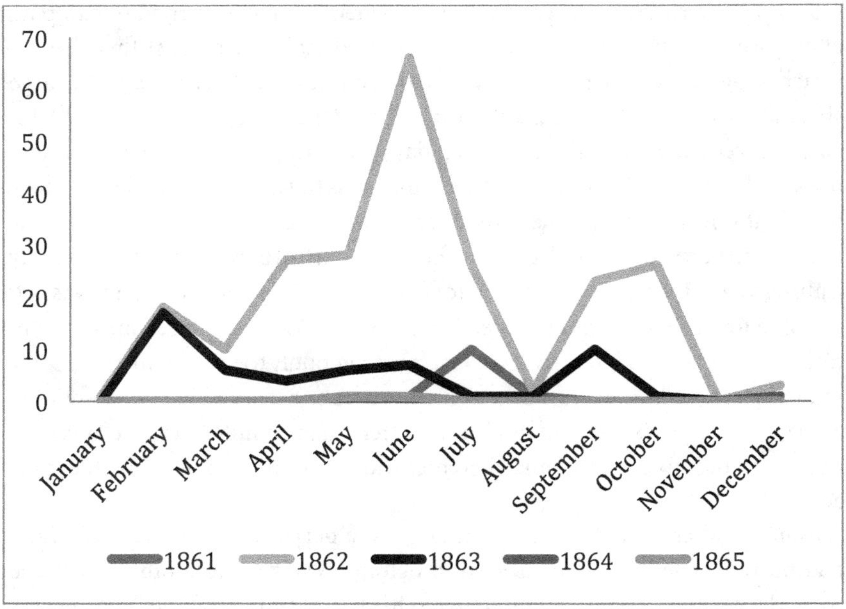


Figure 4 Desertions in the 23rd Illinois by month and year. (Database of Volunteers to Irish Regiments.)

its organization, desertions peaked in that regiment during the late summer of 1864 when the soldiers returned home for their veteran furlough. The patterns of desertion seem to imply that although desertion may have reflected dissatisfaction with military service, it was clearly an act of opportunity and, especially, connected to proximity to home.

Desertion was not an affinity exclusive to Irish soldiers. While the Irish were more likely to desert than soldiers of other ethnicities in their regiments, Irish-born men actually deserted in proportionally fewer numbers when compared to their overall representation in the regiment. These numbers can be slightly misleading, however. For example, of the 52 Irish-born soldiers who deserted the 17th Wisconsin, 32 of the men left the regiment during the tumultuous month of March 1862, when the unit mutinied over issues of pay. Similarly, of the 312 men who deserted the 23rd Illinois, 149 did so during the regiment's reorganization in Chicago in the months leading to their deployment to the Shenandoah Valley, and it is unclear how many of these men were actually deserters or simply failed to report for the reorganization of the regiment.

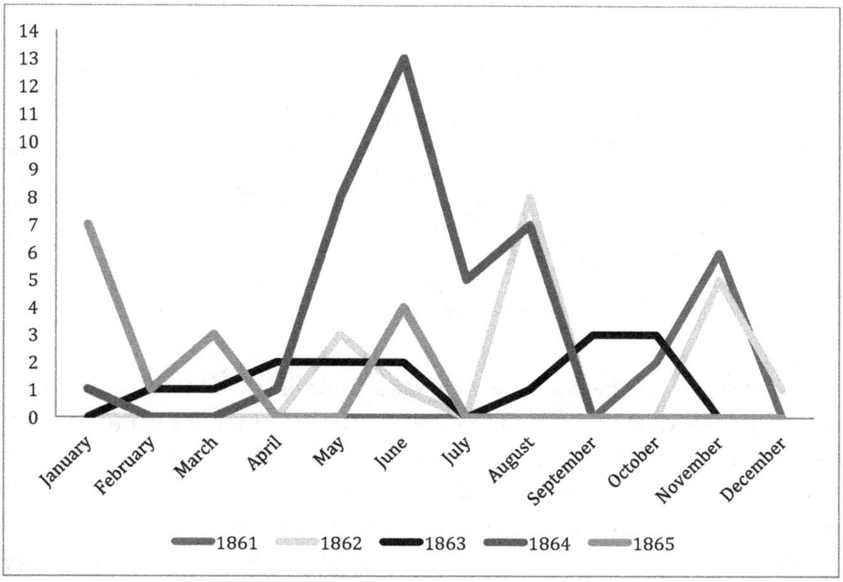


Figure 5 Desertions in the Ninth Connecticut by month and year. (Database of Volunteers to Irish Regiments.)

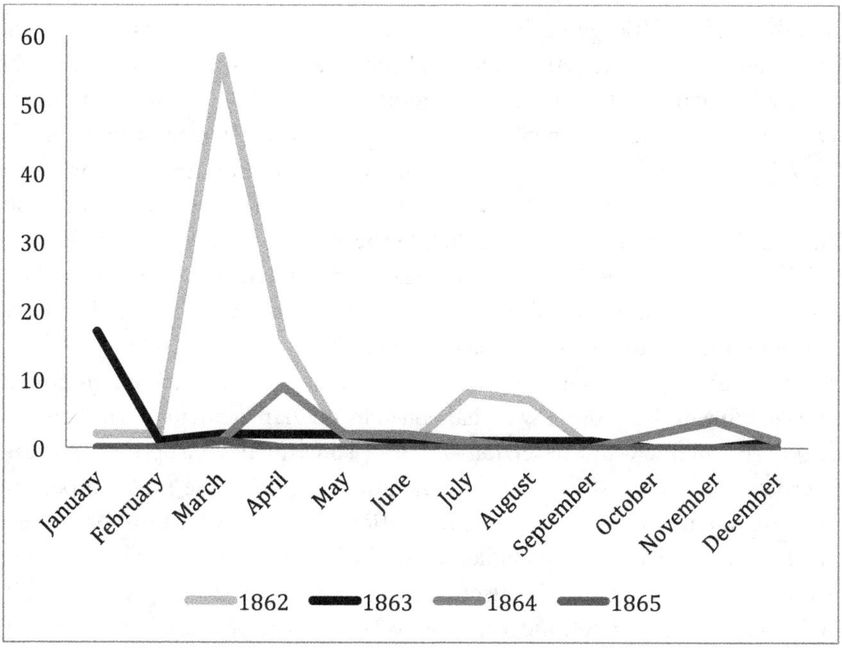


Figure 6 Desertions in the 17th Wisconsin by month and year. (Database of Volunteers to Irish Regiments.)

Table 5-4 Irish and American Desertions Compared to Unit Representation

| Regiment | Percentage of Irish in Regiment | Percentage of Deserters Who Were Irish | Percentage of Americans in Regiment | Percentage of Deserters Who Were American |
|---|---|---|---|---|
| 9th Connecticut | 61% | 43% | 24% | 13% |
| 17th Wisconsin | 32% | 34% | 33% | 22% |
| 23rd Illinois | 48% | 45% | 31% | 40% |

Like disorderly behavior, desertion was a crime of opportunity, and reflected more the individual soldier's commitment to the war than the commitment of the regiment or the home communities as a whole. High desertion rates in the 17th Wisconsin in the spring of 1862 likely reflected soldiers' distress over the well-being of their families. This was the cause of the mutiny, and was reflected in the general sentiment of the men in camp during that time. For other soldiers, such as French-born Private Charles Verdeax of Company K, 23rd Illinois, enlistment, and desertion apparently had little to do with concern for anyone other than themselves. Verdeax joined the regiment in January 1862, was paid in late February, and deserted with a group of men in early March. He was apprehended in Chicago in February 1864 by Lieutenant Thomas Moore, who had resigned his post to return home to become a police officer. Some men who deserted returned home; some simply took leave for a few days to enjoy the cities where they were stationed. Others, like Samuel McClement and his uncle, capitalized on local labor shortages and regimental bounties for their own financial gain. Most returned to service, whether on their own accord or under the guard of the provost marshal. While these incidents may have reflected a lack of character, especially in the context of nineteenth-century ideals about manhood and honor, they did not seem to reflect ethnic peculiarities or the broader loyalty of the men in these regiments.[28]

The nature of Civil War service and the reliance on volunteers led to conflict, as acceptable military order was challenged by civilian behavior. Drunkenness, disorderly conduct, and desertion—often a consequence of opportunity and interpersonal disputes—not only wreaked havoc among the ranks, especially when regiments were stationed in major cities such as New Orleans, but were at times accompanied by open challenges to the very undemocratic military justice system. At first glance the disorder in these three regiments, and especially in the Ninth Connecticut, suggests a period stereotype of drunk and disorderly conduct among recent immigrants. Yet court martial testimonies hint at more nuanced justifications for behavior, as defendants, officers and enlisted men alike, justified their actions in language that often reflected their individual conceptions of their rights as citizens, naturalized or otherwise. The disorder that existed in these regiments largely reflected a private war, as officers struggled to control one another and the men under their command. While some incidents—especially those involving regimental leadership—played out in the public eye, most remained anonymous, occurring in camps and courtrooms, with little to no impact on the ways in which those at home viewed the service of their men-in-arms. Disorder, then, did not affect the legacy of the men in these regiments. When called upon, the soldiers in all three regiments fought fiercely, living up to the precedents and reputations established by their countrymen in other regiments and other armies. Heroics on the battlefield, rather than stereotypical accounts of barroom brawlers and deserters, dominated the war-time and postwar legacy of these units, helping to secure the place of these Irish volunteers as loyal citizen-soldiers while simultaneously rebuking nativist questions of the immigrant's place within these communities.

# 6 Connecticut, Illinois, and Wisconsin React to the New York City Draft Riots

In July 1863, New York City erupted in flames as men and women poured into the streets in protest of the draft and the shifting Federal policies on emancipation. At the height of the success of the Irish regiments from Connecticut, Illinois, and Wisconsin on the battlefield, the national views on Irish American support for the Union were dealt a devastating blow. "I read all about the Riot in New York," Private Thomas Knablin of the Ninth Connecticut wrote to his wife a month after the protests were quelled. "It was a Pitty that one of those Murderers Should escape I hope the Police will furit every one of them out and hang them. You will find that if they Soldiers are Called on they will do their Duty. Those Simpitizers of the North has done more to Injure the Cause than a hundred thousand Rebels in Arms. I hope the whole of them will be hanged." His sentiment rang true for many, both in the ranks and on the home front.[1]

As the war dragged into its third bloody summer, Irish Americans in Connecticut, Illinois, and Wisconsin were drawn into public debate surrounding ethnic loyalty and disloyalty that held far-reaching implications for the place of these ethnic Americans in their adopted homeland. The summer of 1863 provided an opportunity for Irish men and women in these states to express their continued loyalty to the Union while openly rejecting the actions of their countrymen in New York City, the site of America's largest Irish enclave. The Draft Riots also provided an occasion for members of these local communities to comment on the place of these adopted citizens. Irish immigrants reiterated their support for the war effort in language that reinforced attitudes expressed in the accounts of the service of their regiments. At the same time, Democrats and Republicans alike voiced their own views on the loyalty of the immigrants in their towns and cities—and did so in ways that rejected broader attempts to disavow Irish participation and patriotism. Most men and women in these communities rejected the means and motives of the rioters in New York, but they were equally vocal in their support of "their" Irish. The New York City Draft Riots have often been used to define the rise and fall of Irish American support for the war. The reaction to this event in Connecticut, Illinois, and Wisconsin, however, shows the ways that men and women in smaller Irish enclaves, along with their friends and neighbors, understood their relationship to their communities and to the Union war effort.

Nationally, the Draft Riots were appropriated to signify dissatisfaction among the immigrant population, sentiment that was cultivated by vocal opposition to Lincoln's war measures by many prominent Irishmen. Such issues revitalized questions of immigrant place that had proliferated across the antebellum landscape. Yet this is obviously only one component of the narrative of Irish American experience during the Civil War. Publicly, most Irish Americans in Connecticut, Illinois, and Wisconsin rejected the example of the Draft Riots, viewing them as the spontaneous manifestation of a certain class that lived in New York City and were outspoken in the belief that any challenges to federal policy should come legally rather than violently. But this issue was not cut and dried. Professions of loyalty occurred hand in hand with accusations of disloyalty, and men often took conflicting ideological stances on important issues of the day. To fully understand the Irish experience during the Civil War, one must understand the nuanced responses that existed among smaller immigrant communities, for these were as important to defining the political and social lives of Irishmen in these communities as the New York City Draft Riots were to defining broader issues of Irish American dissent during the later part of the nineteenth century.

For Irish Americans, soldiers and civilians alike, the Draft Riots have remained one of the defining events of the war. The motivations behind the riots were, themselves, nuanced; public animosity over the draft, emancipation, and high casualty rates among Irish Union soldiers combined with more personal issues appear to have been what drove men and women to violently protest on New York City's streets. Nevertheless, in the immediate aftermath of this event, there was a distinct shift in national public perception, as Americans largely forgot the battlefield sacrifice of Irish soldiers and replaced this with imagery of rioting and the rhetoric of ethnic disloyalty. However, loyalty and dissent were not black-and-white issues for Irish Americans, and the response of the immigrants in New York was not reflective of a universal attitude among this group. In fact, the responses of Irishmen and their supporters across the North were as much dependent upon broader national policy as they were upon the unique experiences of Irish regiments and their supporters on the home front. Common themes emerged among all these communities: outspoken rejection of the Draft Riots, continued support for the Union and the democratic practices of American government, and a clear sense that the alienation of the New York Irish had not occurred in other regions. As New York burned, the men of the Ninth Connecticut, 23rd Illinois, and 17th Wisconsin continued to bleed on the battlefield, and their families and friends waged a political war on the home front to prove their continued loyalty to the Union cause.[2]

The New Year rang in bleakly for Irish American regiments in the Army of the Potomac. The Federal assault on Fredericksburg, Virginia had been repulsed, with terrible casualties. For the Irish, especially those in eastern cities such as New York and Boston, the slaughter on the fields of Virginia fueled discontent, as the sacrifices of the Irish Brigade appeared to have been in vain. Political issues on the home front, most importantly Lincoln's issuing of the Emancipation Proclamation, further compounded the issue and forced the largely Democratic Irish American population to directly confront the shift in war aims amid increasingly hostile accusations of disloyalty. "Presidents Proclamation published," James Mulligan wrote in early January, "Something about Freeing Niggers. Those Niggers keep this part of the world in business. We kill our white brothers to save our beloved black cousins." Despite his disdain for the shift in war aims and his staunch commitment to the Democratic platform, Mulligan still blamed the South for the war. "We Endanger a Republic," he concluded, "to preserve a plantation." Such sentiment, simply stated yet startlingly profound, speaks to the duality of Irish political thought in Connecticut, Illinois, and Wisconsin over the course of the war.[3]

Irish Americans, like many others North and South, expressed a complex set of loyalties during the war that often changed depending on circumstance and situation. Loyalty was not clear-cut, and ideologies professed loudly from the pages of local newspapers and in the speeches of elected officials in the wake of the New York City riots can be read in a number of ways, especially since Democratic politicians and their Irish constituents in communities outside of Manhattan maintained the rhetoric of loyal dissent throughout the war. Couched in the language of patriotism, the responses to the Draft Riots also served as subtle retorts to lingering nativism and the accusations of disloyalty that had run as undercurrents to the rhetoric of 1861–62 and became increasingly vocal in the summer of 1863. Distancing themselves from the violence in Manhattan, men and women in Irish American communities in Connecticut, Illinois, and Wisconsin loudly proclaimed their continued support for the Union war effort. Republicans and Democrats alike came to the defense of their

Irish American friends and neighbors. These responses played a critical role in defining the local experiences of Irish men and women, distancing them from the violence and the disloyal acts of their countrymen in New York and illustrating a level of social and political inclusion not typically associated with this immigrant group.

While the soldiers of the Irish Brigade bled along the Potomac, animosity grew among communities that supported those regiments. These losses were compounded by larger political moves by the Lincoln administration that often alienated Irish Americans, especially those living in the very visible enclaves within the major urban centers on the East Coast. Irish racism in the nineteenth century stemmed from economic competition; unskilled Irishmen competed for work with unskilled African Americans, and these men clashed in the work place over jobs throughout the antebellum period and during the war. The Emancipation Proclamation, coming as it did in the wake of the devastating losses at Antietam and Fredericksburg, led some immigrants to waver in their loyalty to the Federal government. Similarly, the draft and, in particular, the fact that those with sufficient means could buy their way out by payment of a $300 commutation fee, offended the impoverished masses, who saw this as a sign that the conflict was becoming a "rich man's war but a poor man's fight." Nowhere was there more visible destitution than in the Irish neighborhoods of Lower Manhattan in 1863. In this context, the Draft Riots become understandable as the reaction of the Irish in New York City. It was the confluence of events that ultimately led them to violently reject the implementation of the draft and, by proxy, Republican war measures, in July of 1863.

Meanwhile, in Connecticut, Illinois, and Wisconsin, the debate surrounding emancipation became increasingly contentious. The Emancipation Proclamation, claimed editors of New Haven's *Columbian Register* in January 1863, "will stand forth a huge barrier to any future reconciliation of the sections, and a memento to the Future of the desperate determination of the ruling minority that the Union should never be restored." Such sentiment was hardly new. A year before the Emancipation Proclamation was issued, the *Wisconsin Daily Patriot* had expressed the fears of the working class: "If Abolition Republicans could succeed in their diabolical plot of destroying the Government by the abolition of slavery, we should soon see the sambo transferred from southern cotton fields to the Northern corn and potato fields, for he must go somewhere, and it would not be long before the poor white laborer would be driven to work for fifteen cents a day or starve." Some Chicago editors appeared supportive of liberating slaves as a war measure. Southerners, they wrote, "must be very perverse, very stupid, if they expect that their property shall enjoy an immunity which does not belong to any other property of belligerents under like circumstances." If slaves were used to aid the Confederacy, "it is not only the right, but the absolute duty, of the government to seize them. . . . The question is entirely one of business common sense. . . . [T]his is a very different thing from hostility to slavery *per se*." The idea, however, "that the United States are engaged in an abolition war against slavery, is so absurd as scarcely to merit attention," noted the same newspaper a month later. Such sentiments rang louder as the nation was poised to institute the greatest social realignment in American history.[4]

"If Mr. Lincoln will trample on the constitution," wrote the editors of the *Daily Illinois State Register* in January, 1863, "the people will not stand by him. They will become disheartened in fighting the battles of this country, and they will utterly withdraw from him the affection and respect which every ruler should, by upright conduct, command. . . . The people will stand by the constitution and laws of the Union, and every measure of safety for the preservation of this bleeding republic." The effect of the Emancipation Proclamation in the North, one editor wrote, "will be to widen the division of sentiment now unhappily apparent. While it will have some warm friends, it will have a multitude of bitter enemies. The number of the latter will rapidly diminish if it should prove a valuable accessory in reducing the rebellion." Lincoln, wrote the editor of the *Wisconsin Daily Patriot*, had received "generous, earnest, and sincere popular support . . . in the prosecution of the war." But, he noted, "this support was without condition, save in one respect. The sole condition was that the war should be conducted to the end, as it had been professedly undertaken, for the preservation of the constitution and the restoration of the Union, with all the rights of the states unimpaired." A shift towards abolition would "make it a war not only of the subversion of the political constitution of the country, but of sudden, radical and inevitably ruinous revolution in the social and industrial relations of the people."[5]

"Opposition to abolitionism in all its phases is a cardinal political value," lectured the *Chicago Times* in 1861, "and a war waged to serve abolition or antislavery interest would be alike wicked and unconstitutional." Although emancipation became intertwined with the larger goals of victory a year later, many still had questions. "More than all," the *Times* later reported, responding to claims that volunteers were beginning to support abolition and emancipation, "the soldier wishes it distinctly understood that his creed is a single joined plank—'the constitution and the Union, one and inseparable.' For this, and this only, he fights. For this, and this only he endures hardships, suffers wounds, and even gives his life. . . . So the Union is restored, they care not whether the negro remains on the face of the globe. He is the smallest of the soldier's trouble." "If this is the way the abolitionist wants to free the black cussin [cousin]," a frustrated Albert Phillips of the 23rd Illinois wrote after marching thirty-two miles in pursuit of Confederate cavalry in the Shenandoah Valley, "I don't want any more to do with them." Support McClellan, another urged during the election season in the autumn of 1864, reiterating the belief among many Democrats that change could be made with the ballot, "and tell your friends to support him for he is the only hope of the country now that he is the leader of the democratic party for I tell you that if this country is ever saved it will be by that party."[6]

With emancipation, of course, came questions of African American military service. "We think it is high time that the Government should look into this absurd and dangerous matter," the editors of the *Wisconsin Daily Patriot* wrote, responding to news that the government had authorized African American regiments. "It is nothing but an absolute waste of time and money. . . . In the first place there is no necessity whatever for such auxiliaries; and in the next, the idea can never be carried out to any practical result." It was a "foolish illusion" that these regiments could play an integral part in the war effort, the editorial continued, one that had preoccupied generals throughout the country. Had these men continued to devote themselves "to the care and discipline of the regular white army . . . we should certainly have had fewer reverses and more victories to record."[7]

Responses to African American service were mixed. On April 8, 1863, Brigadier General Lorenzo Thomas arrived at Lake Providence, Louisiana, tasked with recruiting black regiments for the Union war effort. The 17th Division held a dress parade for Thomas, and was presented "in one solid mass in front of headquarters, drawn up by regiments, battalions, and batteries," wrote participant Thomas Christie of the First Minnesota Light Artillery; he noted that the 17th Wisconsin "had been put away back in the rear; there are many men in that regiment who do not believe in arming the black man." The heroics of African American troops at Port Hudson in May 1863 were reported with mixed enthusiasm at home. "All the abolitionist papers took part in the chorus of praise for the negroes [at the Battle of Port Hudson]," noted editors of the *Daily Illinois State Register* of Springfield. "But the truth is out at last. The whole story was a falsehood from beginning to end and was prepared beforehand to reconcile the north to the arming of the slaves." The numbers of African American troops in the field were greatly exaggerated, the same men argued in December 1863, questioning whether black troops were truly willing to participate in the "cause of freedom." In Connecticut, one politician decried a bill calling for the arming of African American troops; he was reportedly protesting "its passage as the most 'disgraceful' and 'vilest' bill ever introduced into the Connecticut Legislator—more disgraceful even than the bills once before the British Parliament, for arming savages. He would sooner let loose the wild Comanchees than the ferocious negro."[8]

Debates surrounding emancipation and African American service continued throughout the war, though ideological shifts can be found among some of the mostly Democratic soldiers in the Ninth Connecticut after their lengthy service in the Deep South. Thomas Cahill wrote home to his wife in disgust after seeing the "splendid summer residences of the southern aristocracy built upon the meanest of all foundations: the unwilling labor of the Black." Another officer in the Ninth reported that "the negro is not that animal he has been represented; far from it . . . he has tasted of that fruit of American culture, *Liberty*, and he is willing to fight for it. *The negro will fight*." That same officer noted that "the regiment to which I belong came South Democrats—that you know—and on my honor as a man, they are this day abolitionists, almost every one of them, and why? Because they have seen slavery in its naked deformity, in its every guise . . . We shall have gained everything in this context if we gain a free country." In the wake of state elections in 1864, *Hartford Daily Courant* readers learned that "in answer to this slanderous intimation that the 'Old Ninth' would vote the copperhead ticket, we state on authority of a Democratic officer . . . that there is not a good soldier in the Regiment who would not vote the Union ticket."[9]

In Illinois, Democrats claimed that Republicans were attempting to organize "an army of black janizaries, by impressing and arming slaves which are property of American citizens. The only circumstance which can possibly mar their scheme, is the fact that negro soldiers, contrary to the assertions of the abolitionists, are nearly worthless." The belief that freedmen would be ineffective on the battlefield and thus unworthy of citizenship was, ultimately, disproven by the actual service of black soldiers. For others, African-American service had the potential to have a more meaningful impact. As part of the larger war effort, one Wisconsin editor concluded, "every negro enlisted saves a white man from the draft, and the white men—even the copperest of them—are beginning to realize this." Democrats in all three states continued to debate the politics of emancipation and African American service long after these became official policy, in ways that reiterated just how important the democratic process was to them during this period.[10]

The national political issue that was next in importance after emancipation was, perhaps, the draft. It was a war measure that Democrats in Connecticut, Illinois, and Wisconsin appeared more inclined to defer to than emancipation, as it marked a less radical means of achieving victory. It was one of the primary issues that motivated the rioters in New York City, but reactions to conscription were subdued in these states, even among the strongest ethnic enclaves of New Haven and Chicago. In these regions the draft served more as a means of enticing recruits than an efficient means of organizing an effective fighting force. The Republican newspaper the *Chicago Tribune* applauded the draft, suggesting that the list of eligible citizens be "printed, and thus thrown open to inspection of the public" for all to see the names of the loyal men. Doing so would also let the citizens of Chicago bear witness to "every disloyal man, who would steal an exemption." Editors in Springfield enthusiastically reported that the draft's "effect upon enlistments [was] magical," as word of impending conscription "electrified the people. In place of depression and despondency, it has given rise to enthusiasm and confidence." It may be more realistic to surmise that it was community pressure, along with a desire to collect federal and state bounties—money not offered to drafted men—that drove later war volunteering.[11]

By the spring of 1863 support for the war had not vanished in Wisconsin, though it had certainly been counterbalanced by loud voices of dissent. As in the arguments over emancipation, political rhetoric largely focused on the means by which the draft was pursued and questions surrounding the commutation fee and the hiring of substitutes. For example, some in Wisconsin saw the $300 commutation fee as necessary to keep the price of substitutes within reason. Refuting the commutation fee, the editors of the *Wisconsin Daily Patriot* suggested that the government simply "'ignore' substitutes, and make *all* go who are drafted. This would put each man on level." They further advocated that the state, counties, or towns "raise a sufficient amount to commute for the number of men required, and that those [men] willing to respond to the draft or volunteer their services, should be paid the three hundred dollars." The *Patriot* also reported that rumors of the pending draft were causing "a good deal of unnecessary alarm in regard to the number that will probably be drafted." Men and women in Connecticut looked upon conscription with some trepidation, and while the Peace Democrats, also known as Copperheads, gained power within the state, resistance to the draft came more as interference than as violent resistance. In the wake of the growing need for soldiers and the impending draft, the Irish citizens of Hartford resolved that "as our proportion of the men who will inevitably be obliged to go to the war will more than fill a complete regiment, it is a duty to ourselves—our children and to history—to form an Irish Regiment in Connecticut." Further, they desired that "we will each and all use our utmost influence to render a draft unnecessary by filling up at once the companies forming for this our own special organization." The draft was met with ambivalence, as the outpouring of patriotism quickly filled county quotas. Some men, though, resisted volunteering, choosing instead to take their chances with a draft that might or might not occur.[12]

As enrollment for the draft continued, some men in Connecticut actively tried to avoid it. "The enrolling for a draft is going on here at present and our folks are flying away 'like chaff before the wind,'" Father Matthew Hart of New Haven wrote to Thomas Cahill; "there will be very few of them here in three weeks time at the rate they are Skeddaddling." The *New Haven Palladium* reported word of men fleeing the city, and reminded those at home "that every-one who leaves makes the obligation resting upon those who remain so much greater." Though things appeared peaceful in his own city, Father Hart noted that "many expect a revolution in N. York if they attempt a draft there, we are on the brink of troublesome times in this part of the Country, all the Secret Societies in N.Y. are pledged to resist the draft, Free Masons, Odd fellows and all so you may look out for Squalls in that direction Certainly."[13]

According to the *Chicago Tribune*, however, only one in six men of military age would be drafted in 1862. In Chicago there were upwards of 25,000 men eligible for the draft, of whom only 4,000 would be qualified for service under the current draft law. Service was a "sacred duty [that would] be cheerfully done," and they urged that all war funds be directed to the aid of those families whose loved ones were sent to the field. Nevertheless, reported the *Chicago Times*, a committee was organized with the purpose of "submitting plans to our people for the purpose of averting the enforcement of conscription." The citizens of Chicago could raise sufficient funds to pay bounties for new volunteers "who will take our place in the armies and navies and fight our battles," and the material interests of the people of Cook County "demand that a sum of money should be immediately raised for this purpose." This committee, the *Times* further reported, also took steps to purge the enrollment lists in an effort to lower the county's quota. As in other states, the overwhelming focus was on fairness when it came to raising volunteers.[14]

Despite the focus on the draft, patriotic rhetoric continued to stress the prowess of the volunteer. Volunteering gave a man the opportunity to join other "brave boys" in defense of the republic, language that underscored the notion that draftees were somehow less loyal than their comrades who had voluntarily joined the service. By the spring of 1863, though, the pending draft bore witness to the reality of declining numbers of volunteers. Supporters of conscription, such as the *Chicago Tribune*, called men to "bear their share in it, stand each in his own lot, and '*go or send a man.*'" Dissenting voices, especially loud among Democrats, continued to reject conscription; as late as 1864 the *Chicago Times* suggested that volunteers would flock to the cause if Lincoln would simply announce "that the war is prosecuted for the restoration of the union under the constitution, and that the south may have peace on these terms whenever she desires it." Many feared that conscription would bring discouragement and disillusionment throughout the North and this, combined with war weariness, would reignite Southern enthusiasm.[15]

Rioting was a very public manifestation of the anger that must have been felt often by men and women who had little to no ability to combat the socioeconomic inequities of the United States in the mid-nineteenth century. Among the Irish in New York, this common act of public protest coincided with growing anger over what was seen as a rich man's war and a poor man's fight. The $300 commutation fee was beyond the reach of the average laborer, and so these men felt they were left without options. Yet the average citizen who was opposed to joining up did have options beyond that of mob violence. Men were fully capable of avoiding the draft. An unknown number of men simply expressed their opposition with their feet, leaving their towns before they could be enrolled in the draft. Men in Connecticut, Illinois, and Wisconsin organized draft groups to pay commutation fees, and newspapers encouraged and offered men suggestions on how to organize to avoid service. "A new and good way is suggested for those who wish to escape the draft," the *Wisconsin Daily Patriot* noted in June of 1863. "Not more than one in six will be taken, and six persons can make up a fund among themselves, by contributing $50 each, to pay for a substitute if any one of them is drafted." Advertisements appeared in the *Chicago Tribune* offering ways for "active men to make enough money to provide substitutes before the draft." Ward associations, through which groups of men all donated to a fund to be used if one of the members was drafted, also organized in many cities to provide a means of collectively providing commutation fees.[16]

Nevertheless, riots over the draft broke out in the summer of 1863. They were worse in New York City than anywhere else, and historian William Burton has argued that these riots "marked the climax of Irish alienation from the Union war effort"; following the New York City Draft Riots and the Irish American community's "outspoken criticism of a victorious administration, and unfailing support of the opposition party . . . [a] shadow of disloyalty would darken the Irish for years to come, and the history of Irish bravery, loyalty, and devotion to the Union would remain buried for decades." Martin Öfele has remarked that in the wake of the draft, the "Irish again were [viewed as] violent hoodlums unfit for civilization." Seemingly no other group experienced such a clear and rapid shift in support during the Civil War as did the Irish. Yet when placing the events of July 1863 within the context of the Irish American experience during the war, it is increasingly clear that the motivations of the rioters were incredibly complex. In addition, even if all of the factors involved could be linked to the war effort, they would be seen to have largely reflected local, rather than national, complaints. For while the Irish Brigade's casualties at the Bloody Lane at Antietam and at Marye's Heights at Fredericksburg were frequently portrayed as representative of the sacrifices being made by Irish Americans, those losses were not the central focus for communities outside of New York, Boston, and Philadelphia. Simply put, men and women on the home front were primarily concerned with the service and sacrifice of their own men-in-arms. This played out in numerous ways, particularly with regard to shifting attitudes regarding emancipation and the draft. In the home states of the 23rd Illinois, Ninth Connecticut, and 17th Wisconsin, continued support for the war effort reflected the conviction that the sacrifice of the soldiers in these regiments was a worthy one.[17]

Even in 1863 some observers recognized that during the several days the New York City riots lasted, there was a noticeable demographic shift among the participants, from those involved on the first day—men who were voicing their opposition to the draft—to those involved in the later days, when events devolved into full-scale violent rioting. But in the days following the riots, the events in New York City were appropriated and misconstrued by some of the largest newspapers in the country into a simplistic and overtly anti-Irish, anti-Democrat account of events. It is clear that the mobs in New York were, in fact, composed largely of Irish Catholics, but the riots themselves were portrayed as broadly symbolic of ethnic disloyalty, and have been intrinsically linked to the place of Irish Catholics in American society. The riots and rioters were not only taken to represent Irish American wartime disloyalty but were also cited as evidence that this group of immigrants could never truly assimilate into American society. The riots, the editors of the *New York Tribune* predicted in late July 1863, would dredge up "a sentiment of deep-rooted hostility against Irish Catholics. No one . . . can have been an eye-witness of the unparalleled, fiendish outrages which were committed by a mob, almost exclusively consisting of Irish

Catholics, without coming to the conclusion that such beings will never be fit to be citizens of a republic."[18]

Critics of the Irish successfully portrayed the events in New York City as emblematic of Irish animosity, lack of patriotism, and disconnection from broader American society. Despite the fact that the riots were much more nuanced than this, Irishmen throughout the nation understood that they would be used as evidence of Irish Catholic disloyalty. Furthermore, the timing of the riots linked them symbolically and intrinsically to larger issues surrounding Democratic loyalty that had emerged by that time, and appeared to be a response to the shifting of war aims in the wake of the Emancipation Proclamation. In the spring and summer of 1861, Irish Americans had rushed to the defense of the flag and were given enthusiastic send-offs by the towns and cities they called home as they marched to war. But this changed, Susannah Ural Bruce has remarked, as "the riots had renewed or reinforced nearly every negative stereotype about the Irish in America." Despite the loyalty and sacrifices of this ethnic group in defense of the Union, "American elites belittled Irish war contributions, excluded or minimized Irish participation in victory celebrations, and cited the New York draft riots of 1863 as continued proof of Irish disloyalty and barbarity," notes Kerby Miller.[19]

The riots in New York in the summer of 1863 were neither isolated nor unprecedented, though they were far more extensive and more destructive than those that had previously rocked other Northern cities. While the first day of rioting in New York was clearly a response to the draft, the white-on-black violence of the following days of turmoil reflected similar trends seen throughout the North. The violent acts perpetrated against African Americans in New York reflected growing Irish animosity toward free black labor, driven by fear of losing socioeconomic viability; these tensions were exacerbated by the industrial demands of a wartime economy and the growing visibility of African Americans in Northern cities as the war progressed. The physical act of rioting reflected, then, the strife that existed on the most local level between workers in major Northern cities. Yet accusations of disloyalty to the nation often emerged in the wake of these events, linking the acts to deeper political expressions of wartime animosity.

In early July 1862, for example, Irish dockworkers in Toledo, Ohio rioted because a sudden influx of workers led to pay cuts in industry throughout the city. Irish workers went on strike, were subsequently dismissed, and were replaced by freed blacks paid at the rate the strikers had initially hoped to negotiate. The riot soon spread throughout the waterfront, the *Wisconsin Daily Patriot* reported, as "the Irish tried to prevent the negroes from working, attacking them with stones, clubs, etc. The negroes in defense, drew knives and pistols, and considerable shooting and cutting was done." The size of the mob and the accompanying violence caused some to question the spontaneity of the event. The riot was "a foretaste of what we may expect as soon as the abolitionists can succeed in getting the north sufficated with negro labor," the *Patriot* editor noted. The *Macon (Ga.) Telegraph* reported that "there were some men [among the rioters] who called themselves Democrats, that were at their heels, telling them to clean out the niggers; that this was a war of capital against white labor, and that if they would clean out the niggers and abolitionists then they would have better prices for labor." The *New York Tribune* saw in the riot the work of supporters of the Ohio politician and Copperhead leader Clement Vallandigham, who sought to disrupt the war effort by any means possible.[20]

In August 1862, the *Chicago Tribune* reported that Irish laborers at the Chicago docks rioted against the presence of freed blacks, which undercut their wages. The same month, workers in Brooklyn clashed over employment practices at the local tobacco manufactories. At one, "the overseer or foreman . . . [was] a colored man, and all the persons employed in the factory, consisting mostly of women and children, are colored to the number from 50 to 75." In another factory, white and black employees worked harmoniously in the months leading up to a riot. On August 5, however, a mob of some two to three thousand gathered outside to protest the employment of African Americans. "The population in the vicinity," the *New York Tribune* pointed out, "are principally Irish, who as is well known, have no great fondness for the colored race." The passions of the mob were fueled by liquor; police officers who investigated the riot found that "nearly every home in the neighborhood was an unlicensed rum shop, where the rioters had wrought themselves up to the fighting point." Stereotypical behaviors, in this case, were prominently featured by the paper as motivating factors. Other newspapers placed blame for the Brooklyn riot elsewhere. "For several days past," the *Weekly Wisconsin Patriot* reported, "the negro population in the vicinity . . . were charged with having used insulting language to white females on several occasions. This conduct, of course, had the effect of exciting the indignation of the Irish laborers in the neighborhood."[21]

In Buffalo, New York, on August 12, 1862, white and black dockworkers battled each other, again over wages. The *New York Tribune* reported that the police were able to quell the fighting only after opening fire on the mob. At the end of August, street fights broke out in Cincinnati, an event that stemmed from a disagreement between an Irishman, Thomas Larkin, and a freedman, George

Brown. People had gathered to watch the fight, and when Brown stabbed Larkin three times in the face, "the crazy crowd made a rush for the negro and his brother," said the *Philadelphia Inquirer.* To the dismay of the crowd, who tried to lynch George Brown and his brother, the police arrived and took the Brown brothers into custody, which caused further rioting, quelled only by the arrival of a police detachment with bayonets fixed. In March 1863, Detroit experienced similar riots caused by "negro mania" and the "settled hatred against the negro, which is continually excited in this vicinity." In April, another round of riots rocked the New York City docks, as reported in such papers as the *New York Tribune* and the *Hartford Daily Courant.* In June in Newburgh, New York, fifty miles north of Manhattan on the Hudson River, a young Irish girl was raped. According to newspapers in New York and Albany, a crowd took the accused man, an African American, from jail and lynched him. A week before the New York City Draft Riots broke out in July 1863, laborers again clashed in Buffalo, an event that according to the *Milwaukee Daily Sentinel* illustrated the "Irish determination to prevent negroes from working."[22]

A common theme links all of these riots—workplace competition. Reacting to a perceived threat to their socioeconomic stability, Irish Americans lashed out against African American workers in acts that were contextualized, at the time, as part of a broader reaction against emancipation. But such incidents also reflected a continuation of the "golden age of riots" that began in the decades before the Civil War; and a *New York Tribune* reporter came to the conclusion that "most of the participants in the late disgraceful scenes were unquestionably honest," and had "supposed that the hour had come when they must expel the negroes, or be exiles themselves." It seems that these riots were as much, if not more, reactions to an immediate threat in the workplace as they were protests over war aims; they were part and parcel of urbanization, and of the socio-economic positions of and workplace competition between white and black workers. With the exception of the riots on Chicago's docks, workplaces in Connecticut, Illinois, and Wisconsin remained relatively strife-free during this period, in large part because so few African Americans called those states home. However, within the broader context of mid-century rioting, the attempts to portray the New York City Draft Riots as something more sinister for the nation at large than they were marked a trend that emerged early in the war, as Republican commentators linked riotous activity to disloyalty. Despite these trends, public rhetoric in Connecticut, Illinois, and Wisconsin reveals outspoken attempts to justify and distance "Irish America" from these accusations of disloyalty. Assertions of ethnic loyalty in these states began early in the war and continued throughout the conflict, forming an important component in the broader public response to the New York City Draft Riots and illustrating the degree to which the riots themselves had an impact (or did not have an impact, in these cases) on notions of Irish inclusion in other parts of the nation.[23]

The responses of ethnic communities in Connecticut, Illinois, and Wisconsin—especially those that sent men to their state's Irish regiments—to shifting war aims, and their open rejection of the Draft Riots as a means of forcing Lincoln's hand on policy, suggest that Irish in these areas were relatively unified in their responses to this event. As the Draft Riots have traditionally defined the ethnic experience in the Civil War, the reactions of these communities speak to the broader historiographical problems that arise when attempting to understand the Irish experience in the Civil War from the perspective of events in New York. Publicly, men and women in these states rejected the means and motives of the rioters, and pledged their continued support for the Union. Although, as Democrats, they differed politically from Lincoln and vocally protested Republican policies throughout the war, these men distanced themselves as well from the Peace Democrats and sought, time and again, to portray their dissent in loyal terms. They were War Democrats who fought unconstitutional policies through the democratic process. Of equal importance, perhaps, was that as the Irish in these areas maintained their faith in the war effort, their non-Irish friends and neighbors championed their patriotism and loyalty time and again.

Had they been asked, it is possible that some of the soldiers who volunteered to serve in the Ninth Connecticut, 23rd Illinois, and 17th Wisconsin would have voiced concern over the possibility that emancipation would mean increased competition for jobs at home. The unskilled workers probably would have had stronger opinions than the skilled workers, artisans, and farmers in these units, simply because they would have faced the greatest threat from unskilled former slaves arriving in Northern cities seeking employment. But if these questions were asked, no one bothered recording the answers, and even if someone had, it would have been hard to tell whether negative responses were based on any real experiences with African Americans in the workplace. The fact is that there were no significant populations of African American men of working age in any of the cities in Connecticut, Illinois, or Wisconsin, and it is unlikely that the Irish Americans in the Ninth Connecticut, 23rd Illinois, or 17th Wisconsin would have encountered African Americans on a daily basis. According to the 1860 U.S. census, African American men of working age in New Haven numbered 280 out of a total population of 12,007 men of that age; in Hartford, 211 out of 9,428; in Chicago, 178 out of 33,607; and in Milwaukee, 19 out of 12,671. It is hard to imagine, then, that the fear and urgency that drove the rioters in New York and other larger industrial centers was present during the war in these areas, simply because of the lack of actual competition.[24]

The impact of the draft in these communities is less clear. Democrats in all states reacted strongly to the implementation of the draft policy and sought measures to counteract what they perceived as an extreme extension of Federal power. But battle lines in the fight over the draft were drawn along political, not ethnic, lines, and despite the riots in Manhattan, the draft was conducted in all states, though with a glaring inefficiency. In Connecticut, for example, only 248 of the 12,000 men drafted actually entered service. Concerning Irishmen in New Haven who were drafted, Matthew Hart noted that "of these 136, more than half were legally exempt and at a town meeting held on last Thursday the Town voted to pay three Hundred Dollars for every Drafted man who was not able to pay it for himself." The *Daily Illinois State Journal* in Springfield reported that the rural communities in Illinois contributed far and above their share of volunteers, and ultimately the state fielded 20,000 men more than its assigned quota. Most likely slighting Chicago, the editor claimed that although the "country districts have furnished liberally of their men for the public defense, the cities have, in a most niggardly manner, been far in arrears. . . . *Is it right, is it just, that the brave and patriotic young men of Illinois should give their lives freely, as they have done, for their country, while the degraded and brutal ruffians, the habitues of the beer saloons, of New York and other cities, remain at home in cowardly and unpatriotic safety?*" More than 44,000 men volunteered for service in Illinois in the wake of the riots in New York, eliminating the need for the draft in the state. The reaction in Illinois to the riots in the East clearly illustrates a local focus and celebration of the late-war enlistees, some of whom volunteered to serve in the five companies organizing in Chicago and set to join the 23rd Illinois.[25]

By mid-July, word began to filter into Wisconsin that resistance to the draft was local to New York and enrollment was continuing peacefully in other large cities. In an effort to approach the draft in an egalitarian way, newspapers such as the *Milwaukee Daily Sentinel* published the names of enrolled men so that citizens would "have ample opportunity to examine them, and report any omissions to the Provost Marshal's office." Such acts were hardly indicative of a community held in check by fear of potential uprisings. With "assurances of the fairness with which the draft is to be conducted . . . there will be few who dream of creating any disturbance or difficulty," wrote the *Sentinel*. Democratic presses in Wisconsin subscribed to the rhetoric that emerged in eastern papers such as the *Boston Post*, which called the draft "a summons to join, not a discomfited and broken-spirited soldiery, but a band of heroes, the monument of many a well-fought field." In Wisconsin the draft continued, and draftees filled the holes in the ranks of regiments in the field, including the 17th Wisconsin. Between 1863 and 1865, 300 draftees and 99 substitutes joined the ranks of the state's Irish regiment, and nearly all loyally served their time. "So you See," Matthew Hart observed, in the wake of the New York City Draft Riots, "the teeth are pulled out of the Draft in this part of the World." His words rang true for many communities throughout the North.[26]

Vocal opposition to Lincoln's policies certainly was a part of the landscape in all states, but the Irish and their supporters in Connecticut, Illinois, and Wisconsin moved quickly to distance themselves from the extreme of the New York City Draft Riots through public professions of loyalty and rejection of the means and aims of the rioters. Collectively, their language rejected any broad linking of ethnicity with a propensity for violent protest of Federal policy. The Irish in these states were unified in their response to the riots and in their rejection of the methods and motivations of the Irish men and women of New York City. This response outside of New York to the riots that occurred there suggests how problematic it can be to portray this event as illustrative of the rise and fall of Irish American support for the Union war effort.

The rioters, the *Wisconsin Daily Patriot* claimed, were encouraged by men for whom "robbing and plunder was the main object." New York was a city of "thieves, gamblers, garroters, shoulder hitters, thugs, and scoundrels of every conceivable hue and grade. Most of this class are never at ease unless they are in a fight." The editors of the *Patriot* expressed the hope "that no resistance will disgrace the West, but that if any think they have cause, to resort to the courts." Many saw the riots in New York as "a scheme for plunder—opposition to the draft being made the pretext. But the leaders only desire plunder and pillage." In Milwaukee, the *Sentinel* noted that "Irish Americans, even of the humblest class, bring with them to this country not one particle of prejudice against the colored race. They acquire it here under the debasing influence of . . . demagogues. . . . No practical Catholic has ever violated law or order in this country. . . . [T]he so-called Catholics who disturb the public peace, are Catholics only in name." True Catholics were "ever unswervingly loyal and ever obedient to authority." In the view of the *Weekly Wisconsin Patriot*, "The Catholics have shown their loyalty to our Government without flinching. They are ready to fight for the Government and its institutions and laws. . . . [A] more chivalrous, patriotic class cannot be found on this or any other continent."[27]

In Connecticut, Matthew Hart wrote "that [far] from being organized to resist the draft, the mob turned out to be one of the most heinous, murdering, robbing, burning crowds that ever cursed any city in the world, it was made up of pick-pockets, thieves, robbers, blackslegs, gerotters and all of that class that infest N.Y." In the wake of the riots, New Haven's Republican mayor Samuel Walker fervently denied the existence of a Democratic plot for insurrection in a speech that concluded with an apology to the Irish of that city. "I feel it due to many of our Irish citizens," he declared, "to inform the public that, in the face of many cruel suspicions against them, I have had kind offers of their assistance in case of any disturbance and I caution the public against an indiscriminant condemnation of a sect or race for the indiscretion of some. I have not learned of but two threats made by this class of our citizens, and those too insignificant to be noticed, which is more than I can say for our native born"—yet more evidence of the loyalty of this group.[28]

The defense of the Irish continued unabated. Since the war began, the *Chicago Times* noted, "the Roman Catholics have been among the most steady and faithful adherents and supporters of the Union cause. . . . None of our people have volunteered more freely or fought more bravely than Catholics." "Who was responsible for the mob [in New York]," asked the editors of the *Chicago Post*. "Every intelligent mind will acquit the poor foolish and misguided men who were the active operators in this disgraceful and shocking tragedy of being the originators of any individual or organized resistance to the laws of this country. If let alone, there would have been no resistance, no mob, no bloodshed. . . . *[T]he whole blame, responsibility, and criminality of the whole affair should rest upon those demagogues, led by Fernando Wood* [New York mayor and Democrat], *who for monthes have been educating the thoughtless men and women of New York that this war was an illegal and unauthorized proceeding*." The editors of the *Daily Illinois State Journal* agreed with this assessment, and urged their readers to look over the *Post's* article. "It has become quite fashionable among the 'loyal' journals of the day to denounce the Roman Catholic and Episcopal churches, generally, as 'disloyal' organizations," the same editors noted at the end of July. "We venture the assertion," they continued, "that an exhibition of the religious creed of men now in the ranks of our armies would show at least as great a proportion of Catholic [belief as of Protestant]. . . . And did we go back to nationalities, we think the proportion of Irishmen fighting the battles of the Union would not suffer in comparison with the men of other birth-place. . . . [T]hese churches and their members, need no defenders of their loyalty." There was a clear difference, then, between the actions of the New York Irish and that of local Irish residents. Viewing those in Manhattan as the "other" was a reflection, perhaps, of the importance that familiarity played in assessing patriotism and loyalty during the war.[29]

For men and women in the communities of Connecticut, Illinois, and Wisconsin, the Draft Riots represented something deeper and of more concern than a simple response to the growth of the Copperhead movement and war weariness. As an extreme expression of Northern political dissent, the rioters represented something far beyond the pale, for their acts illustrated the breakdown of the democratic process. The Ninth Connecticut, 23rd Illinois, and 17th Wisconsin marched south at the height of public enthusiasm for the war effort. Yet the overwhelming support for the war in their home communities (especially during the first year of the conflict) should not diminish the fact that many Democrats saw their opposition to Republican policies, in particular those regarding abolition and the draft, as a legitimate middle ground for bridging the growing divide between North and South. Time and again they justified their opposition as legitimate, citing their dedication to their party and party platform as evidence of their commitment to the republican process. "We have taken the position," noted the *Chicago Times,* the voice of Chicago's Democrats and Mulligan's Irish Brigade, "and shall maintain it to the end, that there ought not to be party lines in the conduct of the war . . . but that does not mean that men shall have no opinions save those that are popular."[30]

The tendency of Republicans to portray their political rivals as disloyal was a point of contention for many Democrats vested in the continued health of the democratic experiment in the United States. "The democrats are now threatened," an editor in Springfield, Illinois wrote, for "if they hold democratic conventions and nominate democratic candidates for the various county offices, they will do so under the pains and penalties of being denounced as 'traitors' by the lick-spittle of Abraham Lincoln." "Democrats were to be stigmatized as 'traitors' for adhering to their own party organization," bemoaned party members in Connecticut a year later, in New Haven's *Columbian Register.* "The idea that two millions of men in the free States are not in favor of the Union because they are not Republicans, is so utterly ridiculous as to attract the denunciation of the more respectable portion of the Republican press," they concluded. In Madison, "well meaning men have serious apprehensions that an attempt will be made to stifle the freedom of political expression at the ballot box in the coming election," the *Wisconsin Daily Patriot* stated, and the *Weekly Wisconsin Patriot* concurred: "It is feared that the signs of the times predict the prohibition of Democrats the exercise of the elective franchise unless they vote the Abolition ticket." Members of the opposition party were on the defensive throughout the war, forced to continually justify their political ideologies against charges of disloyalty. These accusations increased in intensity as the Copperhead movement gained momentum and served to broadly paint all political dissenters, regardless of beliefs, as disloyal.[31]

For Democrats, party principles did not vanish when Confederates fired on Fort Sumter. Concerns over the war and war aims began immediately after the election of Lincoln and continued, in spite of the outward enthusiasm of most Northerners in the months after its outbreak. Yet Democrats understood their opposition as a valuable component of the American political tradition, and as Mark Neely has said, "testified to the culture's internalization of the Constitution over the years." They were active in opposing Republican policy throughout the war, and saw in the shifting political goals of Republican leadership justification for their political antagonism. For example, though the *Chicago Tribune* labeled its rival the *Chicago Times* "the organ of Jeff Davis," the editors of the *Times* justified the criticism expressed by their news outlet via their belief that the war was "against the constitution and laws—a reproach upon the patriots who framed the constitution and the government." But, they poignantly noted, it was "a favorite dodge of some people now-a-days to endeavor to shut up a man who disagrees with them by accusing him of secessionism." "Loyalty," noted the *Wisconsin Daily Patriot,* "is a word which is being distorted to a sense which does not belong to it. Loyalty here and now [winter 1862] means devotion to the Union, and the legitimate government of the United States. It does not mean the adoption of any peculiar theory. . . . [T]o call a man disloyal or a traitor because his sober sense disapproves of your hobby on the right way of ending the war, is simply to prove yourself a narrow-minded, persecution-loving fanatic."[32]

In these states many, but certainly not all, Democrats denounced treasonous activity in favor of change through political means and believed that protest should be expressed at the polls. In 1862, the *Hartford Daily Courant* applauded the loyalty of the typical ethnic citizen of that city: "He ceased to be known by any other designation than that of an Irish-born loyal American citizen, bound not more by his interests than by his oath and his honor to defend his country from foreign and domestic foes. . . . He was not an Abolitionist or a Black Republican, but simply a patriot. If your house is on fire and you have a bucket of water handy to extinguish it, you would not be likely to decline using it because the color of the bucket was unpleasant to you." "There is a great difference between the defense of the government and the support of the administration," echoed the *Chicago Times.* "All citizens owe absolute loyalty to the first, and only such respect to the last as passing events may warrant. . . . The specious cry of 'no party' is becoming the foundation of a despotism which is intolerable, and which, if submitted to, is as harmful as secession itself." In Wisconsin, the opposition party made its stance equally clear. "Our Republic would cease to be a refuge for the oppressed of all nations if broken in twain," noted the *Weekly Wisconsin Patriot*, "and under no circumstances would their condition be tolerable in a Sothern slave Confederacy. . . . Under such circumstances of peril, it behooves every good citizen to stand firmly by the Union, which is the guarantee and mainstay of the Constitution. Secession can only be accomplished through a violation of the Federal compact, a direct breach of faith with those who hold it." These men saw loyalty simply: continued support of their nation and, of equal importance, support of the tenets of the republican process—for one could not exist without the other.[33]

Democrats showed their loyalty to the Union in modest and subtle ways that simultaneously rejected the violence in New York. "A genuine democrat is always a friend of his country. His creed is the constitution and the Union. He has that reverence for his flag which enshrines it among the divinities of his conscience," noted the *Chicago Times* editors. "Loyalty," wrote an editor of the Bridgeport, Connecticut *Republican Farmer* in October 1864, "means, in its true sense, a firm and faithful adherence to the law and the Constitution of the community of which we are members. . . . [This] will accurately characterize the party that is rallying for the UNION, the CONSTITUTION, and the LAWS." Disloyalty, the editors of the *Wisconsin Daily Patriot* countered, was not synonymous with disagreeing with Republican ideology. This succinct definition, a response to national questions regarding wartime support and the place of political dissent during a time of rebellion, perfectly contextualized the efforts made after 1863 in these states to defend the outspoken rejection by Democrats of Republican policies and the subsequent response to growing criticism of those who dared reject the status quo. The same news outlets that worked so diligently to espouse Irish loyalty and patriotism in the face of nativist backlash in 1860–61 renewed their efforts to educate their readers about the continued support of these immigrants in the wake of the Draft Riots. There was a consensus among Democrats that they were loyal to the Union; their vocal protests of Lincoln's policies did not affect their deeply rooted commitment to their nation.[34]

A number of common themes emerged in the press in Illinois, Connecticut, and Wisconsin in the wake of the New York City Draft Riots. First, the focus on the New York "mob" was a rhetorical tool that deflected potential backlash away from the local community while simultaneously creating specific definitions of loyal and disloyal conduct. An intrinsic difference was seen between the rioters who took to the streets in July of 1863, men and women out of control and operating outside of social norms, and the loyal Democrats in Connecticut, Illinois, and Wisconsin. The mob, many believed, was driven to act by external forces, by agents of the Copperheads or Confederates and, as in other labor riots that occurred earlier in the war, the rioters themselves were viewed as not necessarily responsible for their actions. Finally, as political language stressed time and again throughout the war, one could protest particular war aims while remaining loyal to the Union, so long as those protests were manifestations of the democratic experiment. Thus, although most Irish Americans were Democrats and thus differed politically from the Republicans, this did not make them disloyal, nor did it make their political protest synonymous with the actions of the rioters in New York. As the war progressed, their public expressions of loyalty and support for the military aims of the war, first seen in 1861, continued, and were crucial to dispelling charges of ethnic disloyalty.

There was a degree of solidarity among Irish American communities in Connecticut, Illinois, and Wisconsin with regard to views on loyalty and disloyalty. Indeed, denunciation of the acts of the rioters came from New York itself when Archbishop John Hughes spoke out in defense of the Irish of New York City on July 16, 1863. Men and women in communities in the three states examined here, however, vocally and passionately rejected the actions of the mobs in New York, all the while proclaiming their loyalty to the Union. Their responses made clear that the events in New York City in July 1863 were in no way representative of local dissatisfaction with the progress and direction of the war. In fact, in 1863 Irish regiments outside of Virginia experienced a degree of success—this was the case for the 17th Wisconsin—and relatively light service—as seen by the occupation duties of the Ninth Connecticut and 23rd Illinois. The summer of 1863 provided the men in these regiments and those at home with the opportunity to express their continued loyalty to the Union cause as they openly rejected the acts of their countrymen in the East. But their reactions were also important indications of the nature of the Irish communities in these regions. While much has been made of the disconnection between the Irish and their adopted homeland as a result of their religion, politics, and socioeconomic position, the response of these communities illustrates the inclusive nature of Irish life in these areas. Living in smaller towns and cities, with access to employment and land, and in many cases able to develop close personal ties within their communities, these Irish denounced the acts of their countrymen in New York City and, in turn, were showered with support from their friends and neighbors. Disloyalty and disillusionment, then, had seemingly little impact on the lives of Irish American citizens living in these Connecticut, Illinois, and Wisconsin communities, and the New York City riots in fact provided the opportunity for these men and women to reinforce their commitment to the cause of the Union. In these three states, the Irish remained loyal to both their party affiliations and to the broader national war effort, illustrating just how ingrained the ideology of democracy was, even among recent immigrants. Ethnicity reinforced the important link between soldiers and their local communities, and ultimately bound disparate ethnic communities and their soldiers together as loyal defenders of the Union.

Private Josiah Barker, 9th Connecticut Volunteer Infantry. Barker was an eighteen-year-old laborer from Farmington, Connecticut, when he enlisted in Connecticut's Irish Regiment and typical of the American-born volunteers from this unit. After the war, Barker made his home in Philadelphia until his death in 1911.

First Lieutenant James Nugent, company C, 23rd Illinois. Nugent was killed July 24, 1864, at the Battle of Kernstown, Virginia.

Irish-born Lieutenant Patrick Pillion enlisted in Mulligan's Regiment in April 1861 and rejoined Company D when the regiment reformed that winter. A clerk, he was one of the many skilled immigrants living in Chicago when the war broke out.

Kerryman Bartholomew Quirk served as Second Lieutenant of Company K, 23rd Illinois. A carpenter by trade, he enlisted in November 1861 and was discharged at Deep Bottom, Virginia, in January 1865.

Private Edward Bevans, Company I/G, 17th Wisconsin. Bevans enlisted in January 1864 and after his service moved to Missouri and then to Colorado, where he died in 1889. He is pictured here with his wife, Rosetta, and his two children in 1874.

Captain Elliot Curtis, Company I, Ninth Connecticut Volunteers. A native of Bridgeport, Connecticut, Curtis moved to California after the war and died in Los Angeles in the 1890s.

James A. Mulligan, Colonel, 23rd Illinois.

Veterans of the Ninth Connecticut in 1903 at the dedication of a monument to the service of their regiment in New Haven.

# 7 Patriotism and Sacrifice on the Home Front

Democracy, republicanism, and citizenship were vital components of public rhetoric surrounding Irish service and the continued support of the Irish Americans at home. Although Irish immigrants and their children faced tremendous pressure from Anglo-Protestant America before, during, and after the war, between 1861 and the summer of 1863, the service of Irish soldiers was upheld, nationally, as proof of loyalty to the United States that overcame the doubts of even the most ardent nativists. After the New York City Draft Riots and the integration of apparently hesitant volunteers and reluctant draftees into the army, many Americans again began to question the patriotism and loyalty of Irish immigrants, and public rhetoric becoming increasingly acrimonious. Local observers in Connecticut, Illinois, and Wisconsin rejected accusations of Irish disloyalty, insisting that the riots in New York had been the product of a certain class of individuals living in Manhattan and were not emblematic of Irish attitudes generally, assertions that captured well the actual Irish American sentiment in these areas. Furthermore, as the original terms of the volunteers from the Ninth Connecticut, 23rd Illinois, and 17th Wisconsin regiments expired, many chose to reenlist as veteran volunteers, an act that reiterated the pledge to the Union that they had made three years earlier. Despite this, national attitudes were swayed by the events in New York, shifting toward largely negative perceptions of Irish American soldiers and civilians that persevered well into the twentieth century.[1]

Locally, public enthusiasm and support was important to the morale of these Irish American soldiers. Professions of support from the press and from friends and neighbors, however, should not be taken to imply that experiences on the home front were without trials and tribulations. Military service had far-reaching implications for the families of volunteers, and public affirmations of their patriotism and loyalty often went hand-in-hand with private suffering and sacrifice. Families of the men in these three regiments, like those of many soldiers both North and South, suffered over the four years of conflict, and their experiences illustrate the duality of the war years for these men and women: their public support for the war was often countered by private struggles at home, beyond the prying eyes of the judgmental public. For while the contemporary political rhetoric, combined with the struggles of families on the home front, may suggest that there was growing disillusionment among both soldiers and civilians as the war progressed, for these men and their families the realities were much different.

Soldiers and civilians from these regiments and states voiced oppositional political views in the press but never encouraged outright violence or disloyalty as a means to achieving those ends—at least not in public forums. Though they questioned the motives behind emancipation, they remained largely supportive of means that could help lead to the rapid conclusion of hostilities. Debates surrounding the riots in New York reinforced the relationship between the Irish American citizen and the state initially defined by the Irishman's act of enlistment in 1861 and 1862. In the wake of the New York City Draft Riots, reiteration of support for the war, whether through proclamations of loyalty or through visible acts of support for the military effort, were vital for families who had sent fathers and sons to war a year before. Families of the soldiers in the Ninth Connecticut, 23rd Illinois, and 17th Wisconsin were likely attuned to these debates—their prevalence and importance were such that it is hard to imagine that anyone on the home front was not, to some degree—but the perception of the broad commitment of these families to the Union cause throughout the war contributed to relatively positive accounts in the Democratic press about the stability of the home front.

In the late fall of 1863, for example, over one hundred thousand people descended upon Chicago to attend the Northwestern Soldiers' Fair, an event organized by the Sanitary Commission to raise money for supplies for troops. The success of the fair reflected continued support for the war and, especially, for soldiers-in-arms from that region. "To one who stood there, looking on," the masses arriving daily in the city "came like a great whelming torrent of love and power, and solemn earnestness, which was irresistible, carrying everything before it," read a report issued several weeks after the fair's end. Among the influx of patriotic citizens, one family stood out; a "man past middle age, with the clothes and look of one who toiled hard, but he had a thoughtful and kindly face. By his side, with feet over the front of the wagon, for it was filled very full [with supplies for the soldiers], was his wife, a silent, worn-looking woman. . . . Near the rear of the wagon was a girl of fifteen, perhaps, and her sister, dressed in black, carrying in her arms a little child." Asked if he had a son in the army, the man answered "'No, I haven't *now*, but we had one there once; he's buried down by Stone River: he was shot there . . . and' (pointing over his shoulder without looking back) 'that's his wife there with the baby!'"[2]

While the writer left this family and the son and husband they had lost anonymous, this image of the young widow and fatherless child was important to the portrayal of support on the home front and exemplified the sacrifice of Northern families during the war, regardless of political allegiance. Determination, manifest through war work and publicized support for the war effort despite individual loss, has become a vital component of the historical memory of the role that women played in the Federal victory. "*Women* can do that which is rarely considered," proclaimed one reader to the *Chicago Times*, for the war provided the opportunity to "mingle our domestic duties with those we owe our country, and, without fear of neglecting either, prove the importance of the Union." In Connecticut, the *Hartford Daily Courant* quoted a war widow with three young children patriotically stating that she had never "said a word against [his going to war]. I would give up another dear friend if my country needed it, and if I had one to give even if it cost my own life." Her husband "died a noble death—a precious legacy to his children." "To the young wife," urged supporters in the *Weekly Wisconsin Patriot*, "we would say, better far is a widowhood of honor than a lifelong union with a craven who would not defend his home." Inherent here, of course, is the notion that virtuous self-sacrifice was vital to the Union cause. Often reinforced by outpourings of support by local women who organized to send supplies to local regiments, such pleas were not directed at any specific ethnic group. Rather, they were broadly prescribed as traits that *all* women should uphold.[3]

Yet public portrayals of support tended to downplay or overshadow the void that was left when fathers, sons, and husbands enlisted, a void that often became permanent. A year before the first major soldiers' fair in Chicago, William Rickey wrote to James Mulligan. His son-in-law had fought at Lexington in a cavalry company under Mulligan's command. After the young man was killed in battle, "his widow was left almost Entirely Destitute of means of Support and Two Small Children He never Recd any pay for the Services Rendered the

Government nor any pay for his Horse." "Sir," the letter continued, "I wish you to Instruct me How To Act in this Matter . . . if you Will be So Kind as give me Such Information as you may think Proper in this Matter So that She may Receive What is Justly Due Her From the government." As this letter suggests, the experiences of women and families on the home front, often elided from public professions of patriotism and willing sacrifice, provide important insight into daily life and the uncertainty that many faced following a soldier's enlistment, issues that became even more pressing in the wake of injury or death on campaign, in battle, or in camp. The ways in which the war affected the lives of the wives, families, and dependents of soldiers from Connecticut, Illinois, and Wisconsin help illuminate the collision of public and private spheres, as soldiers and civilians were forced to contend with the personal as well as political consequences of the war.[4]

As the war progressed, support networks developed on the home front and served as extensions of the public recognition of the shifting relationship between citizens and government; they marked an important step in the development of a progressive Federal state that expanded during the latter part of the century. Men, women, and children—veterans, widows, and orphans—relied, at times, on these programs as a means of support during and after the war. Their experiences in negotiating the bureaucracy of local and Federal aid provide some insight into life on the home front for men and women during this period—experiences that were often far different from the public portrayals of women's involvement in war work, from the images of stoically patriotic widows, and from the political rhetoric of loyalty and support. In this context, local support continued in spite of both shifting political aims and hardships on the home front. The relationship between adopted citizens and the United States, reinforced in 1861, was not conditional; those at home stayed the course. But there was also a clear expectation that their unconditional support would be rewarded by local, state, and federal governments in times of need and the development and role of these support networks illuminate the inner workings Northern home front during the war.[5]

Soldiers in all three of the regiments examined here left families at home when they volunteered to defend the Union. Of the total of 5,034 soldiers who served in the Ninth Connecticut, 23rd Illinois, and 17th Wisconsin, 2,217 reported their marital status when they enlisted, and of these men 801, or 36 percent, were married. The percentage of men who were married differed significantly, however, by regiment.

Table 7-1 Marital Status by Regiment

| Regiment | Number of Men in Regiment | Number of Men who provided Marital Status | Percentage who provided Marital Status | Number of Married Men | Number of Single Men | Percentage of Married Men |
|---|---|---|---|---|---|---|
| 9th Connecticut | 971 | 420 | 43% | 196 | 224 | 47% |
| 23rd Illinois | 2,235 | 809 | 36% | 142 | 667 | 17% |
| 17th Wisconsin | 1,823 | 973 | 53% | 463 | 510 | 47% |

Among all Irishmen living in these states in 1860, however, marital rates were higher. In Connecticut, 53 percent Irish men of military age living in the state's major cities were married. In Illinois the figure was slightly higher, at 55 percent, and in Wisconsin nearly 70 percent of Irish men of military age were married when war broke out. Thus, military service seems to have been less appealing to Irishmen with families, especially among those living in Illinois.[6]

Married or not, for volunteers who were the primary contributors to the economic well-being of their families, the war posed hardships, especially when pay was inconsistent. For some, enlisting meant leaving their families to fend for themselves. In light of strained finances at home, perhaps the most universally recognizable relationship between soldiers and families was the transfer of pay. Often desperately needed by those left behind, pay could also serve as a point of tension between soldiers and their families. When available, money was sent home by various means, and discharged friends, officers, and priests often served as conduits as they made their way home from the front lines. A variety of issues, however, could delay or prevent the timely arrival of those funds. Soldiers' pay was unreliable, especially during campaigns in the summer months. At times, however, delays were caused by the soldiers themselves, who spent money on food and a variety of sundries to make life more comfortable, or to indulge in bad habits. When soldiers accrued debt, life was often made difficult for those at home.

Local papers periodically and enthusiastically reported the arrival of monies from the troops in the field, and the arrival of these funds reinforced the connection between soldier and family while also serving as a topic of discussion that reinforced social values, stressing the soldier's responsibility to those at home. In the fall of 1862, for example, soldiers of the 17th Wisconsin sent a total of $6,060 home to their families, as reported in the *Sheboygan Post*. The editors of the *Hartford Daily Courant* similarly applauded the Ninth Connecticut for having "more money placed to its credit at the office of the State Paymaster than any other State regiment in the service." So important were these funds that Republicans in Illinois scoffed at distributing state aid to families in part, because they believed that it was the responsibility of the soldiers to care for their own. "The Government lodges, feeds, and clothes that soldier free of expense[,] maintains him in health and cares for him in sickness, without cost to him," wrote a *Chicago Tribune* editor.

> Besides this, it pays him some $900 per year [in reality many soldiers made less than $300] a sum sufficient with economy to comfortably maintain his family. In view of this, should the soldier entirely neglect his family and impost upon the community, the tax of its entire support? Should he squander that $900 in the sutlers store in the purchase of pies, cakes, raisins, candy and other nonsense which only serve to injure his health, leave him penniless at the end of the year, line the pockets of the sutler and leave his family exposed to privation and poverty? The ordinary rules of economy should obtain in war as well as peace.

Responsibility, obligation, and concern for security at home were part of broader public debates surrounding public assistance, as well as figuring in more personal concerns over soldiers' pay.[7]

For soldiers, financial relief was far more personal. In 1863, for example, Ninth Connecticut soldier Thomas Knablin asked his wife Mary to "send me no more [money] except I send for it as it is very little use to me (I do not drink)." In another letter he enclosed a $10 check that he had received for pay, noting "mostly all my company drew [their pay] and sold them. They are continually drunk and it is frightful to hear the oathes of them." Private George Hill expressed considerable concern over the uncertainty of his family's financial situation and his ability to get money to his wife, a result of the lack of timely pay and untrustworthy mail routes home to Connecticut. "We expect to get paid four months pay the first of September and I hope Shall not be disappointed," he wrote, "for I know you need the money as soon as you can get it." Sending those funds home, however, "worried me until I can hear you have got it all." Private Patrick Clancy of the 23rd Illinois felt similar concerns. Sending $30 home to his mother in February 1864, he wrote again in March to see if the money had arrived. "Dear mother," he wrote, "I am uneasy about the money that I send to you because you did not let me know any thing about it in your last letter write as soon as you get this and let me know whether you got it or not." Private James Fowler of the 17th Wisconsin kept meticulous financial records during his time in the army and seems to have been determined not to let the soldiering lifestyle distract him from obligations at home.[8]

For every responsible soldier, there were others who failed in their obligations to their families. Justifying to his wife his expenditures on tobacco and writing paper, Knablin compared his spending to that of his comrades and specifically to their friend Jack Wallace, who "has turned out a very poor Soldier he does very little duty he is very dirty in his person . . . [and] he will hardley ever draw a cent of Pay as he Makes away with so much extra clothing." Thomas Cahill's wife Margaret wrote to her husband on numerous occasions inquiring into the financial situations of certain soldiers. In 1862 she inquired about the pay of a soldier in the regiment. His mother "came to me and wished me to enquire you about her sons wages," she wrote, "She is very poor and needs all she can get from her Son." On another occasion, she wrote, "Please mention B Leynch [and] James Lawler their wives are very much troubled about them." Father Matthew Hart wrote to Cahill that "St. Patrick's is a congregation of Women [and] children, God only knows what will become of them if they lose their husbands [and] Fathers." In Chicago, "the women and children of our volunteers are suffering from the want of the necessities, not to speak of the luxuries of existence," the editors of the *Times* pointed out, calling for charity as one of the primary duties of both soldiers and civilians. In an appeal for aid to soldiers' families published in the *Milwaukee Sentinel*, a Mrs. M. H. Bardwell asked, "what song has been sung for the poor wife? She who sits weary and worn, waiting in dread suspense, perhaps in deepest poverty, for the termination of this terrible war. . . . Shall she not receive a blessing for the sacrifices she is making, some of them greater than the sacrifices of the soldiers?"[9]

Public relief for families began early in the war, offered in the form of enlistment bounties. Soldiers relied on these state and local funds to cover any unexpected costs while they were away. As early as the late spring of 1861 there were discussions of financial incentives as a means of encouraging enlistment; the money was recognized to be necessary for the support of families, and was conceived of as both a reward and encouragement for the patriotic response of men throughout the nation in the wake of the firing on Fort Sumter. The provision of bounties was initially viewed as part of the patriotic duty of local communities, a reward for soldiers who left their families to defend the Union. A public meeting in New Haven, Connecticut on July 9, 1861, for example, raised $20,000 for enlistment bonuses for soldiers. Soon thereafter, the governor and local committees pledged a state bounty of $90 to each volunteer, and local communities pledged an additional $200, which historian John Niven notes "began a policy of competitive biddings by town" for the formation of regiments.[10]

Similar efforts were made in Wisconsin, where the citizens of Fond du Lac, for example, "raised $3,500 to fit out volunteers and support their families," Frank Klement has noted. On February 20, Governor Louis Harvey addressed the state legislature on the matter of support on the home front. Ordering the 14th, 15th, and 16th regiments to St. Louis, Harvey scolded state lawmakers for refusing to provide for the families of these soldiers and suggested the sale of $200,000 worth of war bonds for the support of those left at home. Editors of the *Chicago Tribune* urged those who had second thoughts on volunteering for three years to reconsider their decision, pointing out to their readers that the government was offering a bounty of $100 in gold at the end of service. Many hoped that this would be sufficient motivation for those wavering in their patriotism. By 1862, federal and state bounties reached upwards of $300, a year's salary for a Northern laborer, reflecting the ever-growing need for manpower and the commitment of the state to its soldiers.[11]

As the war continued, local aid societies became systematically organized under the umbrella of the United States Sanitary Commission, an organization that was instrumental to the support of soldiers in the field. For example, the Soldiers' Aid Society in Wisconsin organized and distributed 3,500 cases of supplies to soldiers between 1861 and 1864. In New Haven, men and women purchased materials and, at one point during the war, "within the space of three weeks . . . [stitched] 1,000 sheets, 1,500 towels, and 1,600 handkerchiefs and napkins." Their success was "an example of the systematic effort by which the Auxiliary Societies contribute so largely to the efficiency of our central agency." In the fall of 1863 the Northwest Sanitary Fair in Chicago drew "some hundred thousand people of the great Northwest . . . as if some sudden and mysterious impulse had taken hold of one-quarter of the whole nation, who had suddenly spring to their feet, seized whatever of goods or riches were at hand, and rushed forth led by music and banners." In May 1865 Midwesterners again gathered in Chicago, "the mother of Sanitary Fairs," for the second Northwest Sanitary Fair, which was attended by men and women "each vieing with the other in efforts to do the most for the good cause."[12]

There is no doubt that the arrival of mail at the front, which included not only letters but also a variety of comfort items, was vital to the morale of the troops and reinforced a connection between soldiers and the home front. Yet such focus often overlooks the reality of the war for many. Because the North was ultimately victorious, the impact of the war on many families in the North has been lost in the narrative of the triumph of the Union. Local and Federal support in the North were important indications of the government's willingness to compensate men for their service and were vital to stability on the home front. But public displays of support often downplayed issues at home in favor of the encouragement of soldiers. The comfort of soldiers in the field, in other words, was the primary concern and overshadowed the struggles of families. In fundamental contrast with the public displays of support for soldiers was the implementation of the Federal pension system, an official recognition of the need for an established system of financial support for families that illustrates how endemic these issues were at the time.

While public funds were intended to support those at home, the payment of bounties created problems, for often a soldier was awarded only part of the money when he enlisted, with the remainder to be paid out at the completion of his term. Pensions, too, were available, but awards differed depending on the severity of a soldier's injury, and they provided no funds to support families at home unless a soldier was killed in service. The Sanitary Commission stood as another medium of aid for families, though its influence and impact on the well-being of those on the home front over the course of the war is unclear, as the overwhelming focus of this organization was aiding men in the field.

The collection and distribution of funds subscribed for relief on the home front appears largely blind to antebellum divisions and animosities. For example, an editor of the New Haven, Connecticut *Columbian Register* wrote that "the families of soldiers who are in the army, must be cared for. . . . [T]he poor must be fed; and if labor can find no employment, charity must step in to its assistance." The head of a war committee in Hartford clarified that "support [for families of soldiers] shall not be given as a charity, but as a matter of duty, which we are as much bound to perform as we are to provide for our own households." Robert Bremner has noted that the language of relief, combined with notions of duty and obligation, at times reflected concerns about the creation of a class reliant on social welfare, while simultaneously inducing "governors and state legislatures to depart from the long-established principle that poor relief was strictly a local function." Nevertheless, although relief for soldiers' families was an important component of the local response to the war, the impetus for relief was conditional. As the Republican *Chicago Tribune* complained in the winter of 1861, "many wives of members of the Irish Brigade [the 23rd Illinois] apply daily for relief. Manifestly they are improper subjects. The old Brigade is mustered out of service and the husbands are at home and able to take care of their families. Imposters are plenty and other causes exist which render disbursing of the fund a delicate matter." Less a swipe at Mulligan's Irishmen, this account speaks to the very real fears surrounding charity during this period, including questions of legitimate need and, more importantly, fears of abuse, misuse, and dependence, which often influenced the extent of support.[13]

Northerners were not blind to the implications of military service for families of soldiers and were vocal in their responses to the needs of women and children. Questions of relief came early in the war and were a concern among local communities throughout the conflict. But relief efforts were not new, especially among the Irish communities in Illinois, Connecticut, and Wisconsin. In Chicago, Irish aid societies emerged in the mid-1840s to help deal with systemic poverty among recent immigrants. The arrival of Famine immigrants in Connecticut caused the state legislator in 1851 to debate the direction of poor relief, though there were attempts to minimize these efforts as a means of discouraging dependence. The 1849 Poor Law in Wisconsin authorized local communities to remove paupers to farms or poorhouses, though as in Connecticut and Illinois, the means of dealing with the poor were left up to local, rather than state, authorities or charities. These laws, as an editor of the Racine, Wisconsin *Advocate* claimed, were "mere boons to secure against starvation." While the arrival of Famine immigrants increased awareness of the plight of the poor, aid in the antebellum period focused not only on those deserving of charity but also reflected broader social concerns about the creation of a class permanently reliant on charitable donations for survival.[14]

After war broke out the language of relief continued to be couched in the rhetoric of the deserving poor. "Poor men have enlisted who could get no work and left their families destitute," noted a resident of Springfield in the *Daily Illinois State Journal*. "Relief has not yet come to them from their friends and camp, and even now while we banquet . . . or live daintily every day at home, there are soldiers' families who have not the necessaries of subsistence." Suffering became increasingly evident during the fall and winter, causing further concern. A relief worker in Wisconsin spoke of "these very women now before me, soldiers' wives or widows, waiting for back pay or pension, through months and sometimes for over a year, with the 'hope deferred that maketh the heart sick.'" He described how a wife waited "on such days as this with hungry children cowering round her fireless hearth," while a representative of the Milwaukee Soldiers' Aid Society, visiting the Quartermaster's Department in Washington, D.C.,

> by the power of truth and her pathetic delineations of great and unavoidable suffering among the families whose provider had abandoned home ties for the wider circles of duty, which at every point touches hardship, danger and death, obtained a Government contract for the making up of soldiers' underclothes, and it is by the work and pay afforded them in sewing these clothes, that these poor women get the tea to soften their bread, and the salt to flavor their children's potatoes.

"The Poor and destitute should be looked after during this inclement season of the year," wrote another citizen from Connecticut. "Those who have an abundance should remember those who are in want. Many families no doubt, would be grateful for assistance who much need it, but will rather suffer than ask for it. Are there not some soldiers' families who need help, and who should be sought out? Now is a time for active benevolence, and for exercising charity at home." Impetus for support, first in state bounties and later, through the private organization of charitable donations for families, was cast in the broadest possible terms. While many saw it as the duty of those at home to provide aid and support to women and children who would otherwise suffer in the absence of their husbands or sons, charity was rarely associated with ethnicity or with a specific unit. In all three states, of course, churches and other religious associations were outspoken in their encouragement of charity, especially to benefit orphans and other children, but there is no evidence in the press to suggest any popular bias toward these organizations.[15]

In August 1862, a man wrote to the *Chicago Tribune* noting that during a meeting, "contributions were offered for the families of volunteers. One man . . . gave ten dollars, and offered ten more to any young gentleman that would volunteer. . . . Who dare best that?" In the winter of 1863–64 in Springfield, the citizens were reminded that the day had come for "contributions of wood for soldiers' families. . . . [W]e are certain that we cannot go amiss when we say, that whatever can contribute to the support or add to the comfort of a family can be advantageously and worthily bestowed." The *Chicago Tribune* reported that a women's society had been organized in Chicago specifically to deal with issues of relief at home, and on Thanksgiving Day, 1864, Governor Richard Yates of Illinois asked that "collections be made in all churches, and also that contributions be made everywhere for the relief of families of our soldiers during the coming winter." "It is plain to see," another observer noted for the *Milwaukee Daily Sentinel*, "that there must exist very urgent need of the united and systematic effort to relieve the wants of soldiers' families. It is a duty we owe to these men who are suffering for us; and a most solemn and sacred duty." Thus, relief efforts on the home front became part of "patriotic duty," and communities were quick to respond to needs of families and soldiers throughout the war.[16]

Calls for support were not limited to families of volunteers. In the wake of the 1862 draft in Wisconsin, for example, one citizen wrote that "it becomes the duty of whose who were so fortunate as to escape being drafted to do all in their power to alleviate the distress which will be occasioned by the draft. These families must be supported, and they should not have what justice and humanity requires us to do for them, tendered us an act of charity on our part, but as our imperative duty." "The duty of providing, in some way, for the families of drafted men," echoed the *Hartford Courant*, "seems to us clearly binding, in a moral sense at least, upon the towns from which some men have been drafted." The following year, even as the Draft Riots raged in New York City, the editors of the *New Haven Palladium* supported a similar policy.[17]

Relief was an important component of wartime relationships on the home front. It defined, perhaps to a greater degree than aid for soldiers, the patriotism and sense of community of those who remained at home. Inherent in relief efforts was the recognition that the family unit was an extension of the individual soldier and that the sacrifice of men in the field merited the support of those who stayed behind. In this context, relief was not viewed as charity, but, rather, as the duty of the community. Furthermore, relief efforts focused on socioeconomic necessity and appeared largely blind to pre-existing divisions among communities, though political rivals often vied with one another to claim responsibility for efforts to organize and raise funds for the home front. Furthermore, there is no indication that relief measures waxed or waned in accordance with broader political or military issues or questions of loyalty. Once men enlisted, their families were, by proxy, entitled to some degree of support if they needed it, regardless of their background or political orientation. Consequently, the local community that was so vital to the formation of these regiments was preserved and fostered throughout the war.[18]

Charitable aid played an important role in the rhetoric of support on the home front, but it was when a soldier was killed or severely wounded that questions of long-term financial stability became a truly pressing concern. The death of a soldier meant that his family was no longer supported by his pay, and often, local charities ceased to provide for his widow and children. Furthermore, when a soldier died, the question of his enlistment bounty—often paid after the soldier mustered out of service—became crucial for families in need of money.

Although families may have been psychologically prepared to handle the "good death" of their loved one on the battlefield, the economic realities that came with a soldier's death were another issue altogether. But a soldier's death was only one of the outcomes that could impel a complex shift of responsibility. Perhaps equally significant, and equally difficult to deal with psychologically and otherwise, was the burden a severely wounded or permanently disabled man became for his family. Significantly more men were wounded or severely debilitated than died in service, and returning veterans often found the transition back to civilian life difficult if their role within the family had shifted from provider to dependent.

As early as 1862 the Federal government began to offer pensions to disabled men and to widows and dependents as a means of support. These pensions reflected the government's assumption of responsibility for families of the dead and wounded. Citizens who had become disabled while engaged in the defense of the Union were rewarded and supported through the issuance of monthly stipends that reflected the severity of injury and individual financial needs. The scale of the war made these measures a necessity, as individuals and families were often left without means of support. However, for many widows, filing a pension application was the final stage in a long process of uncertainty and insecurity and was by no means an immediate or guaranteed financial solution.

News of a soldier's death or injury often marked the beginning of a new type of uncertainty. In the late fall of 1864, for example, Mary Kelly wrote to Captain Daniel Quirk of the 23rd Illinois regiment to inquire into the whereabouts of her son Patrick. She had received word from the War Office in October that her son, a thirty-one-year-old laborer from Chicago who had enlisted in the regiment in February 1862, had been wounded and captured in September of that year. A "distressed widow," whose "only means of my support in my old days" was her son, Mrs. Kelly wrote to find out whether he was still alive; if not, she sought to claim his pension and personal effects. Brothers Edward and Edmund Kelly followed their mother's letter with inquiries of their own requesting any information about Patrick, efforts finally rewarded with the news that their brother had been killed at Manchester, Virginia on July 25, 1864. The delay between a soldier's death and the official confirmation of that death, which in this case took nearly six months, was a major issue for women and children teetering on the brink of poverty.[19]

In many respects, the Civil War undercut contemporary notions of dependency, as wartime necessity forced women from the home and into the public sphere. Employment options for women were limited, however, despite concerns about the economic viability of families whose primary breadwinner had left for the army, women on the home front remain relatively anonymous within the narrative of the war, but the experiences of widows of soldiers from these regiments illuminate the uncertainty that accompanied wartime death. The delay between a widow's completion of a Federal pension application and the awarding of that pension raised questions and concerns with regard to the economic survival of women on the home front during this period.[20]

For example, when Private Ambrose Carey, a tailor from New Haven, died of swamp fever on August 19, 1862 at Saint James Hospital in New Haven, he left behind his wife, Ellen, and four children under the age of sixteen. The couple married in Cashel, Ireland in 1843, but did not have their first child until nine years later, after their immigration to New Haven. Ellen applied for a widow's pension in June of 1863, nearly ten months after the death of her husband. It was not until February 1864 that a pension of $8 per month was awarded, and while the funds "commenced" on the date of Ambrose's death, there was an eighteen-month gap in which the family was theoretically without an income. Moreover, $8 per month did little to help families struggling with wartime inflation. By the winter of 1864–65, John Niven has noted, "an estimated 70 per cent of the charity cases in Connecticut cities were soldiers' families."[21]

Such was the case of Margaret Lynch of Wallingford, Connecticut. Margaret and her husband John were married in March 1843 in County Clare, Ireland. Their son, Patrick, was born the same year. The family left Ireland in 1849 and immigrated to Wallingford, a growing factory town north of New Haven. In 1859, when John died after being run over by a rail car, Patrick assumed the role of provider for his family. Before enlisting, he "worked in a factory [in Wallingford] at making spoons, and being a good workman received good wages and . . . he gave his wages or a great portion of his wages to his mother for her support and the support of her young children," a friend of Mrs. Lynch attested. On October 20, 1862, Patrick was killed by rebel guerillas outside of New Orleans. A Federal pension, family friends claimed in November 1863, was necessary for the family's continued survival. Without Patrick's financial support, his mother "would have been deprived of many . . . comforts and necessaries . . . and have been dependent upon the charities of others for a comfortable living."[22]

The larger the family, of course, the greater the impact of a soldier's death. As a result, the government offered support for children under the age of sixteen at a rate of $2 per month per child, though this money was not always guaranteed. Julius Gross was thirty-eight when he enlisted in the 17th Wisconsin in February 1862. A German immigrant, and one of the large minority of Germans in

Wisconsin's Irish Brigade, he and his wife, Bertha, had moved to Milwaukee from Prussia in the late 1840s, and by the time Julius enlisted, their family had grown to include five children, though their eldest, a daughter, married and moved out of the home soon after the war broke out. Before enlisting, Gross had worked as a laborer around the city, doing odd jobs such as sawing wood and gardening for his neighbors. His wife supplemented the family's income by working as a housekeeper. Julius died of disease less than a year after his enlistment in November 1862, while the regiment was stationed at Corinth, Mississippi. Bertha, a "widow in needy circumstances," applied for government aid soon after she received word of her husband's death. Her application was significantly delayed, however, by the fact that her marriage certificate had to be sent from Germany, and that no public records existed to verify the birth dates of their children. She was not awarded a pension until 1867, four years after she submitted her initial application. Despite the fact that many of the affidavits in her pension file allude to the strength of the German community in Milwaukee—or, at the very least, to the presence of a strong support network for this widow—it is unclear how the Gross family survived the four years after the death of Julius, though it was likely through a combination of hard work and local support systems.[23]

Mary Calahan experienced a similar setback when applying for a pension after the death from disease of her husband, a member of the 17th Wisconsin, in July 1862 at Corinth, Mississippi. Mary was unable to provide baptismal or other public records to verify the ages of her five children when she applied for Federal aid. Although she was granted a pension in 1864, two years after her husband's death, her attempt to claim additional benefits from the government in 1867–68 rested solely on depositions from midwives who assisted in the birth of her children. Another soldier of the Ninth Connecticut, Thomas Dunn, worked in the manufacturing industry in Hartford before enlisting. His death in 1863 left his wife, Margaret, and his four children without any means of support. Like her counterparts in Wisconsin, Margaret Dunn had a difficult time convincing the government of her need for assistance, and in 1864 was awarded a pension of a mere $8 per month, hardly enough, it seems, to care for herself and her children. Interestingly, however, none of these women personally commented about the gravity of her financial situations, relying instead on neighbors and friends to speak of the family's destitution.[24]

Perhaps these women were too embarrassed to provide minute details of their situations, or did not see any purpose in doing so. Or perhaps they felt that the true nature of their condition could be better stated by the petitioners who wrote in support of their pension applications. Regardless of their reasons, the fact is that although these pension applications broadly suggest the conditions at home for those on whom the war had a devastating personal impact, for the most part the descriptions of hardship and want appear rather sterile. But this must not be taken as evidence of a lack of emotion in the face of death or poverty, or, worse, as evidence of complacency with regard to the struggle to make a living, or to the family's socioeconomic position. For most Americans during this period, and especially for those in the laboring classes, life was by no means easy, but rarely does correspondence illuminate discontent or include widespread complaints about the situation on the home front, and the pension applications themselves reflect a more stoic acceptance of this reality. And while there must have been some animosity, confusion, and fear among family members following the death of a soldier, it is not so surprising that such sentiments are not in evidence in pension applications, simply because the bureaucratic nature of these application packets left little room for the expression of lingering emotions.

While the welfare of young families often hung the balance in the wake of the death of a husband, dependent mothers seemed to have faced even greater hardships at home, a consequence, perhaps, of their age and lack of broader support networks. Ellen Lane, for example, mother of Private Patrick Lane, faced destitution after her son died on August 15, 1862. Prior to his enlistment, Lane had worked as a carriage painter in the employ of George L. Newhall, a carriage manufacturer in New Haven. Michael Keefe, Patrick Sisk, and Michael Mulcahy, citizens of New Haven, would later attest that his pay, "regularly received every Saturday night, were by him regularly given to his mother, except such small portion of the same which he used to procure his own wearing apparel [and] other necessary purposes—and that his wages were thus given to her by him to be used for her support and maintenance." When Patrick's father died in 1843, Patrick became the sole financial supporter of his mother, a task he took seriously. Keefe, Sisk, and Mulcahy explained in 1864 that "Ellen Lane is very poor, being possessed of no property, that she is too infirm from age to labor at any employment, so as to earn wages and she is therefore wholly dependent upon the Pay of her son and the Pension for which she now makes application." Furthermore, they noted, "if she does not receive the Pension aforesaid She must be almost entirely dependent for support upon gratuitous help which she may receive from her friends, or from the Charitably disposed."[25]

After the death of her son Patrick, Margaret Clancy also found herself in a desperate situation. A widow for nearly fifteen years, the sixty-nine-year-old native of Galway, Ireland found herself without property and without any source of income. Her son, a thirty-five-year-old laborer, had enlisted in 1862 and periodically sent home portions of his pay. His death left his mother dependent "upon the kindness of relatives and friends" for her support, a strain that eventually led her to apply for a Federal pension. Similarly, Rose Curran had been a widow for nine years when her son, Frank, was shot and killed at the Battle of Lexington on September 18, 1861. Frank had supported his mother and invalid brother for at least eight years before he enlisted in the army. In support of a pension, her neighbors noted that the applicant was "very old . . . and is very poor and has no property of any kind she now lives in a shanty belonging to a neighbor." Despite these conditions, Rose did not receive Federal support until April 1864, nearly two and a half years after her son died, leaving her destitute.[26]

In Madison, Wisconsin, Mary Scanlan applied for a Federal pension after her son James was killed outside of Vicksburg, Mississippi. Her husband, John Scanlan, was killed in 1854 while working on the Mississippi and Milwaukee Railroad, and after his death James "provided for her maintenance by having land and working it, as well as by working out as a laborer." After his enlistment Mary "relied upon the states pay then allowed (now no longer paid her since his death) and such money as he from time to time remitted her during his life." After James's death, Mary quickly went through her son's county bonus and back pay and found herself in desperate need of assistance. Although applications for pensions to support dependent mothers of dead soldiers were less common than widows' applications, they tell darker tales. While these files allude to basic levels of community support, the applications also reflect a level of desperation that belies the reports about support networks that appeared throughout local newspapers. These women often became a burden on their local communities, and the applications for Federal pensions suggest that community-based systems of support ultimately failed in meeting the continued needs of such citizens.[27]

As with widows' applications for pensions, there was often a considerable time lag between the submission of pension applications by dependent mothers of soldiers and the awarding of those pensions, and the delay, which often coincided with extensive investigations into the true need of the applicant, could suggest the struggle between the desire to administer widespread aid and lingering questions about the role of a social-welfare system within the American democratic tradition. The time it took to grant pensions was not lost on men and women in the North. "Another class urgently needing assistance," noted the *Milwaukee Daily Sentinel*, "is that of the families of men who have fallen in the service, and have not yet received the pension to which they are entitled. There is almost necessarily a delay of many months before it can be accomplished, and in the meantime these families have nothing to depend on but their own labors." Decisions on pensions often took two years or more and required applicants to submit extensive proof of their need for government assistance. During this time families had no means of support other than what was available on the most local community level. The time between application and award of pensions reflected a dichotomy in American society at the time. There was clear recognition of the need suffered by a portion of the population who struggled to survive in the absence of husbands and/or sons, and pensions were meant to lessen the financial sacrifice of military service. Yet pensions were different than the outpourings of local support during war. Local support ended with the conclusion of the war and the return of soldiers. Pensions, however, continued long after the guns fell silent and had the potential to create a class indefinitely dependent on government aid, which could potentially change the nature of the relationship between the government and American citizens.[28]

As the home communities of the Ninth Connecticut, 23rd Illinois, and 17th Wisconsin rejected the means of protest employed by the rioters in New York City in the summer and fall of 1863, they simultaneously reiterated their support for the war effort and, thus, for their soldiers on the front lines. But public debate should not be our sole means of gauging the impact of the war in these regions. For while Northern citizens at large were engaged in this discourse, the families of soldiers continued to struggle. Soldiers of these three regiments were concerned about the well-being of their families at home, and both local communities and the Federal government took up the call by supporting the wives and children of the volunteers. The move to support soldiers' women and children illustrates the impact of military service on social inclusion and national identity, while also suggesting the degree to which the men of these regiments and their families had been accepted as part of their local communities. Military service, in other words, threw a bridge over the important chasm that antebellum rhetoric had created to cast immigrants, and especially the Irish, apart from the rest of American society. Although the Irish in these three states had visibly contributed to the social, political, and economic spheres of their communities during the years before the war, by volunteering and reenlisting the men solidified the relationship between themselves and the state, becoming *American* soldiers. Furthermore, the experiences of wives, widows, and mothers on the home front in these states provide a glimpse into the very real impacts that military service had on the lives of Americans throughout the North—experiences that transcended antebellum social divisions and had far-reaching implications for men, women, and children.

# 8

# Wounded Warriors, Public Wards: The Consequences of Military Service

The surrender of Confederate forces in the spring and summer of 1865 marked the end of the war for most soldiers in the Union army. For the Irishmen in the Ninth Connecticut, 23rd Illinois, and 17th Wisconsin regiments, though, the final two years of war must have seemed a whirlwind. Taking to the campaign trail, soldiers in all three units not only faced the enemy on numerous battlefields, but also dealt with changes within their units as new volunteers arrived and disabled veterans were sent home, where they often struggled to assimilate to the homes they had left in 1861 and 1862. The question of reenlistment, furthermore, forced men who had not been wounded to choose whether to remain in the fight or muster out after their three years of service expired. As new recruits struggled to assimilate to military life, disabled veterans faced the challenge of readjusting to civilian society. Veteran Irish volunteers, whose patriotism and loyalty to the Union stood in stark contrast to the heinous acts of their countrymen in New York City, faced renewed challenges as they sought to bring the Confederacy to its knees—and then were challenged again as their final muster cast them back to the homes they had left so many years before.

When regiments became depleted of men during the war, most states simply organized new ones. Wisconsin was one of the few that operated on the replacement system, sending new recruits to veteran regiments to replace the men they had lost. As a result, the 17th Wisconsin provides an interesting example of military organization. Over the course of the war, 1,823 men served in Wisconsin's Irish Brigade, 820 more than its original muster of 1,003 volunteers. Between April 1, 1862 and March 8, 1864, when the regiment was furloughed home to Wisconsin, 236 men were mustered into service. Of these men, 189 volunteered, 2 were substitutes, and the status of another 45 was not noted in muster and descriptive rolls, though it is likely that they too were volunteers. Of the soldiers who joined after April 1, 1862, 34 were Irish-born and 103 had been born in the United States; it is possible that around three-quarters of these native-born men were of Irish descent. Many of the new recruits (127) were farmers, and of the rest who provided an occupation (44 did not), nearly all were members of the working class. Furthermore, 98 men joined the regiment as substitutes over the course of the war, and during the fall and winter of 1864 another 290 men joined the regiment as draftees.[1]

Consequently, while the regiment lost nearly half of its original volunteers due to death and disability between December 1861 and March 1862, its numbers were continually replenished with seemingly reliable volunteers, draftees, and substitutes from the home front. One of these new volunteers was Orin Jameson, a twenty-two-year-old farmer from Baraboo, Wisconsin, who enlisted in November 1863. Jameson arrived at Vicksburg with a group of fellow volunteers in December and was immediately taken with the pleasantness of the city and with army life. "I am well and like Soldiering," he wrote home soon after joining the unit. Orin joined the 17th with his friend James B. Fowler, and the two spent the winter in relative ease. It was a period of high activity, but the men were "having a splendid good time now but little duty to do and plenty to eat." Orin was a clerk in charge of the company books, and soldiering suited him. He liked it "a great deal better than I had any idea that I could."[2]

As 1864 dawned, though, so too did questions of reenlistment in all three regiments. During the winter of 1863, soldiers in the 17th Wisconsin had the opportunity to reenlist, a decision that came with a $400 bounty and a thirty-day furlough. Among the men who reenlisted were Ebenezer Wescott and Levi H. Nickel, though each made this choice for very different reasons. For Wescott, the decision to reenlist came from pressure from the other soldiers in his company. He put off the decision until early February, when "the pressure was too strong." When word spread that he did not intend to reenlist, one of his comrades approached and challenged him, saying that Wescott "was a little scared . . . [and] said Bully Boy, I dare you to reenlist," after which Wescott "made a bee line for the Captain's tent and signed the enlistment roll." Levi Nickel's choice was much more ideological. Leaving home after his furlough and, as he wrote in his diary, "not knowing whereafter I would ever see [my friends and family] again," the corporal knew that "my country calls me and I must go to fight my countrys battle and save the union and the Star Spangled Banner. So again I started out for war." For Nickel, soldiering had become a duty, and he reenlisted despite his belief that a soldier was "exposed to a great many hardships and trials, his life is like a string it can be cut short at any moment."[3]

Not all the men who rejoined their regiments were happy with their decision. Opposite Petersburg, Virginia, in trenches along the Bermuda Hundred in the winter of 1864–64, Captain Martin Wallace of the 23rd Illinois eagerly anticipated the expiration of his term. "Simmson, Quirk, and Allen have left service and are gone home I suppose you have seen them ere now," he wrote on February 14, 1865; "all would leave if they could." Although reenlistment numbers in the Ninth Connecticut were high, when the unit returned from furlough so many officers sought to resign that they were eventually forced to draw names to determine who would stay with the men who reenlisted and who would muster out and return home. Despite such attitudes, the question of reenlistment often came with immense pressure from officers and fellow soldiers, which reflected the desire to keep trained men in the field. This push began in the winter of 1863, with veteran furloughs to take place before the start of the 1864 summer campaign season.[4]

The campaign for reenlistment was relatively successful. Approximately 361 men reenlisted in the 23rd Illinois, 263 in the 17th Wisconsin, and 367 in the Ninth Connecticut. As Cahill noted in a letter home, however, the numbers from his unit were not enough to earn the coveted title of "veteran regiment," as less than three-quarters of the regiment reenlisted, and his unit was later consolidated into a battalion. In Bridgeport, Connecticut the *Republican Farmer* reported the return of mustered-out veterans of the Ninth who came home with the "appearance and bearing . . . of veteran soldiers." "Would that we could welcome home every soldier of the state," the article continued, "with this war at an end and peace restored." Ultimately, those who remained in service with the Ninth were consolidated into a battalion of four regiments. And while the veteran ranks of the 17th Wisconsin were supplemented by substitutes, draftees, and late-war volunteers, in Chicago ambitious recruiters began organizing five new companies to join Mulligan's men in the Shenandoah Valley.[5]

Veteran furloughs were cause for excitement among the troops, most of whom were returning home for the first time since their enlistment. Private James Fowler noted that the men of the 17th had a "first rate time" as they prepared for their journey home to Wisconsin. The trip home was exciting and a bit off-putting, with "everybody drunk [and] fighting," Private Orin Jameson confided to his diary. The enthusiasm of the soldiers likely escalated as they traveled through Illinois, where they were met in every town, wrote Private Fowler, by "very patriotic folks' waving hand kerchiefs table cloths and every thing to be got a hold of." The *Columbian Register* described for its New Haven readers the reception the veterans of the Ninth Connecticut received when they landed in

New York, how they were met by "an immense crowd of friends and citizens . . . present to extend to them a hearty welcome home. . . . [T]he street was crowded with the friends of the returning soldiers, while flags were flying and fire-works exploding. The men cheered and the women pressed forward to greet their husbands and brothers." The editors concluded, "The citizens of New Haven may well feel proud of the record of the gallant 9th Conn." After the 23rd Illinois was reorganized in New Creek, Virginia, James Mulligan again was inundated with lecture requests. His regiment, which then numbered fewer than 400, made its way east to Illinois at the end of April for their furlough, and it is likely that his men experienced a homecoming equal to those received by their peers in the other two regiments, especially given the fact that recruiters were busy in Chicago gathering men to refill the ranks of the regiment. Men in all three units marched to war with immense fanfare, and their welcome home after two years' absence, in spite of the political divides on the home front, likely served as an encouragement to continue the fight. The enthusiasm with which the veterans were welcomed home speaks to the continued support for the war effort in these regions outside of New York City and belies the apparent decline of Irish American support that occurred in larger eastern cities during 1863 and afterwards.[6]

After returning from their furlough, the Ninth Connecticut was dispatched to the Shenandoah Valley, where they served under Philip Sheridan in the Second Division of the 19th Corp during his Valley Campaign of 1864. On September 19 the men from Connecticut were on the field at the Third Battle of Winchester, but played no role in the battle itself. Two days later, at Fisher's Hill, they advanced to capture the fords over the North Fork of the Shenandoah River and "drive the enemy's pickets from the bluff." At Cedar Creek on October 19 the battalion was "under arms and at the breast-works [at the center of the Union line] at 5 a.m. At that time a heavy volley of musketry was heard on our left, which was followed soon after by artillery firing and a continuous one of musketry." As the Confederate forces advanced, the regiment struck tents and "formed in line of battle and delivered a well directed fire at the enemy with marked effect." Falling back to the bottom of the hill, the battalion regrouped and again advanced on the enemy lines, firing another well delivered volley. The colors of the Ninth, John Healey reported, were the "first upon the recaptured works" after the regiment had succeeded in driving the rebels back from the positions they had captured in the morning. Although newspapers in Connecticut reported the battle, no specific mention was made of Ninth Connecticut and, importantly, the emphasis on ethnicity in news articles written earlier in the war appears to have dissipated. In the Shenandoah Valley until the winter, the Ninth then moved east to Fortress Monroe, then south to Savannah, Georgia. The regiment was, in fact, more heavily engaged in military operations in 1864 and 1865 than it had been at any other point in the war. Interestingly, though, its service during the final years of the war remained relatively obscure at home.[7]

In April 1864 the 23rd Illinois remustered as a veteran volunteer unit and was granted furlough home to Illinois. As had been the case for the Ninth Connecticut, regimental losses led to the consolidation of the 23rd Illinois into a battalion consisting of five companies, approximately five hundred men. Before their return to Chicago the men fought hard at New Creek in early February 1864, the *Chicago Tribune* reporting heavy losses. After returning from furlough in the late spring, the unit joined General Philip Sheridan on his campaign in the Shenandoah Valley during the summer and fall of 1864. Although they served in the same army as the Ninth Connecticut, the two Irish regiments seemed unaware of each other's presence.[8]

In July of 1864 three bullets momentarily propelled the 23rd Illinois back into the national limelight. As James Mulligan led his regiment in a charge against Confederate lines at what became known as the Second Battle of Kernstown, he was struck in the thigh, shoulder, and side. "His men picked him up and were carrying him from the field, when the Rebels surprised the whole party," reported the *New York Tribune* and other news outlets throughout the North. "The Colonel told the boys to leave him and save the flag." The hero of Lexington "fell while rallying his men. When his troops fell back, outnumbered and outflanked, he was sitting erect in his saddle and with hat off was rallying by voice and example the soldiers of his own regiment—the men who loved him so dearly and were proud of their heroic leader." As he lay wounded on the field, reported the *New World*, the enemy concentrated their fire on the men who had gathered to carry him to the rear. Above their heads "waved the colors of the Irish Brigade. The colors becoming endangered in the struggle, Col. Mulligan gave his last command, the command of a hero: 'Lay me down, and save the flag.'" "There is something touching in the fate of brave Colonel James A. Mulligan, who gave his life to the cause of his adopted country," reported the *Philadelphia Inquirer*, clearly unaware that Mulligan had been born in New York. "Colonel Mulligan was a true soldier." His heroics, first at Lexington, Missouri and then in his death near Winchester, Virginia, ultimately defined the war for the men of the 23rd Illinois; adopted citizens, like their brave colonel they never once flinched from a fight and took whatever steps necessary to save their flag.[9]

At the end of April 1864, the 17th Wisconsin reformed at Camp Washburn in Milwaukee, "in good health and Spirits," according to Corporal Levi Nickel, and began a journey south to join the Army of the Tennessee at Cairo, Illinois. Winter recruiting was aided by the arrival of a number of wounded officers who showed off the regiment's "bullet pierced flag, that shows the shots of Vicksburg [and] Corinth . . . and the other actions in which the 17th has bravely fought." "Honor to the Green Flag," reported the, *Wisconsin Daily Patriot*, in support of their efforts. Wounded while "bearing the green flag against the enemy," they were received by the regiment's "so many proud friends in this city and State." During May the regiment moved south from Clifton, Tennessee, first to Athens, Tennessee, then onward to Decatur and finally to Huntsville, Alabama. On May 25, after three days in that city, the regiment received marching orders and Ebenezer Wescott and his comrades again "start[ed] of[f] on the war path." There, blocking the path to Atlanta, waited a Confederate army commanded by Joseph E. Johnston.[10]

Private Orin Jameson was quick to grasp the enormity of the situation. After dress parade on May 24, he wrote in his diary: "My thoughts when corps were marching past us [was] first the music [acted] splendidly to liven the poor soldier[,] 2nd how many good boys brave and true are following it perhaps for the last time still they never see it in that light always cheerful." Others had less poignant commentary on their movements. "We have no tents with us," Ebenezer Wescott wrote, "we have not slept under tents since we left home. Our roof is the blue sky, providing its not raining, then the roof is somewhat leaky and we are liable to get a little damp."[11]

The Atlanta Campaign of 1864 was a complex series of battles and maneuvers as Joseph Johnston sacrificed ground for ever-stronger fortifications blocking the road to Atlanta. Sherman's army advanced in flanking maneuvers, attempting to nullify the heavily fortified positions Johnston chose. According to Ebenezer Wescott, Johnston's presence was the biggest problem facing the Army of the Tennessee, for if Sherman "would only step [to] one side there would be no trouble going to Atlanta, but he says 'No,' and the dispute will have to be settled another way, a very hard and costly way"—the pursuit of Johnston's army. Another frustrated soldier wrote that Sherman was "not trying to take Atlanta he is trying to get Johnston and his army and is waiting to see how Genl Grant comes out at Richmond."[12]

Despite the larger confluence of events surrounding the campaign against Atlanta, the men of the 17th Wisconsin were largely focused on the events in their immediate vicinity, and their diaries recount the monotony of short moves, entrenching, and "occasional shot from the pickets." On July 20 at Decatur, six miles from Atlanta, the men were once again asked to charge rebel works. Unlike their experiences at Vicksburg, though, they successfully drove the Confederate forces from their position, though they lost a number of their own men. "There will be mo[u]rning in Farmington [Wisconsin] when the news reaches there," Wescott wrote to his mother, listing four men from that city cut down by rebel fire. The Confederates counterattacked in a ferocious way on the night of July 21–22. "They came almost up to our works several times and finally about four o'clock gave up," Wescott wrote; "I do not see how men could charge such a battery as we had there behind strong works and plenty of support. They treble shotted those guns and just simply moved them down." Unbeknownst to them at the time, the men of the 17th were witness to one of the last desperate measures of the Army of Tennessee to save Atlanta.[13]

On September 2 Atlanta fell, and soon thereafter, Sherman's men began their famous march across Georgia to Savannah. Letters and diaries from the men in the 17th Wisconsin do not provide significant insight into this trek, other than the fact that they were constantly on the move, forced to forage for supplies, all the while pushing back local Confederate forces under Generals Joseph Wheeler and Wade Hampton. The move across Georgia was an incredible feat, as Sherman strayed from his supply lines and fed his men off the Georgia countryside. Compared to the fight for Atlanta, however, the occupation of Savannah was in itself anticlimactic. On the morning of December 21, Union forces approached the city and "found that the rebs had vacated their works and our pickets went in and found none so they went on and found that the rebs had left the city of Savannah," Levi Nickel wrote in his diary. For their part, Wisconsin newspapers followed Sherman's siege of Atlanta and his March to the Sea, but, as in coverage by local papers of large actions in which the Ninth Connecticut participated, the 17th Wisconsin was lost within the broader combat narrative, as men and women on the home front became captivated with Sherman's moves as a whole rather than with small unit actions. The ethnic designations that had so defined early service disappeared after the regiment left Wisconsin for veteran service.[14]

As the war drew to an end, the men from Connecticut, Illinois, and Wisconsin were spread throughout the South. The 23rd was participating in operations in the Shenandoah Valley, the 17th Wisconsin was on the move through North Carolina with Sherman, and the Ninth Connecticut was in Savannah, Georgia, where they celebrated St. Patrick's Day with the city's local Irish militia, the Jasper Greens, who loaned the Connecticut men their Irish flag for the occasion. By late summer, troops from all three units began arriving home, where they received a hero's welcome. In July, on their way to their home state, 465 veterans of the 17th Wisconsin arrived in Chicago, where they were "received with due ceremony by a large representation of the Fenian Brotherhood and one company of the 99th regiment Illinois volunteers, who escorted [them] through the streets," reported the *Milwaukee Daily Sentinel*. The *New York Times* wrote that on their way home to New Haven in August, the men from the Ninth made an impression on New Yorkers when they landed in Manhattan "for the great number of pets brought home by the men. Numerous cages of blackbirds, robins and mocking-birds accompanied the regiment, while dogs of all sizes and breeds trotted along, seemingly quite satisfied with their first visit to the populous North. Several raccoons and opossums clung to the knapsacks of their owners." The families and friends of the 23rd Illinois organized a rally in Chicago to honor the returning veterans. The men of this brigade, noted the *Chicago Tribune*, would "continue to exist in history, where their gallantry will never be forgotten."[15]

Irish American veterans faced a complex set of struggles after they mustered out of Union service. This was a period, notes Susannah Ural Bruce, during which "Irish Americans began to make a concerted effort to create a clear identity for themselves in the United States," fighting against "the prejudice they had faced since the first famine immigrants began pouring into American ports despite all they had accomplished in American." A revival of nativism aimed at limiting the growing Irish presence and Irish political power coincided with "accounts of pandemic Irish poverty" in urban centers. Nativists, however, struggled to contain the rise of this group as the Irish asserted themselves in major cities throughout the North. They did so, according to Bruce, through clarifying "within and outside their communities, their role in the defining American experience: the Civil War."[16]

Certainly, though, the plight of the urban Irish that had defined the antebellum experience for many recent immigrants did not end with the return of veterans, and the loyalty and patriotism of these men did little to abridge the economic hardships of their countrymen and women in America's cities. As historians such as Kerby Miller, Noel Ignateiv, Tyler Anbinder, and Matthew Frye Jacobson have illustrated, the processes of growth, mobility, and acceptance were slow ones for these immigrants and their children. Veterans from Connecticut, Illinois, and Wisconsin must have been attuned, to some degree, to the complex relationships that existed between their immigrant group and their adopted nation, for significant immigrant communities existed in all three states. Yet there were personal, individual aspects to the experiences of these veterans that were both intertwined with and separate from broader sociopolitical issues that defined the Irish experience in the postwar era. Their return home marked a period of personal trials, and these experiences expand on our understanding of the ways in which Union veterans, Irish and otherwise, negotiated their postwar spaces and fought to secure a place for themselves and their families within their communities.[17]

Veterans returned home during and after the war. The presence of wounded veterans at home while the war carried on helped to ensure a close relationship between soldiers and the home front. Regiments were in constant flux as men were discharged from service for a wide array of diseases and injuries, and at times the wounded returned home within weeks, not years, of their initial muster. Men who returned home during the war were walking reminders of the realities and horrors of warfare and service in Civil War armies. Their comrades who served through their final muster, healthy enough to reenlist and fight until the surrenders of Lee and Johnston's armies, lived a more convoluted existence after the war. Although eager to reenter the workplace, these men often suffered from a variety of injuries that ultimately affected their lives to varying degrees. Returning to towns left unscathed by the war, they took part in the vibrant, if at times volatile, national growth that occurred during the latter half of the nineteenth century. As pension applications suggest, however, veterans from these regiments were relentless in their pursuit of gainful employment and long-term stability in ways that embodied the burgeoning notions of individualism and advancement that characterized American society during this period.

Historians have traditionally focused on Civil War veterans in two distinct ways. The first is the role that veterans and their families played in shaping the postwar social and political environment and in memorializing their military service. As purveyors of their individual causes, these men and women sought to preserve the legacy of wartime service, sacrifice, and honor while negotiating a new and at times unsettling postwar society. The second is the experiences of Civil War veterans themselves. Scholars have compiled impressive and varied accounts of the difficulties faced by veterans in the postwar period. For many, an empty sleeve stood as a constant reminder of sacrifice for the cause. Other veterans suffered from less visible, psychological wounds—injuries lingering just beyond the view of family and friends. For these soldiers, post-traumatic stress and other nervous disorders could be devastating, preventing them from completely rejoining society. These men were intrinsically linked together through their shared postwar experience. Their status as veterans, in other words, made them fundamentally different from other Americans; men who donned the blue led a unique existence. The experiences of the veterans from these Irish American regiments, or at least the experiences of those who applied for and received pensions from the Federal government during and after the war, do not fit any one particular mold. Some became outcasts; many more were active agents in their own growth and the growth of their communities. The postwar experiences of these regiments' pensioners expand on the already rich narrative of Civil War veterans in the later half of the nineteenth century. Though historians often highlight the struggles of veterans as evidence of the tumultuous lives of men after muster-out, the reality was that many returning soldiers were fundamentally connected to their larger communities and, despite lingering disabilities, fought to ensure a better life for themselves and their families.[18]

Debilitating medical conditions, as a consequence of battle or of camp life, plagued soldiers from all three regiments and often led to medical discharges. For the Ninth Connecticut, 23rd Illinois, and 17th Wisconsin, it was camp life, rather than battle, that had the greatest lasting effect on the health of the soldiers, whether they were medically discharged during the war or stayed in arms until the surrender of the Southern armies. In all three regiments, as throughout the rest of the Union army, the number of men who died from disease was far greater than the number who died in battle. The number of men from these regiments wounded in battle was comparatively small, considering that these units were actively campaigning throughout the war. Most of the injuries sustained were incurred in camp, and the location of these camps and the amount of time the regiment stayed often dictated the men's health. Campaigning also depleted the physical condition of the men, especially when marches were conducted in foul weather. While medical conditions varied among soldiers and were attributable to a variety of experiences, the impact that military service had on the physical health of the soldiers is undeniable.[19]

At Corinth, Mississippi in the summer and fall of 1862, for example, Ebenezer Wescott wrote to his parents of the steady decline of regimental strength, explaining that "there is a good deal of sickness here." The only available water source for the army was located seven miles from town. Although details were sent from each company twice a day to retrieve water, by the time they returned with the water it was "not fit to drink," and unclean water bred widespread illness. According to regimental muster rolls, 83 men died of disease between April and December of 1862, while the 17th Wisconsin was stationed at or near

Corinth. By early September 1862, the regiment had dwindled to 600 men, and the surgeon in charge of the regiment's hospital acknowledged that reports had begun to circulate suggesting that the 17th was a "sickly regiment." "The mortality of the regiment is truly discouragingly frightful," Colonel Doran wrote in exasperation. Movement south, along with a mild winter and access to clean drinking water, assuaged disease among the men, and though the strength of the regiment further declined to 454 soldiers during this time, by the end of the winter of 1863 there were only 11 men sick in hospital.[20]

The move to Vicksburg during the summer of 1863, though, proved devastating for the regiment. The *Watertown Democrat* back home in Wisconsin urged those on the home front to "weep for the soldiers when the weather is bad." Soldiering, they reminded civilians, was a constant struggle. "Put a man in the field and soak him with rain; he has no warm change of clothing to comfort him; chill his hands or feet, he has no register and slippers to thaw out the frost; weary his body, he has no soft bed to charm the ache away. . . . [W]hen a man tells you feebly that he isn't strong enough to go to war, you may feel like believing it more than you have." The sickly Southern summer that Jefferson Davis so hoped would "compell their baffled and defeated forces to abandonment of an expedition on which was based their chief hope of success in effecting our subjugation" slowly wore upon the men from Wisconsin, and the affects lingered on through the winter.[21]

Disease was their constant companion. Corporal William O'Brien, for example, a twenty-one-year-old native of Franklin, Maryland, attested in his pension application that he was stricken by fever and ague while on duty at Vicksburg; he was "subject to such sickness during the balance of his terms [that only] occasionally he was well enough to do duty, then would be taken down again." Due to sickness, O'Brien was placed on detached duty driving an ordnance train and was unable to return to his company until April 1865. Likewise, Peter Fahn, a thirty-four-year-old German immigrant who enlisted in the regiment in early January 1862, was afflicted with "Janduce Chronic Diarrhea complicated with acute rheumatism" while stationed in the rifle pits in front of Vicksburg, due to exposure while lying on the wet ground. He was sent to St. Louis to recuperate and was finally discharged in April 1864. All accounts from pensioners speak to the hardships of military life, and the far-reaching impact that local environment had on the well-being of troops in the field.[22]

Soldiers in the Ninth Connecticut, too, were struck down with disease and injury at a startling rate. Their difficulties began soon after the regiment landed at Ship Island, and disease continued to decimate the ranks during their time in the Gulf region. Men suffered not only from disease but also from the physical breakdown that often accompanied military service. As James Mullen aged, his legs became stricken with varicose veins, a condition that he attributed to the hardships of life on Ship Island. In December 1890 Michael McCarten, who served as captain of Company C, wrote to the Pension Bureau in support of Mullen's claim. "I knew James Mullen since he could walk and knew that when he enlisted in my company he was sound in body and mind," he recalled. Mullen "was sound and well until March 1862 when we were at Ship Island and during that month we had heavy drilling which was very bad on account of the sand and Mr Mullen being then a young man was strained and weakened by the drill and working in the sand." Martin Burke, a private in Company B, was injured in early April 1862 when he fell "between two ships or vessels while working unloding munitions of war and commissaries Stores. The ships were lying at anchor near the fort and while working along a plank between two transports slipped and falling between the boats was badly injured by being caught between the sides."[23]

Another soldier, Peter Morris, a thirty-one-year-old cabinetmaker from London, England, was injured in July 1862 "while working under orders . . . in the tearing down of a brick structure on [Ship Island] for the purpose of getting materials to construct a bakery." Edward Murray, a private in Company H, was disabled while collecting wood for the regiment. "One of the biggest men in the regiment," Murray was tasked with lashing logs together to make a raft, which would then be floated to the regiment. While pushing the raft, he slipped and hit a piece of log. As Patrick Foley recalled, "I saw him wade out of the water holding his hands over his privates and squeezed in that shape [doubled over]." By the next morning, his scrotum had swollen considerably. The surgeon reportedly drained a nearly a pint of fluid from the afflicted area.[24]

Malarial fever also ran rampant within the ranks of Connecticut's soldiers, compounded by exposure and poor water. Sherman Multhrop of Company I attested in his original pension claim that when the regiment landed on Ship Island, "the men were without tents for three or four weeks and were obliged to wade through water and sleep out on the sand in the open air without any protection." Similarly, Moses Mills, a private in Company D, was afflicted with neuralgia and deafness as a consequence of exposure on Ship Island; the debility became more severe as the war progressed, and he was left totally deaf by 1864.[25]

Thirty-four-year-old Orlando Yale developed such bad kidney disease in the spring of 1862 "that his legs were badly swollen and he complained of deafness."

Hospital steward Gary Scot never expected to see the stretcher-bound Yale alive again after parting ways with the private at New Orleans that summer. Yale was discharged in August of 1862, returned to his wife in Bristol, Connecticut, and was awarded a pension for disability nearly thirty years later, in April 1892. Continual exposure to contaminated water and mosquitoes plagued the regiment, especially during the warmer months in the South. Diseases contracted at Ship Island worsened in June and July of 1862, when the already weakened regiment moved north to Vicksburg. Like their peers in the 17th Wisconsin, the men from Connecticut were stricken down with disease in large numbers. Although news of disease filtered home over the course of the war, it was the arrival home of discharged veterans that served as a vivid reminder of the grim realities of military service.[26]

The soldiers of the 23rd Illinois suffered from an equally diverse set of ailments. During the winter of 1862–63 the regiment was unusually active, and from all accounts Mulligan's Irish Brigade was almost constantly on the move, trooping through the Shenandoah Valley. On January 2, Albert Phillips noted optimistically in his diary that the men began "cutting timber for to build log houses," in preparation for a winter encampment. Two days later, though, the men were ordered to arms and began a march during which they eventually covered more than sixty miles over the course of five days, and which took the regiment to Winchester and then to New Creek. On Monday, January 5, Phillips wrote that after marching forty miles, "at roll call every man was greatly crippled," and the following day, "All the men was w[e]akened." For Phillips, the personal consequence of this forced march was that his brother fell so ill that their father traveled from Illinois to accompany the sick soldier home. Veterans from the regiment often cited these forced marches as the cause of their disabilities. James Wilson, for example, later attested on behalf of Elias Shaw that "on or about the 24th day of September 1864 after a very hard days marching and as we were about to go into camp for the night a short distance from harpers Ferry—the Said Elias Shaw did not answer his name at Roll Call a search was made for him and he was found resting beneath a tree with his left leg exposed and very much swollen with enlarged veins."[27]

Others suffered similar fates. Thomas Moore, who enlisted as a private in Company K of the 23rd Illinois and was later promoted to lieutenant of Company H, resigned from the service in September 1862. He cited sunstroke, a consequence of a forced march in the autumn of 1861 from Jefferson City to Hickory Hill, Missouri, as his reason for leaving the service. Returning to Chicago, he married and took a position with the city's police force. Private James

Holland was discharged from New Creek, Virginia after he was stricken with chronic disease of the throat and lungs while "doing guard service during a severe storm" at Camp Douglas in Chicago in the summer of 1862. By the time the regiment arrived in Virginia, his respiratory infection had been complicated by the onset of severe diarrhea. He was discharged in August. Sergeant John Haley returned home to Detroit after he was discharged from Company A in 1864. Eighteen months earlier, when returning from picket duty, he and his comrades were ordered to discharge and clean their weapons. The musket of one of the soldiers discharged accidentally, and the ball "struck his [Haley's] left arm just below the elbow joint, passing through the arm just touching the bone and destroying some of the cords and muscles of the arm." He returned home and took up work as a painter in an effort to support his elderly mother. Like their peers from the other units in this study, the experiences of these men of the 23rd Illinois illustrate the hardships of military life and the far-reaching impacts that disease and injury had on men after they returned home.[28]

Although many men attributed their chronic disabilities to their wartime experiences, not all of these injuries necessarily impaired soldiers to the point of keeping them from the line of duty. Many veterans, of course, argued extensively that the long-term effects of subtle wounds were devastating—it was necessary to do so to secure a pension—but it is often hard to gauge the true extent of these injuries, when they occurred, and whether they were actually related to military service. What these pension file accounts do provide is unique insight into the day-to-day struggles of men who often left no other written account of their service. Interestingly, too, many of the injuries that men later reported became debilitating were only passively acknowledged while in the service. In fact, Colonel Cahill once referred to sick men in his regiment as "old stagers," suggesting that many of the injuries incurred in camp were not deemed serious enough by many to warrant acknowledgement on the regiment's sick roll. Furthermore, few of these injuries were severe enough to result in a soldier's immediate discharge, and most likely reflected, instead, the normal day-to-day conditions for soldiers during the war.[29]

Disease struck heavily during the first year for most soldiers, but disease was not something new to the Irish who lived in the heavily populated wards of Eastern cities. Nor was it uncommon in Illinois or Wisconsin, where there were periodic outbreaks of cholera and other epidemics during the two decades prior to the war. Disease and exposure, along with accidents at work, led one Irish American observer to comment, "It is a well established fact that the average length of life of the emigrant after landing here is six years; and many insist it is much less." "How often do we see such paragraphs in the paper," exclaimed one emigrant, "as an Irishman drowned—an Irishman crushed by a beam—an Irishman suffocated in a pit . . . and other like causalities and perils to which honest Pat is constantly exposed, in the hard toils for his daily bread." The unique experiences and inherent dangers of military life, however, compounded typical hardships, and lingered with soldiers long after their discharge.[30]

At least 355 men were discharged from the Ninth Connecticut, 23rd Illinois, and 17th Wisconsin between 1862 and 1864 as a result of disabilities incurred while in the army. Returning home, they tried to rejoin communities to which they had only recently said goodbye—though their status and health had drastically changed and often made seamless reentry difficult. Just as families of soldiers and, especially, poor widows were often displaced over the course of the war, returning veterans faced similar hardships. Like the plight of widows, the struggles of veterans who were discharged during the war have often been overshadowed in historical narrative by a focus on military organizations such as the Invalid Corps, later renamed the Veterans Reserve Corps, a unit that allowed men to continue the defend their nation despite disabilities. Many soldiers with crippling wounds or debilitating diseases, however, left the army for good after their discharge, returning home to towns and cities that were both familiar and different. Veterans discharged during the war faced tremendous struggles when reentering civilian life. Wounds or diseases that forced a man to leave the army were serious, often life-threatening. These crippled soldiers, unqualified to serve, faced an uphill battle to reenter civilian society given that their wounds inhibited their ability earn a living.[31]

Civilian life was considerably more difficult for these men because of their wounds, and veterans often struggled to negotiate their new reality as disabled or partially disabled wage earners. Simply put, men who were discharged during the war because of disease or injury were not only unfit for military service, but were often unfit for work once they returned home. Although they were reunited with their family and friends, many men were often mere shells of their former selves and became more a burden upon their families than anything else. The men who marched to war were, on average, twenty-seven years old and were considered by acquaintances to be active, sound of body, and able to work and provide for their families and dependents. The experiences of George Winfrey appear typical. His family was large and desperately poor, and while he was "not very bright [he] was able to work." Known before the war as "a man around the town," he had been employed by a number of men in Dowagiac, Michigan, for odd jobs such as ice packing, wood cutting, and gardening. One employer noted that Winfrey was a "good stout man for a days work." Through his efforts, George was able to provide for his parents and a younger brother. Winfrey was taken prisoner at Lexington, Missouri with other members of the 23rd Illinois. After he was paroled, he reenlisted in the 12th Michigan. At the Battle of Shiloh Winfrey was wounded in the left groin by a shell and received a gunshot wound to his head and a bayonet wound to his nose. He was subsequently discharged from the army and sent home. Despite attempts to regain employment after leaving the army, by the time Winfrey applied for a pension, the examining officer found him in "indigent circumstances."[32]

Difficulty reentering the workplace posed perhaps the greatest challenge for soldiers and their families, as it severely limited their income and stability. When Winfrey was discharged from the service in 1862, he returned home a broken man. Suffering from a ruptured hernia, among other ailments, the veteran was no longer capable of manual labor; a neighbor attested that Winfrey had become "known in the neighborhood as a Disabled Soldier, always in poor health and unfit to perform the ordinary labor expected from a stout able bodied man." Another neighbor noted that Winfrey "could not perform one half the common work of a sound man as a laborer." John Alexander, a private in Company F of the Ninth Connecticut, experienced a similarly difficult transition back to civilian life. He first became sick in the summer of 1862 while the regiment was stationed across from Vicksburg working on the failed canal project. Sent south to Baton Rouge and, after three months in the field hospital there, to New Orleans, Alexander remained sick with fever, chills, and chronic diarrhea, ultimately leading to his discharge from the army in December of 1862. He was furnished with passage from New Orleans to New York City where, upon his arrival, Alexander stayed for a time with a close friend, Ann Flannigan. Flannigan attested that Alexander returned home "very much emaciated. . . . He then had no retention or control of his bowels for over two years." Not only was this veteran plagued by continual bouts of diarrhea for the remainder of his life, but his illnesses so weakened his eyes that often "he would pass a friend [on the street] without noticing him." Unable to perform manual labor except for odd jobs and chores "which did not really support him," he and his family survived off his wife's wages as a domestic servant and charity from a New York City infirmary.[33]

These situations must have been trying for families. The return of wounded men, many of whom, before the war, had been the primary providers for their families, must have caused some degree of strife and uncertainty. It is clear that in many cases veterans' injuries forced a reversal of roles of dependency within the family, as these once strong men returned from the front lines as shadows of their former selves. James McCarthy's experience in the wake of his discharge, though extreme, provides some insight into the way these tensions could tear families apart. McCarthy was born in 1828 in Cork, Ireland and immigrated to the United States in 1847 along with thousands of other Famine refugees. He found work as a shoe crimper in New Haven. He enlisted in the Ninth Connecticut and served as the regiment's Color Sergeant until the summer of 1862, when, in mid-July, he was injured while lifting a heavy box of clothing aboard a transport. McCarthy strained his legs to such a degree that he was confined to bed, unable to stand. By August, still unable to move his left leg, he was discharged and sent home to New Haven.[34]

Returning home crippled, on crutches, McCarthy received little support from his wife Ann, who told him "that she had no more use for him"; he reported that she "did not treat him right." The marital problems between James and Ann appear to have stemmed from a combination of his disability and the large amount of debt that Ann had incurred on the family's small grocery business while her husband was away in the army. It is not hard to imagine that Ann's concern over the growing debt was compounded by the realization that her husband had returned from war unable to contribute to the family's welfare. At some point between 1865 and 1870, Ann left James and took her children to live in a boarding house. After publicly avowing "that she had left his bed and board and that he would not be responsible for her debts," James filed for divorce, assigned a guardian for his children, and moved west to Dubuque, Iowa, where he went to work for his uncle. There, despite his disabilities, he was able to find gainful employment, and, as his employers later noted, was "moral, temperate, truthful . . . [and] industrious, although not at all times able to work constantly." He also remarried. The dissolution of his first marriage was linked, to a large degree, to his wartime service. His absence from home led to the ruin of his family's business and, upon his return, his wife was either unwilling or unable to accept his condition. It is difficult to assess how typical this kind of conflict was, though it is not hard to imagine that it affected more families than we know. Certainly, for many of those who volunteered, life had not been easy before the war; the stress of financial instability may have been a permanent fixture, especially among the laboring classes. But the war magnified the issue, when former wage earners returned home incapable of working. Their disabilities often led to financial crises for families, while simultaneously disrupting the gender roles that were so important within nineteenth-century American society.[35]

Soldiers and their families experienced an array of challenges that tested their abilities to negotiate the new wartime society. Men returning from the front lines confronted not only the difficulties of finding and sustaining employment, but also struggled to regain acceptance at home. Private and state-sponsored charities grew as the war continued and casualties mounted. The women in Milwaukee, for example, pledged themselves to serve returning soldiers as "a good Samaritan . . . [and] adopted the best means we could devise for meeting them with kindness and refreshment on their homeward journey," providing tickets and meals for those in need. This charity, like many similar efforts, were viewed as a duty, but the relief was not intended for long term support. The primary form of long-term financial assistance for wounded men and their families came in the form of Federal pensions, though these were difficult for wounded men and war widows alike to obtain both during and after the war. Organizations founded for the long-term care of seriously wounded veterans, such as the soldiers' and sailors' homes, were run with military strictness, in an effort, it seems, to make life for residents unpleasant enough to discourage veterans from seeking asylum. As veterans transitioned back to civilian life, at times their experiences were often denied by lingering illnesses and injuries as well as a society unprepared to deal with the often debilitating consequences of military service.[36]

There is little doubt that military service had far-reaching consequences for many of the soldiers who served in the Union armies. For men who served out their terms of enlistment without sustaining significant apparent injury, however, assessing the true impact of their time in arms is difficult. Soldiers from all three regiments suffered from an array of diseases and physical ailments after they were mustered out of service, and they almost always claimed that their time in the military directly impaired their ability to earn a living. Strong, sound men in their physical prime when they entered the army in 1861 and 1862, many argued that the war had left them a shadow of their former selves. It is sometimes difficult, however, to draw a direct line between wartime service and the declining health of these veterans as they aged. Most veterans from these regiments refrained from applying for pensions until the 1880s, and thus it is nearly impossible to gauge—apart from the claims of the men themselves—what the war truly may have contributed to the severity of physical ailments that could just as easily have stemmed from aging and the physical toll taken by nineteenth-century working environments.

Military service affected men, however, both physically and emotionally. In a few instances, men exposed to the severe conditions of the war clearly exhibited psychological symptoms in the years after their discharge similar to what psychologists now diagnose as war neurosis or post-traumatic stress syndrome. William Donovan, for example, was twenty-two when he enlisted as a private in Company D of the 17th Wisconsin. A farmer from Watertown, Wisconsin, Donovan reenlisted as a veteran volunteer in the winter of 1864 and was mustered out with his regiment in June of 1865. A healthy young man when he marched off to war, he returned home changed. Hearing of his pending arrival, his family planned to meet him at the train depot to welcome him home. When they arrived, Donovan was not there. He had "gone across the prairie to town from the junction [and] they found him drilling in the street alone with his gun." When his family finally found him "he shook hands and was glad to see them, but [could give them] no reason why he had left the junction." In a state of constant excitement, "he would run around after his sisters and keep laughing; would get angry if he didn't have his own way." The officer assigned to investigate Donovan's pension application in 1885 noted that the soldier's dementia first appeared during service and had plagued him ever since.[37]

Thiron Ingham was close to Donovan's age when he enlisted in Company A of the 17th Wisconsin in March of 1862. He was discharged at war's end in April of 1865. Like Donovan, Ingham also returned from the war suffering from severe mental debilities, noted by doctors in 1896 to be chronic melancholia, or severe depression. By 1898, when a pension application was submitted in his name, Thiron was fifty-five and in a desperate state. He had returned to his hometown, and though his family and relatives had taken care of him for many years, it seems they had become incapable of continuing to do so. By 1898, if still alive his father would have been ninety-one and his mother approaching seventy. The family owned upwards of $6,000 in property in 1870, and Thiron was the oldest of nine children. Yet by 1898 he found himself confined to the county poor house, his family having seemingly deserted the aging and feeble-minded veteran, and the soldiers' home refusing to take in a man who required round-the-clock attention.[38]

Ingham's situation was dire, and it is not difficult to imagine how men with psychological disorders were greeted on their arrival home and in their everyday interactions with the community at large. Physically whole, they must have appeared an odd and sometimes terrifying reminder of the far-reaching impact of the war. Not all psychological issues were, however, as readily apparent as the examples described above. James Begley, for example, returned home to Bridgeport, Connecticut in 1866 and attempted to return to work as a bricklayer for mason and builder John Barr. Patrick McCarrick, Barr's foreman, was forced to lay Begley off after three weeks because "he did not seem to have any control over himself, showed great nervousness, his hands trembled so, and he trembled bodily, so much that he could not do the brick laying and plastering in which he was employed." Other soldiers in the Ninth Connecticut filed pensions citing similar complaints of "nervousness" or "nervous debility" as a component of their disability. For veterans such as Ebenezer Wescott, who sat for months in trenches outside of Vicksburg and Atlanta and whose letters illuminate the stress that the men were under day in and day out, it would not be implausible to suggest that they, too, may have experienced at least minor psychological debility, though it did not noticeably limit their daily activities.[39]

While men often noted "nervousness" in their pension claims, it usually appeared as a secondary condition, just one component of their numerous debilities. Thus, among the pensioners in this study, psychological trauma as the contributing factor to postwar disability seems to be the exception rather than the norm. Very few pensioners made specific reference to these types of problems as the sole factor in their debility, and even where veterans' home records for a large sample exist, it is difficult to determine how widespread psychological issues or difficulties were. For example, 66 veterans from these regiments (57 from the 23rd Illinois, 8 from the 17th Wisconsin, and 1 from the Ninth Connecticut) were admitted to the veteran's home at Quincy, Illinois between 1887 and 1915. Physicians cited only three of these men as exhibiting mental instability, though it is impossible to determine with any degree of accuracy what exactly their psychological issues were. In addition, as is case with myriad other issues that befell soldiers in the years after the war, it is rather difficult to assess what noncombat injuries were actually caused by the veterans' time in the army.[40]

Many veterans returned from war, reentered the workforce, and actively pursued opportunities at home and afar with the hope of advancing themselves. It is reasonable to assume that most veterans returned to their antebellum homes after they mustered out of service, though the time they spent there varied based on access to employment, a struggle for the nearly one million men left unemployed after the war. Notions of Manifest Destiny and the relationship between American freedom and perceptions of socioeconomic success may very well have motivated veterans to venture off in pursuit of opportunities, just as they had motivated generations of Americans, immigrant and native born. Opportunities could be seized, fortunes could be won, so long as one was willing to reach for them.[41]

Pensioners moved. Of the pensioned veterans from the Ninth Connecticut traced in this study, 60 percent made Connecticut their permanent home. By the end of the century, the remaining 40 percent had scattered throughout the country. For pensioners from Mulligan's Irish Brigade, only 32 percent remained permanently in Illinois, and the rest spread across the United States, though Kansas and Minnesota appear to have been the preferred destinations for nearly one-quarter of those men. A little more than half of the men who mustered out of the 17th Wisconsin remained close to their prewar residences. As with the veterans from the other two regiments, many others moved throughout the nation in pursuit of employment and financial stability.[42]

Employment and security encouraged some returning veterans to set down roots in the hometowns they had left four years before. John Curtis, recipient of the Congressional Medal of Honor for his courage at the Battle of Baton Rouge in 1862, had left school in 1861 to join the Ninth Connecticut. A clerk by trade, Curtis found work after his discharge at a small grocery store in Hilton Head, South Carolina, where he was employed for one year from 1864 until 1865. Returning to Bridgeport, Connecticut shortly thereafter, he went to work as an accountant with the Adams Express Company. Curtis claimed that his service in the army had incapacitated him for any type of manual labor. Furthermore, his disability restricted his opportunities, as he could only work in occupations where he could sit at a desk. Yet this claim belies the fact that he held what could be considered white-collar positions. Ultimately, his inability to perform manual labor did not affect his ability to earn a living as a clerk in the offices of the Adams Express. But Curtis's administrative and clerical duties gave him some degree of job security, and he noted, somewhat proudly, that during this whole period he "still retained my residency in Bridgeport . . . never losing my voting privilege" there. Curtis's pride in his hometown is subtle, but within a very mobile late-nineteenth-century society, by maintaining his voting privileges he illustrated a sense of loyalty and security within that community that was reinforced by his stable job.[43]

Lieutenant Thomas Moore returned to Chicago, where he received a commission in the city's police force and served in that capacity from 1865 until his death in 1881. Hugh Dorsey was twenty-four when he was mustered out of the service in July of 1865. Though a prewar resident of Fond du Lac, Wisconsin, immediately after the war Dorsey moved to Chicago, where he worked as a laborer for twenty years at the North Chicago Rolling Mill. Though his work suffered from war-related disabilities, according to associates Dorsey was favored by his foreman, and was allowed to come and go as he pleased. This situation gave him relative security despite being an unskilled laborer, though his pay suffered from his inability to work full time. For many returning veterans, however, and especially for those employed as common laborers, this type of stability was not guaranteed, and this could be attributed to a combination of factors including an excess number of unemployed men as well as disabilities attributed to war-time service. Similarly, Adam Blaul returned home to Chicago immediately after the war. A German-born farmer, Blaul served with the 23rd Illinois at Lexington, was taken prisoner and paroled, and traveled around Illinois and Wisconsin in search of work before he reenlisted in the First Wisconsin Heavy Artillery in 1864. After the war Blaul returned to Chicago where in 1868 he met and married recent immigrant Louise Netz (she had been in the United States for just three weeks when they first met). The two lived in Chicago until Blaul's death, with the exception of the three years between 1878 and 1881 when the couple moved to Terre Haute, Indiana, most likely in search of work.[44]

Economically motivated moves, even excursions that lasted only a few years and took the veteran and his family relatively short distances from their hometown, appear to have been relatively commonplace for pensioners from these regiments. Mobility was a large part of the lives of Irish men and women before, during, and after the war, as Americans of all ethnic backgrounds sought opportunities to advance themselves. Members of the laboring classes, especially those living in the Midwest, often moved during the antebellum period as they chased after the many jobs that came with the sudden growth of communities in those areas. Daniel Quirk's experiences prior to the war, though extreme, provides some insight into these types of economically motivated moves. Discharged from the regular army in 1857, Quirk returned home briefly to visit his family in Chicago before taking a contract for mason work in St. Louis, where he stayed for over a year. When that contract expired he again returned to Chicago where he was hired as an agent for a liquor house, a job that sent him to New Orleans, where he lived and worked until the outbreak of war in 1861. Private Thomas Heffernan was equally mobile in the decade before the war, though his movement was a result of family hardship rather than any active search for employment. He and his mother migrated from Ireland to New York in 1850 when he was only a child. They lived in New York until 1853, when they moved to Chicago. His mother died the following year, and Thomas, only thirteen at the time, bounced from family member to family member in Illinois and Missouri before finally enlisting in the 23rd Illinois in 1861. Such as evidence of the birthplace of children noted in the 1860 census further illustrates, many immigrants, especially those living in Wisconsin at that time, made a number of stops on their journey to their adopted state.[45]

Movement after the war seems to have been motivated by a number of factors. Financial hardship, word of work opportunities, desire for land, and friendships that continued after the war all played some role in decisions to move away from the familiar community. Soldiers often moved within states in search of employment. Such was the case of Addis Payne who, during the five years prior to his enlistment, moved between Watertown and Bridgeport, Connecticut, where he was employed in the manufacturing of sewing machines and sewing machine needles. Many soldiers, however, before setting off to work, returned home to the towns where they had grown up. Thomas Dolan's affidavit provides significant insight into his decision to eventually move across the country from New Haven, Connecticut to Oakland, California. Born in County Clare, Ireland, Dolan worked as a clockmaker in New Haven before he enlisted in the Ninth Connecticut. He contracted rheumatism in his arms and left side in the spring of 1862 while in Mississippi, and the disease left him unable to continue in a trade that required precision craftsmanship. Returning to New Haven in 1865, Dolan worked for three weeks at the New Haven Clock Company before taking a job at the American Needle and Fishhook Company, a position that "was not hard but it required some skill." In 1870 he took another position at Malary Wheeler and Company, Lock Maker, where he worked as a contractor until the financial panic of 1873 caused the company to close, forcing Dolan to return to his job making fishhooks. In 1887 he left for California and began "working for firm of McGovern and Cahil doing boys work my pay is small and I dust furniture sweep the store and do errand for the men." The firm was owned by "an officer in the same Regiment [the Ninth Connecticut] and thats why I happened to get the work."[46]

In 1868 James Orr left his wife Mary in Manchester, Connecticut, to travel to California. The veteran "left for California to better himself not because of any trouble." He arrived in San Francisco in April, with plans to move north to Oregon as soon as he earned enough money to pay his passage. Soon after his arrival he wrote encouragingly home that "i have not got any work yet but i expect it in a few days work will be plenty in one month and i like the Country verry well it is the nicest Country i have been in yet." He asked her to make all the preparations to be ready to travel to join him as soon as possible. Apparently they did not have the money to travel to California as a family, and his letters suggest that they had decided he would go first with the purpose of raising money to bring the rest of the family west to join him. In May he sent further instructions to her for her trip, warning Mary to be careful of herself and her belongings during her stay in New York, and suggesting that she purchase her ticket for a second-class cabin with the North American Company in Hartford before she and their young son William began their trek west.[47]

By December, the chance of the family reuniting appeared bleak. "Dear Mary," James wrote, "i got your letter and i think by the way you write that you dont Care whether you write to me any more or not i dont know what is the reason of it." For a couple that married just before the war and spent four years apart, the apparent change in heart is fascinating. Mary justified her decision on the grounds of her husband's drinking, which he in fact addressed in his last letter to her, noting his temperate lifestyle. His letters stopped after 1868, leading Mary to believe that he had died in California. Curiously, though, one wonders whether Mary's hesitancy to join her husband, and James's predilection for alcohol, were both derived from his disfiguration by a wound that had left him with one eye and a mangled nose. Regardless of the reasons, the lack of communication between James and Mary seems to have destroyed the marriage, though James appears to have held to the belief that he would eventually save a bit of money to return to his family.[48]

For some, the war instilled a sense of adventure and desire for advancement that occasionally led them to foreign countries. Silas Sawyer, formerly of the Ninth Connecticut, returned to New Orleans after the war, and became a fairly wealthy and influential man. His experiences during the occupation of that city had clearly helped him recognize the potential economic opportunities for a Northern officer with access to some funds. By 1870 he was married and owned two sugar plantations south of New Orleans as well as some property back north in Vermont. A member of the Levee Board in New Orleans, he was seen by some locals as a man of "a roving disposition and possessing the untiring energy and ambition of the typical yankee." He was also nearly bankrupt, having "so many irons in the fire that he finally had to sacrifice all he had." Ambition bred ambition and Sawyer, in pursuit of fortune, "went to that Mecca of the fortune-hunter of this section, Central America," where he worked at a variety of endeavors, "always dabbling in something [as] a first class hustler." He continued, according to affidavits, to pursue various undertakings until July 11, 1897, when he was found murdered at his camp in Belize. In both Orr's and Sawyer's cases, the men left their families to pursue fortune abroad, and as years passed, their letters home became less and less frequent. These individuals demonstrate the lengths to which men were willing to go in the postwar years to secure financial stability for themselves and their families.[49]

Opportunities in the West provided men with access to land and improved working conditions not necessarily available in their home communities. Irish immigrant Michael Doolan, for example, was a brass worker in Derby, Connecticut when he and his brother James enlisted in the Ninth Connecticut. He was single and owned no property and, for these reasons, it is easy to see why he may not have been drawn to return home to Connecticut after the war. After he mustered out of the Ninth Connecticut, Doolan joined the regular army. He seems to have had few connections in Connecticut outside of his immediate family, which may have made it easier for him to decide to leave home, both to join the Ninth as a volunteer, and then to enlist in the regular army. Four years later, in 1869, he was discharged from the army at Fort Stanton, New Mexico. Though the discharged soldiers were given the opportunity to travel home before the winter, Doolan rejected that offer and instead took up residence in Texas. Doolan worked at a number of jobs as a teamster for the Government, constructing public works and hauling goods to the frontier. Between 1873 and 1876 he found work as a railroad man, before settling in Cladwell, Texas, where he married and had six children. Although he never owned land, he did rent a substantial farm of nearly one hundred acres.[50]

Patrick Murphy followed a similarly transient lifestyle in the Pacific Northwest. An eighteen-year-old farmer when he enlisted in the 17th Wisconsin, Murphy was wounded during operations outside of Atlanta in 1864, struck by a minié ball in the left ankle, an injury that inhibited him from pursuing his trade as a lumberman after he left the army. Instead of returning home, he went west, living in six different places, following his job "teaming"—working as a teamster—which "did not remain long in any place." Murphy was part of what he referred to as a "floating population" and made no permanent acquaintances in any of those areas. He became one of America's transient workers, and his experiences provide stark imagery of the realities of postwar experience for many veterans, who sought financial stability for themselves and their families after they left the army.[51]

The movements of the aforementioned veterans may have been the extreme, but a large number of veterans were quite mobile, moving in search of employment; that was what drew men from place to place. In 1881, at age fifty-five, James Holland applied for a pension from the government. Holland had enlisted in the 23rd Illinois in the summer of 1861, then reenlisted and was discharged because of his health at New Creek, Virginia in August 1862. Unlike other soldiers who returned home too ill or disabled to find work, Holland returned home and reentered the workplace with vigor, which raises questions about the severity of the throat and lung disease that led to his discharge. During the war he moved throughout Illinois as an insurance agent for a company based in Chicago, a job he held for nearly eight years and one that ultimately took him to Kansas, where he settled with his wife and son. There Holland worked as a stock trader, and in the 1880 census noted his occupation as that of a farmer. When he applied for his pension in 1888 he stated that he was a sickly man; an affidavit described him as one who "if not for his iron will and general ambition . . . would have been dead years ago." Though he was unable to perform manual labor, this note provides a subtle clue into the realities of postwar life. Although Holland claimed he was disabled from physical labor, it seems that Holland had never had to make his living as a laborer, but also that this was not a man without control over his environment or the direction of his life. While ambition did not always manifest itself through socioeconomic success, the desire to advance nevertheless seems to have been a prevalent attitude among these veterans as they actively sought to make better lives for themselves and their families.[52]

In Connecticut, John McKenna was similarly mobile in the years after the war. After his discharge he moved slowly east from Norwich, living in towns along the Connecticut shore and Rhode Island before finally settling in East Brookfield, Massachusetts. A painter, McKenna claimed that he worked "when able to." But that statement downplays that fact that, apart from the diarrhea and fever that plagued him during his service in Louisiana, his moves reflected his constant search of work and were not a unique manifestation of trauma sustained while in the service. He was married, and while the family's living conditions do not appear to have been stable—they moved ten times between 1865 and 1888—it seems that these moves were directly related to a search for employment, as neither McKenna nor his wife claimed abject poverty in their pension applications.[53]

When McKenna finally applied for a pension, he did so not because of inability to operate within New England's postwar economy, but, more probably, due to the simple fact that as he got older there would have been growing appeal to a guaranteed monthly allowance as a form of compensation for his service thirty years before. Life for McKenna and his wife most likely continued as it had before the war. John pursued his trade and took steps to better his position through the pursuit of employment outside of his hometown. He made no great fortune, as evidenced by his application for a federal pension, but there never had been a guarantee that military service would lead to prosperity for the average volunteer. This type of movement from place to place, whether within the a home state or beyond, must have been part of the reality for most returning veterans as they, along with hundreds of thousands of their comrades, attempted to reintegrate themselves into society after four years at war.

John Connelly's experiences illuminate this trend more clearly than the previous examples. Connelly was twenty-five years old and working as laborer in Janesville, Wisconsin when he enlisted in the 17th Wisconsin. Two months after he mustered out of service he returned home, married, and spent the next sixteen years in Wisconsin, working at various occupations, peddling ice and laboring in the town's mill and foundry. In 1870 the family lived in the fourth ward of Janesville, where John had accumulated real estate valued at $1,000. Nine years later, the family decided to move to Minnesota, where they purchased a large farm of 160 acres. At the time of his death in 1905, John's holdings had expanded to nearly 220 acres of land, valued at nearly $3,000. The family made a conscious decision to move to Minnesota specifically to purchase a farm. This was a marked shift from the urban lifestyle that Connelly was accustomed to when he lived and worked in Janesville.[54]

Both John and his wife were Irish immigrants, and perhaps their decision to purchase a farm reflected a sort of nostalgia for the rural Irish lifestyle that grew as time and distance came between these immigrants and their original homeland. Or maybe they had simply grown tired of Janesville and sought to try their luck on the Minnesota frontier. Regardless of the reason, their decision ended up being a financially sound one, and the family appears to have done well for themselves. When John finally did apply for a pension, he made clear in the application that his debility had only recently manifested itself. Able to do a full day's work for most of his life, only in his old age did the veteran relent and apply for a pension, claiming disability from the combination of rheumatism and diarrhea. A veteran and his family need not have moved every year or every two years in order to fit the broad trend found among these men and their families. A single significant move motivated by the hope of socioeconomic advancement is enough. Veterans such as John Connelly, who moved with his family from Wisconsin to Minnesota in 1878 before settling and establishing roots in a new community, were still members of a somewhat transient group, part of a continuing trend of mobility among the midwestern population that can be traced to the early nineteenth century.[55]

While experiences at home during and after the Civil War are typically analyzed through a lens of individual and public patriotism and support for the Union war effort, the experiences of men who mustered out during and after the war provide important insight into the impact of military service on the men who donned blue uniforms. The reassimilation of veterans into their communities, or the attempts of veterans to reenter the social worlds they had left behind, has been largely glossed over in the historiography, which has tended to create what Peter Carmichael has characterized as a "distorted portrait of Civil War veterans as a lost generation."[56] The narrative of the disaffected veteran, wounded and cast apart from society, was certainly true for some men who returned home as broken shells of their former selves. Many veterans experienced hardship as they negotiated postwar America in search of stability and success. But their experiences were by no means unique, because many Americans, veterans and otherwise, immigrants and native born, struggled to secure their place in the burgeoning cities and towns of late-nineteenth-century America. For the veterans of these Irish regiments from Connecticut, Illinois, and Wisconsin, their postwar lives were a mixture of success and failure, of hardship and triumph. Ancillary information from their pension files suggests that although the war stayed with them, their wounds and debilities often serving as constant reminders of their sacrifice for their nation, they were by no means disconnected from or rejected by their communities. Often proud of their service, these veterans were active participants in the social and economic development of the United States after mid-century and actively pursued opportunities to better themselves and solidify their place within American society.

The men and their families quickly transitioned back to civilian life, though the move from soldier back to civilian was not always easy. These veterans can be broadly divided into two categories. The first is the walking wounded, those who were mustered out during the war and returned home to become constant reminders of the true impact of military service on troops. These men struggled; the debilities that kept them from the front lines also kept them from finding gainful employment, and their lingering difficulties affected their families as well. The second category is men who served their time and mustered out after the surrender of Confederate forces in the spring of 1865. Able enough (even if they had been constantly plagued by various illnesses during the war), these volunteers returned home and attempted to reenter the workforce they had left years before. Although they often claimed that whatever chronic health problems or disabilities they coped with resulted from military service, and while these veterans were likely reminded daily of their time in the army, there is little to suggest that those four years significantly influenced how the men viewed their relationship to American society. These veterans, as their pension files illustrate, were proud of their service. Their pension applications provide a glimpse into the lives of a group of men who were active participants in the social and economic development of the United States after mid-century. Their experiences illuminate the pursuit of economic opportunities and the availability of advancement to men, regardless of ethnic background, and the lengths to which veterans from these regiments would go to secure a place for themselves in postwar America.

# Conclusion. Irish Americans in the Civil War: Myth and Memory

In 1903 veterans of the Ninth Connecticut, along with their friends and family and other prominent members of the New Haven community, dedicated a monument in honor of the regiment's service in Bay View Park, within sight of Long Island Sound. This monument represented "a world of memories, a world of deeds, a world of tears, and a world of glories." The veterans hoped that this stark column of granite, topped with a Union infantryman, would "look down upon the boys of this city and state, that may tread upon these beautiful walks leading to our handsome park, for generations to come and will not let them sleep when their country calls them." The monument still stands in honor of the fallen soldiers of the Ninth Connecticut, even though Bay View Park has been dissected by Interstate 95. Every November a number of family members, re-enactors, and members of the Knights of Columbus gather in a wreath-laying ceremony. The ceremony is not large, but it is rife with Irish and Catholic symbolism, a tribute to the unit's heritage. It is attended by the few men and women most dedicated to preserving the memories of their relatives who fought in Connecticut's Irish Regiment. The descendants of these men are, rightly, bothered by the fact that the Ninth Connecticut has been largely left out of the historical narrative of Irish service in the war, and some years ago they successfully petitioned for its inclusion in a number of memorials including, in 2009, a monument at Vicksburg National Military Park dedicated to the regiment's service in the summer of 1862 building Grant's Canal.[1]

Veterans of the 23rd Illinois and 17th Wisconsin also met periodically during the late nineteenth and early twentieth centuries. In the summer of 1907 the state of Wisconsin placed ten monuments at Vicksburg to commemorate the Wisconsin regiments, including the 17th Volunteer Infantry, who served there in the summer of 1863. That same year the state appropriated over $100,000 to construct a state monument on the battlefield. During the latter half of the nineteenth century, veterans of the 23rd Illinois periodically gathered at Chicago's Calvary Cemetery, where James Mulligan lies buried, to decorate his grave and the graves of their comrades in arms. A monument to the colonel was erected there in 1885. These were celebrations very befitting of the late colonel, whose final words were allegedly "Lay me down and save the flag." Even in death his prominence continued to overshadow the deeds of the men who served in his command.[2]

The legacy of all three of these Irish regiments is complex, reflecting a collision of ethnic and American identities in the postwar era. While efforts were made to memorialize Irish American service to the Union cause by men such as David Conyngham, William Corby, and St. Clair Mulholland, who wrote about the Irish Brigade, the men from Connecticut, Illinois, and Wisconsin remained largely obscure in these efforts. The paucity of published postwar accounts from veterans of these units, combined with the fact that these regiments were not part of the famed Irish Brigade, have most likely contributed to the fact that accounts of their actions have been missing from broader postwar attempts to secure a place for the Irish in histories of the war. In fact, only one regimental history was published, and this in 1903 by a historian who did not himself serve in the Ninth Connecticut, the regiment he wrote about. The lack of published accounts certainly does not mean that the veterans did not remember or were not proud of their service, but it has meant that few aside from the veterans themselves would ever know of their exploits. Many veterans, though, returned home after their mustering out and participated in a variety of civic and political activities, and expressed an array of fluid identities in the postwar years that can be traced to their service.[3]

Fenianism, a movement present in all three states prior to the outbreak of war in 1861, continued to play a significant role in Irish American politics after the war and contributed to strengthening the identity of the Irish American diaspora. In 1864 a Fenian Congress met in Chicago. From New Creek, Virginia, James Mulligan sent $100 in support of the endeavor, concluding his note that "if, by the grace of God, and the consent of the United States, we come to blows in support of this same holy cause [of Irish independence], then, having first solidly settled the present question in favour of the Union, I devote all my heart, and all my strength, and whatever experience I possess, 'to aid in establishing and maintaining the cause of Irish Nationality.'" The congress promised to be the "largest ever held in this country . . . [and] the first of its kind," and its immediate result was an increase in American control over Fenian activity, both in the United States and in Ireland. Animosity had grown between James Stephens, the founder and "Head Center" of the Irish Republican Brotherhood (the official name of the organization, used mainly in Ireland) and the American Fenians over funds and organization in Ireland. Broadly, Irish organizers in the United States became increasingly weary of delays in Ireland and viewed Stephens's leadership with concern, attitudes that were compounded by questions surrounding misuse by the "Fenian Chief" of monies from the Irish American community.[4]

Driven by the notion that the "Irish people are a distinct nationality and have a right to self-government," Fenian organizers in the United States increasingly focused on support for what they assumed was the pending revolution in Ireland. Discord grew between the Irish and American branches, however, as leaders in the United States grew increasingly frustrated with the Stephens's idleness. For his part, Stephens was equally frustrated with his American counterparts, who he felt did not know or did not appreciate the political situation in Ireland. He wrote succinctly to the Fenian Brotherhood Central Council in July 1865, "It has become difficult—that is *dangerous*—to meet in any numbers." Increased English presence in Ireland during the 1860s as a means of curtailing revolutionary activity hampered the organizational capability of the Irish Republican Brotherhood, and belied the initial assessment by Stephens in the late 1850s that "Ireland was never in a better condition for such a project" as the organization of a revolutionary movement. Interestingly, as Irish organization floundered—despite overtly optimistic accounts by Stephens that suggested a widespread commitment to his cause—Irish Americans became increasingly motivated, and early difficulties in raising funds in support of the movement seemed to vanish during the first half of the 1860s. "I am firmly impressed," one American observer in Ireland wrote optimistically in the summer of 1865, "with the belief that at least three-fourths of the population are patriotic and that the greater part of that number would readily join in any movement calculated to free the country from the hated yoke of England."[5]

References to Fenian organization appeared throughout the war. The *New Haven Palladium* described the Fenians as a group of "citizens of the United States of Irish birth or descent," who "declare their allegiance to the constitution and the laws of the United States . . . [and] . . . ask the moral influence of every American loyal to the principles of self-government" for their support. As the spring of 1865 turned to summer and the news of Lee's surrender and Lincoln's assassination faded into not-too-distant memory, the Irish nationalist movement gained increasing notoriety among the press for its organization efforts and the growing animosity between the movement and the Catholic Church—an issue that editors in Connecticut, Illinois, and Wisconsin all commented on with an interest that suggests that subtle currents of nativist ideology still ran just beneath the surface in all three states. In August 1865 in Milwaukee, a Fenian speaker addressed a packed crowd. The *Milwaukee Daily Sentinel* described his standing on a stage "ornamented with the American flag, side by side with the green silk banner bearing the harp of Erin," and how the orator, "after dwelling eloquently upon the glory and shame of Ireland, the patriotism of her sons, both in the land of their nativity and that of their adoption, and their love of liberty, as shown both here and there, explained the objectives of the Fenian brotherhood." The response of the crowd, noted the editors of the *Sentinel*, suggested that Fenian membership would grow quickly in Milwaukee. In Connecticut that same month, a "Grand Fenian Picnic" was held in Terryville, attracting a number of observers. Another rally in early September was well attended, and the crowd listened to a speech about "the past wrongs, present hope, and future prospects of Ireland."[6]

The soldiers in the Ninth Connecticut, 17th Illinois, and 23rd Wisconsin were undoubtedly attuned to the political environment both at home and abroad during this period. Broadly, the mens' decision to enlist under commanding officers who were known Fenians, a trend found in both the Ninth Connecticut and 23rd Illinois, suggests an awareness of the Irish national question, an impression reinforced by the fact that before the war many of the enlistees had openly participated in militia and community organizations that espoused ties to Ireland and Irish heroes. The relationship in Wisconsin was less pronounced, though the prevailing attitudes among the Democratic press in the state suggest a fairly strong Fenian presence there as well. There were soldiers in all three regiments who were very open in their political allegiances, although they were the exception rather than the norm. Political activity in support of Irish nationalism at home and abroad provides some insight into the varied postwar experiences of soldiers who had fought in these regiments as they sought to preserve a place for themselves and their ideologies within the broader historical narrative.

Members of avowed Fenian militia units in Connecticut played a vital role in the organization of the Ninth Connecticut, and in Chicago James Mulligan was a vocal supporter of the movement. The Fenian presence was also strong in the Midwest, and while there are few record of veterans from these regiments returning to Ireland, they nevertheless threw themselves into the political fray. When the 17th Wisconsin arrived home from the war the regiment was met "by a large representation of the Fenian Brotherhood . . . who escorted it through the streets." Newspapers in the Badger State reported with interest the growing

"Fenian excitement" in Ireland, England, Canada, and the United States during the fall and winter of 1865. Observers in Illinois were equally fascinated with the growth of Fenianism. This society "seems to comprise a very liberal and intelligent class of our Irish population," noted editors of the Bloomington, Illinois *Pantagraph*. "We trust that the Fenians are yet destined to exert a powerful influence in behalf of the regeneration of Ireland." At a large picnic in August 1865 held in that city, guests were treated to a lengthy oration on Irish nationalism. The spirits of past revolutionaries, the speaker noted, were "looking down upon them and smiling upon their efforts, there [where] the Irish soldiers of the Irish republic meet and swear to free their native land or die." Calling for more than $2 million to arm the revolutionaries in Ireland, the speaker, pointing to an Irish banner, promised that "before the next summer's sun sends down his warm rays upon the wheat fields of Ireland, this flag will be unfurled, surrounded by a hundred thousand bayonets," and his words were met with "tumultuous applause." The *Madison County Courier* of Edwardsville, Illinois, a town that was home to a large contingent of the original volunteers to Mulligan's Irish Brigade, reported Fenian celebrations in New York City on the anniversary of the British evacuation of Manhattan in 1783. In January 1866 Fenians in Chicago met and subscribed five hundred rifles and saw "arrangements made for the arming and equipping of two regiments, to be ready when required."[7]

Ultimately, the Fenian movement that emerged in the 1860s was unsuccessful in its stated goal of overthrowing English rule in Ireland. English authorities quickly put down the 1867 uprising in Ireland, and Irish American invasions of Canada that were launched between 1866 and 1871 were more comical than anything else. In Connecticut, Illinois, and Wisconsin, the Fenian Brotherhood remained an important social and political organization among the Irish American community, and funds raised by these men directly contributed to growth of the Irish Republican Army and the successful overthrow of British rule in 1921. The prevalence of Irish nationalist ideology in these communities illustrates the continuity of ethnic identity and nationalist memory among Irish Americans in these states and suggests, perhaps, that military service reinforced the militancy of this immigrant group.

The memory of Irish service was reinforced in other ways as veterans sought to preserve their place in postwar America. The growth of the Grand Army of the Republic allowed veterans—regardless of their ethnicity—to commemorate their service and sacrifice in the defense of the Union war effort. Of the three regiments, only men from the 23rd Illinois actively organized a regiment specific GAR post, which was first composed primarily of soldiers from that regiment and was named for their commanding officer. The Col. James A. Mulligan Post was chartered in Chicago on July 20, 1883 to serve as a living legacy to the man who had laid down his life on the field of battle in the Shenandoah Valley twenty years before. The Mulligan Post played a vibrant role in Chicago's community during the last two decades of the nineteenth century, and the organization was key to the preservation of the legacy of Mulligan and the exploits of the 23rd Illinois. A major component of the memorialization of the war was the involvement of the veterans in Memorial Day celebrations. In particular, these men planned grand celebrations at Chicago's Calvary Cemetery, where "exercises centered around the grave of Colonel James A. Mulligan."[8]

The Mulligan Post sponsored innumerable social outings during the last years of the century, but its political involvement illuminates a shift in attitudes among veterans as the nation moved ever closer to reconciliation. When Grover Cleveland visited Chicago in 1887, the Irish of the city turned out en masse. Members of the Mulligan Post marched in line with local militia, the Hibernian Rifles, and the Clan-na-Gael Guards, to the tune of "Marching through Georgia." Their presence was well received by observers. Two years later they travelled to Milwaukee to attend the twenty-third national encampment of the Grand Army of the Republic. Chicago's *Daily Inter Ocean* reported that behind a banner on which was printed "Who Said We Wouldn't Come?" the men from the Mulligan Post intermingled with a number of other GAR posts, including "the John Brown Post (colored)." At least for a moment, then, the goals of the war had been realized and reinforced by veterans on the streets of Milwaukee.[9]

Sentiment seems to have shifted by the early 1890s. In 1893, for example, the post was "expected to participate in the ceremony to honor Confederates at Oakwoods Cemetery" in Chicago. Two years later, the issue of commemorating the Confederate dead divided the post. In May 1895 the post's commander spoke out against a proposed Confederate memorial for the city. It was, he noted, "idle to try and inculcate a patriotic spirit in the young generation by object lessons of devotion to the American flag if veterans are to take hand in honoring the Confederate dead." Two weeks later, however, at a ceremony at Calvary Cemetery, an opposing chord was struck when another speaker proclaimed,

> The Colonel Mulligan post is significant, because it has come not only to decorate the grave of Colonel Mulligan and other Union dead, but while a tear is shed for the memory of our old-time comrades, we are present also to place a wreath upon the resting places of our former foemen, whose memory

> we honor. There is no North, no South, no embitterment's, no sectionalism; but one Union forever and honor to the American soldier, contender and defender.

It is unclear whether this reflected the broader shift toward reconciliation that historians such as David Blight and John Neff have identified as part of the nation-building process that occurred in the late nineteenth and early twentieth centuries, or whether this was something more personal—for the men of the 23rd had stood guard over Confederate prisoners at Camp Douglas during 1861 and 1862. Regardless of what drove the commemoration of Confederate dead, what is important here is the public role that the Mulligan Post played in reinforcing, at least locally, the service and sacrifice of the men of the 23rd Illinois.[10]

Veterans in Connecticut and Wisconsin seemingly made no effort to form GAR posts to preserve the legacy of their individual Irish regiments. A number of officers from the 9th Connecticut were members of the Admiral Foote Post in New Haven, a socially and politically active GAR post, but one that did not reinforce or memorialize any ethnic or regimental-specific ideologies. In both these states, the service of the Irish regiments largely slipped into obscurity, save for occasional reunions and, in the case of the Ninth Connecticut, the dedication of the monument in New Haven at the turn of the century.

The memory and memorialization of these Irish regiments is complex. Locally, men from each state sought to preserve the memory of their service and sacrifice to the Union cause. In public commemorations two key identities, Irish and American, were often intertwined. These volunteers had defended the Union and, in doing so, had also proven the loyalty of the much-maligned Irish American population.

In spite of their sacrifice, however, all three of these regiments have remained mere footnotes within the broader narrative of ethnic experience in the Civil War, overshadowed by the exploits of the units in the Irish Brigade and more famous Irish American soldiers such as Philip Sheridan, Michael Corcoran, William Corby, and St. Claire Mulholland. It is probable that the theaters where these regiments served kept them from the national spotlight during the war. Certainly the heroics of the 23rd Illinois at Lexington in 1861 caught the attention of a much-beleaguered Northern public, but the darlings of Mulligan's Irish Regiment were soon overshadowed by the larger confluence of military events. The men from Connecticut, in spite of their close relationship before the war with the men of the 69th New York, and those from Wisconsin, marched to war in 1861 and 1862 with little fanfare outside of what was provided by their local newspapers. Though they served valiantly throughout the war, little attention was paid to the sacrifice of these Irishmen in the far-flung battles of the Western theater. Certainly, a degree of fate was involved in the rise in popularity of the Irish Brigade in the Army of the Potomac. The Eastern theater, along the Washington-Richmond axis, was viewed by many as the chief theater of the war, and the battles there took on a significance that was driven as much by perception as by tactical importance. This, combined with the incredibly high casualty rates sustained by the regiments in the Irish Brigade at Antietam, Fredericksburg, Gettysburg, and Cold Harbor, cast these specific ethnic soldiers into a class of their own, and their heroics became synonymous with Irish service. It is not too far-fetched, perhaps, to think that veterans from Connecticut, Illinois, and Wisconsin took some comfort in the conclusions that many Americans drew, linking Irishness to ferocity on the battlefield.

But geography alone is insufficient to explaining the historical obscurity of these regiments. More important, perhaps, was the lack of physical memorialization in the wake of the war. While members of the 23rd Illinois did honor their fallen commander, references to ethnic heritage appeared of secondary importance. But perhaps more interesting is the fact that not a single regimental history was written by a veteran of any of these three regiments. In a postwar society that championed the regimental history, the lack of this type of memorialization is in and of itself a subtle commentary on the connection (or lack-thereof) that the soldiers felt with their units and the atmosphere to which they returned. Regimental histories of ethnic units published in the aftermath of the war were imbued with the rhetoric of inclusion and assimilation. Regimental historians who sought to preserve the role of their ethnic units within the broader narrative of the war created works that were, as Craig Warren has remarked, "remarkable for [their] propensity to mythologize Irish participation in the Civil War, North and South." Furthermore, within the framework of the growth of American nationalism during the postwar era, Irish military service took on what Warren Young has called the "theme of 'quid pro quo,' that is, full support of the war effort on the part of the minority and its leadership in return for full citizenship rights or other benefits for minority-group members." The fact that the men from all three of these regiments seemed to simply melt back into their communities seems to imply that these veterans felt little need to underline their service to the Union through the ethnic language espoused by their counterparts in the Irish Brigade.[11]

Certainly consciousness of ethnicity was not absent from the initial organization of the regiments in Connecticut, Illinois, and Wisconsin, and men flocked to join these units and prove not only their loyalty to the Union but also the prowess of the Irish. Ethnic imagery was complemented by ethnicity-based hierarchies within the regiments themselves, for although they were not completely manned by Irish-born volunteers, clear trends existed in all three units. Among officers and noncommissioned officers, for example, Irish-born men far outnumbered those from the United States and other nations. The Irish-born presence in the ranks in all three regiments was significant, and even the 17th Wisconsin, which had, proportionally, the smallest contingent of ethnic soldiers, boasted a visibly Irish component that drew the attention of observers. The Irish were boisterous in their displays of ethnic pride during the recruiting and initial organization of all three of these regiments. The connections between these units and the Irish communities at home were reinforced at times throughout the war, although publicly these connections were in no way as strong as those that existed among the Irish regiments from New York, Massachusetts, and Pennsylvania and their hometowns.

Unfortunately, however, little direct evidence remains to help us understand what motivated soldiers to enlist in the Ninth Connecticut, 23rd Illinois, and 17th Wisconsin. Recruiting rhetoric certainly alluded to dual motives—loyalty to the Union and to Ireland—and the success that recruiters had in convincing men to volunteer certainly suggests the intrinsic appeal of these messages, at least among Irish-born and Irish American soldiers. But to make any broad assertions regarding individual motivations is problematic, as the evidence simply does not exist in either wartime or postwar writings. What we can derive though, is equally important. Volunteers in these three regiments enlisted from communities throughout their states, and the relationships between recruits—ethnic and non-ethnic—often flourished first in these smaller communities before the war began. Men often chose to enlist together in a company under a known community leader, and while ethnic ties did sometimes appear to influence this decision, more often than not recruiting patterns followed those typically associated with Civil War enlistments broadly.

Enlistment practices and, in particular, ethnic enlistments varied by community and state. Enlistments in the Ninth Connecticut appear to have followed more traditional ethnic recruiting trends, namely, large cohorts of Irish-born men enlisting together from a specific town or city, while much more diverse patterns were found in company-level organization in Illinois and Wisconsin.

Nevertheless, a common theme does emerge—the lack of a common urban-ethnic recruiting center. While historians have often viewed the ethnic ward or neighborhood as the single most important factor in the formation of ethnic regiments, none of these regiments exhibited this characteristic. Units were geographically diverse and came together from communities throughout their individual states, uniting ethnic and non-ethnic soldiers in regiments that reflected the demographics of the state more than they did individual ethnic neighborhoods. What is abundantly clear is that for many of these soldiers, local communities were as important to their identity as their ethnic heritage. While their decision to serve in an Irish unit made them unique, the reality was that Irish regiments were themselves diverse manifestations of local and state communities, linked together only by a loose ethnic identity. This diversity among the regiments—in their wartime experiences, on the home front, and in the preservation and memorialization of their service—highlights the truly complex nature of ethnic service. Put simply, although the memory and legacy of these regiments has been shrouded in the emerald green of Ireland—drawing these men into a shared ethnic experience that began in 1861 and continues through this day—service in an Irish regiment did not necessarily yield shared experiences, and Irish regiments were not all the same. The experiences of these American soldiers serving in Irish regiments and the experiences of their families provide important insights into the impact of the Civil War and illuminate the complexity of the immigrant experience during the nineteenth century.

# Appendices

# Appendix A

*Nationality of Volunteers by Company*

| 9th Connecticut, Company A | |
|---|---|
| Canada | 1 |
| England | 2 |
| Germany | 1 |
| Holland | 1 |
| Ireland | 79 |
| Scotland | 1 |
| United States | 13 |

| 9th Connecticut, Company B | |
|---|---|
| Canada | 1 |
| England | 1 |
| Ireland | 81 |
| Scotland | 2 |
| United States | 7 |
| Unknown | 2 |

| 9th Connecticut, Company C | |
|---|---|
| Canada | 1 |
| England | 5 |
| Ireland | 71 |
| United States | 13 |
| Unknown | 1 |

| 9th Connecticut, Company D | |
|---|---|
| Canada | 3 |
| England | 3 |
| France | 1 |
| Germany | 8 |

| | |
|---|---|
| Ireland | 58 |
| Scotland | 3 |
| United States | 14 |
| Unknown | 8 |

| 9th Connecticut, Company E | |
|---|---|
| England | 2 |
| Germany | 1 |
| Ireland | 60 |
| United States | 12 |

| 9th Connecticut, Company F | |
|---|---|
| England | 4 |
| Germany | 5 |
| Ireland | 21 |
| Switzerland | 1 |
| United States | 3 |

| 9th Connecticut, Company G | |
|---|---|
| Austria | 1 |
| Canada | 2 |
| England | 8 |
| France | 2 |
| Germany | 18 |
| Ireland | 46 |
| Italy | 1 |
| Scotland | 1 |
| Spain | 1 |
| Switzerland | 1 |
| United States | 12 |

| 9th Connecticut, Company H | |
|---|---|
| Cuba | 1 |
| Denmark | 1 |
| England | 5 |
| France | 1 |
| Germany | 1 |
| Holland | 1 |
| Ireland | 72 |
| Scotland | 1 |

| | |
|---|---|
| United States | 23 |
| Unknown | 1 |

| 9th Connecticut, Company I | |
|---|---|
| Canada | 2 |
| England | 3 |
| Ireland | 12 |
| United States | 74 |
| Unknown | 1 |

| 9th Connecticut, Company K | |
|---|---|
| Austria | 1 |
| Canada | 2 |
| England | 2 |
| France | 1 |
| Germany | 10 |
| Holland | 1 |
| Ireland | 30 |
| Scotland | 1 |
| Spain | 1 |
| United States | 33 |

| 23rd Illinois, Company A | |
|---|---|
| At Sea* | 2 |
| Canada | 8 |
| England | 11 |
| Germany | 3 |
| Ireland | 49 |
| Scotland | 4 |
| United States | 57 |
| Unknown | 48 |

*Born at sea, while immigrating

| 23rd Illinois, Company B | |
|---|---|
| Canada | 2 |
| England | 2 |
| Germany | 7 |
| Ireland | 72 |
| Scotland | 4 |
| United States | 15 |
| Unknown | 5 |

| 23rd Illinois, Company C | |
|---|---|
| At Sea | 1 |
| Canada | 8 |
| England | 12 |
| France | 2 |
| Germany | 7 |
| Ireland | 59 |
| Norway | 2 |
| Scotland | 3 |
| Sweden | 1 |
| United States | 81 |
| Unknown | 1 |

| 23rd Illinois, Company D | |
|---|---|
| Canada | 7 |
| England | 9 |
| France | 1 |
| Germany | 5 |
| Ireland | 12 |
| Norway | 1 |
| Sweden | 2 |
| United States | 76 |
| Unknown | 75 |

| 23rd Illinois, Company E | |
|---|---|
| Canada | 2 |
| England | 2 |
| Germany | 9 |
| Ireland | 26 |
| Scotland | 2 |
| United States | 35 |
| Unknown | 84 |

| 23rd Illinois, Company F | |
|---|---|
| Canada | 3 |
| France | 3 |
| Germany | 1 |
| Holland | 1 |
| Ireland | 135 |
| Scotland | 4 |

| | |
|---|---|
| United States | 21 |
| Unknown | 2 |

| 23rd Illinois, Company G | |
|---|---|
| Canada | 2 |
| England | 6 |
| Germany | 2 |
| Ireland | 71 |
| Norway | 1 |
| United States | 37 |
| Unknown | 59 |

| 23rd Illinois, Company H | |
|---|---|
| Canada | 3 |
| England | 5 |
| France | 1 |
| Germany | 3 |
| Ireland | 63 |
| Scotland | 1 |
| United States | 36 |
| Wales | 1 |
| Unknown | 1 |

| 23rd Illinois, Company I | |
|---|---|
| Canada | 3 |
| England | 2 |
| Germany | 1 |
| Ireland | 51 |
| Scotland | 1 |
| United States | 22 |

| 23rd Illinois, Company K | |
|---|---|
| Canada | 2 |
| England | 6 |
| France | 4 |
| Germany | 2 |
| Ireland | 84 |
| Scotland | 2 |
| Switzerland | 3 |
| United States | 24 |

| 17th Wisconsin, Company A | |
|---|---|
| Canada | 3 |
| England | 3 |
| Germany | 2 |
| Hungary | 1 |
| Ireland | 15 |
| Poland | 1 |
| Scotland | 1 |
| Switzerland | 2 |
| United States | 19 |
| Unknown | 10 |

| 17th Wisconsin, Company B | |
|---|---|
| Canada | 1 |
| England | 3 |
| France | 3 |
| Germany | 12 |
| Ireland | 46 |
| Norway | 2 |
| Scotland | 2 |
| United States | 25 |
| Unknown | 3 |

| 17th Wisconsin, Company C | |
|---|---|
| Canada | 9 |
| England | 6 |
| Germany | 2 |
| Ireland | 55 |
| Norway | 2 |
| Scotland | 3 |
| United States | 16 |
| Unknown | 4 |

| 17th Wisconsin, Company D | |
|---|---|
| Austria | 1 |
| Canada | 4 |
| England | 2 |
| France | 1 |
| Germany | 27 |

| | |
|---|---|
| Holland | 2 |
| Ireland | 20 |
| Scotland | 1 |
| United States | 27 |
| Unknown | 9 |

| 17th Wisconsin, Company E | |
|---|---|
| England | 1 |
| Germany | 3 |
| Ireland | 37 |
| Norway | 2 |
| Scotland | 3 |
| United States | 34 |
| Unknown | 8 |

| 17th Wisconsin, Company F | |
|---|---|
| Canada | 2 |
| England | 5 |
| France | 5 |
| Germany | 1 |
| Ireland | 75 |
| Norway | 1 |
| Scotland | 1 |
| Sweden | 3 |
| United States | 15 |
| Unknown | 2 |

| 17th Wisconsin, Company G | |
|---|---|
| Belgium | 22 |
| Canada | 30 |
| Denmark | 2 |
| France | 1 |
| Germany | 3 |
| Ireland | 2 |
| Norway | 1 |
| Scotland | 1 |
| Sweden | 3 |
| United States | 12 |
| Unknown | 7 |

| 17th Wisconsin, Company H | |
|---|---|
| Austria | 1 |
| Canada | 3 |
| Denmark | 1 |
| England | 3 |
| Germany | 6 |
| Ireland | 33 |
| Mexico | 1 |
| Netherlands | 1 |
| Switzerland | 1 |
| United States | 37 |
| Wales | 2 |
| Unknown | 9 |

| 17th Wisconsin, Company I | |
|---|---|
| Canada | 1 |
| Germany | 24 |
| Ireland | 7 |
| Norway | 1 |
| United States | 65 |
| Unknown | 3 |

| 17th Wisconsin, Company K | |
|---|---|
| Canada | 5 |
| England | 4 |
| Germany | 7 |
| Ireland | 8 |
| Scotland | 1 |
| Switzerland | 1 |
| United States | 66 |
| Unknown | 1 |

# Appendix B

*Counties of Birth of Irish Volunteers*

| 9th Connecticut Volunteers | |
|---|---|
| Antrim | 8 |
| Armagh | 8 |
| Carlow | 4 |
| Cavan | 24 |
| Clare | 19 |
| Cork | 48 |
| Derry | 5 |
| Donega | 19 |
| Down | 7 |
| Dublin | 25 |
| Fermanagh | 7 |
| Galway | 26 |
| Kerry | 18 |
| Kildare | 14 |
| Kilkenny | 21 |
| Kings | 10 |
| Laois | 2 |
| Leitrim | 55 |
| Limerick | 37 |
| Londonderry | 1 |
| Longford | 6 |
| Louth | 3 |
| Mayo | 7 |
| Meath | 17 |
| Monaghan | 3 |
| Offaly | 3 |
| Queens | 10 |
| Roscommon | 19 |
| Sligo | 8 |

| | |
|---|---|
| Tipperary | 41 |
| Tyrone | 11 |
| Waterford | 13 |
| Westmeath | 25 |
| Wexford | 4 |
| Wicklow | 1 |
| Unknown | 11 |
| **Total** | **530** |

23rd Illinois Volunteers

| | |
|---|---|
| Antrim | 5 |
| Armagh | 5 |
| Carlow | 2 |
| Cavan | 6 |
| Clare | 27 |
| Cork | 48 |
| Derry | 3 |
| Donegal | 5 |
| Down | 8 |
| Dublin | 22 |
| Femoy | 1 |
| Fermaugh | 1 |
| Galway | 78 |
| Kerry | 49 |
| Kildare | 5 |
| Kilkenny | 12 |
| Kings | 11 |
| Leittrim | 10 |
| Limerick | 35 |
| Longford | 8 |
| Louth | 4 |
| Mayo | 27 |
| Meath | 11 |
| Queens | 4 |
| Roscommon | 13 |
| Sligo | 7 |
| Tipperary | 32 |
| Tyrone | 3 |
| Waterford | 4 |
| Westmeath | 4 |

| | |
|---|---|
| Wexford | 5 |
| Wicklow | 5 |
| Unknown | 163 |
| **Total** | **623** |

| 17th Wisconsin Volunteers | |
|---|---|
| Antrim | 1 |
| Bangor | 1 |
| Cavan | 1 |
| Clare | 1 |
| Cork | 6 |
| Down | 2 |
| Dublin | 2 |
| Galway | 1 |
| Kerry | 1 |
| Kildare | 3 |
| Kilkenny | 2 |
| Limerick | 2 |
| Mayo | 1 |
| Meath | 1 |
| Monahan | 1 |
| Roscommon | 4 |
| Sligo | 1 |
| Tipperary | 3 |
| Waterford | 2 |
| Unknown | 262 |
| **Total** | **298** |

# Appendix C

*General Courts Martial*

| Regiment | Last Name | First Name | Rank | Ethnicity | Date of Offense | Location | Major Offense 1 | Offense 2 |
|---|---|---|---|---|---|---|---|---|
| 9 | Barker | Joshua | Pvt | US | 3/1/62 | Ship Island, MS | Slept on Guard | |
| 9 | Baylies | John | Pvt | US | 4/1/62 | Biloxi, MS | Insulting Language Officer | |
| 9 | Bently | Henry | Pvt | ENG | 9/1/63 | New Orleans, LA | Drunk on Duty | Drunk as a Sentinel |
| 9 | Buggy | Patrick | Pvt | UNK | 11/1/83 | New Orleans, LA | Left Guard Post | |
| 9 | Bulger | Anthony | Pvt | ENG | 11/1/63 | New Orleans, LA | Drunk and Disorderly | Struck a Sgt |
| 9 | Bulger | John | Lt | IRE | 8/1/64 | Washington, DC | Drunk and Disorderly | |
| 9 | Bulger | Anthony | Pvt | ENG | 6/1/62 | Baton Rouge, LA | Absence without leave | |
| 9 | Burke | John | Cpl | IRE | 1/1/63 | New Orleans, LA | Drunk and Disorderly | Language to Lt |
| 9 | Burns | Bernard | Pvt | IRE | 6/1/62 | Baton Rouge, LA | Drunk and Disorderly | |
| 9 | Burns | Lawrence | Pvt | IRE | 10/1/63 | New Orleans, LA | Absence without leave | |
| 9 | Carey | Thomas | Pvt | IRE | 1/1/63 | New Orleans, LA | Drunk on Duty | |

| | | | | | | | | |
|---|---|---|---|---|---|---|---|---|
| 9 | Clarke | Robert | Pvt | US | 1/1/63 | New Orleans, LA | Drunk and Disorderly | |
| 9 | Condon | Morris | Pvt | IRE | 1/1/63 | New Orleans, LA | Absence without leave | |
| 9 | Connell | Henry | Pvt | IRE | 2/1/65 | Savannah, GA | Disobedience | Disrespect |
| 9 | Connell | Henry | Pvt | IRE | 1/1/63 | New Orleans, LA | Absence without leave | |
| 9 | Connor | Thomas | Lt | IRE | 2/1/64 | | Neglect | Conduct Prejudicial |
| 9 | Corner | Charles | Pvt | ENG | 1/1/65 | New Orleans, LA | Desertion | |
| 9 | Costello | James | Pvt | IRE | 7/1/65 | Hilton Head, SC | Absence without leave | |
| 9 | Costello | James | Pvt | IRE | 10/1/63 | New Orleans, LA | Absence without leave | Language to Sgt |
| 9 | Costello | James | Pvt | IRE | 1/1/63 | New Orleans, LA | Quit his guard | |
| 9 | Cronan | Patrick | Pvt | IRE | 10/1/63 | New Orleans, LA | Drunk on Duty | Left post and commited nuisance |
| 9 | Cummings | Thomas | Pvt | IRE | 1/1/63 | New Orleans, LA | Drunk and Disorderly | Language to Lt |
| 9 | Cummings | James | Pvt | IRE | 10/1/63 | New Orleans, LA | Quit his guard | Brought prisoners Liquor |

| Regiment | Last Name | First Name | Rank | Ethnicity | Date of Offense | Location | Major Offense 1 | Offense 2 |
|---|---|---|---|---|---|---|---|---|
| 9 | Daly | Jeremiah | Pvt | | 10/1/63 | New Orleans, LA | Desertion | Enlisted in anotherr Regt |
| 9 | Dolan | Michael | Pvt | IRE | 8/1/64 | New Orleans, LA | Conduct Prejidicual | |
| 9 | Donohue | Patrick | Pvt | IRE | 9/1/63 | New Orleans, LA | Left Guard Post | |
| 9 | Dougherty | Robert | Pvt | IRE | 11/1/63 | New Orleans, LA | Desertion | |
| 9 | Doyle | Nicholas | Pvt | IRE | 6/1/72 | Baton Rouge, LA | Insulting Language Officer | Tried to kill Capt |
| 9 | Doyle | Nicholas | Pvt | IRE | 1/1/63 | New Orleans, LA | Conduct Prejidicual | |
| 9 | Duffy | John | Pvt | IRE | 2/1/64 | | | |
| 9 | Dunn | Thomas | Pvt | IRE | 3/1/63 | New Orleans, LA | Quit his guard | Conduct Prejudicial |
| 9 | Ellis | Thomas | Pvt | US | 1/1/63 | New Orleans, LA | Absence without leave | |
| 9 | Ellis | Thomas | Pvt | US | 4/1/62 | Biloxi, MS | Disobedience | |
| 9 | Flanagan | Peter | Pvt | IRE | 4/1/62 | Biloxi, MS | Conduct Prejidicual | |
| 9 | Foley | John | Pvt | IRE | 1/1/63 | New Orleans, LA | Conduct Prejidicual | Contempt |

| | | | | | | | | |
|---|---|---|---|---|---|---|---|---|
| 9 | Gordon | William | Pvt | IRE | 10/1/63 | New Orleans, LA | Quit his guard | |
| 9 | Gray | Patrick | Pvt | IRE | 9/1/63 | New Orleans, LA | Desertion | Conduct Prejudicial |
| 9 | Gregg | Dennis | Pvt | IRE | 1/1/63 | New Orleans, LA | Conduct Prejidicual | |
| 9 | Hagarty | John | Pvt | IRE | 1/1/63 | New Orleans, LA | Drunk and Disorderly | Language |
| 9 | Healy | John | Pvt | IRE | 2/1/65 | | Stealing | |
| 9 | Heavey | Michael | Pvt | IRE | 1/1/63 | New Orleans, LA | Contempt | Mutiny |
| 9 | Hefferman | John | Pvt | IRE | 1/1/63 | New Orleans, LA | Drunk on Duty | Conduct Prejudicial |
| 9 | Ingoldsby | Patrick | Lt | IRE | 3/1/63 | New Orleans, LA | Conduct Unbecoming | |
| 9 | Ingoldsby | Patrick | Lt | IRE | 6/1/63 | New Orleans, LA | Conduct Unbecoming | Conduct Prejudicial |
| 9 | Kelly | Michael | Pvt | IRE | 6/1/62 | Baton Rouge | Absence without leave | tried to strike colonel |
| 9 | Kelly | Thomas | Pvt | IRE | 9/1/63 | New Orleans, LA | Desertion | Absence without Leave |

| Regiment | Last Name | First Name | Rank | Ethnicity | Date of Offense | Location | Major Offense 1 | Offense 2 |
|---|---|---|---|---|---|---|---|---|
| 9 | Layden | James | Pvt | IRE | 1/1/63 | New Orleans, LA | Absence without leave | |
| 9 | Leader | John | Pvt | ENG | 1/1/63 | New Orleans, LA | Quit his guard | |
| 9 | Lynch | Hugh | Pvt | IRE | 5/1/65 | | Conduct Prejidicual | |
| 9 | Lynch | John | Pvt | IRE | 1/1/63 | New Orleans, LA | Drunk on Duty | |
| 9 | Lynch | Michael | Pvt | IRE | 3/1/62 | Ship Island, MS | Disobedience | |
| 9 | Lych | Hugh | Pvt | IRE | 10/1/63 | New Orleans, LA | Quit his guard | Drunk on Duty |
| 9 | Mahoney | Patrick | Pvt | IRE | 3/1/62 | Ship Island, MS | Conduct Prejidicual | |
| 9 | Maragin | Louis | Cpl | CUB | 11/1/63 | New Orleans, LA | Desertion | |
| 9 | McClune | John | Pvt | FRA | 1/1/63 | New Orleans, LA | Conduct Prejidicual | |
| 9 | McCormack | Peter | Pvt | IRE | 6/1/62 | Baton Rouge, LA | Absence without leave | |
| 9 | McGriff | Joseph | Pvt | IRE | 11/1/63 | New Orleans, LA | Slept on Guard | |
| 9 | McKern | James | Pvt | IRE | 10/1/64 | | Desertion | |
| 9 | McQuirk | Philip | Pvt | ENG | 4/1/62 | | Conduct Prejidicual | |

| | | | | | | | | |
|---|---|---|---|---|---|---|---|---|
| 9 | Mehan | William | Pvt | US | 1/1/63 | New Orleans, LA | Absence without leave | |
| 9 | Moore | William | Pvt | | 11/1/63 | New Orleans, LA | Absence without leave | Conduct Prejudicial |
| 9 | Morrow | John | Pvt | IRE | 2/1/64 | | Desertion | |
| 9 | Mulvey | John | Pvt | IRE | 11/1/63 | New Orleans, LA | Drunk on Duty | Conduct Prejudicial |
| 9 | Murphy | John | Pvt | US | 10/1/63 | New Orleans, LA | Insulting Language Officer | Conduct Prejudicial |
| 9 | Obrien | Dennis | Pvt | US | 4/1/62 | | Insulting Language Officer | Insubordinate |
| 9 | Odonnell | Phillip | Pvt | IRE | 3/1/62 | Biloxi, MS | Drunk and Disorderly | |
| 9 | Odonnell | Phillip | Pvt | IRE | 1/1/63 | New Orleans, LA | Conduct Prejidicual | |
| 9 | Otoole | Garrett | Pvt | IRE | 10/1/63 | New Orleans, LA | Desertion | Enlisted in anotherr Regt |
| 9 | Ryan | Daniel | Pvt | | 1/1/63 | New Orleans, LA | Absence without leave | |
| 9 | Ryan | Nathan | Pvt | | 9/1/63 | New Orleans, LA | Left Guard Post | |

| Regiment | Last Name | First Name | Rank | Ethnicity | Date of Offense | Location | Major Offense 1 | Offense 2 |
|---|---|---|---|---|---|---|---|---|
| 9 | Scott | George | Pvt | | 1/1/63 | New Orleans, LA | Left Guard Post | |
| 9 | Scott | Michael | Pvt | IRE | 6/1/62 | Baton Rouge | Drunk and Disorderly | |
| 9 | Scully | John | Pvt | | 9/1/63 | | Murder | |
| 9 | Shea | James | Pvt | IRE | 1/1/63 | New Orleans, LA | Absence without leave | |
| 9 | Sheridan | Terrence | Cpt | IRE | 11/1/63 | New Orleans, LA | Drunk and Disorderly | |
| 9 | Sheridan | Patrick | Pvt | IRE | 1/1/65 | Washington, DC | Desertion | |
| 9 | Sheridan | Patrick | Pvt | IRE | 9/1/64 | | Desertion | |
| 9 | Smith | Charles | Pvt | | 2/1/65 | Alexandria, VA | Desertion | |
| 9 | Smith | John | Pvt | | 9/1/63 | New Orleans, LA | Left Guard Post | Language to Capt |
| 9 | Sullivan | John | Pvt | IRE | 1/1/65 | Alexandria, VA | Desertion | |
| 9 | Sweetman | John | Pvt | IRE | 1/1/63 | New Orleans, LA | Drunk on Duty | |
| 9 | Truman | John | Pvt | US | 9/1/63 | New Orleans, LA | Slept on Guard | |
| 9 | Welch | John | Pvt | IRE | 2/1/64 | | Desertion | |

| | | | | | | | | |
|---|---|---|---|---|---|---|---|---|
| 9 | Whalan | John | Pvt | IRE | 1/1/63 | New Orleans, LA | Absence without leave | |
| 9 | Wright | William | Cpt | IRE | 9/1/62 | Baton Rouge, LA | Conduct Unbecoming | |
| 9 | Wright | William | Cpt | IRE | 1/1/63 | New Orleans, LA | Drunk on Duty | Conduct Unbecoming |
| 17 | OConner | Patrick | Cpt | IRE | 6/1/62 | Corinth, MS | Drunk on Duty | |
| 17 | McCauley | Patrick | cpt | | 11/1/62 | | Assault with intent to Kill | |
| 17 | Dwyer | William | Pvt | US | 2/1/63 | | Conduct Prejidicual | Rape |
| 17 | Dwyer | William | Pvt | US | 2/1/63 | | Stealing | |
| 17 | Harrington | John | Pvt | IRE | 2/1/63 | | Desertion | |
| 17 | Ulrich | Julius | Pvt | GER | 4/1/65 | Kingston, GA | Desertion | |
| 17 | Thomas | Reilly | Lt | US | 11/1/63 | Vicksburg, MS | Disobedience | |
| 17 | Pohl | Christian | Pvt | GER | 2/1/64 | | Absence without leave | |
| 17 | Kelly | John | Pvt | IRE | 12/1/63 | Vicksburg, MS | Disrespect | |
| 17 | Ginnesty | James | PVT | IRE | | 10/10/64 | Absence without leave | |
| 17 | Sullivan | John | PVT | IRE | | | Desertion | |
| 17 | Smith | John | PVT | IRE | | 8/18/64 | Struck Commanding Officer | |

| Regiment | Last Name | First Name | Rank | Ethnicity | Date of Offense | Location | Major Offense 1 | Offense 2 |
|---|---|---|---|---|---|---|---|---|
| 17 | Huff | Thomas | PVT | US | | | Absence without leave | |
| 17 | Huff | Thomas | PVT | US | 3/18/62 | | Absence without leave | |
| 17 | McMullen | Daniel | | | | | Desertion | |
| 17 | Powderly | Jason | PVT | IRE | | | Desertion | |
| 23 | Patrick | Higgins | Lt | IRE | 6/1/62 | Chicago, IL | Aid in POW Escape | Treason |
| 23 | Moore | Thomas | Cpt | IRE | 11/1/62 | | Drunkeness | Conduct Unbecoming |
| 23 | Van Falkenburg | Abram | Pvt | US | 4/1/63 | | Stealing | |
| 23 | Rush | Thomas | Pvt | IRE | 4/1/63 | | Stealing | |
| 23 | Whomble | James | Pvt | ENG | 4/1/63 | | Absence without leave | Drunkeness |
| 23 | Reed | Henry | Pvt | US | 2/1/63 | | Disobedience | Threatened Officer |
| 23 | Martin | Andrew | Pvt | US | 2/1/63 | | Desertion | |
| 23 | Fitzgerald | Michael | Pvt | IRE | 2/1/63 | | Desertion | |
| 23 | Doyle | John | Pvt | | 2/1/63 | | Struck Commanding Officer | |
| 23 | King | Owen | Pvt | IRE | 9/1/63 | | Conduct Prejidicual | |
| 23 | Fitzgerald | James | Pvt | IRE | 12/1/63 | | Desertion | |
| 23 | Hayden | Patrick | Pvt | IRE | 12/1/63 | | Desertion | |
| 23 | Obrien | Simon | Pvt | IRE | 12/1/63 | | Desertion | |
| 23 | Budrow (Burden) | Stephen | Pvt | FRA | 7/1/64 | | Desertion | |

| | | | | | | | | |
|---|---|---|---|---|---|---|---|---|
| 23 | Keegan | Phillip | Pvt | IRE | 7/1/64 | | Desertion | |
| 23 | Brees | William | Pvt | US | 1/1/65 | | Desertion | |
| 23 | Downey | Edward | Pvt | US | 1/1/65 | | Desertion | |
| 23 | McCarty (McCarthy) | Dennis | Pvt | IRE | 12/1/62 | | Assault with intent to Kill | Tried to Stab Sgt |
| 23 | McAndrew | William | Pvt | IRE | 5/1/63 | | Left Guard Post | Took arms and gone three days |
| 23 | Oshea | James | Pvt | IRE | 5/1/63 | | Absence without leave | Stealing |
| 23 | Daly | John | Lt | US | 1/1/64 | | Disobedience | Absence without Leave |
| 23 | Dow (Dowe) | John | Pvt | IRE | 4/1/64 | | Burglary | |
| 23 | Battle | Edward | Sgt | IRE | 3/1/64 | | Desertion | |
| 23 | Sweeney | Thomas | Pvt | IRE | 3/1/64 | New Creek, VA | Desertion | |
| 23 | Haley (Haney) | Patrick | Pvt | IRE | 2/1/64 | Petersburg, WV | Desertion | |
| 23 | Oshea | James | Pvt | IRE | 4/1/64 | New Creek, VA | Desertion | |
| 23 | Preston | John | Pvt | IRE | 3/1/64 | New Creek, VA | Desertion | |
| 23 | Downey | Edward | Pvt | US | 1/1/64 | | Desertion | |
| 23 | Ohara | William | Pvt | | 2/1/65 | | Desertion | Enlisted in another Regt |

# *Acknowledgments*

This project is the product of the love and support of many people who have entered my life over the past fifteen years. That this book exists is, in large part, a testament to Andy Slap's patience and excellence as an editor. We first spoke about this project at the 2012 meeting of the Society of Civil War Historians in Lexington, Kentucky. His support, and the long hours that he, along with the staff and board of Fordham University Press, has put into this project, has made this an enjoyable and fruitful process.

My decision to study history was encouraged by a number of people to whom I will be forever indebted. At Holy Cross, Noel Cary's enthusiasm for teaching lit a fire in me, and it was in one of his classes that I determined to pursue this field of study. During that same time Anthony Cashman and Stephanie Yuhl became close friends and mentors. They challenged me, their student, to become a better thinker and writer and, outside of the confines of the classroom, a better person. They have spent countless hours advising me through the transition from undergraduate to graduate student, and I am forever grateful for their insight and support. Ed O'Donnell was also instrumental in this journey. His passion for Irish American history is contagious, and his encouragement over the years kept me focused on the end goal. While I was at Trinity College, Dublin, Jane Ohlmeyer and Anne Dolan offered support and advice to a poor graduate student far from home and in over his head. Their combination of kindness and patience is something that I strive daily to replicate with my own students.

At Fordham, a number of faculty members made lasting impressions. Dan Soyer and Sal Acosta kindly read draft after draft of my work as it slowly morphed from a mass jumble of ideas into a coherent finished product. I spent hours with Nancy Curtin on the golf course where she offered insight and advice while beating me by, on average, twenty strokes. Brian Purnell, who started at Fordham as an Assistant Professor around the same time as I began as a student there and who has now moved on to Bowdoin College, continues to be a sounding board and has helped guide me through my early career. During my time in the Bronx I also had the pleasure of becoming close friends with a number of other excellent young historians: Patrick Hege, Alessandro Saluppo, Brandon

Gauthier, Elizabeth Stack, Megan Monahan, Pedro Cameselle, and Noel Wolf. You all kept me sane. Thank you.

I also must thank all my colleagues at California State University, San Bernardino, who welcomed me into the History Department in 2013 with open arms and who have provided me with unquestioned support. You have fostered a port of calm in a sea of crazy. Accepting the position at CSUSB was one of the best decisions I have ever made.

A number of friends and colleagues have provided valuable help, insight, and unparalleled support over the years. Susannah Ural has been most gracious in her support of this project. Her work inspired my own, and I consider myself lucky to call her a friend. Chris Samito, a fellow Crusader, also read numerous drafts and offered invaluable comments and support. Julie Mujic, Dave Thompson, Barb Gannon, Lorien Foote, Will Kurtz, Brian Miller, Thaddeus Romansky, and Frank Towers have always been quick to respond to texts and e-mails and have always been willing to chat about work and life. Finally, the database for this project would not have existed without Tim Cannon. Tim offered his IT expertise way back in the early stages of this project and spent many hours scrubbing data and helping me streamline the database. He is a fabulous computer scientist and a great friend.

Mark Snell at the George Tyler Moore Center for the Study of the Civil War at Shepherd University awarded me my first grant, and our conversations at the Schindler House and the back porch of his farmhouse close to the Gettysburg battlefield helped turn a mass of raw ideas into a discernible research question. I hope he finds, when he reads this, that I have answered (to the best of my ability) the most difficult question he ever posed to me: "So what?" In Wisconsin, Tom Garver and the Friends of the UW–Madison Libraries provided me with the financial assistance to spend a month in the Wisconsin state archives. This book would not exist without their support. Funds from the King V. Hostick Foundation allowed me to spend three weeks in Springfield and Chicago in the summer of 2011, and I was there able to complete a majority of my research on the 23rd Illinois. Finally, generous assistance from the United States Army Center for Military History made it possible for me to complete much of the initial draft of this book. A number of other individuals were instrumental in the completion of my research. Robert Larkin graciously welcomed me into his home on numerous occasions and provided me with invaluable material on the Ninth Connecticut that he has compiled over the years. His commitment to preserving the legacy of this unit is second to none, and I can only hope that I have done Thomas Cahill's men, and their descendants, justice in my account of their war. He is joined in this work by Joseph Kelly, Jeffery Cook, Charles Sibley, and Neil Hogan, to all of whom I express a great degree of gratitude for their preserving many of the materials from the Ninth Connecticut that appear in this book. Garrett Eucalitto, then working for Senator Joe Lieberman, worked diligently and put me in touch with Dennis Edelin at the National Archives, who pulled hundreds of pension files for me before my research trips. He went above and beyond in support of a young graduate student, and I am forever grateful for his assistance. Finally, Clint and Annie Lyons opened their home to me time and again during my research trips to Washington, and I could not have completed the research for this book without their hospitality.

My family and friends were unwavering in their support of this project. My father fostered my love of history from a very young age, and my mother has played an equally important part in this, for she encouraged all of her children to pursue their dreams and has been there for me through good times and bad. My siblings—Casey, Mickey, and Jack—inspire me daily. For my friends—especially Matt, Mike, Jonny, Jason, Brandon, Sean, Wade, and Tyler—thanks for always being there, and here is what I have been working on for the past nine years.

When I arrived in the Bronx in 2007, I met Paul Cimbala, who agreed to take me on as a student soon after I started at Fordham and, since then, has been the best mentor and advisor that one could have asked for; he has also become a close friend. Everything I have in my career I owe to him. He has been a part of this project since its earliest stages and has been an unwavering supporter of it. I hope it lives up to his expectations. My son, Owen, came into this project when it was about halfway done, and he has been the driving force behind its completion. He has patiently waited for me to finish sentences, paragraphs, and footnotes before our excursions to the park, the pool, or market night, and I hope that someday he will understand what this book represents. And finally, for Christina, who came into this as it was nearing its chaotic conclusion. You have grounded me and inspired me in ways I never knew possible and remind me daily of why this is all worthwhile. I consider myself extremely fortunate to have you in my life. Thank you all.

# *Notes*

## Introduction

1. See William Corby, *Memoirs of Chaplin Life: Three Years with the Irish Brigade in the Army of the Potomac*, ed. Lawrence Frederick Kohl (New York: Fordham University Press, 1992); St. Clair A. Mulholland, *The Story of the 116th Regiment, Pennsylvania Volunteers, in the War of the Rebellion*, ed. Lawrence Frederick Kohl (New York: Fordham University Press, 1996); David Power Conyngham, *The Irish Brigade and Its Campaigns, with Some Account of the Corcoran Legion*, ed. Lawrence Frederick Kohl (New York: Fordham University Press, 1994); Frank A. Boyle, *A Party of Mad Fellows: The Story of the Irish Regiments in the Army of the Potomac* (Dayton, Ohio: Morningside, 1996); William Burton, *Melting Pot Soldiers: The Union's Ethnic Regiments* (New York: Fordham University Press, 1998); Martin Öfele, *True Sons of the Republic: European Immigrants in the Union Army* (Westport, Conn. and London: Praeger, 2008); Susannah Ural Bruce, *The Harp and the Eagle: Irish American Volunteers in the Union Army, 1861–1865* (New York: New York University Press, 2005); Christian Samito, *Becoming American under Fire: Irish Americans, African Americans, and the Politics of Citizenship during the Civil War Era* (Ithaca, N.Y.: Cornell University Press, 2009); and Craig Warren, "'Oh God What a Pity!' The Irish Brigade at Fredericksburg and the Creation of a Myth," *Civil War History* 47, no. 3 (2001): 193–221.

2. "The Fruits of the American War," *Irish People* (Dublin), December 26, 1863.

3. John Higham, *Strangers in the Land: Patterns of American Nativism, 1860–1925* (New Brunswick, N.J.: Rutgers University Press, 2002); Noel Ignatiev, *How the Irish Became White* (New York: Routledge, 1995).

4. For discussions of the changing nature of American society during the Industrial Revolution, see Carol Sheriff, *The Artificial River: The Erie Canal and the Paradox of Progress* (New York: Hill and Wang, 1996); Daniel Howe Walker, *What Hath God Wrought: The Transformation of America, 1815–1848* (New York: Oxford University Press, 2007); Charles Sellers, *The Market Revolution: Jacksonian America, 1815–1846* (New York: Oxford University Press, 1991); Paul E. Johnson, *A Shopkeeper's Millennium: Society and Revivals in Rochester, New York, 1815–1837* (New York: Hill and Wang, 1978); "Our Noble 69th (Irish) Regiment," *Wisconsin Daily Patriot* (Madison), July 27, 1861.

5. With regard to the phrase "Irish race": Irish nationalists utilized a language of race to distinguish their countrymen from the English ruling class, as a means of emphasizing a difference between English and Irish and justifying independence. The role of the United States in the salvation of the "Irish race," especially during and immediately after the Famine, has played a major part in the larger debates over how the Irish viewed their position within the country at the outbreak of the war. Primary research

into Irish nationalist movements in the United States during the antebellum period, however, shows that Irish dedication to the republican tradition only applied to the United States when these men viewed the U.S. government as upholding this ideology. While many viewed the United States as evidence of what they themselves could achieve at home, there were instances in which Irish faith in the United States waned—especially during the outpouring of emotions over the 1860 visit of the Prince of Wales (see ch. 1, n. 18). However, as Fenian leader John O'Mahony stated numerous times in the Irish American newspaper the *Phoenix*, American laws allowed for Irish political organization, and thus he urged the Irish, whose primary loyalty should be to Ireland, to operate within the bounds of American laws and regulations. Quotation from Daniel William Cahill: "Anniversary Dinner in Honor of Saint Patrick's Day: Address at Glasgow," in *The Works of the Rev. D. W. Cahill, D.D.* (Boston: Patrick Donahoe, 1855), 54; and D. W. Cahill, "To the Small Tenant Farmers, the Tradesmen, and Laboring Classes of Ireland," reprinted in the *Phoenix* (New York, N.Y.), January 21, 1860.

6. "The Lawrence Massacre," *Phoenix*, January 21, 1860; letter to the editor from "An Irishman," *Phoenix*, February 4, 1860. This ideology is also seen in letters to the editor published in the *Phoenix* well after Cahill's various "Letters from America" were reprinted in Irish American newspapers. Specifically, on January 26, 1861, the *Phoenix* reprinted a letter from a William Lalor of Wisconsin addressed to the editor of the *Irish News* that harshly critiqued Cahill's analysis of the situation in the United States, questioning why numerous events, including the burning of a nunnery, were not reported to the people back home in Ireland. Many Irish Americans believed that Cahill was exaggerating the situation in their country and giving false hope to the unfortunate in Ireland.

7. "Island, Race and Doom," *Irish People* (Dublin), November 28, 1863.

8. Tyler Anbinder, *Nativism and Slavery: The Northern Know-Nothings and the Politics of the 1850s* (New York: Oxford University Press, 1992).

9. David Montgomery, "The Shuttle and the Cross: Weavers and Artisans in the Kensington Riots of 1844," *The Journal of Social History* 5, no. 4 (1972), 411–46; "The Platform of the American Party," *Chicago Times*, June 28, 1855.

10. Anbinder, *Nativism and Slavery*, 11–12; 111–13.

11. Christine Kinealy, *This Great Calamity: The Irish Famine 1845–52* (Dublin: Gill and Macmillan, 1994); Mary Daly, *The Famine in Ireland* (Dublin: Dundalgan Press, 1986), 26–30; Kinealy, *This Great Calamity*, 18.

12. Kerby Miller, *Emigrants and Exiles: Ireland and the Irish Exodus to North America* (New York: Oxford University Press, 1985), 21–22; Sean J. Connoly, *Religion, Law, and Power: The Making of Protestant Ireland, 1660–1760* (Oxford: Clarendon Press, 1992); Robert Kee, *The Green Flag: A History of Irish Nationalism* (London: Penguin Books, 1972), 19.

13. Miller, *Emigrants and Exiles*, 295.

14. Miller, *Emigrants and Exiles*, 315, 321; *Morning Courier and New-York Enquirer*, January 13, 1847, *Report of the Council of Hygiene and Public Health* (New York, 1865), and *Harper's Weekly*, February 21, 1857, quoted in Tyler Anbinder, *Five Points: The Nineteenth-Century New York City Neighborhood* (New York: Free Press, 2008), 73, 75; see also ch. 4.

15. Reverend Theodore Parker, quoted in Thomas H. O'Connor, *The Boston Irish: A Political History* (Boston: Northeastern University Press, 1995), 60–61; William H. Shannon, *The American Irish: A Political and Social Portrait* (New York: McMillan, 1963), 183; John Prescott Bigelow, quoted in O'Connor, *The Boston Irish*, 63; ibid., 64–65.

16. "Opinions of the Whig Press," *Ohio Statesman* (Columbus), December 12, 1843. Spelling and punctuation in all quotations reflects the original document.

17. Christian Samito, *Becoming American under Fire*, 27.

18. Susannah J. Ural, "'Ye Sons of Green Erin Assemble': Northern Irish American Catholics and the Union War Effort, 1861–1865," in *Civil War Citizens: Race, Ethnicity, and Identity in America's Bloodiest Conflict*, ed. Susannah J. Ural (New York: New York University Press, 2010), 100; Mitchell Snay, *Fenians, Freedmen, and Southern Whites: Race and Nationality in the Era of Reconstruction* (Baton Rouge: Louisiana State University Press, 2007), 7; Christian Samito, *Becoming American under Fire*; William Burton, *Melting Pot Soldiers*. The discussion of the impact of war on the creation of national sentiment, or the "Americanization" of certain groups, is not confined to the historiography of the Civil War. Gary Gerstle in *American Crucible: Race and Nation in the Twentieth Century* (Princeton: Princeton University Press, 2001) suggests that military service and notions of citizenship are intricately linked within the American mindset. In *Good Americans: Italians and Jewish Immigrants during the First World War* (New York: Oxford University Press, 2003), Christopher M. Sterba argues that the organization of ethnic militia units in New Haven, which dated to the early 1850s, was a means of both challenging nativism and demonstrating loyalty to the United States through willingness to participate in the larger defense of the state and country (14, 186). The notion of the "good American" during wartime was a reaction to the reliability of a soldier rather than to his ethnic background. The inclusion in the larger nation of those marked by ethnicity or race was not limited to male soldiers. See Lizabeth Cohen, *A Consumers' Republic: The Politics of Mass Consumption in Postwar America* (New York: Knopf, 2003), and Meg Jacobs, *Pocketbook Politics: Economic Citizenship in Twentieth-Century America* (Princeton: Princeton University Press, 2005). In an analysis of the home front in the twentieth century, these historians suggest that purchasing power provided women and families with the means of protecting the democratic interests of the United States while at the same time participating in an economic Americanization. Similarly, the impact of the Civil War on issues of inclusion or nationalism must not be limited solely to those men directly participating in the military. Melinda Lawson, in *Patriot Fires: Forging a New American Nationalism in the Civil War* (Lawrence: University Press of Kansas, 2002), has taken the first steps in illustrating the impact of the war on larger issues of nationalism and identity through the participation of men and women on the home front in activities that supported the larger war effort. Despite the fact that the data informing *Shades of Green* is gender-specific, there is little reason why ethnic communities cannot be examined for trends similar to those noted above, reflecting an appreciation of the organic relationship that existed between citizens and soldiers.

19. Craig Warren, "'Oh God What a Pity!' The Irish Brigade at Fredericksburg and the Creation of a Myth." The first historical account of Irish American service, David Powers Conyngham's *The Irish Brigade and Its Campaigns, with Some Account of the*

*Corcoran Legion*, was published in 1867. A six-hundred-page tome focusing on what has arguably become recognized as the most important ethnic unit in the Northern war effort, Conyngham's work is notable not only for its extensive discussion of Irish service in the Eastern Theater but also for his attempt to contextualize Irish sacrifice through the lens of American patriotism. *The Irish Brigade and Its Campaigns* was followed in the later half of the nineteenth and early part of the twentieth century by other works on Irish American units, such as William Corby's *Memoirs of Chaplain Life: Three Years with the Irish Brigade in the Army of the Potomac* (1893), Daniel George Macnamara's *The History of the Ninth Regiment, Massachusetts Volunteer Infantry, June 1861–June 1864* (1899), St. Clair Mulholland's *The Story of the 116th Regiment, Pennsylvania Volunteers, in the War of the Rebellion* (1903), and Thomas Hamilton Murray's *The History of the Ninth Regiment, Connecticut Volunteer Infantry, "The Irish Regiment," in the War of the Rebellion, 1861–65* (1903).

20. See Susannah Ural Bruce, *The Harp and the Eagle*; Christian Samito, *Becoming American under Fire: Irish Americans, African Americans, and the Politics of Citizenship during the Civil War Era* (Ithaca, N.Y.: Cornell University Press, 2009); Martin Öfele, *True Sons of the Republic*; and David Gleeson, *The Green and the Gray: The Irish in the Confederate States of America* (Chapel Hill: University of North Carolina Press, 2013).

21. Burton, *Melting Pot Soldiers*, 14.

22. Issues of patriotism and loyalty, identity, and manhood during the Civil War era are incredibly complex. For discussions of patriotism and loyalty, see: Robert Sandow, *Deserter Country: Civil War Opposition in the Pennsylvania Appalachians* (New York: Fordham University Press, 2009); Jennifer L. Webber, *Copperheads: The Rise and Fall of Lincoln's Opponents in the North* (New York: Oxford University Press, 2006); David Williams, *Bitterly Divided: The South's Inner Civil War* (New York: The New Press, 2008); Margaret M. Storey, *Loyalty and Loss: Alabama's Unionists in the Civil War and Reconstruction* (Baton Rouge: Louisiana State University Press, 2004); Frank Klement, "Catholics as Copperheads during the Civil War," *Catholic Historical Review* 8, no. 1 (January 1994): 36–57; Matthew Warshauer, *Connecticut in the Civil War: Slavery, Sacrifice, and Survival* (Middletown, Conn.: Wesleyan University Press, 2011); Mark V. Wetherington, *Plain Folk's Fight: The Civil War and Reconstruction in Piney Woods, Georgia* (Chapel Hill: University of North Carolina Press, 2005); David William, Theresa C. Williams, and R. David Carlson, *Plain Folk in a Rich Man's War: Class and Dissent in Confederate Georgia* (Gainesville: University Press of Florida, 2002); Judkin Browning, *Shifting Loyalties: The Union Occupation of Eastern North Carolina* (Chapel Hill: University of North Carolina Press, 2011); Bruce, *The Harp and the Eagle*; and Samito, *Becoming American under Fire*.As I illustrate throughout the book, patriotism and loyalty, especially among Irish Americans, was vague and shifting. Men made clear their allegiances to both the United States and Ireland, but support for the war often changed, reflecting local as well as national concerns. The complexity of patriotism and loyalty, however, was a vital part of the experience of nineteenth-century Americans and deserves the attention given to it in this study, for by illuminating local manifestations of patriotism and support we may better understand the impact of the war on the ideologies of men and women across the North. For

discussions of manhood and, in particular, Victorian notions of masculinity and military service, see Lorien Foote, *The Gentlemen and the Roughs: Violence, Honor and Manhood in the Union Army* (New York: New York University Press, 2010); Nina Silber, *Daughters of the Union: Northern Women Fight in the Civil War* (Cambridge: Harvard University Press, 2005); Patricia L. Richard, *Busy Hands: Images of the Family in the Northern Civil War Effort* (New York: Fordham University Press, 2003); Judith Giesberg, *Army at Home: Women and the Civil War on the Northern Home Front* (Chapel Hill: University of North Carolina Press, 2005); Jeanie Attie, *Patriotic Toil: Northern Women and the American Civil War* (Ithaca, N.Y.: Cornell University Press, 1998); Steven J. Ramold, *Across the Divide: Union Soldiers View the Northern Home Front* (New York: New York University Press, 2013); Catherine Clinton and Nina Silber, *Divided Houses: Gender and the Civil War* (New York: Oxford University Press, 1992); Catherine Clinton and Nina Silber, *Battle Scars: Gender and Sexuality in the American Civil War* (New York: Oxford University Press, 2006); Chandra Manning, *What This Cruel War Was Over* (New York: Vintage Books, 2007); James McPherson, *For Cause and Comrades: Why Men Fought in the Civil War* (New York: Oxford University Press, 1997); and Brian Craig Miller, *Empty Sleeves: Amputation in the Civil War South* (Athens: University of Georgia Press, 2015). For the sake of this study, "manhood" refers to traditionally defined roles, ideals, and values, in particular the notion that military service provided a vehicle through which men could prove their masculinity. Similarly, discussion of gender during the war falls in line with the excellent framework created by the aforementioned historians. It is abundantly clear that the war shifted the paradigm of traditional gender roles, but, like notions of manhood, gender roles were most often defined by nineteenth-century Victorian ideals. The war simultaneously challenged and reinforced social norms.

23. The database is as thorough and accurate as possible given the availability of records. The demographic data is not complete, however, for every soldier. For example, a number of the companies of the 23rd Illinois lost their muster and descriptive rolls when the regiment surrendered to General Sterling Price at Lexington, Missouri in the fall of 1861. Officers recreated those rolls as accurately as possible when the regiment re-mustered in the winter of 1861, but there are nevertheless some missing pieces. Another difficulty was posed by the array of spellings. Soldiers' names and ages were often recorded differently on different rolls. The initial database, which reflected *all* of the captured data from the various descriptive rolls, contained well over seven thousand names.

## 1. Illinois and Mulligan's Irish Brigade

1. "Letter to the Editor," *Chicago Democrat*, February 17, 1834, quoted in Weston A. Goodspeed and Daniel D. Healy, eds., *History of Cook County, Illinois* (Chicago: Goodspeed Historical Association, 1909), 1:101; *Chicago Democrat*, April 30, 1834, quoted in Goodspeed and. Healy, History of Cook County, Illinois, 1:101. Goodspeed and Healy, *History of Cook County*, 1:115; Susanna Ural Bruce, *The Harp and the Eagle: Irish-American Volunteers and the Union Army, 1861–1865* (New York: New York University Press, 2006), 13.

2. *Chicago American*, August 3, 1839, quoted in Goodspeed and Healy, *History of Cook County, Illinois*, 1:332; Goodspeed and Healy, *History of Cook County Illinois*, 1:332–33. Locofoco Democrats were a radical Jacksonian branch of the Democratic Party that first emerged in New York in 1835, led by labor unions and labor activists and based in working-class urban neighborhoods. They supported hard-money reform, antimonopoly, and rights of labor. See Matthew S. R. Bewig, "Locofoco Democrats," in *Encyclopedia of U.S. Labor and Working-Class History*, ed. Eric Arnesen (New York: Routledge, 2007), 1:817–18.

3. "The Know-Nothings and Slavery," *Illinois State Chronicle* (Decatur), June 23, 1855.

4. *Chicago Tribune*, February 25, 1856, quoted in Bruce, *Harp and Eagle*, 15; *Chicago Democratic Press*, March 6, 1855, quoted in Goodspeed and Healy, *History of Cook County, Illinois*, 1:360; "Nativism in Whig Mouths," *Daily Illinois State Register* (Springfield), December 27, 1844; "Know-Nothings Unveiled," *Chicago Times*, May 10, 1855; "Freedom of Conscience," *Chicago Times*, August 9, 1855.

5. Statistics for the major cities, cited here and in all chapters of this book, are from a database developed from the 1860 U.S. Census and constructed specifically for this project. Socioeconomic statistics from each city were derived from a database composed of a random sampling of census returns for 20 percent of the Irish-born male population of military age (18–45) living in each city before the outbreak of the war. Men were categorized by their employment: the groups identified were White Collar/Nonmanual; Blue Collar/Working Class; Farmer. Subcategories were created within each of these. White Collar/Nonmanual workers were divided into high nonmanual and low nonmanual (denoting, for example, differences between men who identified themselves as businessmen and lawyers and those who identified as teachers and clerks). Blue Collar/Working Class men were divided into unskilled laborers (those who listed their employment simply as, for example, "laborer," "day laborer," or "factory worker") and artisans (workers with a specific job requiring a specific skill). Agricultural workers were differentiated between those who worked their own farms and those who were farm laborers. While the terms "white collar" and "blue collar" may be a bit anachronistic, these categories were extremely useful in describing the vibrant socioeconomic cross section in these cities. On the growth of Irish neighborhoods and the growing number of Catholic churches and Irish organizations, including militia, see Lawrence J. McCaffrey, "The Irish American Dimension," in *The Irish in Chicago*, ed. Lawrence J. McCaffrey, Michael F. Funchion, Ellen Skerrett, and Charles Fanning (Urbana and Chicago: University of Illinois Press, 1987), 3; Alfred Theodore Andreas, *History of Chicago* (Chicago: A. T. Andreas, 1884), 1:291; ibid., 1:285.

6. *History of La Salle County, Illinois, Together with Sketches of Its Cities, Villages and Towns. . . .* (Chicago: Inter-State Publishing Co., 1886), 1:740; ibid., 1:743; ibid.,1:744.

7. Elmer Baldwin, *History of La Salle County, Illinois: Its Topography, Geology, Botany, Natural History. . . .* (Chicago: Rand, McNally and Co., 1877), 1:165.

8. *History of La Salle County, Illinois, Together with Sketches*, 1:469; ibid., 1:473.

9. "The Irish Press on the Crisis," which originally appeared in the *Irish American* (New York), was reprinted in the *Appleton (Wis.) Crescent*, May 11, 1861.

10. Bruce, *The Harp and the Eagle*, 2. Bruce notes that approximately 150,000 Irish-born men enlisted in the Union Army.

11. "Spirit of Chicago Democracy," *Daily Illinois State Journal* (Springfield), April 16, 1861; "War Times—The State of Feeling Yesterday—Our Volunteers," *Chicago Tribune*, April 17, 1861; "An 'Irish Brigade,'" *Daily Illinois State Journal*, April 29, 1861.

12. "The Meeting of the Irish Citizens," *Rock River Democrat* (Rockford, Ill.), April 20, 1861; "The Uprising: Patriotism in the Northwest," *Chicago Tribune*, April 25, 1861.

13. "Our Irish Fellow Citizens and the War," *Daily Illinois State Journal*, May 21, 1861; "Devoted Patriotism of the Irish Catholics—Its Probable influence on their Secession Countrymen," *Daily Illinois State Journal*, May 23, 1861.

14. "The Irish," *Rock River Democrat* (Rockford, Ill.), October 15, 1861.

15. Mulligan's participation in the Shields Guards is noted in the *Phoenix*, the newspaper of the Fenian movement, published by John O'Mahony in New York between 1859 and 1861. In *Special Sorrows: The Diasporic Imagination of Irish, Polish, and Jewish Immigrants in the United States* (Cambridge, Mass.: Harvard University Press, 2002), Matthew Frye Jacobson implies that nationalist impulses were often greater among men born in the United States to immigrant parents than they were in immigrants themselves. In 1858 Mulligan was selected to chair the Smith O'Brien Reception Committee. William Smith O'Brien, a former member of the revolutionary Young Ireland movement, was exiled to Australia after the failure of the 1848 uprising in Ireland. In the late 1850s he traveled throughout the United States and reported that the nativism and poverty Irish immigrants confronted had made them "so uncomfortable that they would willingly have left the United States if their circumstances had enabled them to quit that country without great loss." Nevertheless, Smith O'Brien remained an icon of Irish nationalism. Mulligan's role as chairman of the Smith O'Brien Committee is alluded to in Daniel McIlrow to James Mulligan, 19 April 1859, James A. Mulligan Papers, Chicago Museum of History; information on Smith O'Brien's role in the 1848 uprisings is provided in Kerby Miller, *Emigrants and Exiles: Ireland and the Irish Exodus to North America* (New York: Oxford University Press, 1985), 343; Smith O'Brien is quoted in Miller, *Emigrants and Exiles*, 343.

16. "The F.F.V's and the F.F.I's," *Daily Milwaukee News*, July 2, 1861.

17. "Visit of the Prince of Wales," *New York Times*, August 1, 1860; "Visit of the Prince of Whales," *Phoenix*, October 13, 1860; "Open Letter to the Phoenix, by Michael Corcoran," *Phoenix*, March 15, 1861; Bruce, *The Harp and the Eagle*, 48–49.

18. Records of the Executive Committee of the Irish Brigade, 25 April 1861 and 7 May 1861; letter of Henry S. Monroe to Hannibal Hamlin, 21 May 1861; all in the Mulligan Papers, Chicago.

19. Dunne's response is dated April 26; see P. W. Dunne to James A. Mulligan, 26 April 1861, Mulligan Papers, Chicago. "The Objects and the Duty of the Phoenix," *Phoenix*, June 4, 1859.

20. For a list of Fenian militias see, see, for example, *Phoenix*, August 20, 1859, though this list grew in length over the two years before the war. Over 350 men are named as militia officers dedicated to the Fenian movement. It is difficult to determine how many of them served in non-Irish regiments, but it is likely that many did. For information on the Fenian involvement in the organization of the Ninth Massachusetts, see Daniel George Macnamara, *The History of the Ninth Regiment, Massachusetts Volunteer Infantry, June, 1861 to June, 1864* (1899; reprint, New York: Fordham University

Press, 2000). Patrick Dunne's reply to James Mulligan: P. W. Dunne to James A. Mulligan, 26 April 1861, Mulligan Papers, Chicago.

21. R. F. Farrell to James Mulligan, 26 April 1861, Mulligan Papers, Chicago. Based on the letter of April 30, and the offer of a commission in a Detroit Zouave company, it is likely that R. F. Farrell is Roderick F. Farrell, who later served as captain of Company C, 15th Michigan Volunteer Infantry. This is the only R. F. Farrell from Michigan who served in the Civil War as a commissioned officer. P. Flynn to James Mulligan, 20 May 1861, Mulligan Papers, Chicago; Matthew Cushman to Thomas, 12 June 1861, Records of the Adjutant General's Office, Illinois State Archives, Springfield. Cushman's correspondence illuminates the early problems the men from Ottawa faced when trying to enlist for the war. These were primarily due to the overwhelming response of volunteers in the immediate aftermath of the attack on Fort Sumter.

22. "The Irish Brigade," *Chicago Tribune*, June 15, 1861.

23. "Presentation," *Chicago Times*, June 15, 1861; "The Irish Brigade," *Chicago Times*, June 20, 1861; "The Mustering," *Chicago Times*, June 16, 1861; "The Ladies' Meeting," *Chicago Times*, June 27, 1861; "Help the Brigade," *Chicago Times*, June 28, 1861; "More Uniforms and Blankets for the Brigade," *Chicago Times*, July 10, 1861.

24. Anne Wallace to Will Wallace, 1 July 1861, Wallace-Dickey Collection, Abraham Lincoln Presidential Library, Springfield, Ill. (ALPL, Springfield). Interestingly, Anne Wallace's husband William Wallace does not appear in the Muster and Descriptive Rolls for the regiment until 1864, when the 23rd was consolidated.

25. Charles Coffee to R. Thorn, 30 June 1861, Wallace-Dickey Collection, ALPL, Springfield.

26. "A Card," *Chicago Tribune*, July 16, 1861.

27. *Portrait and Biographical Record of Saginaw and Bay Counties, Michigan . . .* (Chicago: Biographical Publishing Co.,1892), 837–38.

28. "Resolution of the Detroit Soldiers," *Chicago Times*, June 19, 1861.

29. "The Irish Brigade," *Chicago Tribune*, July 16, 1861.

30. Ethnic background can be difficult to determine. The 1860 Census does not provide information on the place of birth of an individual's parents, and thus unless a soldier was living with his parents in 1860, there is no way to determine his ethnic background. Furthermore, the size of the ethnic communities and problems with spelling and age make it difficult, if not impossible, to determine whether a particular soldier and an individual in the Census is the same person. Furthermore, the mobility of men after the war makes any assumption about residence problematic and makes difficult the matching-up of soldiers and individuals identified in postwar census data, such as the 1870 U.S. Census (which merely notes whether parents were foreign born) and the 1880 U.S. Census (which actually lists place of birth for father and mother). The difficulty is further complicated by the simple fact that there were many men of the same name. The solution, for this project, was to rely on data from the New York Passenger Lists (1820–1957) compiled by Ancestry.com. Search by last names provides the number of passengers with that name who arrived in New York City, the primary port of entry for most Irish immigrants to the United States. I searched for the last names of all the soldiers from these three regiments in my database who were born in the United States and ranked them according to the likelihood that their names were

Irish, based on birthplace of immigrants entering the United States between 1820 and 1957 with that same last name, as recorded in the New York Passenger Lists. Where more than 50 percent of the immigrants with a particular name arrived in New York from Ireland, I attributed "probable Irish descent" to men with that last name. Where between 15 and 49 percent of the immigrants with a given last name arrived from Ireland, most arrived from Ireland, England, or Great Britain, and only a small number with that name arrived from Continental Europe, I attributed "likely Irish descent" to men with that last name. Given the immigration patterns between Ireland and England during the nineteenth century, and the fact that these men all chose to serve in a regiment that identified itself as Irish, I felt comfortable that this range would be the most inclusive. Where between 5 and 14 percent of the immigrants with a particular last name arrived from Ireland and there were also a large number of British/English/Scottish immigrants of that name, as well as a large number of immigrants from the Continent, I attributed "possible Irish descent" to men with that name. Where between .01 and 4 percent of the immigrants with a particular name were from Ireland, or a majority of immigrants with that name were from the Continent, I defined men with that name as "unlikely." I assigned a "no" to men with names that showed no link to Ireland, and also created a separate category for names that were not found at all in the New York Passenger Lists. The 70 percent mentioned in the main text is the proportion of American-born soldiers whose names fell into the first two categories, "probable" and "likely." This method was used throughout.

31. "Mulligan and the Irish Brigade," *Journal of the Illinois State Historical Society* 56, no. 2 (1963): 164–76; David A. Wilson, *United Irishmen, United States: Immigrant Radicals in the Early Republic* (Ithaca: Cornell University Press, 1998), 20–22, 51; William Henry Condon, *Life of Major-General James Shields: Hero of Three Wars and Senator from Three States* (Chicago: Blakely Printing Co., 1900). Company names were made available through the Civil War database project sponsored by the Illinois GenWeb Project, civilwar.illinoisgenweb.org.

32. Muster dates for the men in this section are from April 12, 1861 through July 27, 1861. Information about James Barnes (Co. B, 23rd IL Vol. Inf., Civil War) is from pension application no. 672,372, certificate no. 700,060, Case Files of Approved Pension Applications, 1861–1934; Civil War and Later Pension Files, Records of the Veterans Administration, Record Group 15, National Archives and Records Administration, Washington, D.C. (hereafter RG 15, NARA). Information about John Ward (Cpl. Co. D, 23rd Vol. Inf., Civil War) is from pension application no. 982,434, certificate no. 698,366, RG 15, NARA. Civil War pension files show numerous incidents such as the marriage of John Ward and the widow of William Scully. Such marriages speak to the close-knit communities that developed during this period, and one wonders if there was some notion of duty felt among returning soldiers to care for the widows of their comrades in arms. William and Mary Scully had been married for only two years when William was killed, and he left behind not only a wife but also a small child, for whom a pension application was submitted.

33. "The Irish Brigade," *Chicago Tribune*, July 16, 1861; Harold F. Smith, "Mulligan and the Irish Brigade," *Journal of the Illinois State Historical Society* 56, no. 2 (1963), 164–76; James McPherson, *Battle Cry of Freedom: The Civil War Era* (New York: Oxford University Press, 1988), 350–51.

34. McPherson, *Battle Cry of Freedom*, 351–53. The quotation is from "The Battle of Wilson's Creek [Correspondence of the St. Louis Democrat]," *Boston Daily Advertiser*, August 19, 1861For an overview of the battle, see William Garrett Piston and Richard W. Hatcher III, *Wilson's Creek: The Second Battle of the Civil War and the Men Who Fought It* (Chapel Hill: University of North Carolina Press, 2000).

35. Smith, "Mulligan and the Irish Brigade," 167. For examples of the national scope of attention to the battle, see "The Rebels Defeated at Lexington," *Jamestown (N.Y.) Journal*, September 20, 1861; similar articles appeared in the *Boston Liberator, Lowell Daily Citizen and News*, and *the New York Tribune.* Account of Mulligan's initial defense of the city appeared in an article entitled "The Latest War News," *New-York Daily Tribune*, September 20, 1861. Mulligan's reply was printed that same day in an article entitled "Important from Missouri."

36. Accounts of the Brigade's defensive position appeared in an article entitled "Interesting from Missouri; The Battle of Lexington," *New-York Daily Tribune*, September 21, 1861. For "brave defense" see "Late from Lexington," *North American and United States Gazette* (Philadelphia), September 21, 1861; for surrender, see "The Latest War News," *New-York Daily Tribune*, September 23, 1861.

37. Bruce, *The Harp and the Eagle*, 74. Bruce provides a fine overview of the action of the 69th New York at First Bull Run and their subsequent emergence in the eyes of the American public as an extremely important unit. Christian Keller, in *Chancellorsville and the Germans: Nativism, Ethnicity, and Civil War Memory* (New York: Fordham University Press, 2008), 77–91, argues that perceptions of cowardice that emerged surrounding the mostly German 11th Corps in the wake of the Battle of Chancellorsville seriously inhibited German assimilation during and after the war. The surrender of Irish forces in the early months of the war had no such impact. The *Albany Evening Journal* of September 24, 1861 reported a *New York Tribune* dispatch stating that "it is not unlikely that Gen. Frémont will be considered responsible, and the disaster may be the immediate occasion of his removal."

38. "Who Is Colonel Mulligan?" *Albany Evening Journal*, September 24, 1861; "Col. Mulligan," *Appleton (Wis.) Crescent*, October 12, 1861.

## 2. An Irish Regiment in the Nutmeg State

1. On the role of Irish soldiers of Connecticut prior to the Civil War, see Thomas Hamilton Murray, *History of the Ninth Regiment, Connecticut Volunteer Infantry* (New Haven: Price, Lee and Adkins Co., 1903), 10–15. Histories of the area include Everett Gleason Hill, *A Modern History of New Haven and Eastern New Haven County*, 2 vols. (New York: S. J. Clarke Publishing Co., 1918); John L. Rockey, ed., *History of New Haven County, Connecticut* (New York: W. W. Preston and Co., 1892); *Commemorative Biographical Record of Hartford County, Connecticut, Containing Biographical Sketches of Prominent and Representative Citizens, and Many of the Early Settled Families* (Chicago: J. H. Beers and Co., 1901); Henry Howe, *An Outline History of New Haven (Interspersed with Reminiscences)* (New Haven: O. A. Dorman, 1884).

2. Rockey, *History of New Haven County*, 1:107–8; *Connecticut Gazette* quoted on p. 169.

3. Michael Sletcher, *New Haven: From Puritanism to the Age of Terrorism* (Chicago: Arcadia Publishing, 2004), 102.

4. "Immigrants Should Go West," *Constitution* (Middletown, Conn.), February 14, 1855.

5. "The Sword of Jackson," *Columbian Register* (New Haven), March 10, 1855; "The Voice of Henry Clay," *Columbian Register*, May 19, 1855.

6. William T. Minor to Justin Hodge, Adjutant General, August 24, 1855, reprinted in Murray, *History of the Ninth Regiment*, 17; untitled article, *Constitution* (Middletown, Conn.), February 14, 1855; untitled article, *Albany Evening Journal*, March 21, 1855; "In Senate," *Daily Globe* (Washington, D.C.), January 26, 1855 .

7. "The Militia Disbandment," *Columbian Register* (New Haven), October 6, 1855; "Opinion," *Connecticut Courant* (Hartford), October 6, 1855; "One of the Documents," *Columbian Register*, October 6, 1855.

8. *The Metropolitan Catholic Almanac and Laity's Directory: For the United States, Canada, and the British Provinces* (Baltimore: John Murphy and Co., 1861.

9. Murray, *History of the Ninth Regiment*, 22–23.

10. Robert Emmet, quoted in Robert Kee, *The Green Flag: A History of Irish Nationalism* (New York: Penguin Books, 1972), 167–69.

11. Bruce Alan Clouette, "'Getting Their Share': Irish and Italian Immigrants in Hartford, Connecticut, 1850–1940" (Ph.D. diss., University of Connecticut, 1992), 52–62.

12. Joseph Anderson and Anna Lydia Ward, eds., *The Town and City of Waterbury, Connecticut, from the Aboriginal Period to the Year Eighteen Hundred and Ninety-Five* (New Haven: Price and Lee, 1896), 2:431; Samuel Orcutt, *A History of the Old Town of Stratford and the City of Bridgeport, Connecticut* (New Haven: Press of Tuttle, Morehouse and Taylor , 1886), 2:693.

13. "Irish Volunteers," *Constitution* (Middletown, Conn.), April 24, 1861.

14. *Palladium* (New Haven), April 22, 1861, quoted in Murray, *History of the Ninth Regiment*, 27.

15. Untitled article, *Columbian Weekly Register* (New Haven), May 11, 1861; "In the Days of Know-Nothingism," *Columbian Weekly Register*, May 11, 1861.

16. "A Priest's War Speech," *Hartford Daily Courant*, June 25, 1861; "Connecticut Correspondence," *Irish-American Weekly*, October 12, 1861; "Grand Union Meeting on the Park," *Connecticut Courant* (Hartford), September 21, 1861.

17. "The Departure for the War of the Sixty-Ninth," *Hartford Daily Courant*, April 25, 1861; "The Baptism of One of the Big Guns of the New York Sixty Ninth by Father Mooney," *Columbian Weekly Register* (New Haven), June 29, 1861.

18. "The Great Battle," *Hartford Daily Courant*, July 24, 1861; "A Letter from Washington," *Hartford Daily Courant*, July 25, 1861; "The Irish Soldiers," *Columbian Weekly Register* (New Haven), August 10, 1861.

19. Susannah Ural Bruce, *The Harp and the Eagle: Irish American Volunteers in the Union Army, 1861–1865* (New York: New York University Press, 2006), 79.

20. "Colonel Mulligan," *Hartford Daily Courant*, September 25, 1861; "The Siege of Lexington—Detailed Account," *Hartford Daily Courant*, September 25, 1861; "News from Washington," *Columbian Weekly Register* (New Haven), September 28, 1861; "Col. Mulligan," *Constitution* (Middletown, Conn.), October 2, 1861.

21. "Response to Irish Peace Democrat," *Constitution* (Middletown, Conn.), September 4, 1861; Murray, *History of the Ninth Regiment*, 33; "Meriden Volunteers," *Hartford Daily Courant*, September 21, 1861; "Irish Regiment," *Constitution*, September 4, 1861.

22. See Murray, *History of the Ninth Regiment*, 30–33; "One of the Documents," *Columbian Weekly Register* (New Haven), October 6, 1855; and "The Militia Disbandment," *Columbian Weekly Register*, October 6, 1855.

23. "The Emmet Guard Going," *Palladium* (New Haven), September 5, 1861, quoted in Murray, *History of the Ninth Regiment*, 34; *Palladium*, September 10, 1861, quoted in Murray, *History of the Ninth Regiment*, 35; untitled article, *Hartford Daily Courant*, September 12, 1861; "Father Quinn's Lecture," *Hartford Daily Courant*, September 13, 1861.

24. Murray, *History of the Ninth Regiment*, 334; 14.

25. Murray, *History of the Ninth Regiment*, 21; 39.

26. Orcutt, *History of the Old Town of Stratford*, 2:865.

27. James McCarty (Pvt. Co. E, 9th CT Vol. Inf., Civil War), pension application no. 12,299, certificate no. 40,193, Case Files of Approved Pension Applications, 1861–1934; Civil War and Later Pension Files, Records of the Veterans Administration, Record Group 15, National Archives and Records Administration, Washington, D.C. (hereafter RC 15, NARA).Information exists for some 664 soldiers who enlisted between April 1861 and December 1861, before the regiment reached Ship Island. There were more men who joined the regiment after it reached Louisiana, who are not included in this count. The average age of the Irish recruits was twenty-eight, while the American-born men were, on average, four years younger.

28. Francis McKeon (Co. E, Ninth CT Vol. Inf., Civil War), pension application no. 500,246, certificate no. 467,560, RC 15, NARA.

29. Edward Murray (Co. H, 9th CT Vol. Inf., Civil War), pension application no. 590,717, certificate no. 702,044; John Hanlon (Co. D, 9th CT Vol. Inf., Civil War), pension application no. 464,568, certificate no. 420,415; Michael McCarten (Co. C, 9th CT Vol. Inf., Civil War), pension application no. 709, 696, certificate no.720,831, RG 15, NARA.

30. "For the War," *Constitution* (Middleton, Conn.), October 16, 1861; untitled article, *Constitution*, October 16, 1861.

31. *New Haven Register*, September 11, 1861, quoted in Murray, *History of the Ninth Regiment*, 37.

32. A Friend to Thomas Cahill, 31 October 1862, Cahill Collection, held by Charles Sibley, Hamden, Connecticut.

33. "Local News," *Columbian Weekly Register* (New Haven), September 14, 1861; "Military Affairs," *Hartford Daily Courant*, November 1, 1861; John Niven, *Connecticut for the Union: The Role of the State in the Civil War* (New Haven: Yale University Press, 1965), 67.

34. Niven, *Connecticut for the Union*, 67.

35. Major-General Benj. F. Butler to the Adjutant-General, November 18, 1861, in *The War of the Rebellion: Official Records of the Union and Confederate Armies*, series 3 (Washington, D. C.: GPO, 1899–1900), 1:653.

36. Niven, *Connecticut for the Union*, 67.

37. Murray, *History of the Ninth Regiment*, 35; "The Ninth Regiment," *Hartford Daily Courant*, November 5, 1861.

38. "The Ninth Regiment," *Hartford Daily Courant*, November 12, 186; Murray, *History of the Ninth Regiment*, 37; "The Ninth Regiment," *Hartford Daily Courant*, November 5, 1861; "The Ninth Regiment," *Hartford Daily Courant*, November 12, 1861.

39. "The Ninth Regiment," *Hartford Daily Courant*, November 13, 1861; "The Ninth Regiment," *Connecticut Courant*, November 9, 1861.

40. Murray, *History of the Ninth Regiment*, 49.

41. Daniel O'Sullivan to Friend, 25 December 1861, Daniel O'Sullivan and George Hill Collection held by Joseph Kelly, Toms River, N.J. (hereafter cited as O'Sullivan Collection).

42. "City Marshall," *Lowell Daily Citizen*, November 13, 1861.

43. "The Expedition from Boston; Steamship Constitution at Portland; The Trip to the Capes of Virginia; The Weather; The Passengers, and How They Stood the Passage," *New York Times*, November 29, 1861.

44. Daniel O'Sullivan to Friend, 25 December 1861, O'Sullivan Collection.

45. Daniel O'Sullivan to Friend, 25 December 1861, O'Sullivan Collection; John D. Winters, *The Civil War in Louisiana* (Baton Rouge, Louisiana State University Press, 1963), 28, 50.

46. Daniel O'Sullivan to "Sir," 23 March 1862, O'Sullivan Collection; Thomas Cahill to Margaret Cahill, 18 January 1862, Cahill Collection.

47. Captain Michael McCarten, in James Mullen (Co. C, 9th CT Vol. Inf., Civil War), pension application no. 740,032, certificate no. 634,359, RG 15, NARA. The letters of Thomas W. Cahill contained in the Cahill Collection from this period emphasize the focus on regimental drill and discipline during the time the Ninth Connecticut was stationed on Ship Island. That just one man was discharged during the Ninth Connecticut's time at this post is from the database of the Ninth Connecticut, 23rd Illinois, and 17th Wisconsin regiments developed for this project, referred to as the Database of Volunteers to Irish Regiments and compiled from the Descriptive and Muster Rolls of Civil War Regiments, Records of the Adjutant General's Office, 1780s—1917, RG 94, National Archives and Records Administration, Washington, D.C. (NARA); Company Muster Rolls of Illinois Regiments, RS 301.019, Military and Naval Department (Civil War), RS 301, Illinois State Archives, Springfield; and Regimental Muster and Descriptive Rolls, Wisconsin Adjutant General's Office, State Historical Society of Wisconsin, Madison.

48. Proclamation of Brigadier-General Phelps to the loyal people of the Southwest, December 4, 1861, U.S. Department of the Navy, *Official Records of the Union and Confederate Navies in the War of the Rebellion*, series 1 (Washington, D.C.: GPO, 1903), 17:18–20

49. "From Washington," *Hartford Daily Courant*, December 12, 1861; "General Phelps," *Hartford Daily Courant*, February 12, 1862; untitled article, *Columbian Weekly Register* (New Haven), February 22, 1862; "Proclamation of Flag Officer Foote," *Columbian Weekly Register*, March 1, 1862.

50. Thomas Cahill to Margaret Cahill, 7 December 1861, Cahill Collection. It is impossible to determine the percentage of Catholics in the three regiments in this study. However, in all three units, Catholic priests accompanied the men into the field and were supported by parishes on the home front.

51. Thomas Cahill to Margaret Cahill, January 7, 1862, Cahill Collection; Thomas Cahill to Margaret Cahill, February 26, 1862, Cahill Collection; Daniel O'Sullivan to Unknown, March 23, 1862.

## 3. The Formation of the 17th Wisconsin

1. M. Justille McDonald, *History of the Irish in Wisconsin in the Nineteenth Century* (Washington, D. C.: Catholic University of America Press, 1952), 11–13; David Noel Doyle, "The Irish as Urban Pioneers in the United States, 1850–1870," *Journal of American Ethnic History* 10, no. 1/2 (Fall 1990–Winter 1991); *History of Milwaukee, Wisconsin: From Pre-Historic Times to the Present Date* (Chicago: Western Historical Company, 1881), 1:118, ibid., 197; La Vern J. Rippley, *The Immigrant Experience in Wisconsin* (Boston: Twayne, 1985), 2; McDonald, *History of the Irish in Wisconsin*, 8.

2. Daniel S. Durrie, *A History of Madison, the Capital of Wisconsin; Including the Four Lake Country to July, 1874* (Madison: Atwood and Culver, 1874), 15–16; ibid., 32–34; ibid., 162; ibid., 264.

3. *History of Fond du Lac County, Wisconsin* (Chicago: Western Historical Company, 1880), 765; ibid., 423–27; Dennis O'Laughlin to Laurence O'Laughlin, undated, State Historical Society of Wisconsin, Madison, SC 2063.

4. *Annual Report of the Emigration Commissioner of the State of Wisconsin for the Year 1853* (Madison: Beriah Brown, 1854), 6, quoted in McDonald, *History of the Irish in Wisconsin*, 10–11.

5. Louis Phelps Kellogg, "The Story of Wisconsin, 1634–1848: Foreign Immigration in Territorial Times," *Wisconsin Magazine of History* 3, no. 3 (March 1920): 316, quoted in Rippley, *Immigrant Experience in Wisconsin*, 3. McDonald (*History of the Irish in Wisconsin*, 127) also notes the "capacity for political action" (Kellogg, "Foreign Immigration," 316) of the Irish in the Wisconsin territory and their involvement in the territorial and later state legislature in the 1840s and 1850s. "Qualifications of Voters," *Milwaukee Sentinel*, October 12, 1844.

6. Joseph Schafer, "Know-Nothingism in Wisconsin," *Wisconsin Magazine of History* 8, no. 1 (September 1924): 8–9; quotation from American Party in ibid., 9; untitled article, *Wisconsin Daily Patriot* (Madison), October 14, 1854; "Black Republicans and Know Nothings Melted Together," *Weekly Wisconsin Patriot*, June 28, 1856. McDonald, *History of the Irish in Wisconsin*, 135; Schafer, "Know-Nothingism in Wisconsin," 12; McDonald, *History of the Irish in Wisconsin*, 137; Robert C. Nesbit, *Wisconsin: A History* (Madison: University of Wisconsin Press, 1930), 238–40.

7. "Devoted Patriotism of the Irish Catholics—Its Probable Influence on their Secession Countrymen," *Daily Illinois State Journal*, May 22, 1861; "The Adopted Citizens of the Union," *Weekly Wisconsin Patriot*, January 5, 1861; "Saint Patrick's Day at Madison," *Daily Milwaukee Press and News*, April 2, 1861; "The American Flag on the Cathedral," *Milwaukee Sentinel*, April 26, 1861; "From Fond du Lac," *Wisconsin Daily Patriot*, April 19, 1861.

8. "Governor's Message," *Wisconsin Daily Patriot*, January 12, 1861; untitled article, *Milwaukee Sentinel*, April 27, 1861; "The Irish and the War," *Wisconsin Daily Patriot*, April 24, 1861.

9. "Irish True to the Union," *Wisconsin Daily Patriot*, April 17, 1861. Stories about Irish support for the Union included "Latest News: Military Spirit Thoroughly Aroused!" *Milwaukee Daily Sentinel*, April 14, 1861; "The Foreign Element in the Federal Army," *Albany Evening Journal*, reprinted in the *Milwaukee Morning Sentinel*, June, 20, 1861; "The Irish and the War," *Weekly Wisconsin Patriot* (Madison), April 27, 1861; "The War Feeling in the State," *Hartford Daily Courant*, April 23, 1861; "Irish Volunteers," *Constitution* (Middletown, Conn.), April 24, 1861. "The War Feeling in the State," *Hartford Daily Courant,* April 23, 1861; untitled article, *Columbian Weekly Register*, May 11, 1861; "An Irish Company," *Janesville Daily Gazette*, April 29, 1861; "All Sorts of Paragraphs," *Janesville Daily Gazette*, June 18, 1861.

10. See "Terrible Catastrophie!" *Wisconsin Daily Patriot*, September 10, 1860; "The Calamity on the Lady Elgin—Is Gov. Randall Responsible?" *Wisconsin Daily Patriot,* September 14, 1860; William George Bruce, *History of Milwaukee, City and County* (Chicago: S. J. Clarke Publishing Co., 1922), 128–29; Charles Martin Scanlan, *The Lady Elgin Disaster, September 8, 1860* (Canon Printing Co., 1928); Brian A. Kangas, "Tragedy, Myth and Memory: The Sinking of the *Lady Elgin* and Its Impact on Irish American Nationalism in Milwaukee, 1850–1870" (Ph.D. diss.,University of Wisconsin, Milwaukee, 2011); McDonald, *History of the Irish in Wisconsin*, 55. McDonald notes that Scanlan in *The Lady Elgin Disaster* suggests that the sinking of the *Lady Elgin* pushed the Milwaukee community back at least twenty years, while allowing the Irish community in Chicago to thrive.

11. "Communicated," *Daily Milwaukee News*, June 4, 1861; *Weekly Wisconsin Patriot*, August 23, 1862; "Governor Randall and the Union Guards," *Wisconsin Daily Patriot*, March 12, 1860.

12. "Progress of the War," *Milwaukee Daily Sentinel*, April 27, 1861; "Interesting War Items," *Weekly Wisconsin Patriot*, May 4, 1861; "Departure of Meagher's Irish Zouaves," *Weekly Wisconsin Patriot*, June 1, 1861.

13. "Lieutenant Simpson's Account of the Battle of Bull's Run," *Weekly Wisconsin Patriot*, August 3, 1861; "The Great Battle," *Wisconsin Daily Patriot*, July 26, 1861; "News from the Sixty-Ninth Regiment," *Daily Milwaukee News,* July 28, 1861; "Our Noble 69th (Irish) Regiment," *Wisconsin Daily Patriot*, July 27, 1861; Kerby Miller, *Emigrants and Exiles: Ireland and the Irish Exodus to North America* (New York: Oxford University Press, 1985). Miller discusses at length the Irish diaspora in North America, with particular attention to the impact of the shared notions of exile that united this broadly dispersed group.

14. "The Irish Brigade, Chicago," *Wisconsin Daily Patriot*, June 25, 1861; "Col. Mulligan's Answer," *Janesville Daily Gazette*, September 20, 1861.

15. "The Lexington Fight; Additional Particulars," *Weekly Wisconsin Patriot*, September 28, 1861; "The Surrender of Lexington," *Janesville Daily Gazette,* September 24, 1861; "Particulars of the Lexington Fight," *Wisconsin Daily Patriot*, September 24, 1861; "Our Noble 69th (Irish) Regiment," *Wisconsin Daily Patriot*, July 27, 1861.

16. "Irishmen! Rally to the Rescue," *Watertown Democrat*, November 7, 1861; "How It Works," *Appleton Crescent*, August 10, 1861; "An Irish Regiment," *Wisconsin Daily Patriot*, September 24, 1861; "Let Us Fill Up the Ranks," *Janesville Daily Gazette,* September 25, 1861.

17. On John Doran , see *History of Milwaukee, Wisconsin: From Pre-historic Times to the Present Date*, 1:689; Jerome A. Watrous, *Memoirs of Milwaukee County, from the Earliest Historical Times Down to the Present* (Madison: Western Historical Association, 1909), 96; and Bruce, *History of Milwaukee, City and County*, 1:141."Seventeenth Regiment," *Janesville* Daily Gazette, reprinted in the *Wisconsin Daily Patriot*, December 8, 1861.

18. "Seventeenth Regiment," *Janesville Daily Gazette* reprinted in the *Wisconsin Daily Patriot*, December 8, 1861.

19. Reports on Watertown recruiting appear in "Irishmen at Home and in America," *Watertown Democrat*, November 21, 1861, and "The Irish Brigade," *Watertown Democrat*, December 5, 1861. "Col. Doran's Irish Brigade," *Janesville Daily Gazette*, November 29, 1861; "Recruits Wanted for the Irish Regiment," *Milwaukee Daily News*, January 10, 1862.

20. "Military Items," *Wisconsin Daily Patriot*, January 4, 1862; Ebenezer Wescott to Mother, 19 January, 1862, M. Ebenezer Wescott Papers, River Falls Area Research Center, University of Wisconsin–River Falls (hereafter cited as Wescott Papers, River Falls).

21. Names of the companies were published in "The Seventeenth, or the Irish Regiment," newspaper clipping, Quiner Scrapbooks: Correspondence of Wisconsin Volunteers, 1861–1865, 6:25; Mss 600, State Historical Society of Wisconsin, Madison (hereafter cited as Quiner Scrapbooks, SHSW). The Quiner Scrapbooks were organized during the war by an E. B. Quiner, who collected, organized, and stored newspapers clippings dealing with Wisconsin regiments during the war, including correspondence from soldiers published in local papers. In some instances the sources of clipped articles have been identified. In those cases, the article will be cited from the original newspaper source. If the newspaper source is unidentifiable, the article will be cited by its volume and page in the Quiner Scrapbooks. For further reading on Harvey, the United Irishmen, and the Peep O'Day Boys, see Robert Kee, *The Green Flag: A History of Irish Nationalism* (London: Penguin Books, 1972), and Nancy Curtain, *The United Irishmen: Popular Politics in Ulster and Dublin, 1791–1798* (New York: Clarendon Press, 1998).

22. Sylvanus Cadwallader, *Three Years with Grant* (New York: Knopf, 1955), 30.

23. A. T. Glaze, *Incidents and Anecdotes of Early Days and History of Business in the City and County of Fond du Lac from Early Times to the Present* (Fond du Lac, Wis.: P. B. Haber Printing Co., 1905), 6–7.

24. On McCauley and Crane, see William J. K. Beaudot and Lance J. Herdegen, eds., *An Irishman in the Iron Brigade: The Civil War Memoirs of James P. Sullivan* (New York: Fordham University Press, 1993), and Rufus Robinson Dawes, *Service with the Sixth Wisconsin Volunteers* (Marietta, Ohio: E. R. Alderman and Sons, 1890), 26–27 and 25; on Feagan and McGowery, see Carl Ziller, *History of Sheboygan County, Wisconsin, Past and Present*, vol. 2 (Chicago: S. J. Clarke Publishing Co., 1912.); on Darius Palmer, see Harry Ellsworth Cole, *A Standard History of Sauk County, Wisconsin*, vol. 1 (Chicago: Lewis Publishing Co., 1918); on David Bishop, see J. W. Stearns, ed., *The Columbia History of Education in Wisconsin* (Milwaukee: State Committee on Educational Exhibit for Wisconsin, 1893); on Charles Armstrong and John Doran, see *The History of Sauk County, Containing an Account of Its Settlement, Growth, Development*

*and Resources* (Chicago: Western Publishing Co., 1880), and Waltrous, *Memoirs of Milwaukee County*, 96. An overview is provided by Andrew S. Bledsoe, *Citizen-Officers: The Union and Confederate Volunteer Junior Officer Corps in the Civil War* (Baton Rouge: Louisiana State University Press, 2015), 40–42.

25. S. Hanson, "True Patriotism," Quiner Scrapbooks, 6:25, SHSW.

26. Hugh Dorsey (Co. C, 17th WI Vol. Inf., Civil War), pension application no. 507,593, certificate no.568,465; Dennis Harkins(Co. C, 17th WI Vol. Inf., Civil War), pension application no. 20,292, certificate no. 19,469; James Connelly (Co. F, 17th WI Vol. Inf., Civil War), pension application no. 321,243, certificate no. 375,450; all in Case Files of Approved Pension Applications, 1861–1934, Civil War and Later Pension Files, Records of the Veterans Administration, Record Group 15, National Archives and Records Administration, Washington, D.C. (hereafter RG 15, NARA).

27. Victor Melin (Co. G, 17th WI Vol. Inf., Civil War), pension application no. 511,080, certificate no. 343,610, RG 15, NARA.

28. Nathan Phillips (Co. K, 17th WI Vol. Inf., Civil War), pension application no. 21,300, certificate no. 340,616; Edward Riley (Co. F, 17th WI Vol. Inf., Civil War), pension application no. 1,304,119, certificate no. 1,076,128; William Copeland (Co. D, 17th WI Vol. Inf., Civil War), pension application no. 764,866, certificate no. 874,407, RG 15, NARA.

29. Frank L. Klement, *Wisconsin in the Civil War: The Home Front and the Battle Front, 1861–1865* (Madison: State Historical Society of Wisconsin, 2001), 11; "Soldiers' Relief Bounty," *Wisconsin Daily Patriot* (Madison), February 22, 1862.

30. "The Seventeenth, or the Irish Regiment," Quiner Scrapbooks, 6:25, SHSW; "Fire at Camp Randall—Loss of Life—Mutinous Conduct of the Regiment—A Part Refuse to Obey the Order of Departure," Quiner Scrapbooks, 6:25, SHSW; Thomas Davis (Co. D, 17th WI Vol. Inf., Civil War), pension application no. 210, 933, certificate no. 154,666, RG 15, NARA; "Fire at Camp Randall—Disorganization of the 17th," *Wisconsin Daily Patriot* (Madison), March 20, 1862.

31. "Fire at Camp Randall," *Wisconsin Daily Patriot*, March 22, 1862.

32. "Fire at Camp Randall," *Wisconsin Daily Patriot*, March 22, 1862; "The 17th Regiment—Numerous Desertions—Apprehensions and Excitement in the City last evening," Quiner Scrapbooks, 6:26, SHSW.

33. "Nine Cheers for Capt. McAully," *Wisconsin Daily Patriot*, March 22, 1862; "The Effect of Pluck and Spirit," Quiner Scrapbooks, 6:26, SHSW.

34. Louis Powell Harvey to James Mulligan, 20 March 1862, James A. Mulligan Papers, Chicago History Museum; Louis Powell Harvey to James Mulligan, 22 March 1862, Mulligan Papers.

35. "Departure of 200 more of the 17th Regiment: How some Things can be Done as well as Others—The men of Lexington in Madison—How boys that Would not go were Made to go—Nobody hurt," Quiner Scrapbooks, 6:27, SHSW; Richard Curran to Mother, 31 March 1862, Regimental Correspondence of the 17th Wisconsin, 1861–62, box 90, folder 4, Records of Civil War Regiments, Series 1200, Wisconsin Adjutant General's Office, State Historical Society of Wisconsin, Madison (hereafter cited as Regimental Correspondence of the 17th, SHSW); "Letter to the *Advocate*," Quiner Scrapbooks, 6:28, SHSW.

36. Riccardo Herrera, "A People and Its Soldiers: The American Citizen as Soldier, 1775–1861," *International Bibliography of Military History* 33, no. 1 (2013), 11.

37. Warren L. Young, *Minorities and the Military: A Cross-National Study in World Perspective* (Westport, Conn.: Greenwood Press, 1982), 255; "The 17th Regiment—Numerous Desertions," Quiner Scrapbooks, 6:26. SHSW; "Fire at Camp Randall—Loss of Life," Quiner Scrapbooks, 6:26, SHSW; "Departure of 200 more of the 17th Regiment: How some Things can be Done as well as Others," Quiner Scrapbooks, 6:27, SHSW.

38. Richard Curran to Mother, 31 March 1862, Regimental Correspondence of the 17th, SHSW; "The Effect of Pluck and Spirit," Quiner Scrapbooks, 6:26, SHSW.

39. "War Correspondence: Camp Benton, St. Louis, March 24, 1862," Quiner Scrapbooks, 6:29, SHSW. Concerning the sympathies of the people of Missouri, see William C. Harris, *With Charity for All: Lincoln and the Restoration of the Union* (Lexington: University Press of Kentucky, 1997), 18–20. Despite the fact that Missouri remained in the Union and St. Louis was largely a pro-Union city, Southern sympathy still existed and the correspondence suggests that soldiers in the 17th Wisconsin were aware of the various loyalties at play in this border state.

40. "Letter from the 17th Wisconsin Regiment" (Capt. D. D. Scott, April 13, 1862), Quiner Scrapbooks, 6:32, SHSW; Ebenezer Wescott to Mother, 3 April 1862, Wescott Papers, River Falls; "Letter from the 17th Wisconsin" (Scott, April 13, 1862), Quiner Scrapbooks, 6:32, SHSW. Scott notes that the 17th was visited by members of the 16th Wisconsin, who discussed the battle in detail. He also suggests that the men of the 17th could see the physical impact of battle on the men of the 16th Wisconsin.

41. See Christian Keller, *Chancellorsville and the Germans* (New York: Fordham University Press, 2007) for discussions of the national attention given to the mostly German 11th Corps after the Battle of Chancellorsville. See also Thaddeus Romansky, "Disunion in the Ranks: Soldiers, Citizenship, and Mutiny in the Union Army," Ph.D. diss., Texas A&M University, 2015.

## 4. Ethnicity and Combat

1. James Tompkins to James Mulligan, 18 November 1861; George A. Hamilton to James Mulligan, 2 December 1861; William Cassidy to James Mulligan, 5 December 1861; all in James A. Mulligan Papers, Chicago Museum of History.

2. "Serenade to Col. Jas. A. Mulligan," *Daily Illinois State Register* (Springfield), January 28, 1862; "The Hero of Lexington Coming," *Rock River Democrat* (Rockford, Ill.), January 28, 1862; "The Orator and Warrior," *Rockford (Ill.) Republican*, February 13, 1862.

3. Adam Blaul (Co. E, 23rd IL Vol. Inf., Civil War), pension application no. 780,511, certificate no. 559,999; George Winfrey (Co. A, 23rd IL Vol. Inf., Civil War), pension application no. 62,490, certificate no. 369,740; William Crowell (Co. A, 23rd IL Vol. Inf., Civil War) pension application no. 1,284,728, certificate no. 676,690; all in Case Files of Approved Pension Applications, 1861–1934, in Civil War and Later Pension Files, Records of the Veterans Administration, Record Group 15, National Archives and Records Administration, Washington, D.C. (RG 15, NARA); John McDermott to James Mulligan, 4 January 1862, Mulligan Papers, Chicago.

4. The loss of muster and descriptive rolls at Lexington poses some problems with regard to the men who were members of the original Illinois 23rd, recruited in summer 1861, but the numbers provided here, while not exact, reflect as accurately as possible the regiment that reformed between October 1861 and August 8, 1862. Diary of Albert V. B. Phillips, Albert V. Phillips Papers, 1860–1872, SC 1171, folder 2, Abraham Lincoln Presidential Library, Springfield, Ill. (hereafter cited as Phillips Papers, ALPL).

5. Diary of Albert V. B. Phillips, Phillips Papers, ALPL.

6. Martin Simmons (Co. C, 23rd IL Vol. Inf., Civil War), pension application no. 112,116, certificate no. 191,827, RG 15, NARA; Eighth Census of the United States, 1860.

7. "Three Year Volunteers," *Chicago Tribune*, June 6, 1861.

8. Thomas Cahill to Margaret Cahill, April 8, 1862, Cahill Collection, held by Charles Sibley, Hamden, Conn.; George Hill to Wife, April 6, 1862, Daniel O'Sullivan and George Hill Collection, held by Joseph Kelley, Toms River, N.J.

9. "News," *Hartford Daily Courant*, April 30, 1862; William Buckingham, quoted in Thomas Hamilton Murray, *The History of the Ninth Regiment, Connecticut Volunteer Infantry, "The Irish Regiment," in the War of the Rebellion, 1861–65* (New Haven: Price, Lee and Adkins Co., 1903), 85; Major-General Butler, General Orders, no. 10, Headquarters Department of the Gulf, April 12, 1862, *The War of the Rebellion: Official Records of the Union and Confederate Armies*, series 1, vol. 6 (Washington, D. C.: GPO, 1882), 709–10.

10. Thomas Cahill to Margaret Cahill, March 23, 1862, Cahill Collection.

11. Franklin Terrell quotations from Franklin Terrell (Co. E, 9th CT Vol. Inf., Civil War), pension application no. 1,368,978, certificate no. 1,142,774, RG 15, NARA. For a nuanced discussion of the sentiment in New Orleans in the spring of 1861, see Chester G. Hearn, *When the Devil Came Down to Dixie: Ben Butler in New Orleans* (Baton Rouge: Louisiana State University Press, 1997). Although many of the city's inhabitants were Confederates, there was a large immigrant population with divided allegiances. See Michael D. Pierson, *Mutiny at Fort Jackson: The Untold Story of the Fall of New Orleans* (Chapel Hill: University of North Carolina Press, 2008) for an excellent account of social and political issues in New Orleans during the first year of the war and the military action in and around the defenses of the city in the spring of 1862.

12. Pierson, *Mutiny at Fort Jackson*; Thomas Cahill to Margaret Cahill, May 2, 1862, Cahill Collection.

13. Murray, *History of the Ninth Regiment*, 105; Thomas Cahill to Margaret Cahill, May 26, 1862, Cahill Collection; pension file of Charles Michalk (Co. G, 9th CT Vol. Inf., Civil War), pension application no., 884,800, certificate no., 681,090, RG 15, NARA.

14. On living conditions at Camp Parapet, see Thomas Dolan (Co. E, 9th CT Vol. Inf., Civil War), pension application no. 659,452, certificate no. 732,080, RG 15, NARA. On strategies and troop movements in the Mississippi Valley in spring 1862, see Brian Holden Reid, *America's Civil War: The Operational Background* (New York: Prometheus Books, 2008), 143, and Francis Vinton Green, *Campaigns of the Civil War: The Mississippi* (New York: Charles Scribner's Sons, 1892), 29–33. Green provides an excellent military analysis oversight of campaigns in the Mississippi Valley during the war from the perspective of a lieutenant in the U.S. Army Corps of Engineers.

15. For accounts of the movement of the 17th Wisconsin in the summer of 1862, see "Letter from the 17th Wisconsin Regiment" (Capt. D. D. Scott, April 13, 1862), Quiner Scrapbooks :Correspondence of Wisconsin Volunteers, 1861–1865, 6:25, Mss 600, State Historical Society of Wisconsin, Madison (hereafter cited as Quiner Scrapbooks, SHSW); Ebenezer Wescott to Mother, 14 May 1862, M. Ebenezer Wescott Papers, River Falls Area Research Center, University of Wisconsin–River Falls (hereafter cited as Wescott Papers, River Falls); "From the Seventeenth Regiment," Quiner Scrapbooks, 6:33, SHSW; "Affairs at Corinth Just Previous to the Evacuation—Great Boasting," *New York Times*, June 2, 1862; Ebenezer Wescott to Parents, 5 June 1862, Westcott Papers, River Falls; James McPherson, *Battle Cry of Freedom: The Civil War Era* (New York: Oxford University Press, 2003), 416; and "The Evacuation of Corinth," *New York Times*, June 2, 1862. The relationship between Halleck and Grant, the movement of the army toward Corinth, and the retreat of the Confederates are described in "The Evacuation of Corinth," *New York Times*, June 2, 1862, and Carl R. Schenker, Jr., "Ulysses in His Tent: Halleck, Grant, Sherman, and 'The Turning Point of the War,'" *Civil War History* 56, no. 2 (2012): 175–221. Schenker's work contextualizes the post-Shiloh relationship between Grant and Halleck and specifically Special Field Order No. 35, which historians have suggested effectively removed from Grant any real control by promoting him to second in command of the army organizing at Pittsburg Landing in April 1862. Schenker suggests that historians have misrepresented Halleck's post-Shiloh treatment of Grant as "rooted in 'envy' of his success, or 'disdain' for his shortcomings, or shock at Shiloh's casualty list" (188). Rather, in Schenker's view, Halleck appeared to act in support of Grant in the wake of the battle, though this relationship appears to have soured as the army struggled south towards Corinth. For brief counterpoints to this argument see Brian J. Murphy, "The Secret War between Grant and Halleck," *Civil War Times* 45, no. 6 (2006): 44–52; John W. Marszalek, "Halleck Captures Corinth," *Civil War Times* 45, no. 1 (2006): 46–52; and Marszalek, *Commander of All Lincoln's Armies: A Life of General Henry W. Halleck* (Boston: Harvard University Press, 2004), 119–23.

16. Thomas Cahill to Margaret Cahill, 27 June 1862, Cahill Collection. The situation at Vicksburg is further described in Thomas Cahill to Margaret Cahill, 5 July 1862, Cahill Collection; "Important from Vicksburg," *Columbian Register* (New Haven), July 12, 1862; "From Vicksburg," *New London Daily Chronicle*, July 7, 1862; and "Rebel Reports from Vicksburg," *Hartford Daily Courant*, July 16, 1862. The feelings of one soldier in Chicago are described in Amaziah Hadden to Charlotte Hadden, 8 June 1862, and the Hadden quotation in text is from Amaziah Hadden to Charlotte Hadden, 12 June 1862; both letters in the Amaziah Hadden Letters, SC 2060, Abraham Lincoln Presidential Library (ALPL), Springfield, Ill. Diary of Albert V. B. Phillips, 14 June 1862, Phillips Papers, SC 1171, ALPL; "Departure of the Irish Brigade," *Chicago Times*, June 15, 1862.

17. Work on the canal is described in glowing terms in "Important from Vicksburg," *Columbian Register*, July 12, 1862; "From Vicksburg," *New London Daily Chronicle*, July 7, 1862; and "Rebel Reports from Vicksburg," *Hartford Daily Courant*, July 16, 1862.Thomas Cahill to Margaret Cahill, 27 June 1862, Cahill Collection; Lt. Col. Richard Fitzgibbon quote is from Franklin Tyler (Co. I, 9th CT Vol. Inf., Civil War), pension application no. 233,870, RG 15, NARA; Capt. Lawrence O'Brien quoted in Murray,

*History of the Ninth Connecticut*, 111, and Matthew Warshauer, *Connecticut in the Civil War: Slavery, Sacrifice, and Survival* (Middletown, Conn.: Wesleyan University Press, 2011), 81. Letters from Thomas Knablin to Mary Knablin, 28 July 1862 and 22 July 1863, in Thomas Knablin (Co. D, 9th CT Vol. Inf., Civil War), pension application no. 429,164, certificate no. 399,850, RG 15, NARA.

18. Thomas Knablin to Mary Knablin, 28 July 1862, in pension file of Thomas Knaplin; Matthew Warshauer, *Connecticut in the Civil War*, 81.

19. Thomas Cahill to Margaret Cahill, 5 July 1862, Cahill Collection; John D. Winters, *The Civil War in Louisiana* (Baton Rouge: Louisiana State University Press, 1963), 113–14. The Confederate attack was supposed to coincide with the arrival of the ram *CSS Arkansas*, but the ironclad ship did not leave Vicksburg, three hundred miles from Baton Rouge, until the morning of the battle, and the lack of Southern naval presence was key to the Union victory.

20. "Victory at Baton Rouge," *Hartford Daily Courant*, August 19, 1862. Only 5,100 men were engaged at Baton Rouge (Winters, *Civil War in Louisiana*, 123). In comparison, at Fair Oaks, Virginia on May 31, 1862, nearly 84,000 men had been engaged. At Gaines' Mill, Virginia a month later, 85,000 men fought as Lee attempted to push McClellan away from Richmond (Donald Stoker, *The Grand Design: Strategy and the U.S. Civil War* [New York: Oxford University Press, 2010), 140–56). Thomas Knablin to Mary Knablin, 7 September 1862, pension file of Thomas Knablin; "News," *Hartford Daily Courant*, August 27, 1862; Thomas Cahill to Sister, 20 October 1862, Cahill Collection; "A Better Look," *Hartford Daily Courant*, August 19, 1862.

21. "Private Letter from an Officer of the Irish Brigade," *Chicago Times*, September 16, 1862; diary of Albert V.B. Phillips, Phillips Papers, SC 1171, ALPL; diary of James Mulligan, January 16, 1863, Mulligan Papers, box 10, Chicago Museum of History.

22. "The Seventeenth Wisconsin on the Alert," *Wisconsin Daily Patriot*, September 27, 1862.

23. The details of the campaigns in Mississippi between July and October 1862 that led to the battles of Iuka and Corinth are not essential for the purposes of this discussion. But F. V. Green, *Campaigns of the Civil War: The Mississippi*, 29–54, provides useful military analysis of these campaigns and battles and is worth reading for details of the events that occurred during these months. For a more contemporary account of the Corinth campaign, see Steven E. Woodworth, *Nothing but Victory: The Army of the Tennessee, 1861–1865* (New York: Knopf, 2005), 219–40.

24. "From the Seventeenth Regiment," October 19, 1862, and "From the 16th and 17th regiments," Quiner Scrapbooks, 6:34, SHSW. See also Woodworth, *Nothing but Victory*, 226. Colonel John M. Oliver's command was part of the Sixth Division. The 17th Wisconsin was also part of the Sixth, attached to a brigade under Brigadier General John McArthur.

25. "From the Seventeenth Regiment," October 19, 1862, Quiner Scrapbooks, 6:35, SHSW. The author of this letter is adamant about the fact that the 17th Wisconsin acted alone in their charge. He notes that "I see it stated in the Chicago journals that Baldwin's brigade assisted, or made the charge. Such is not the case; the 17th alone made it." Other published accounts of the 17th Wisconsin's heroism include "A Gallant Oconto Boy," Quiner Scrapbooks, 6:34; "Compliment to a Brave Milwaukeean," *Milwaukee*

*Sentinel*, October 14, 1862; and "The Battle Near Corinth," *Watertown Democrat*, October 16, 1862. *The Democrat* noted that "the Seventeenth Wisconsin made a charge through the lines of the enemy, wheeled and charged back again."

26. Thomas Cahill to Margaret Cahill, May 6, 1863, and Thomas Cahill to Margaret Cahill, May 9, 1863, Cahill Collection. The Confederates moved down Bayou Teche by boat, around Cahill's men, and landed at Brashear on the morning of June 22, 1863, surprising the Federal garrison of some 700 men (only 400 effective) and causing considerable anxiety among the Union high command (Winters, *Civil War in Louisiana*, 285–92). Correspondence from this period illustrates the confusion regarding Confederate feints on Thibodaux, southwest of New Orleans. Reports reached General William Emory that rebel forces in the region numbered some 7,000 men, and that they had captured the town of Brashear on June 24, 1863. That same day, Cahill was ordered to spike his artillery pieces and retreat by rail back toward New Orleans, destroying bridges as he went. Emory seemed confused about Cahill's delay in retiring from the area, ordering him, at 10:00 pm: "If you cannot bring your horses, kill every one on the spot. Kill them with a knife, so the enemy will not hear your guns. Don't let anything fall into their hands. Destroy all the bridges, including the one at La Fourche, after your rear has passed. . . . Destroy the telegraph office and all its records. Blow up your caissons, but make no fires until your main body is at least 10 miles off." General William Emory to Thomas Cahill, June 24, 1863, *War of the Rebellion: Official Records*, series 1, vol. 26, part 1 (Washington, D.C.: GPO, 1889), 594.

27. Diary of James Mulligan, March 25, 1863, Mulligan Papers, Chicago; Report of Capt. Martin Wallace, Twenty-third Illinois Infantry, of skirmish at Greenland Gap, New Creek, Va., June 11, 1863, *War of the Rebellion: Official Records*, series 1, vol. 25, part 1 (Washington, D.C.: GPO, 1889), 108–10; "Mulligan Reported to Have Lost 250 Men as Prisoners," *Chicago Tribune*, May 4, 1863.

28. "The 17th Regiment," *Watertown Democrat*, June 4, 1863; Ebenezer Wescott to Parents, 27 May 1863, Wescott Papers, River Falls; "'Parvus' to 'Friend Ballou,'" *Watertown Democrat*, June 11, 1863; Ebenezer Wescott to Parents, 27 May 1863, Wescott Papers, River Falls. For an overview, see Michael B. Ballard, *Vicksburg: The Campaign that Opened the Mississippi* (Chapel Hill: University of North Carolina Press, 2004), 282–308, and Stoker, *Grand Design*, 266–67. The battle of Champion's Hill occurred on May 16, 1863, shortly after the Federal occupation of Jackson, Mississippi on May 14. Confederate casualties numbered 3,800, and Union casualties numbered 2,400.

29. "Bravery of the 17th Regiment: Camp of the 17th Wisconsin, Near Vicksburg, June 8, 1863," Quiner Scrapbooks, 9:256, SHSW. General Ransom is quoted in "Bravery of the 17th Regiment: Camp of the 17th Wisconsin."

## 5. Disorder and Discipline

1. Ebenezer Wescott to Parents, 7 February 1863; Ebenezer Wescott to Parents, 20 August 1863, in M. Ebenezer Wescott Papers, River Falls Area Research Center, University of Wisconsin–River Falls. Also published in M. Ebenezer Wescott, *Civil War Letters, 1861 to 1865, Written by a Boy in Blue to His Mother* (1909).

2. Drew Gilpin Faust, *This Republic of Suffering: Death and the American Civil War* (New York: Knopf, 2008), 137–210; David Rolfs, No Peace for the Wicked: Northern Protestant Soldiers and the American Civil War (Knoxville: University of Tennessee Press, 2009), 35–37; Foote, *The Gentlemen and the Roughs: Violence, Honor, and Manhood in the Union Army* (New York: New York University Press, 2010), 72; Thaddeus Romansky, "Disunion in the Ranks: Soldiers, Citizenship, and Mutiny in the Union Army (Ph.D. diss., Texas A&M University, 2015).

3. See Kenneth Noe, *Reluctant Rebels: The Confederates Who Joined the Army after 1861* (Chapel Hill: University of North Carolina Press, 2010); Robert M. Sandow, *Deserter Country: Civil War Opposition in the Pennsylvania Appalachians* (New York: Fordham University Press, 2009); Mark H. Dunkleman, *Brothers One and All: Esprit de Corps in a Civil War Regiment* (Baton Rouge: Louisiana State University Press, 2004); Foote, *The Gentlemen and the Roughs*; and Ricardo Herrera, "Self-Governance and the American Citizen as Soldier, 1775–1861," *Journal of Military History* 65, no. 1 (January 2001): 21–52.

4. "Military," *Hartford Courant*, October 18, 1861; Thomas Cahill to Margaret Cahill, February 11, 1862; Thomas Cahill to Margaret Cahill, March 22, 1862,Cahill Collection, held by Charles Sibley, Hamden, Conn.

5. Margaret Cahill to Thomas Cahill, 23 January 1862; Thomas Cahill to Margaret Cahill, 11 July 1862, Cahill Collection. Resignations were pulled from a database of soldiers of the Ninth Connecticut, 23rd Illinois, and 17th Wisconsin Volunteer Infantries, compiled from the Descriptive and Muster Rolls of Civil War Regiments, Records of the Adjutant General's Office, 1780s—1917, RG 94, National Archives and Records Administration, Washington, D.C. (NARA); Company Muster Rolls of Illinois Regiments, RS 301.019, Military and Naval Department (Civil War), RS 301, Illinois State Archives, Springfield; and Regimental Muster and Descriptive Rolls, Wisconsin Adjutant General's Office, State Historical Society of Wisconsin, Madison. Hereafter this database will be referred to as Database of Volunteers to Irish Regiments.

6. Untitled article, referring to Sheboygan (Wis.) *Post* in Quiner Scrapbooks: Correspondence of Wisconsin Volunteers, 1861–1865, 6:33; Mss 600, State Historical Society of Wisconsin, Madison (hereafter cited as Quiner Scrapbooks, SHSW). John L. Doran to Edward Salomon, 7 June 1862, in Regimental Correspondence of the 17th Wisconsin, 1861–62, box 90, folder 4, Records of Civil War Regiments, Series 1200, Wisconsin Adjutant General's Office, State Historical Society of Wisconsin, Madison (collection hereafter cited as Regimental Correspondence of the 17th, SHSW). The letter was reprinted in the *Milwaukee Morning Sentinel*, July 22, 1862.

7. John L. Doran to Edward Salomon, 7 June 1862, Regimental Correspondence of the 17th, SHSW; Commissioned and Non-Commissioned Officers of the 17th Wisconsin to Governor Edward Salomon, 29 August 1862, Regimental Correspondence of the 17th, SHSW.

8. Special Field Order No. 22, undated, Regimental Correspondence of the 17th, SHSW; A. G. Malloy to Colonel William Walson, Military Secretary, undated, Regimental Correspondence of the 17th, SHSW; "Col. Doran," *Chicago Times*, reprinted in the *Milwaukee Daily Sentinel*, December 2, 1862; Lt. Col. Adam G. Malloy, quoted in John Y. Simon, ed.,*The Papers of Ulysses S. Grant*, vol. 6, *September 1—December 8, 1862*

(Carbondale: University of Southern Illinois Press, 1977), 455–56; Sylvanus Cadwallader, *Three Years with Grant* (New York: Knopf, 1955), 30–31; Petition of Commissioned Officers of the 17th Wisconsin Volunteer Infantry to Governor Edward Salomon in support of the promotion of Adam G. Malloy, 26 November 1862, Regimental Correspondence of the 17th, SHSW; see also "Letter from the 17th Regiment," Quiner Scrapbooks, 9:251, SHSW. Without any more specific evidence, it is very difficult to assess the underlying issues that existed between Doran and his officers. In *The Gentlemen and the Roughs*, Lorien Foote points out that these types of altercations were not uncommon and arose from any number of reasons. The nature of the citizen-army also appears to have affected the attitudes of men and officers alike, as many seemed hesitant to accept the undemocratic system of military rank. This attitude is clear in the petitions by company-grade commissioned and noncommissioned officers seeking promotions based on a very democratic system of merit-based election that disregarded the traditional idea of promotion by seniority. For the 17th Wisconsin, the rejection of Doran's choice for the position of lieutenant colonel in favor of the internal promotion of "local" men could be understood using Thomas Goss's analysis of the dual military traditions of professional soldier and citizen leader that existed in the United States in the antebellum period; see Thomas J. Goss, *The War within the Union High Command: Politics and Generalship during the Civil War* (Lawrence: University Press of Kansas, 2003), and Andrew S. Bledsoe, *Citizen-Officers: The Union and Confederate Volunteer Junior Officer Corps in the American Civil War* (Baton Rouge: Louisiana State University Press, 2015).

9. Sergeants and Corporals of Company G to Governor Richard Yates, 12 June 1862; Michael Gleeson to Adjutant General Fuller, 9 December 1863; John J. Healy to Richard Yates, 11 March 1863; all from Administrative Files of Companies and Regiments, RG 301.018, Military and Naval Department (Civil War), RS 301, Illinois State Archives, Springfield (hereafter cited as Illinois Administrative Files, ISA).

10. Specification of Charges, Court Martial of William Wright, case KK 629; Account of Lieutenant Colonel Fitzgibbon, Court Martial of William Wright, case KK 629; Account of Captain Patrick Garvey, Court Martial of William Wright, case KK 629; all in Records of the Office of the Judge Advocate General (Army), RG 153, NARA. Hereafter, Records of the Judge Advocate General (Army), RG 153, NARA.

11. Court Martial of Patrick O'Connor, case KK 223; Court Martial of Patrick McCaully, case LL 185; both Records of the Judge Advocate General (Army), RG 153, NARA.

12. Court Martial of Thomas Sheridan, December 29, 1863, case LL 1642, Records of the Judge Advocate General (Army), RG 153, NARA.

13. "More Trouble at Camp Douglas," *Chicago Tribune*, February 5, 1862.

14. The total numbers of trials were compiled from the Index Project, Inc. database, managed by Thomas P. Lowry, Woodbridge, Va. The Index Project is a database of all Federal court martial trials held during the Civil War. With 23 and 9 men, respectively, tried by general courts martial, the 23rd Illinois and 17th Wisconsin—Irish regiments actively engaged in campaigns along the Mississippi and in the Shenandoah Valley—had significantly fewer instances of disobedience, as reflected by court martial trials, than the Ninth Connecticut. These numbers are even more interesting when consid-

ered in light of the number of soldiers who served in the 23rd Illinois, 17th Wisconsin, and Ninth Connecticut. Nearly 2,000 men served in each of the first two regiments over the course of the war, compared with approximately 971 in the Ninth Connecticut.

15. Number of charges compiled from the Index Project, Inc. database.

16. The nationality of the soldier on trial was not provided in trial records and was pulled from the Database of Volunteers to Irish Regiments. Nearly 40 percent of the cases in the 17th Wisconsin and 62 percent of those in the 23rd Illinois involved men of Irish birth. Only 21 percent of the soldiers in the 17th Wisconsin and 36 percent of those in the 23rd Illinois were of Irish birth.

17. Numbers of charges compiled from the Index Project, Inc. database.

18. Thomas Knablin to Mary Knablin, 22 September 1863, in Thomas Knablin (Co. D, 9th CT Vol. Inf., Civil War), pension application no. 429,164, certificate no. 399,850, Case Files of Approved Pension Applications, 1861–1934; Civil War and Later Pension Files, Records of the Veterans Administration, RG 15, NARA; Margaret Cahill to Thomas Cahill, 10 October 1862, Cahill Collection.

19. Court Martial of Thomas Cummings, case LL 316, Records of the Judge Advocate General (Army), RG 153, NARA. On the temperance movement and Father Mathew, see Kerby Miller, *Emigrants and Exiles: Ireland and the Irish Diaspora to North America* (New York: Oxford University Press, 1995), 249. Thomas Hamilton Murray, in *The History of the Ninth Regiment,, Connecticut Volunteer Infantry, "The Irish Regiment," in the War of the Rebellion, 1861–65* (New Haven: Price, Lee and Adkins Co., 1903), 322, notes that Thomas Cahill was among the number of New Haven Irish who took Mathew's pledge when the reformer visited the city in 1849.

20. Foote, *Gentlemen and the Roughs*, 29–30, discusses the contribution of alcohol abuse to discipline problems and the number of general courts martial. Court Martial of John Foley, case LL 316; Court Martial of Headquarters Defenses of New Orleans, March 7, 1863, case LL 316, Records of the Judge Advocate General (Army), RG 153, NARA. *Republicanism* here denotes a complex set of ideologies professed by nineteenth-century Americans as well as observers abroad. As Gordon Wood notes in *The Radicalism of the American Revolution* (New York: Knopf, 1991), the notion of republicanism was difficult to define, though broadly it "offered new conceptions of the individual, the family, the state, and the individual's relationship to the family, the state, and other individuals" (96). Daniel T. Rodgers, in his 1992 article "Republicanism: The Career of Concept," *Journal of American History* 79, no. 1 (June 1992), provides an excellent synthesis of the way that republicanism has been analyzed, defined, and appropriated by historians. "Republicanism," he notes, "was neither an ideological map to more than a small piece of experience, nor a paradigmatic language. . . . Neither was it a *tradition*"; it was, and still is, a contested term (37–38). In the context of this study, however, "republicanism" refers not to the term's ideology and culture as debated by historians, but rather to the way nineteenth-century Americans understood the political ideas and practices taking place within their nation. Observers, both at home and abroad, viewed the United States as having a republican form of government, and thus the legal, political, and social practices taking place therein were expressions of republicanism. In the context of the Civil War, this has been illustrated

by Ricardo Herrera, Lorien Foote, and Andrew S. Bledsoe in their recent studies on the citizen-soldier, as well as by Thaddeus Romansky in his dissertation "Disunion in the Ranks: Soldiers, Citizenship, and Mutiny in the Union Army" (Ph.D. diss., Texas A&M University, 2015). In *For Liberty and the Republic: The American Citizen as Soldier, 1775–1861* (New York: New York University Press, 2015), Herrera identifies republicanism as a set of values that "reminded officers and men of their national past and future, and of the standards they had to maintain and uphold if they were to keep faith with the military element of republican citizenship" (165). Soldiers, Herrera argues, held "shared military and civic identities" that were "inseparable" and reflective of "commonly held beliefs that had been firmly rooted in American society and culture since 1775" (165–66). Foote's *The Gentlemen and the Roughs* (2010) offers a detailed analysis of the military justice system in the Union armies that expands on the ways that Americans "struggled to reconcile the authoritarian and hierarchical nature of an army with the republican foundational principles of their Union" (9). In *Citizen-Officers,* Bledsoe illustrates nineteenth-century connections between volunteering and the notion of the republican tradition. Americans were driven by "democratic prerogatives, or the web of rights, customs, behaviors, traditions and values that Alexis de Tocqueville refers to as the 'manners of democracy,'" which had "a long and distinguished pedigree in America's military tradition" (6–7). Men in the regiments in this study expressed an understanding of their place in American society and of the tradition of republicanism, broadly. They saw themselves as part of an American tradition that stressed, among other things, notions of fairness, equality, and individual freedom.

21. Court Martial of Headquarters Defenses of New Orleans, March 7, 1863, case LL 316; Court Martial of Thomas Cummings, case LL 316, Records of the Judge Advocate General (Army), RG 153, NARA.

22. Court Martial of Henry Reed, case LL 444; Court Martial of John Doyle, case LL 444, Records of the Judge Advocate General (Army), RG 153, NARA.

23. Court Martial of John Kelly, case OO 110; Court Martial of William Dwyer, case OO 582, Records of the Judge Advocate General (Army), RG 153, NARA.

24. Dora Costa and Matthew Kahn, *Heroes and Cowards: The Social Face of War* (Princeton: Princeton University Press, 2008), 13–15.

25. The number of deserters from the 23rd Illinois provided in the text (148) does not include men listed as deserters who were actually only guilty of not rejoining the regiment after re-muster in the fall of 1861. Of the total number of men who served in the 23rd Illinois from original muster in July 1861 until the end of the war, 312 men are classified as having deserted, though a large number of these are men who simply did not return to the regiment after the reorganization of the unit in the fall of 1861.Only 148 men deserted from the 23rd Illinois after it was reorganized in the winter of 1862. Numbers for the Ninth Connecticut are only available for six of the ten companies in the regiment. All of the numbers provided come from the Database of Volunteers to Irish Regiments.

26. Court Martial of James Costello, case LL 1676; Court Martial of James Ginnesty, case LL 2725; Court Martial of Andre Anderson, case MM 2087, Records of the Judge Advocate General (Army), RG 153, NARA.

27. Court Martial of Daniel McMullen, case MM 1832; Court Martial of John Harrington, case LL 101; Court Martial of Edward Downey, case LL 3083; Court Martial of John Sullivan, case LL 1715; Court Martial of Jerry Daly, case LL 1676; Court Martial of Garret O'Tolle, case LL 1676; all in Records of the Judge Advocate General (Army), RG 153, NARA.

28. Thomas Moore to James Mulligan, 24 February 1864, Illinois Administrative Files, ISA.

## 6. Connecticut, Illinois, and Wisconsin React to the New York City Draft Riots

1. Thomas Knablin to Mary Knablin, 12 August 1863, in Thomas Knablin (Co. D, 9th CT Vol. Inf., Civil War), pension application no. 429,164, certificate no. 399,850, Case Files of Approved Pension Applications, 1861–1934; Civil War and Later Pension Files, Records of the Veterans Administration, Record Group 15, National Archives and Records Administration, Washington, D.C. (RG 15, NARA).

2. Despite their very visible sacrifice in defense of the Union, Irish Americans were forced to continually justify and validate their service during the later half of the of the nineteenth century as positive recognition of their loyalty was replaced by negative memories of disloyal conduct that were intrinsically linked to the Draft Riots. Furthermore, the decline of Irish American support for the war during the winter and spring of 1863 is fascinating because the sentiment was so at odds with the enthusiasm exhibited, especially in New York, by immigrants in 1861 and early 1862. In spite of the very visible decline of Irish American support for the war effort in New York City, ethnic heritage did not necessarily yield similar attitudes among local communities, and although ethnic associations can be deduced from regimental designations, local relationships and associations often contributed as much, if not more, to the identity and experiences of soldiers in these units as did national ones. Similarities existed among Irish immigrants, but Irish Americans outside of large urban areas experienced a significantly different relationship with their adopted communities as a consequence of more liberal notions of acceptance and assimilation. To define Irish loyalty through the experiences of the New York Irish would be to overlook the nuanced responses of Irish in other areas of the country to shifting war measures. For evidence of this see, for example, William Corby, *Memoirs of Chaplin Life: Three Years with the Irish Brigade*, ed. Lawrence Frederick Kohl (New York: Fordham University Press, 1992); David Power Conyngham, *The Irish Brigade and Its Campaigns*, ed. Lawrence Frederick Kohl (New York: Fordham University Press, 1994); Thomas Hamilton Murray, *The History of the Ninth Regiment, Connecticut Volunteer Infantry, "The Irish Regiment," in the War of the Rebellion, 1861–1865* (New Haven: Price, Lee and Adkins Co.,1908); St. Clair A. Mulholland, *The Story of the 116th Regiment, Pennsylvania Volunteers, in the War of Rebellion*, ed. Lawrence Frederick Kohl (New York: Fordham University Press, 1996); William Burton, *Melting Pot Soldiers: The Union's Ethnic Regiments* (New York: Fordham University Press, 1988), 14, 17; John Gjedge, *The Minds of the West: Ethnocultural Evolution in the Rural Middle West, 1830–1917* (Chapel Hill: University of North Carolina Press, 1997); and Christian Samito, *Becoming American under Fire: Irish Americans,*

*African Americans, and the Politics of Citizenship in the Civil War Era* (Ithaca, N.Y.: Cornell University Press, 2009), 126.

3. Diary of James Mulligan, January 2, 1863, James A. Mulligan Papers, Chicago History Museum (hereafter Mulligan Papers, Chicago).

4. "The Abolition Proclamation" *Columbian Register* (New Haven), January 10, 1863; "The Army and the Nigger Question," *Wisconsin Daily Patriot*, December 2, 1861; "The War," *Chicago Times*, June 15, 1861; "Abolitionism," *Chicago Times*, July 12, 1861.

5. "The Emancipation Proclamation," *Daily Illinois State Register*, January 3, 1863; "The Proclamation of Emancipation," *Milwaukee Sentinel*, December 31, 1862; "The Democratic Party and the War," *Wisconsin Daily Patriot*, December 27, 1862.

6. "Abolitionism," *Chicago Times*, July 12, 1861; "Why the People Oppose the Administration," *Daily Illinois State Register* (Springfield), April 23, 1863; "Refutation of a Republican Slander: The Soldiers Not Becoming Abolitionized," *Chicago Times*, October 29, 1862; diary of Albert V. B. Phillips, 29 October 1864, Albert V. Phillips Papers, Abraham Lincoln Presidential Library, Springfield, Ill. (hereafter Phillips Papers, ALPL); Tom to Friend Martin, September 3, 1864, Mulligan Papers, Chicago.

7. "The Enrolment of Negro Regiments—Utter Futility of the Idea," *Wisconsin Daily Patriot*, April 29, 1863.

8. Thomas Christie to James Christie, April 10, 1863, in Hampton Smith, ed. *Brother of Mine: The Civil War Letters of Thomas and William Christie* (St. Paul: Minnesota Historical Society, 2010), 120–21; "Negro Heroism," *Daily Illinois State Register*, August 15, 1863; untitled article, *Daily Illinois State Register*, December 29, 1863; "Negrophobia," *Connecticut Courant* (Hartford), November 21, 1863.

9. Thomas Cahill to Margaret Cahill, 8 April 1862, Cahill Collection, held by Charles Sibley, Hamden, Conn.; "Extract from a letter written by a well known officer of the 9th C.V., and an Irishman, who was a strong Democrat when he left Connecticut, to a friend in this city," *Connecticut Courant* (Hartford), August 28, 1863; "Now the election is over, it is deemed safe to let the old Ninth visit home," *Hartford Daily Courant*, April 12, 1864.

10. Untitled article, *Daily Illinois State Register*, January 22, 1864; "The Coming Draft," *Wisconsin Daily Sentinel*, June 13, 1863.

11. "Let the List be Printed," *Chicago Tribune*, August 21, 1862; "Effect of the New Order," *Daily Illinois State Journal*, August 7, 1862. See also "300,000 More Men Called for! *Look Out for a Draft!*" *Hartford Daily Courant*, August 6, 1862; "Bounty Money for Families," *Milwaukee Sentinel*, August 6, 1862; Frank Klement, *Lincoln's Critics: The Copperheads of the North* (Shippensburg, Pa.: White Maine Books, 1999), 12, 25; and James W. Geary, *We Need Men: The Union Draft in the Civil War* (DeKalb: Northern Illinois University Press, 1991), 112–13, 80–83.

12. "Secretary Stanton; Madison; Mr. Copperhead," *Wisconsin Daily Patriot*, May 30, 1863; "Commutation at Public Expense," *Wisconsin Daily Patriot*, June 9, 1863; "The Coming Draft," *Wisconsin Daily Sentinel*, June 13, 1863; "City Intelligence: Adopted Citizens Meeting," *Hartford Daily Courant*, August 27, 1862. On dissent in Wisconsin, see Tyler Anbinder, "Which Poor Man's Fight? Immigrants and the Federal Conscription of 1863," *Civil War History* 52, no. 4 (December 2006), and Lawrence H. Larson, "Draft Riot in Wisconsin, 1862," *Civil War History* 7, no. 4 (December 1961). On the

Peace Democrats, see Matthew Warshauer, "Copperheads in Connecticut: A Peace Movement that Imperiled the Union," in *This Distracted and Anarchical People: New Answers for Old Questions about the Civil War–Era North*, ed. Andrew L. Slap and Michael Thomas Smith (New York: Fordham University Press, 2013), 77. Men taking their chances on being drafted was noted in a letter from Margaret Cahill to Thomas Cahill, 11 September 1862, Cahill Collection.

13. Matthew Hart to Thomas Cahill, 11 June 1863, Cahill Collection; untitled article, *New Haven Palladium*, June 9, 1863; Matthew Hart to Thomas Cahill, 11 June 1863.

14. "The Draft," *Chicago Tribune*, August 8, 1862; "Call for a Mass Meeting," *Chicago Times*, September 3, 1864; "Call for a Mass Meeting," *Chicago Times*, September 3, 1864; "Our City and County Grossly Imposed Upon," *Chicago Times*, September 5, 1864; James McPherson, *Battle Cry of Freedom: The Civil War Era* (New York: Oxford University Press, 2003), 492.

15. "Only One More Day," *Chicago Tribune*, August 15, 1862; "And Now We Commence," *Chicago Tribune*, April 16, 1863; untitled article, *Chicago Times*, December 27, 1864; "The Conscription Act," *Daily Illinois State Journal*, March 9, 1863.

16. Untitled article, *Wisconsin Daily Patriot*, June 8, 1863; "Avoid the Draft," advertisement, *Chicago Tribune*, August 27, 1862; "Fifth Draft Ward Association," *Milwaukee Daily Sentinel*, July 20, 1863.

17. Burton, *Melting Pot Soldiers*, 127, 232; Martin W. Öfele, *True Sons of the Republic: European Immigrants in the Union Army* (Westport, Conn. and London: Praeger, 2008), 135.

18. "The German and French Press of New York on the Riot," *New York Tribune*, July 23, 1863. Iver Bernstein, in *The New York City Draft Riots: Their Significance for American Society and Politics in the Age of the Civil War* (Lincoln: University of Nebraska Press, 1990), 23–38, explores not the question of loyalty or disloyalty, but rather the nuances of the relationships among members of the working class in New York City. Intrinsic to the riots was the fear of competition among Irish circles, especially among men and women who understood their place at the bottom of the socioeconomic ladder and saw African Americans as potentially undermining their tenuous hold on jobs. See also Samito, *Becoming American under Fire*, 128–33, and Susannah Ural Bruce, *The Harp and the Eagle: Irish American Volunteers and the Union Army, 1861–1865* (New York: New York University Press, 2005), 180–90. Samito and Bruce illustrate Republican attempts to link the Draft Riots to larger issues of Irish disloyalty over the course of the war.

19. Bruce, *The Harp and the Eagle*, 181; Kerby A. Miller, *Emigrants and Exiles: Ireland and the Irish Exodus to North America* (New York: Oxford University Press, 1985), 324. On the Irish understanding of the riots' impact, see Bernstein, *New York City Draft Riots*, 6.

20. "Bloody Riot among the Stevedores at Toledo," *Wisconsin Daily Patriot* (Madison), July 7, 1862; untitled article, *Macon (Ga.) Telegraph*, July 25, 1862; "The Hiberno-African Riots in the West," *New York Tribune*, August 1, 1862.

21. "Rioting Among Laborers," *Chicago Tribune*, August 10, 1862; "Riot in South Brooklyn," *New York Tribune*, August 5, 1862; "Riot at a Tobacco Factory," *Weekly Wisconsin Patriot*, August 9, 1862.

22. "Riot in Buffalo," *New York Tribune,* August 13, 1862; "Another Riot between Irish and Negroes," *Philadelphia Inquirer,* August 27, 1862; "Riot in Detroit," *The Liberator,* March 9, 1863; "Riot in New York," *New York Tribune,* April 14, 1863, and "Riot in New York," *Hartford Daily Courant,* April 14, 1863; "Riot at Newburgh, N.Y.," *New York Tribune,* June 24, 1863, and "Disgraceful Riot and Murder," *Albany Evening Journal,* June 23, 1863; "Riot in Buffalo," *Milwaukee Daily Sentinel,* July 7, 1863.

23. Jack Tager, *Boston Riots: Three Centuries of Social Violence* (Boston: Northeastern University Press, 2001), 81; "The Hiberno-African Riots in the West," *New York Tribune,* August 1, 1862.

24. In *The Union War* (Cambridge, Mass.: Harvard University Press, 2012),Gary W. Gallagher argues that most Northerners would not have had enough significant interactions with African Americans to have developed any firm stance on slavery or emancipation.

25. Figures for Connecticut are from Matthew Warshauer, *Connecticut in the American Civil War; Slavery, Sacrifice, and Survival* (Middletown, Conn.: Wesleyan University Press, 2011), 131. Matthew Hart to Thomas Cahill, 25 July 1863, Cahill Collection; "The Infamy of Resistance to the Draft," *Daily Illinois State Journal,* July 18, 1863 (emphasis in original); "A Glorious Record," *Daily Illinois State Journal,* September 18, 1863.

26. "List of Enrolled Men," *Milwaukee Daily Sentinel,* July 18, 1863; "The Draft in this State," *Milwaukee Daily Sentinel,* July 18, 1863; *Boston Post,* quoted in "How A Democratic Paper Talked About the Draft," *Milwaukee Daily Sentinel,* July 18, 1863; Matthew Hart to Thomas Cahill, 25 July 1863, Cahill Collection. Lorien Foote, in *The Gentlemen and the Roughs; Violence, Honor, and Manhood in the Union Army* (New York: New York University Press, 2010), 129, contends that there was a growing trend of stringent army discipline after 1863, by which time the Northern recruits, draftees, and substitutes were disproportionately immigrants or poor native-born Americans who were coerced into fighting. Among the men who are the focus of this study, of the 290 men who joined the 17th Wisconsin as draftees in the fall and winter of 1864, only 4 deserted, suggesting that the draftees who served in this unit were not necessarily more prone to undisciplined behavior because of the fact that they were conscripted into service. See Descriptive and Muster Rolls of Civil War Regiments, Records of the Adjutant General's Office, RG 94, National Archives and Records Administration, Washington, D.C.

27. "The Great Riot in New York," *Wisconsin Daily Patriot,* July 18, 1863; "The Draft and Riots," *Wisconsin Daily Patriot,* July 18, 1863; untitled article, *Wisconsin Daily Patriot,* July 17, 1863; "How Catholics Regard the Late Riot," *Milwaukee Sentinel,* July 25, 1863; untitled article, *Weekly Wisconsin Patriot,* August 23, 1863.

28. Matthew Hart to Thomas Cahill, 25 July 1863, Cahill Collection; "To the Public," *Constitution* (Middletown, Conn.), July 22, 1863.

29. Untitled article, *Weekly Wisconsin Patriot,* August 23, 1863; "An Able and Truthful Article," *Chicago Post,* reprinted in the *Daily Illinois State Journal,* July 17, 1863; "The Catholic Church and the War," *Daily Illinois State Register,* July 25, 1863.

30. "No Party," *The Chicago Times,* June 27, 1861.

31. "Another Kind of Treason," *Daily Illinois State Register,* August 27, 1861; "Shame on Them," *Columbian Register* (New Haven), October 18, 1862; "Freedom of Political

Expression," *Wisconsin Daily Patriot*, October 11, 1862; "What a Traitor Says," *Weekly Wisconsin Patriot*, March 28, 1863.

32. Mark Neely, *The Union Divided: Party Conflicts in the Civil War North* (Cambridge, Mass.: Harvard University Press, 2002), 120; "Is This Democracy?" *Chicago Tribune*, January 29, 1863; "Freedom of Speech," *Chicago Times*, August 16, 1862; "Loyalty," *Wisconsin Daily Patriot*, December 10, 1862. See also George M. Frederickson, *The Inner Civil War: Northern Intellectuals and the Crisis of the Union* (New York: Harper and Row, 1965), 65–69; Neely, *The Union Divided*, 158–159; and Jean H. Baker, *Affairs of Party: The Political Culture of Northern Democrats in the Mid-Nineteenth Century* (New York: Fordham University Press, 1998), 78–86. Baker argues that the intersection of politics and American society began when the nation was young, and that by the outbreak of war in 1860, "generations of Northern schoolboys had absorbed a standard view of American history and government, and their cognitive perceptions in turn framed public values, attitudes, and behavior" (86).

33. "Mass Meeting," *Hartford Daily Courant*, June 7, 1862; "No Party," *Chicago Times*, June 21, 1861; "The Adopted Citizens of the Union," *Weekly Wisconsin Patriot*, January 5, 1861.

34. "A Genuine Democrat," *Chicago Times*, April 7, 1862; "Loyalty Means," *Republican Farmer* (Bridgeport, Conn.), October 18, 1864; "Lying vs. Copperheads," *Wisconsin Daily Patriot*, February 23, 1864.

## 7. Patriotism and Sacrifice on the Home Front

1. Historians have associated numerous events, political, military, and economic, with the ascension of Irish immigrants into mainstream America. In *The Wages of Whiteness: Race and the Making of the American Working Class* (New York: Verso, 1991), David R. Roediger suggests a direct correlation between wages and perceptions of "whiteness" within American society in which the term *working class* suggests an "identification of whiteness and work so strong that it need not even be spoken" (19). The author points to the formation of the Irish American working class as justification for his argument, claiming that it exemplifies the development of racial distinctions within this group as Irish Americans were able to transition ethnic distinctions previously defined by the nativist movement into racial distinctions through the organization of white European immigrants against the "colored races," thereby creating the valuable "white worker." Noel Ignatiev, in *How the Irish Became White*, discusses Irish revolutionary Daniel O'Connell's antislavery stance. There was a political disconnection between the Irish at home and abroad, as the social and economic circumstances of the Irish in the United States molded political sentiment within the immigrant community. Like Roediger, Ignatiev suggests a relationship between notions of whiteness and belonging within larger American society. Numerous historians have also pointed to the role that military service, both in the Civil War and later conflicts, played with regard to the transition of these men and women from "Irish" to "American." Perhaps most pertinent to this discussion is William Burton, *Melting Pot Soldiers: The Union's Ethnic Regiments* (New York: Fordham University Press, 1998); Susanna Ural Bruce, *The Harp and the Eagle* (New York: New York University Press,

2005); and Christian Samito, *Becoming American under Fire: Irish Americans, African Americans, and the Politics of Citizenship during the Civil War Era* (Ithaca: Cornell University Press, 2009). Though the approaches of the authors vary, all of these texts suggest the importance that Civil War service played in the process of becoming American. Finally, the acceptance of Irish Americans as Americans was aided by their participation in the social mobility of the late nineteenth century, as many of them moved away from the slums and ethnic neighborhoods of cities such as New York, where they were replaced by poorer groups from Eastern and Southern Europe. Furthermore, it is important to note that the role Irish American Catholics played in the fight against Communism contributed to lessening the nativism and the Protestant backlash against the Roman Catholic Church that lingered from the nineteenth century.

2. "The Great Northwestern Sanitary Fair," *Sanitary Commission Bulletin* 1, no. 3 (New York, December 1, 1863): 65, 66–67. None of the regiments in this study fought at Stone River, but the point here is the public support and sacrifice for the war effort.

3. "Woman's Right to Be Patriotic," *Chicago Times*, October 1, 1862; "A Woman's Patriotism," *Hartford Daily Courant*, March 20, 1863; "The Test of Female Heroism," *Weekly Wisconsin Patriot*, November 2, 1861.

4. William Rickey to James Mulligan, 18 February 1862, James A. Mulligan Papers, Chicago Museum of History.

5. Richard Franklin Bensel, *Yankee Leviathan: The Origins of Central State Authority in America, 1859–1877* (New York: Cambridge University Press, 1990); Heather Cox Richardson, *The Greatest Nation of the Earth: Republican Economic Policies during the Civil War* (Cambridge, Mass.: Harvard University Press, 1997); Andrew Slap, *The Doom of Reconstruction: Liberal Republicans in the Civil War Era* (New York: Fordham University Press, 2006).

6. These percentages are derived from a database of Irish-born men of military age, constructed from a 20 percent sample of men between the ages of 13 and 50 living in twelve cities, as recorded in the 1860 U.S. Census. The cities were Bridgeport, Hartford, New Haven, and Waterbury, Connecticut; Chicago, LaSalle, and Ottawa, Illinois; Detroit, Michigan; and Beloit, Fond du Lac, Madison, and Milwaukee, Wisconsin. These were the cities that sent the largest numbers of Irish soldiers to serve in the Ninth Connecticut, 23rd Illinois, and 17th Wisconsin regiments, *and* were also the cities in their states housing the largest concentrations of persons of Irish birth.

7. Untitled article, *Sheboygan Post*, undated, Quiner Scrapbooks: Correspondence of Wisconsin Volunteers, 1861–1865, 6:33; Mss 600, State Historical Society of Wisconsin, Madison (hereafter cited as Quiner Scrapbooks, SHSW). "Military Items," *Hartford Daily Courant*, April 26, 1864; "The County War Fund," *Chicago Tribune*, December 12, 1861.

8. Thomas Knablin to Mary Knablin, 22 July 1863, and Thomas Knablin to Mary Knablin, 22 September 1863, in Thomas Knablin (Co. D, 9th CT Vol. Inf., Civil War), pension application no. 429,164, certificate no. 399,850, Case Files of Approved Pension Applications, 1861–1934, Civil War and Later Pension Files, Records of the Veterans Administration, Record Group 15, National Archives and Records Administration, Washington, D.C. (pension files hereafter cited by certificate numbers and RG 15,

NARA); George Hill to Wife, 27 August 1862, Daniel O'Sullivan and George Hill Collection, held by Joseph Kelly, Toms River, N.J. The correspondence of Thomas Cahill (in the Cahill Collection, held by Charles Sibley, Hamden, Conn.) also illustrates the uncertainty of communication between New Orleans and Connecticut during the first half of the war. This was not the case, it seems, for those in the Midwest who advanced south down the Mississippi and had more direct routes of communication with home. Patrick Clancy to Mother, 21 March 1864, in Margaret Clancy (mother, Patrick Clancy, Co. K, 23rd Il Vol. Inf., Civil War), widow's pension certificate no. 69,339, RG 15, NARA; Diary of James B. Fowler, Wis Mss 119S, State Historical of Wisconsin, Madison.

9. Thomas Knablin to Mary Knablin, 12 July 1862, Thomas Knablin pension file, RG 15, NARA; Margaret Cahill to Thomas Cahill, 30 January 1862; Margaret Cahill to Thomas Cahill, 10 July 1862; and Matthew Hart to Thomas Cahill, 26 August 1862, Cahill Collection; "Destitution in the City During the Coming Winter," *Chicago Times*, October 5, 1862; "An Appeal to the Women of Wisconsin in Behalf of Soldier's Families," *Milwaukee Sentinel*, May 2, 1863.

10. John Niven, *Connecticut for the Union: The Role of the State in the Civil War* (New Haven: Yale University Press, 1965), 80–81.

11. Frank L. Klement, *Wisconsin in the Civil War: The Home Front and the Battle Front, 1861–1865* (Madison: State Historical Society of Wisconsin, 2001), 11; "Soldiers' Relief Bounty," *Wisconsin Daily Patriot* (Madison), February 22, 1862; "Three Year Volunteers," *Chicago Tribune*, June 6, 1861.

12. "Wisconsin Soldier's Aid Society," letter to the editor from Alfred J. Bloor, Milwaukee, December 9, 1864, *Sanitary Commission Bulletin* 3, no. 29 (Philadelphia, January 1, 1864): 909; "Meeting at New Haven, Connecticut," *Sanitary Commission Bulletin* 3, no. 27 (Philadelphia, December 1, 1864): 856–57; "The Great Northwestern Sanitary Fair," *Sanitary Commission Bulletin* 1, no. 3 (New York, December 1, 1863): 65; Joseph Parish, "The Great Gathering at the Northwest," report datelined Chicago, June 9, 1865, *Sanitary Commission Bulletin* 3, no. 39 (Washington, D.C., July 1, 1865): 1222. (The articles from *Sanitary Commission Bulletin* vols. 1 and 3 are reprinted in *United States Sanitary Commission Bulletin*, vols. 1–3 [New York: Sanitary Commission, 1866].) See also Nina Silber, *Daughters of the Union: Northern Women Fight in the Civil War* (Cambridge, Mass.: Harvard University Press, 2005), 175–200, and Patricia L. Richard, *Busy Hands: Images of the Family in the Northern Civil War Effort* (New York: Fordham University Press, 2003), 176–215.

13. "Good Move," *Columbian Register* (New Haven), August 31, 1861; "War Committee," *Hartford Daily Courant*, July 21, 1862; Robert H. Bremner, *The Public Good: Philanthropy and Welfare in the Civil War Era* (New York: Knopf, 1980), 75; "The County War Fund," *Chicago Tribune*, December 12, 1861.

14. "Exemption of Real Estate," *Racine Advocate*, March 3, 1847. On aid societies and poor relief in Illinois, Connecticut, and Wisconsin, see Harvey Strum, "Famine Relief from the Garden City to the Green Isle," *Journal of the Illinois State Historical Society* 93 (Winter 2000/2001): 392; Hannah J. McKinney, *The Development of Local Public Services, 1650–1860: Lessons from Middletown, Connecticut* (Westport, Conn.: Greenwood Press, 1995), 62–64; and Thomas Woodside Bentley Crafer, "The Administration of

Public Poor Relief in Wisconsin and Minnesota: A Comparative Study" (Ph.D. diss., University of Wisconsin, 1910), 9–10.

15. "Don't Forget Them," *Daily Illinois State Journal* (Springfield), December 20, 1861; "Wisconsin Soldier's Aid Society," 909; untitled article, *Constitution* (Middletown, Conn.), December 17, 1862.

16. "Worthy of Imitation," *Chicago Tribune*, August 7, 1862; "Contributions for Soldiers' Families," *Daily Illinois State Journal* (Springfield), January 8, 1864; "Relief for Soldiers' Families," *Chicago Tribune*, January 11, 1864; "Thanksgiving Proclamation of Gov. Yates," *Chicago Tribune*, November 22, 1864; "Relief of Soldiers' Families," *Milwaukee Daily Sentinel*, December 12, 1863.

17. "Letter to the Editor," *Milwaukee Daily Sentinel*, November 21, 1862. Although this letter deals specifically with the draft, the overall sentiment is clear. Families of soldiers needed support from those who remained at home. Such support was the duty of the state and local communities, as the complement to the willingness of men to sacrifice themselves for the larger cause of the Union. "The Families of Drafted Men Must Be Provided For," *Hartford Daily Courant*, September 12, 1862; "Relief for Drafted Men," *New Haven Palladium*, July 13, 1863.

18. See for example "Praiseworthy," *Wisconsin Daily Patriot*, July 2, 1863, and "Aid to Families of Soldiers, *Milwaukee Daily Sentinel*, October 10, 1862.

19. Mary Kelly to Daniel Quirk, undated, Administrative Files of Civil War Companies and Regiments, RS 301.018, Military and Naval Department (Civil War), RS 301, Illinois State Archive, Springfield (Illinois Administrative Files, ISA); Edward Kelly to Adjutant General of Illinois, undated, Illinois Administrative Files, ISA. Refocusing analysis towards the daily issues faced by men and women at home helps us better understanding the impact of the Civil War on the Northern home front. As the Kelly correspondence illuminates, those on the home front often faced pressing individual issues that, while a product of the war, had little to do with the ideological arguments that surrounded the conflict. The families of the men in the regiments explored here no doubt were attuned to the political issues of the time, but essential to their survival was their ability to negotiate both daily life at home and the economic and bureaucratic spheres of their respective states. The well-being of a soldier's family was affected by the flow of funds he sent home, and by his ability to earn a living after the war; or, by the length of time between a soldier's death and the family's hearing of that death, the time it took to learn about and file a pension application, and the interval until the granting of a pension. A focus on immediate, practical needs plays a major role in the Cahill correspondence. Margaret Cahill's primary concerns lay more in the day-to-day workings of her family and the well-being of her husband than in the broader political issues at play during the war. See Ryan Keating, "Margaret Cahill and the 9th Regiment Connecticut Volunteer Infantry (Irish): A Middleclass Woman on the Urban Homefront and the Forced Changes of Domesticity," *Connecticut History* 50, no. 1 (Spring 2011): 16–36. Also, much of the correspondence available from the men in all three regiments in this study makes it clear that their primary concern lay in the well-being of their families rather than in any broader ideology.

20. Rachel Filene Seidman, "A Monstrous Doctrine? Northern Women on Dependency during the Civil War," in *An Uncommon Time: The Civil War and the Northern*

*Home Front*, ed. Paul A. Cimbala and Randal M. Miller (New York: Fordham University Press, 2002), 177–79.

21. Niven, *Connecticut for the Union*, 319. The account of Ellen Carey is based on Ellen Carey (widow, Ambrose Carey, Co. B, 9th CT Vol. Inf., Civil War), widow's pension application file, certificate no. 19,628, RG 15, NARA. Ellen was theoretically without an income, as these pension funds were established to provide money to women and children who had relied solely on their husbands and fathers for support; the implication was that they were not able, whether due to personal disability or to the number and age of children at home, to seek outside employment. On wartime inflation see Mark R. Wilson, *The Business of Civil War: Military Mobilization and the State, 1861–1865* (Baltimore: Johns Hopkins University Press, 2006), 228. Wilson notes that consumer prices rose in the North by approximately 75 percent during the war.

22. These accounts came in the support of the pension application of Margaret Lynch (mother of private Patrick Lynch, Co. A, 9th CT Vol. Inf., Civil War), widow's pension application file, certificate no. 12,242, RG 15, NARA.

23. Bertha Gross (widow of Julius Gross, Co. D, 17th WI Vol. Inf., Civil War), widow's pension application file, application no. 16764 certificate no. WC6325, RG 15, NARA.

24. Mary Calahan (widow of Thomas Calahan, Co. E, 17th WI Vol. Inf., Civil War), widow's pension application file, application no. 44,392 certificate no. WC30643, RG 15, NARA.

25. Affidavits in Ellen Lane (mother of private Patrick Lane, Co. A, 9th CT Vol. Inf., Civil War), widow's pension application file, application no. 46, 342, certificate no. WC27,979, RG 15, NARA.

26. Margaret Clancy (mother of private Patrick Clancy, Co. K, 23rd IL Vol. Inf., Civil War) widow's pension file, application no. 57, 236, certificate no. 69,339; Rose Curran (mother of private Frank Curran, Co. B, 23rd IL Vol. Inf., Civil War), widow's pension application file, application no. 15,448, certificate no. WC18,747, both RG 15, NARA.

27. Mary Scanlan (mother of Private James Scanlan, Co. B, 17th WI Vol. Inf., Civil War), widow's pension application file, application no. 25,991, certificate no. WC30,452, RG 15, NARA.

28. "Relief of Soldiers' Families," *Milwaukee Daily Sentinel*, December 2, 1863. In their analyses of the "home front" in the twentieth century, historians Lizabeth Cohen and Meg Jacobs suggest that purchasing power provided women and families with the means of protecting the democratic interests of the United States while at the same time participating in an economic Americanization; see Lizabeth Cohen, *A Consumers Republic: The Politics of Mass Consumption in Post War America*, (New York: Knopf, 2003); Meg Jacobs in *Pocketbook Politics: Economic Citizenship in 20th Century America* (Princeton: Princeton University Press, 2005). Analogously, the impact of the Civil War on issues of inclusion or nationalism must not be relegated solely to those men directly participating in the military. See Melinda Lawson, *Patriot Fires: Forging a New American Nationalism in the Civil War North* (Lawrence: University Press of Kansas, 2002). Lawson has taken the first steps in illustrating the impact of the war on larger issues of nationalism and identity through the participation of men and women on the home front in activities that supported the larger war effort.

## 8. Wounded Warriors, Public Wards: The Consequences of Military Service

1. Frank L. Klement, *Wisconsin in the Civil War: The Home Front and the Battle Front, 1861–1865* (Madison: State Historical Society of Wisconsin, 2001), 87. Wisconsin sent only fifty-two infantry regiments to serve in Union Armies during the course of the Civil War. In *Melting Pot Soldiers: The Union's Ethnic Regiments* (Ames: Iowa State University Press, 1988), 47, William L. Burton cites patronage possibilities along with Congress's lack of adequate provision for the organization of replacements as the reason behind the creation of new units. See also Armin Rappaport, "The Replacement System during the Civil War," in *Military Analysis of the Civil War*, ed. T. Harry Williams (Millwood, N.Y : KTO Press, 1977), 115–26. All numbers from this paragraph were derived from the Database of Volunteers to Irish Regiments (see n.6, ch. 5).

2. Orin Jameson to Katie Crandall, 13 December 1863; Orin Jameson to Robert Crandall, 30 January 1864, Crandall Family Correspondence, 1854–1911, Mss 203, State Historical Society of Wisconsin, Madison (SHSW hereafter).

3. Ebenezer Wescott to Mother, 13 February 1864, M. Ebenezer Wescott Papers, River Falls Area Research Center, University of Wisconsin–River Falls; diary of Levi H. Nickel, 1–2,4, Wis Mss 138S, SHSW. On reenlistment, see Joseph T. Glatthaar, *The March to the Sea and Beyond: Sherman's Troops in the Savannah and Carolinas Campaigns* (New York: New York University Press, 1985), 39–40. Glatthaar notes that although men had enlisted for a variety of reasons, by 1863–64 the notions of patriotism and duty served as the motivation for the nearly 50 percent of the men who reenlisted as veteran volunteers.

4. Martin Wallace to "Martin," 14 February 1865, James A. Mulligan Papers, Chicago Museum of History; James W. Geary, *We Need Men: The Union Draft in the Civil War* (DeKalb: Northern Illinois University Press, 1991), 112–13. Thomas Cahill discusses the issues with reenlistment at length in his correspondence with Margaret Cahill after his return to the front from veteran furlough (Cahill Collection, held by Charles Sibley, Hamden, Connecticut). On the reenlistment campaign and veteran furloughs see Mulligan Papers, box 3, folder 4, and "Return of the Ninth C.V.: Grand Reception and Immense Turn Out of Citizens," *Columbian Register* (New Haven), April 23, 1864.

5. Numbers of men reenlisting in each regiment are based on the Database of Volunteers to Irish Regiments (see ch. 5, n. 5)."The Ninth Connecticut," *Republican Farmer* (Bridgeport, Conn.), October 28, 1864. Thomas Cahill to Margaret Chill, 20 July, 1864, Cahill Collection).

6. Diary of James B. Fowler, entry of 5 January 1864, and "Memoranda," 18 February 1864, Wis Mss 119S, SHSW; diary of Orin Jameson, 15–16 March 1864, Wis Mss 118S, SHSW; diary of James B. Fowler, 16 March 1864; "Grand Reception and Immense Turn Out of Citizens," *Columbian Register* (New Haven), April 23, 1864; Alfred Theodore Andreas, *The History of Chicago*, vol. 2, *From 1857 until the Fire of 1871* (Chicago: A. T. Andreas, 1885), 194.

7. The account of the Ninth Connecticut at Third Winchester and Fisher's Hill draws on *The War of the Rebellion: Official Records of the Union and Confederate Armies*, series 1, vol. 43 (Washington, D. C.: GPO, 1880), 326–27 (cited hereafter as OR);

account of Cedar Creek draws on OR, series 1, 43:329, and on "Col. Mulligan's Irish Brigade Attacked by a Rebel Force," *Chicago Tribune*, February 4, 1864; account of Strasburg and Font Royal Pike, on OR, series 1, 43:319, 282. Thomas Hamilton Murray, *History of the Ninth Regiment, Connecticut Volunteer Infantry, "The Irish Regiment," in the War of the Rebellion, 1861–65* (New Haven: Price, Lee and Adkins, 1903), 200–04, describes the Ninth at Cedar Creek, Fortress Monroe, and in Savannah.

8. The 23rd Illinois's actions at New Creek are covered in OR, series 1, 33:29–40. Correspondence in the Mulligan Papers, box 3, folder 4 (Chicago) deals with reenlistments and specifically the order that notes that men may not preemptively reenlist as veteran volunteers.

9. "Affairs on the Upper Potomac," *New York Tribune*, July 29, 1864; "An Irish Catholic Patriot," *The New World*, November 29 (no year), in Papers of the Executive Committee of the Irish Brigade, Mulligan Papers, Chicago; "Col. James A. Mulligan; Gallant Commander of the Irish Brigade (23rd Illinois)," newspaper clipping (newspaper title unknown), November 30, 1896, in Papers of the Executive Committee of the Irish Brigade, Mulligan Papers; "Lay Me Down and Save the Flag," *Philadelphia Inquirer*, August 6, 1864.

10. Diary of Levi H. Nickel, 2, SHSW; "Reception of the Gallant 17th," *Wisconsin Daily Patriot*, March 21, 1863; "Honor to the Green Flag," *Weekly Wisconsin Patriot*, November 28, 1863; diary of Levi H. Nickel, 6; Ebenezer Wescott to Mother, 20 May 1864, Wescott Papers, River Falls.

11. Diary of Orin Jameson, "Memoranda," 27 May 1864, SHSW; Ebenezer Wescott to Mother, 20 May1864, Wescott Papers, River Falls.

12. Ebenezer Wescott to Mother, 9 June 1864, Wescott Papers, River Falls; Orin Jameson to Kittie (Katie) Crandall, 15 July 1864, Crandall Family Correspondence, SHSW. On the summer 1864 Atlanta Campaign, see for example Craig L. Symonds, *Stonewall of the West: Patrick Cleburne and the Civil War* (Lawrence: University Press of Kansas, 1997), 202–41; Richard McMurry, *Atlanta: 1864* (Lincoln: University of Nebraska Press, 2000); Robert G. Tanner, *Retreat to Victory? Confederate Strategy Reconsidered* (Wilmington, Del.: Scholarly Resources, 2001), 11–12; Steven E. Woodworth, *Nothing but Victory: The Army of the Tennessee, 1861–1865* (New York: Knopf, 2005), 459–568; and James McPherson, *Battle Cry of Freedom: The Civil War Era* (New York: Oxford University Press, 2003), 750–55.

13. Diary of Levi Nickel, 20, SHSW; Ebenezer Wescott to Mother, 24 July 1864; Ebenezer Wescott to Mother, 11 August 1864,Wescott Papers, River Falls.

14. Confederate forces under Wheeler and Hampton are discussed in Glatthaar, *March to the Sea and Beyond*, 159; diary of Levi Nickel, 62, SHSW; Glatthaar, *March to the Sea and Beyond*, 160–67.

15. Murray, *History of the Ninth Regiment, Connecticut Volunteer Infantry*, 203. "Returning Troops: The 6th and 17th Wisconsin Regiments," *Milwaukee Daily Sentinel*, July 19, 1865. The Fenians had gained an increasing presence in Wisconsin, and a number of articles appeared in the *Appleton (Wis.) Crescent* and the *Daily Sentinel* during the last year of the war that dealt with the goals of the Fenians, as made clear by the Fenian Fair held in Chicago in 1864, and evidenced by the invasion of Canada in the immediate aftermath of the Civil War. "The Homeward March: Arrival and

Departure of the Ninth Battalion," *New York Times*, August 8, 1865; "Meeting of the Friends of the 23rd Illinois Veteran Volunteers," *Chicago Tribune*, July 31, 1865; "The Twenty-Third Regiment Illinois Volunteers," *Chicago Tribune*, August 1, 1865.

16. Susannah Ural Bruce, *The Harp and the Eagle: Irish American Volunteers and the Union Army, 1861–1865* (New York: New York University Press, 2005), 249, 246–247, 233. See also Christian Samito, *Becoming American under Fire: Irish Americans, African Americans, and the Politics of Citizenship during the Civil War Era* (Ithaca: Cornell University Press, 2009).

17. On the obstacles to integration and the gradual acceptance of the Irish within American society, see Kerby Miller, *Emigrants and Exiles: Ireland and the Irish Exodus to North America* (New York: Oxford University Press, 1985); Noel Ignatiev, *How the Irish Became White* (New York: Routledge, 1995); Tyler G. Anbinder, *Nativism and Slavery: The Northern Know Nothings and the Politics of the 1850s* (New York: Oxford University Press, 1992); and Matthew Frye Jacobson, *Special Sorrows: The Diasporic Immigration of Irish, Polish, and Jewish Immigrants in the United States* (Cambridge, Mass.: Harvard University Press, 1995).

18. For recent work on veterans see: Brian Matthew Jordan, "'Living Monuments': Union Veteran Amputees and the Embodied Memory of the Civil War," *Civil War History* 57, no. 2, (June 2011); Eric T. Dean, "'We Will All Be Lost and Destroyed': Post Traumatic Stress Disorder and the Civil War," *Civil War History* 37, no. 2 (June 1991); Matthew Warshauer and Michael Sturges, "Difficult Hunting: Accessing Connecticut Patient Records about Post-Traumatic Stress Disorder during the Civil War," *Civil War History* 59, no. 4. (December 2013); David W. Blight, *Race and Reunion: The Civil War in American Memory* (Cambridge, Mass.: Harvard University Press, 2001); Barbara A. Gannon, *The Won Cause: Black and White Comradeship in the Grand Army of the Republic* (Chapel Hill: University of North Carolina Press, 2011); Caroline Janney, *Remembering the Civil War: Reunion and the Limits of Reconstruction* (Chapel Hill: University of North Carolina Press, 2013); Donald Shaffer, *After the Glory: The Struggles of Black Civil War Veterans* (Lawrence: University Press of Kansas, 2004); Brian Matthew Jordan, *Marching Home: Union Veterans and Their Unending Civil War* (New York: Liveright, 2015); Paul A. Cimbala, *Veterans North and South: The Transition from Soldier to Civilian after the American Civil War* (Santa Barbara: Praeger, 2015). Jordan's recent study of Civil War veterans, *Marching Home*, continues the broader trend within the historiography of focusing on the struggles of veterans and their mistreatment in postwar America. Cimbala's work, on the other hand, illustrates the diverse range of experiences of veterans in the postwar North. While it is compelling to focus on the trials of veterans, a brief survey of the literature finds that the permanently disabled represented only one small portion of the veteran community during the latter half of the nineteenth and the early twentieth century. As Cimbala illustrates, and as this chapter also hopes to redress, the methodological approach traditionally used to study veterans, involving a heavy reliance on records from soldiers' homes and similar institutions, is fundamentally flawed in that it highlights one particular group of men, ignoring the hundreds of thousands of others who returned home, lived, and died without any relationship with such organizations and institutions. Certainly the suffering of veterans speaks volumes about the implications of military service and the

problematic postwar relationship between former soldiers and the state, especially when it came to dealing with the lingering physical and psychological ramifications of military service, and that suffering deserves the attention that historians have given it. But as Cimbala suggests, this narrative must be balanced by stories of other kinds of lives lived by veterans, in order for us to better understand the true implications of military service for Northern veterans, nationally.

19. In the 17th Wisconsin, 269 men died during the war, 228 from disease and 41 from battle. In the Ninth Connecticut, 253 men died during the war, 243 from disease and 10 from battle. In the 23rd Illinois, 149 men died during the war, 93 from disease and 50 from battle. Casualty rates available online at the Civil War Soldiers and Sailors Database, http://www.itd.nps.gov/cwss.

20. Ebenezer Wescott to Parents, 28 June 1862, Wescott Papers, River Falls; letter of E. Jackson, M.D., to Editors, from Camp Hospital, near Corinth, 2 September 1862, headlined "The 17th Wisconsin—A Healthy Regiment," in Quiner Scrapbooks: Correspondence of Wisconsin Volunteers, 1861–1865, vol. 6, 16th–29th Regiments, 33, Mss 600, State Historical Society of Wisconsin, Madison (hereafter Quiner Scrapbooks, SHSW); John L. Doran to Edward Salomon, 7 June 1862, in Regimental Correspondence of the 17th Wisconsin, 1861–62, Series 1200, box 90, folder 4, State Historical Society of Wisconsin, Madison (hereafter cited as Regimental Correspondence of the 17th, Series 1200, SHSW) ; Andrew McIlwaine Bell, "Mosquito Soldiers: The Impact of Malaria and Yellow Fever during the American Civil War" (Ph.D. diss., George Washington University, 2007). Bell provides an excellent discussion of the history of disease in the South and the impact of diseases on Northern soldiers unaccustomed to the conditions of the South during the summer months. Letter from W. Denniston, Sergt. Major, to "Friend Ballou," March 2, 1863, from Lake Providence, Louisiana, headlined "Letter from the 17th Regiment," Quiner Scrapbooks, 9:251, SHSW. Denniston's addressee would have been D. W. Ballou, editor of the *Watertown Democrat* of Fort Atkinson, Wisconsin. An editorial in the *Wisconsin Chief,* February 20, 1861, which followed the reprinting of an editorial from the *Democrat*, noted that "Ballou is one of the rare things in partizan newspaperdom—a fearless and outspoken editor." The *Dictionary of Wisconsin History* , http://www.wisconsinhistory.org/Content.aspx?dsNav=N:1575, notes that Ballou moved to Wisconsin sometime between the years 1852 and 1853, establishing the *Watertown Democrat* in 1854. A Democrat, he nevertheless consistently supported the Lincoln administration throughout the war.

21. "The Realities of a Soldier's Life," *Watertown Democrat* (Fort Atkinson), May 28, 1863; "Jeff Davis Issues an Address," *Wisconsin Daily Patriot,* April 18, 1862.

22. William O'Brien (Co. H, 17th WI Vol. Inf., Civil War), pension application no. 563,021, certificate no. 406,454, Case Files of Approved Pension Applications, 1861–1934, Civil War and Later Pension Files, Records of the Veterans Administration, Record Group 15, National Archives and Records Administration, Washington, D.C. (hereafter RG 15, NARA); Peter Fahn (Co. A, 17th WI Vol. Inf., Civil War), pension application no. 430,429, certificate no. 324,755, RG 15, NARA.

23. James Mullen (Co. C, 9th CT Vol. Inf., Civil War), pension application no. 740,032, certificate no. 634,359; Martin Burke (Co. B, 9th CT Vol. Inf., Civil War), pension application no. 241,966, certificate no.159,935, RG 15, NARA.

24. Peter Morris (Co. D, 9th CT Vol. Inf., Civil War), pension application no. 394,391, certificate no.238,324; Edward Murray (Co. H, 9th CT Vol. Inf., Civil War), pension application no. 590,717, certificate no. 702,044, RG 15, NARA.

25. Sherman Multhrop (Co. I, 9th CT Vol. Inf., Civil War), pension application no. 394,404. Case Files of Denied Pension Applications, 1861–1934; Civil War and Later Pension Files, Records of the Veterans Administration, RG 15, NARA; Moses Mills (Co. D/I, 9th CT Vol. Inf., Civil War), pension application no. 195,959 certificate no. 184,620, Case Files of Approved Pension Applications, 1861–1934, RG 15, NARA.

26. Orlando Yale (Co. I, 9th CT Vol. Inf., Civil War), pension application no. 492,699, certificate no. 757,510, RG 15, NARA.

27. Diary of Albert V. B. Phillips, January 2, 1863, January 5, 1863, Albert V. Phillips Papers, SC 1171, folder 2, Abraham Lincoln Presidential Library, Springfield, Illinois. Albert's father arrived on February 27 and left with Albert's brother on March 3, 1863. Elias Shaw (Co. G, 23 IL Vol. Inf., Civil War), pension application no. 548,238, certificate no. 346,414, RG 15, NARA.

28. Thomas Moore (Co. K, 23rd IL Vol. Inf., Civil War), pension application no. 283,546, certificate no. 215, 240; James Holland (Co. D, 23rd IL Vol. Inf., Civil War), pension certificate no. 404,856; John Haley (Co. A, 23rd IL Vol. Inf., Civil War), pension certificate no. 75,733, RG 15, NARA.

29. Studies traditionally focus on the horrors and magnitude of death in the war. See for example Drew Gilpin Faust, *This Republic of Suffering*; Mark S. Schantz, *Awaiting This Heavenly Country;* and David Rolfs, *No Peace for the Wicked: Northern Protestant Soldiers and the American Civil War* (Knoxville: University of Tennessee Press, 2009). While the nature of death during the war was much different from what most Americans were used to, especially as it occurred so far from home, the reality was that Americans did understand death, disease, and injury, which were not uncommon during this period, especially in the workplace.

30. John Moses and Joseph Kirkland, *History of Chicago, Illinois,* vol. 2 (Chicago: Munsell and Co., 1895), 232–33; Peter T. Harstad, "Disease and Sickness on the Wisconsin Frontier: Cholera," *Wisconsin Magazine of History*, 43, no. 3 (Spring, 1960); P. K. Walsh, letter in the *Cork Examiner*, June 11, 1860, quoted in Miller, *Emigrants and Exiles,* 319; George Potter, *To the Golden Door: The Story of the Irish in Ireland and America*, 165, quoted in Miller, *Emigrants and Exiles,* 267.

31. Paul A. Cimbala, "Soldiering on the Home Front: The Veteran Reserve Corps and the Northern People," in Paul A. Cimbala and Randall M. Miller, *Union Soldiers and the Northern Home Front: Wartime Experiences, Postwar Adjustments* (New York: Fordham University Press, 2002); Paul A. Cimbala, *Under the Guardianship of the Nation: The Freedmen's Bureau and the Reconstruction of Georgia, 1865–1870* (Athens: University of Georgia Press, 1997), 35–36.

32. George Winfrey (Co. A 23rd IL Vol. Inf., Civil War), pension application no. 62,490 certificate no. 369,740, RG 15, NARA.

33. Pension file of George Winfrey, RG 15, NARA; John Alexander (Co. F, 9th CT Vol. Inf., Civil War), pension application no. 17,400, certificate no. 347,083, RG 15, NARA.

34. James McCarthy (Co. H, 9th CT Vol. Inf., Civil War), pension application no. 12,299 certificate no. 40,193, RG 15, NARA.

35. Pension file of James McCarthy, RG 15, NARA.

36. "Ladies' Soldiers' Relief Association," *Milwaukee Daily Sentinel,* November 24, 1862. Other relief efforts are described in: "Connecticut Legislature," *Columbian Register* (New Haven) June 6, 1863; "State Items," *Hartford Daily Courant,* March 3, 1864; "Wisconsin Soldiers in the Hospitals Near Washington," *Milwaukee Sentinel,* July 29, 1862; "Stand Back Soldiers," *Weekly Wisconsin Patriot,* July 26, 1862; "From Madison," *Chicago Tribune,* March 20, 1863; "Relief for Wounded Western Soldiers," *Chicago Tribune,* June 24, 1862. Veterans' homes were often run in the manner of military camps. In Illinois, for example, residents were required not only to state their disability, but once admitted they were not to leave unless they received an "honorable discharge" from the home. Men who left without proper authorization could be charged by a provost marshal. Veterans' Case Files, Record Series 259.002, Illinois Soldiers' and Sailors' Home, Record Series 259, Illinois State Archive, Springfield (cited hereafter as Veterans' Case Files, RS 259.002, ISA). In 1890 the federal government passed the Dependent Pension Act that opened the pension system to all disabled Union veterans of the Civil War. Prior to this, veterans had to claim that their injury was directly related to military service.

37. See for example Eric T. Dean, *Shook Over Hell: Post-Tramautic Stress, Vietnam, and the Civil War* (Cambridge: Harvard University Press, 1999) and Eric J. Leed, *No Man's Land: Combat and Identity in World War One* (New York: Cambridge University Press, 2009), 186–192. William Donovan (Co. D, 17th WI Vol. Inf., Civil War), pension application no. 457,971, certificate no. 307,364, RG 15, NARA.

38. *Ninth Census of the United States,* 1870; Thiron Ingham (Co. A, 17th WI Vol. Inf., Civil War), pension application no. 987,098, certificate no. 963,101, RG 15, NARA.

39. John Begley (Co. K, 9th CT Vol. Inf., Civil War), pension application no. 412,499, certificate no. 308,747; see also Orlando Yale (Co. I, 9th CT Vol. Inf., Civil War), pension application no. 492,699, certificate no. 757,510; and John Kleiter (Co. G, 9th CT Vol. Inf., Civil War), pension application no. 350,238, certificate no. 643,352, all in RG 15, NARA. However, it is difficult to find mention of these types of afflictions in the pension files from soldiers who served in Wisconsin and Illinois (with the exception of the obviously insane). After reading through over five hundred pension files as part of this project, it became clear that men in different states were advised differently as to what constituted a disability and how to appeal to the government to receive money for those disabilities. For example, in the Ninth Connecticut, there were a significant number of men who received money for varicocele, a medical disorder involving the swelling of veins leading to the testicles. The men of the Ninth were largely successful in arguing that this was caused by the strain of marching (though in reality varicocele is a medical condition that affects one of every four men) and received pensions for this disability. In the files for the men of the 17th Wisconsin and 23rd Illinois, rarely is this mentioned as a physical disability. The same appears to be true for nervous disorders.

40. Veterans' Case Files, RS 259.002, ISA.

41. Robert H. Bremner, *The Public Good: Philanthropy and Welfare in the Civil War Era* (New York: Knopf, 1980), 144.

42. Pension files from 133 veterans of the 23rd Illinois Volunteers (who enlisted between 1861 and 1863), 110 veterans of the 17th Wisconsin, and 130 veterans of the Ninth Connecticut were consulted for this analysis. For the Wisconsin and Illinois regiments, these pensioned veterans constitute approximately 20 percent of the pensioners in each regiment. For the Ninth Connecticut, these pensioned veterans constitute more than 50 percent of the pensioners. There were significantly more pensioned veterans from Wisconsin and Illinois than there were from Connecticut. Mobility was judged based on the addresses used and the pension agencies through which veterans applied for their pensions in the latter part of the nineteenth and the early twentieth centuries. The movement of many of these veterans did not consist of a single move away from their prewar community. Many of them undertook numerous moves over the course of the latter half of the century, arguably in pursuit of every greater opportunity. For those who remained in the state that was their home when they enlisted, their residence was not necessarily unchanged; there were instances of movement within the state itself, though in these cases the pensioner often stayed close to his antebellum home.

43. John Curtis (Co. I, 9th CT Vol. Inf., Civil War), pension application no. 450,598, certificate no. 243,759, RG 15, NARA.

44. Thomas Moore (Co. K, 23rd IL Vol. Inf., Civil War), pension application no. 168,737, certificate no. 132,902; Hugh Dorsey (Co. C, 17th WI Vol. Inf., Civil War), pension application no. 507,593, certificate no. 568,465; Adam Blaul (Co. E, 23rd IL Vol. Inf., Civil War), pension application no. 780,511 certificate no. 559,999, all RG 15, NARA.

45. David E. Schob, *Hired Hands and Plowboys: Farm Labor in the Midwest, 1815–1860* (Chicago: University of Illinois Press, 1975), especially 5–20; Susan Sessions Rugh, *Our Common Country: Family Farming, Culture, and Community in the Nineteenth-Century Midwest* (Bloomington: Indiana University Press, 2001). Schob provides an excellent study of mobility in the antebellum period as men traveled from state to state engaged in tasks that aided in the winning of the Midwest. Daniel Quirk (Co. B, 23rd IL Vol. Inf., Civil War), pension application no. 571,702, certificate no. 469,856 (widow's pension); and Thomas Heffernan (Co. B, 23rd IL Vol. Inf., Civil War), pension application no. 1,162,568, certificate no. 911,314, RG 15, NARA.

46. Addis Payne (Co. H, 9th CT Vol. Inf., Civil War), pension application no. 236,103, certificate no. 156,180; Thomas Dolan (Co I, 9th CT Vol. Inf., Civil War), pension application no. 659,452, certificate no. 732,080, RG 15, NARA.

47. The letters from Orr were found in his pension file and appear as James Orr to Mary Orr, 4 April 1868; James Orr to Mary Orr, 10 May 1868, James Orr (Co. G, 9th CT Vol. Inf., Civil War), pension application no. 222,990, certificate no. 184,623, RG 15, NARA.

48. James Orr to Mary Orr, 5 December 1868, pension file of James Orr, RG 15, NARA.

49. Silas Sawyer (Co. H, 9th CT Vol. Inf., Civil War), pension application no. 625,863, certificate no. 754,489, RG 15, NARA.

50. Michael Doolan (Co. E, 9th CT Vol. Inf., Civil War), pension application no. 1,201,601, certificate no. 1,065,910, RG 15, NARA.

51. Patrick Murphy (Co. C, 17th WI Vol. Inf., Civil War), pension application no. 77,001, certificate no. 59,379, RG 15, NARA.

52. James Holland (Co. D, 23 IL Vol. Inf., Civil War), pension application no. 631,019, certificate no. 404,856, RG 15, NARA.

53. John McKenna (Co. H, 9th CT Vol. Inf., Civil War), pension application no. 774,778, certificate no. 607,150, RG 15, NARA.

54. John Connelly (Co. F, 17th WI Vol. Inf., Civil War), pension application no. 321,243 certificate no. 375,450, (widow's pension) RG 15, NARA.

55. Pension file of John Connelly; David E. Schob, *Hired Hands and Plowboys*, 1–3; Susan Sessions Rugh, *Our Common Country*.

56. Peter Carmichael, "Relevance, Resonance, and Historiography: Interpreting the Lives and Experiences of Civil War Soldiers," *Civil War History* 62, no. 2 (June 2016), 184. See also Paul A. Cimbala, *Veterans North and South: The Transition from Soldier to Civilian after the American Civil War* (Santa Barbara: Praeger, 2015), and also Edward J. Blum, *Reforging the White Republic: Race, Religion, and American Nationalism, 1865–1898* (Baton Rouge: Louisiana State University Press, 2005).

## Conclusion. Irish Americans in the Civil War: Myth and Memory

1. Ninth Connecticut Volunteers Monument Committee, "Dedication Book" (1903), 15, in Daniel O'Sullivan and George Hill Collection, held by Joseph Kelly, Toms River, N.J. The monument in honor of the service of the Ninth Connecticut at Vicksburg was dedicated in October 2008 and was the culmination of nearly a decade of work by Robert Larkin of Cheshire, Connecticut. Larkin became interested in preserving the legacy of the regiment's service at Vicksburg after researching his ancestor, Private John Marlow of Company C. An Irish immigrant, Marlow died in the service from malaria contracted during the time the regiment spent in the swamps across from Vicksburg. Larkin was able to organize considerable support from organizations throughout Connecticut, and the monument stands as a testament to both the efforts of the soldiers of the Ninth and Larkin's own commitment to preserving the memory of this regiment.

2. *Wisconsin Memorial Day Annual, 1907* (Madison: Democrat Printing Company, State Printer, 1907), 32–33; "Cavalry," *Chicago Tribune*, May 31, 1892; "Colonel Mulligan's Memory," *Chicago Tribune*, May 31, 1895; "Many Visit Mulligan's Grave," *Chicago Tribune*, May 31, 1894; "Dedication of the Mulligan Monument at Cavalry," *Chicago Tribune*, May 31, 1885; *Report of the Proceedings of the 42nd and 43rd Reunions of the Society of the Army of the Tennessee* (Cincinnati: Backarach Press, 1915), 142.

3. Thomas Hamilton Murray, *History of the Ninth Regiment, Connecticut Volunteer Infantry, "The Irish Regiment," in the War of the Rebellion, 1861–65* (New Haven: Price, Lee and Adkins, 1903).

4. "James Mulligan to the Committee of the Irish National Fair," *Irish People* (Dublin), February 27, 1864. Growing animosity between Stephens and the Fenians in the United States appears as a running theme in the Fenian Brotherhood Records and

O'Donovan Rossa Personal Papers, ACUA 014, American Catholic History Research Center and University Archives, Catholic University of America, Washington, D.C. (Fenian Brotherhood Records and O'Donovan Rossa Papers, CUA).

5. Joseph Denieffe, *A Personal Narrative of the Irish Revolutionary Brotherhood, Giving a Faithful Report of the Principle Events from 1855 to 1867* (New York: Gael Publishing, 1906), 17; ibid., 20; Desmond Ryan, *The Fenian Chief: A Biography of James Stephens* (Dublin: Gill, 1967), 90; F. F. Millen to John O'Mahony, 24 June 1865, Fenian Brotherhood Records and O'Donovan Rossa Papers, box 1, folder 7, CUA.

6. "The Fenian Brotherhood," *New Haven Daily Palladium*, November 13, 1863. On press coverage of tensions between the movement and the Catholic Church , see, for example, "The Fenian Brotherhood, Bishop Duggan," *Chicago Tribune*, February 16, 1864, and untitled article, *Hartford Daily Courant,* September 9, 1865. "Fenian Meeting," *Milwaukee Daily Sentinel*, August 26, 1865; "Grand Fenian Picnic," *Hartford Daily Courant*, August 28, 1865; "State Matters," *Hartford Daily Courant*, September 6, 1865.

7. The Seventeenth Wisconsin Regiment," *Milwaukee Daily Sentinel*, July 19, 1865; "Fenian Meeting," *Milwaukee Daily Sentinel*, August 26, 1865; "Great Fenian Excitement in Canada," *Milwaukee Daily Sentinel*, November 6, 1865; "The Fenian," *Pantagraph* (Bloomington, Ill.), March 22, 1864; "The Fenian Brotherhood," *Pantagraph*, August 16, 1865; untitled article, *Madison County Courier* (Edwardsville, Ill.), November 30, 1865; "The Chicago Fenians," *Belvidere Standard* (Belvidere, Ill.), January 9, 1866.

8. "In Loving Remembrance: Memorial Day Observed in the City," *Daily Inter Ocean* (Chicago), May 31, 1881.

9. "A Distinguished Guest: The President of the United States Makes His First Visit to Chicago,"*Daily Inter Ocean,* October 6, 1887; "March of Union Victors," *Daily Inter Ocean*, August 28, 1889.

10. "Ex-Confederates," *Daily Inter Ocean*, May 29, 1893; untitled article, *Daily Inter Ocean*, May 17, 1895; "At Cavalry Cemetery," *Daily Inter Ocean*, May 31, 1895.

11. Craig Warren, "'Oh God What a Pity!' The Irish Brigade at Fredericksburg and the Creation of a Myth," *Civil War History* 47, no. 3 (2001), 193–221; Warren L. Young, *Minorities and the Military: A Cross-National Study in World Perspective* (Westport, Conn.: Greenwood Press, 1982), 255.

# *Bibliography*


## Primary Sources

*Abraham Lincoln Presidential Library, Springfield, Illinois*

Phillips, Albert V., Papers, 1860–1872. SC 1171.
Mulligan, James A., Letter, January 29, 1864. SC 1088.
Wallace-Dickey Collection
High, James L., Family Papers.
Haddan, Amaziah. Letters. SC 2060.
Shields, James B., Papers. SC 1385 B.
The Fenian Raid at Fort Erie (1866). F82-D396f.
Federal Writers Project, 1935–1944.

*Archives, U.S. Army Military History Institute, Carlisle Barracks, Pennsylvania*

Greene, John B., Letter. Misc Box 39.
Leigh, Lewis. Collection, 1861–1865.
10th Connecticut Infantry Regiment, Army of the James. Misc Box 39.

*Cahill Collection, held by Charles Sibley, Hamden, Connecticut*

*Catholic University of America, Washington, D.C.*

Fenian Brotherhood Records and O'Donovan Rossa Personal Papers. American Catholic History Research Center and University Archives. ACUA 014.

*Chicago Museum of History*

Mulligan, James A., Papers.

*Connecticut State Historical Society, Hartford*

Connecticut Infantry, Ninth Regiment. Pay, clothing, food, and subsistence voucher for Captain S. W. Sawyer, Company H, dated July 10, 1863. MS Civil War Box 1, Folder 7.
Sedgwick, Charles. Letter to D. W. Gooch. MS 93558.
Thresher, Seneca S., Diary, dealing with legal affairs of families of soldiers. MS 73236.

*Connecticut State Library and Archives, Hartford*

Grand Army of the Republic, Department of Connecticut, 1862–1938. RG 113.
Griffin A. Stedman, Camp 6, Sons of Union Veterans of the Civil War. Connecticut Division, 1909–13. RG 114.

Incoming Letters Concerning Pensions, Nov. 1864–Dec. 1881. Known as "Index Books." RG 13:49.
Muster Rolls, Descriptive Lists, Pay Rolls, and Related Papers, 1861–65. RG 13:32.
Office of the State Comptroller, 1758–1954. RG 008.
Paymaster and Quartermaster Accounts, 1861–65. RG 8:67.
Records of the Military Department, 1776–1986. RG 13.
Records of Payments to Civil War Soldiers and Families, 1861–66. RG 8:72.

*Daniel O'Sullivan and George Hill Collection, held by Joseph Kelly, Toms River, N.J.*
*llinois State Archives, Springfield*

Administrative Files of Civil War Companies and Regiments. RS 301.018, Military and Naval Department (Civil War). RS 301
Company Muster Rolls, 1862–1865. RS 310.019. Military and Naval Department (Civil War). RS 301
Military Censuses, 1861–1863. RS-301.029. Military and Naval Department (Civil War). RS 301.
Muster and Descriptive Rolls, 1861–1865. RS 301.020. Military and Naval Department (Civil War). RS 301.
Veterans' Admission Record, 1887–1967. RS 259.001. Illinois Soldiers' and Sailors' Home. RS 259.
Veterans' Case Files, 1887–1963. RS 259.002. Illinois Soldiers' and Sailors' Home. RS 259.

*Lawrence O'Brien Collection, held by Jeffery Cook, Trumbull, Connecticut*
*National Archives and Records Administration, Washington, D.C.*

Compiled Records Showing Service of Military Units in Volunteer Union Organizations. M594.
Case Files of Approved Pension Applications, 1861–1934. Civil War and Later Pension Files, Records of the Veterans Administration. RG 15.
Records of the Adjutant General's Office, 1780s –1917. RG 94.
Records of the Office of the Judge Advocate General (Army). RG 153.Seventh Census of the United States, 1850.
Eighth Census of the United States, 1860.
Ninth Census of the United States, 1870.
United States Census of Union Veterans and Widows of Union Veterans of the Civil War, 1890. M123.

*River Falls Area Research Center, University of Wisconsin–River Falls*

Wescott, M. Ebenezer. Papers.

*State Historical Society of Wisconsin, Madison*

Allen, Benjamin. Letters to Colonel Benjamin Allen. SC 512.
Crandall Family Correspondence, 1854–1911. Mss 203.

Fowler, James B., Diary. Wis Mss 119S.
Jameson, Orin M., Diary. Wis Mss 118S.
Nickel, Corporal Levi H., Diary. Wis Mss 138S.
Quiner, E. B. Quiner Scrapbooks: Correspondence of Wisconsin Volunteers, 1861–1865. Mss 600.
Records of Civil War Regiments, 1861–1900. Series 1200. Wisconsin Adjutant General's Office.
Regimental Correspondence of the 17th Wisconsin. Box 90, folder 4. Records of Civil War Regiments, 1861–1900. Series 1200. Wisconsin Adjutant General's Office.
Regimental Muster and Descriptive Rolls. Series 1142. Wisconsin Adjutant General's Office.
Regimental Muster and Descriptive Rolls. Series 1144. Wisconsin Adjutant General's Office.

## Newspapers

*Albany (N.Y.) Evening Journal*
*Appleton (Wis.) Crescent*
*Belvidere Standard* (Belvidere, Ill.)
*Boston Daily Advertiser*
*Boston Pilot*
*Chicago Citizen*
*Chicago Evening Journal*
*Chicago Journal*
*Chicago Republican*
*Chicago Times*
*Chicago Tribune*
*Columbian Register* (New Haven)
*Columbian Weekly Register* (New Haven)
*Connecticut Courant* (Hartford)
*Connecticut War Record* (New Haven)
*Constitution* (Middletown, Conn.)
*Daily Constitution* (Middletown, Conn.)
*Daily Illinois State Journal* (Springfield)
*Daily Illinois State Register* (Springfield)
*Daily Inter Ocean* (Chicago)
*Daily Milwaukee News*
*Daily Milwaukee Press and News*
*Daily Wisconsin* (Madison)
*Detroit Free Press*
*Hartford Daily Courant*
*Hartford Times*
*Irish-American Weekly* (New York, N.Y.)
*Irish Citizen* (New York, N.Y.)

*Irish People* (Dublin, Ireland)
*Illinois Daily State Journal* (Springfield)
*Illinois State Chronicle* (Decatur)
*Janesville (Wis.) Daily Gazette*
*Lowell (Mass.) Daily Citizen*
*Macon (Ga.) Telegraph*
*Madison County Courier* (Edwardsville, Ill.)
*Milwaukee Daily Sentinel*
*Milwaukee Sentinel*
*New Haven Daily Palladium*
*New Haven Palladium*
*New Haven Register*
*New London (Conn.) Daily Chronicle*
*New York Herald*
*New York Times*
*New York Tribune*
*New-York Daily Tribune*
*North American and United States Gazette* (Philadelphia)
*Ohio Statesman* (Columbus)
*Phoenix* (New York, N.Y.)
*Pantagraph* (Bloomington, Ill.)
*Republican Farmer* (Bridgeport, Conn.)
*Rockford (Ill.) Republican*
*Rock River Democrat* (Rockford, Ill.)
*Watertown (Wis.) Democrat*
*Weekly Wisconsin Patriot* (Madison)
*Wisconsin Chief* (Fort Atkinson)
*Wisconsin Daily Patriot* (Madison)
*Wisconsin State Journal* (Madison)

## Secondary Sources

Ackerman, Kenneth. *Boss Tweed.* New York: Carroll and Graf, 2005.

Adams, Michael C. *The Best War Ever: America and World War II.* Baltimore: Johns Hopkins University Press, 1994.

Anbinder, Tyler G. *Five Points: The Nineteenth-Century New York City Neighborhood that Invented Tap Dance, Stole Elections, and Became the World's Most Notorious Slum.* New York: Free Press, 2008.

———. *Nativism and Slavery: The Northern Know Nothings and the Politics of the 1850s.* New York: Oxford University Press, 1992.

———. "Which Poor Man's Fight? Immigrants and the Federal Conscription of 1863." *Civil War History* 52, no. 4 (December 2006).

Anderson, Joseph, and Anna Lydia Ward, eds. *The Town and City of Waterbury, Connecticut, from the Aboriginal Period to the Year Eighteen Hundred and Ninety-Five.* Vol. 2. New Haven: Price and Lee, 1896.

Andreas, Alfred Theodore. *History of Chicago from the Earliest Period to the Present Time*. Vol. 1, *Ending with the Year 1857*. Chicago: A. T. Andreas, 1884.

———. *History of Chicago from the Earliest Period to the Present Time*. Vol. 2. *From 1857 until the Fire of 1871*. Chicago: A. T. Andreas, 1885.

Arnesen, Eric, ed. *Encyclopedia of U.S. Labor and Working-Class History*. Vol. 1. New York: Routledge, 2007.

Arnold, James R. *Grant Wins the War: Decision at Vicksburg*. New York: John Wiley, 1997.

Attie, Jeanie. *Patriotic Toil: Northern Women and the American Civil War*. Ithaca, N.Y.: Cornell University Press, 1998.

Baker, Jean H. *Affairs of Party: The Political Culture of Northern Democrats in the Mid-Nineteenth Century*. New York: Fordham University Press, 1998.

Baldwin, Elmer. *History of La Salle County, Illinois: Its Topography, Geology, Botany, Natural History, History of the Mound Builders, Indian Tribes, French Explorations and a Sketch of the Pioneer Settlers of Each Town to 1840*. Chicago: Rand, McNally and Co., 1877.

Ballard, Michael B. *Vicksburg: The Campaign that Opened the Mississippi*. Chapel Hill: University of North Carolina Press, 2004.

Beaudot, William J. K., and Lance J. Herdegen, eds. *An Irishman in the Iron Brigade: The Civil War Memoirs of James P. Sullivan*. New York: Fordham University Press, 1993.

Bee, Robert L. *The Boys from Rockville: Civil War Narratives of Sgt. Benjamin Hirst, Company D, 14th Connecticut Volunteers*. Knoxville: University of Tennessee Press, 1998.

Bell, Andrew McIlwaine. "Mosquito Soldiers: The Impact of Malaria and Yellow Fever during the Civil War." Ph.D. diss., George Washington University, 2007.

Bensel, Richard Franklin. *Yankee Leviathan: The Origins of Central State Authority in America, 1859–1877*. New York: Cambridge University Press, 1990.

Beringer, Richard E., Herman Hattaway, Archer Jones, and William N. Still, Jr. *Why the South Lost the Civil War*. Athens: University of Georgia Press, 1986.

Bernstein, Iver. *The New York City Draft Riots: Their Significance for American Society and Politics in the Age of the Civil War*. New York: Oxford University Press, 1990.

Bhroimeil, Una Ni. *Building Irish Identity in America, 1870–1915*. Dublin: Four Courts Press, 2003.

Bledsoe, Andrew S. *Citizen-Officers: The Union and Confederate Volunteer Junior Officer Corps in the Civil War*. Baton Rouge: Louisiana State University Press, 2015.

Blight, David W. *Race and Reunion: The Civil War in American Memory*. Cambridge, Mass.: Harvard University Press, 2001.

Blum, Edward J. *Reforging the White Republic: Race, Religion, and American Nationalism, 1865–1896*. Baton Rouge: Louisiana State University Press, 2005.

Boyle, Frank A. *A Party of Mad Fellows: The Story of the Irish Regiments in the Army of the Potomac*. Dayton, Ohio: Morningside, 1996.

Brady, Kevin T. "Fenians and the Faithful: Philadelphia's Irish Republican Brotherhood and the Diocese of Philadelphia, 1859–1870." Ph.D. diss., Temple University, 1999.

Brandt, Dennis W. *From Home Guards to Heroes: The 87th Pennsylvania and Its Civil War Community*. Columbia: University of Missouri Press, 2006.

Bremner, Robert H. *The Public Good: Philanthropy and Welfare in the Civil War Era.* New York: Knopf, 1980.

Browning, Judkin. *Shifting Loyalties: The Union Occupation of Eastern North Carolina.* Chapel Hill: University of North Carolina Press, 2011.

Bruce, Susannah Ural. *The Harp and the Eagle: Irish-American Volunteers and the Union Army, 1861–1865.* New York: New York University Press, 2006.

———. "'Remember Your Country and Keep Up Its Credit': Irish Volunteers and the Union Army, 1861–1865." *Journal of Military History* 69, no. 2 (April 2005).

———, ed. *Civil War Citizens: Race, Ethnicity, and Identity in America's Bloodiest Conflict.* New York: New York University Press, 2010.

Bruce, William George. *The History of Milwaukee, City and County.* Chicago: S. J. Clark Publishing, 1922.

Burke, Davis. *They Called Him Stonewall: The Life of Lt. General T. J. Jackson, CSA.* New York: Rinehart, 1954.

Burton, Orville Vernon. *The Age of Lincoln.* New York: Hill and Wang, 2007.

Burton, William. *Melting Pot Soldiers: The Union's Ethnic Regiments.* New York: Fordham University Press, 1998.

Cadwallader, Sylvanus. *Three Years with Grant, as Recalled by War Correspondent Sylvanus Cadwallader.* Edited with introduction and notes by Benjamin P. Thomas. New York: Knopf, 1955.

Cahill, Daniel W. *First American Edition of the Works of the Rev. D. W. Cahill, D.D., the Highly Distinguished Irish Priest, Patriot and Scholar; Containing a Brief Sketch of His Life. . . .* Boston: Patrick Donahoe, 1855.

Callaghan, Daniel M. *Thomas Francis Meagher and the Irish Brigade in the Civil War.* London: McFarland and Co., 2006.

Callaghan, James. "The San Patricios." *American Heritage* 46, no. 7 (1995).

Carmichael, Peter. "Relevance, Resonance, and Historiography: Interpreting the Lives and Experiences of Civil War Soldiers." *Civil War History* 62, no. 2 (June 2016).

Carter, Susan B., Scott Sigmund Gartner, Michael R. Haines, Alan L. Olmstead, and Richard Sutch, and Gavin Wright, eds. *Historical Statistics of the United States: Earliest Times to the Present.* Millennium Edition, vol. 1. New York: Cambridge University Press, 2006.

Casey, John A., Jr. *New Men: Reconstructing the Image of Veterans in Late-Nineteenth-Century American Literature and Culture.* New York: Fordham University Press, 2015.

Cimbala, Paul A. *Under the Guardianship of the Nation: The Freedmen's Bureau and the Reconstruction of Georgia, 1865–1870.* Athens: University of Georgia Press, 1997.

———. *Veterans North and South: The Transition from Soldier to Civilian after the Civil War.* Santa Barbara: Preager, 2015.

Cimbala, Paul A., and Randall M. Miller, eds. *An Uncommon Time: The Civil War and the Northern Home Front.* New York: Fordham University Press, 2002.

———. *Union Soldiers and the Northern Home Front: Wartime Experiences, Postwar Adjustments.* New York: Fordham University Press, 2002.

Clinton, Catherine, and Nina Silber. *Battle Scars: Gender and Sexuality in the American Civil War.* New York: Oxford University Press, 2006.

———. *Battle Scars: Divided Houses: Gender and the Civil War.* New York: Oxford University Press, 1992.

Clouette, Bruce Alan. "'Getting Their Share': Irish and Italian Immigrants in Hartford, Connecticut, 1850–1940." Ph.D. diss., University of Connecticut, 1992.Cohen, Lizabeth. *A Consumers' Republic: The Politics of Mass Consumption in Postwar America.* New York: Knopf, 2003.

Cole, Harry Ellsworth. *A Standard History of Sauk County, Wisconsin.* Vol. 1. Chicago: Lewis Publishing Co., 1918.

*Commemorative Biographical Record of Hartford County, Connecticut, Containing Biographical Sketches of Prominent and Representative Citizens, and Many of the Early Settled Families.* Chicago: J. H. Beers and Co., 1901.

Condon, William Henry. *Life of Major-General James Shields: Hero of Three Wars and Senator from Three States.* Chicago: Blakely Printing Co., 1900.

Connoly, Sean J. *Religion, Law, and Power: The Making of Protestant Ireland, 1660–1760.* Oxford: Clarendon Press, 1992.

Conyngham, David Power. *The Irish Brigade and Its Campaigns, with Some Account of the Corcoran Legion, and Sketches of the Principal Officers.* 1867. Reprint, edited and with an introduction by Lawrence Frederick Kohl, New York: Fordham University Press, 1994.

Conzen, Kathleen Neils. *Immigrant Milwaukee, 1836–1860: Accommodation and Community in a Frontier City.* Cambridge, Mass.: Harvard University Press, 1976.

Cole, Harry Ellsworth. *A Standard History of Sauk County, Wisconsin.* Chicago: Lewis Publishing Co., 1918.

Corby, William. *Memoirs of Chaplain Life: Three Years with the Irish Brigade in the Army of the Potomac.* 1893. Reprint, edited by Lawrence Frederick Kohl, New York: Fordham University Press, 1992.

Costa, Debra, and Matthew Kahn. *Heroes and Cowards: The Social Face of War.* Princeton: Princeton University Press, 2008.

Crafer, Thomas Woodside Bentley. "The Administration of Public Poor Relief in Wisconsin and Minnesota: A Comparative Study." Ph.D. diss., University of Wisconsin, 1910.

Curtin, Nancy. *The United Irishmen: Popular Politics in Ulster and Dublin, 1791–1798.* New York: Oxford University Press, 1998.

Daly, Mary. *The Famine in Ireland.* Dublin: Dundalgan Press, 1986.

Dawes, Rufus Robinson. *Service with the Sixth Wisconsin Volunteers.* Marietta, Ohio: E. R. Alderman and Sons, 1890.

Dean, Eric T. *Shook Over Hell: Post-Traumatic Stress, Vietnam, and the Civil War.* Cambridge, Mass.: Harvard University Press, 1999.

———. "'We Will All Be Lost and Destroyed': Post-Traumatic Stress Disorder and the Civil War." *Civil War History* 37, no. 2 (June 1991).

Denieffe, Joseph. *A Personal Narrative of the Irish Revolutionary Brotherhood, Giving a Faithful Report of the Principle Events from 1855 to 1867.* New York: Gael Publishing, 1906.

Doyle, David Noel. "The Remaking of Irish America, 1845–1880." In *Making the Irish American: History and Heritage of the Irish in the United States*, ed. by Joseph J. Lee and Marion R. Casey. New York: New York University Press, 2006.

———. "The Irish as Urban Pioneers in the United States, 1850–1870." *Journal of American Ethnic History* 10, no. 1/2 (Fall 1990–Winter 1991).

Duncan, Jason K. *Citizens or Papists? The Politics of Anti-Catholicism in New York, 1865–1921*. New York: Fordham University Press, 2005.

Dunkleman, Mark H. *Brothers One and All: Esprit de Corps in a Civil War Regiment*. Baton Rouge: Louisiana State University Press, 2004.

Durrie, Daniel S. *A History of Madison, the Capital of Wisconsin; Including the Four Lake Country to July, 1874*. Madison, Wis.: Atwood and Culver, 1874.

Efford, Alison Clark. *German Immigrants, Race, and Citizenship in the Civil War Era*. New York: Cambridge University Press, 2013.

Elshtain, Jean Bethke. *Women and the War*. New York: Basic Books, 1987.

Fallows, Marjorie R. *Irish Americans: Identity and Assimilation*. Englewood Cliffs, N.J.: Prentice-Hall, 1979.

Faust, Drew Gilpin. *This Republic of Suffering: Death and the American Civil War*. New York: Knopf, 2008.

Fitzharris, Joseph C. "Field Officer Courts and U.S. Civil War Military Justice." *Journal of Military History* 68, no. 1 (January 2004).

Foner, Eric. *Free Soil, Free Labor, Free Men: The Ideology of the Republican Party before the Civil War*. New York: Oxford University Press, 1995.

Foote, Lorien. *The Gentlemen and the Roughs: Violence, Honor, and Manhood in the Union Army*. New York: New York University Press, 2010.

Foreman, Amanda. *World on Fire: Britain's Crucial Role in the American Civil War*. New York: Random House, 2012.

Frank, Joseph Allen. *With Ballot and Bayonet: The Political Socialization of American Civil War Soldiers*. Athens: University of Georgia Press, 1998.

Frederickson, George M. *The Inner Civil War: Northern Intellectuals and the Crisis of the Union*. New York: Harper and Row, 1965.

Gallagher, Gary W., ed. *The Shenandoah Valley Campaign of 1864*. Chapel Hill: University of North Carolina Press, 2006.

———. *The Union War*. Cambridge: Harvard University Press, 2012.

Gannon, Barbara. *The Won Cause: Black and White Comradeship in the Grand Army of the Republic*. Chapel Hill: University of North Carolina Press, 2010.

Geary, James W. *We Need Men: The Union Draft in the Civil War*. DeKalb: Northern Illinois University Press, 1991. Gerstle, Gary. *American Crucible: Race and Nation in the Twentieth Century*. Princeton: Princeton University Press, 2001.

Gienapp, William E. *The Origins of the Republican Party, 1852–1856*. New York: Oxford University Press, 1987.

Giesberg, Judith Ann. *Army at Home: Women and the Civil War on the Northern Home Front*. Chapel Hill: University of North Carolina Press, 2009.

———. *Civil War Sisterhood: The U.S. Sanitary Commission and Women's Politics in Transition*. Boston: Northeastern University Press, 2000.

Gjerde, Jon. *From Peasants to Farmers: The Migration from Balestrand, Norway, to the Upper Middle West*. New York: Cambridge University Press, 1985.

———. *The Minds of the West: Ethnocultural Evolution in the Rural Middle West, 1830–1917*. Chapel Hill: University of North Carolina Press, 1997.

Glatthaar, Joseph T. *Forged in Battle: The Civil War Alliance of Black Soldiers and White Officers*. Baton Rouge: Louisiana State University Press, 2000.

———. *General Lee's Army: From Victory to Collapse*. New York: Free Press, 2008.

———. *The March to the Sea and Beyond: Sherman's Troops in the Savannah and Carolinas Campaigns*. New York: New York University Press, 1985.

———. *Soldiering in the Army of Northern Virginia: A Statistical Portrait of the Troops Who Served under Robert E. Lee*. Chapel Hill: University of North Carolina Press, 2011.

Glaze, A. T. *Incidents and Anecdotes of Early Days and History of Business in the City and County of Fond du Lac from Early Times to the Present*. Fond du Lac, Wis.: P. B. Haber Printing Co., 1905.

Glazer, Walter S. "Wisconsin Goes to War: April, 1861." *Wisconsin Magazine of History* 50, no. 2 (Winter 1967).

Gleeson, David. *The Green and the Gray: The Irish in the Confederate States of America*. Chapel Hill: University of North Carolina Press, 2013.

Goodspeed, Weston A., and Daniel D. Healy, eds. *History of Cook County, Illinois: Being a General Survey of Cook County History, Including a Condensed History of Chicago and Special Account of Districts Outside the City Limits; From the Earliest Settlement to the Present Time*. Vol. 1. Chicago: Goodspeed Historical Association, 1909.

Gordon, Lesley. *A Broken Regiment: The 16th Connecticut's Civil War*. Baton Rouge: Louisiana State University Press, 2014.

Goss, Thomas J. *The War within the Union High Command: Politics and Generalship during the Civil War*. Lawrence: University Press of Kansas, 2003.

Green, Francis Vinton. *Campaigns of the Civil War: The Mississippi*. New York: Charles Scribner's Sons, 1892.

Harris, Howard. "'The Eagle to Watch and the Harp to Tune the Nation': Irish Immigrants, Politics, and Early Industrialization in Paterson, New Jersey, 1824–1836." *Journal of Social History* 23, no. 3 (Spring 1990).

Harris, William C. *With Charity for All: Lincoln and the Restoration of the Union*. Lexington: University Press of Kentucky, 1997.

Harris, William J. *Plain Folk and Gentry in a Slave Society: White Liberty and Black Slavery in Augusta's Hinterlands*. Middletown, Conn.: Wesleyan University Press, 1985.

Hareven, Tamara K., and Maris A. Vinovskis, eds. *Family and Population in Nineteenth-Century America*. Princeton: Princeton University Press, 1978.

Heaney, Michael K. "Uncounted Costs: The Civil War's Impact on an Infantry Company's Men and Their Families." Ph.D. diss., Rutgers University, 2008.

Hearn, Chester G. *When the Devil Came Down to Dixie: Ben Butler in New Orleans*. Baton Rouge: Louisiana State University Press, 1997.

Hearne, John, and Rory Cornish, eds. *Thomas Francis Meagher: The Making of an Irish American*. Dublin: Irish Academic Press, 2005.

Heidicker, Roy William. "Yankee Workers and Rebel Gentlemen: The Triumph of Free Labor Soldiers in the American Civil War." Ph.D. diss., University of Southern California, 2002.

Herrera, Ricardo. *For Liberty and the Republic: The American Citizen Soldier, 1775–1861.* New York: New York University Press, 2015.

———. "A People and Its Soldiers: The American Citizen as Soldier, 1775–1861." *International Bibliography of Military History* 33, no. 1 (2013).

———. "Self-Governance and the American Citizen as Soldier, 1775–1861." *Journal of Military History* 65, no. 1 (January 2001).

Hess, Earl J. *Liberty, Virtue, and Progress: Northerners and Their War for the Union.* New York: Fordham University Press, 1997.

———. *The Rifle Musket in Civil War Combat: Reality and Myth.* Lawrence: University Press of Kansas, 2008.

Hicken, Victor. *Illinois in the Civil War.* Urbana: University of Illinois Press, 1966.

Higham, John. *Strangers in the Land: Patterns of American Nativism, 1860–1925.* New Brunswick, N.J.: Rutgers University Press, 2002.

Hill, Everett Gleeson. *A Modern History of New Haven and Eastern New Haven County.* 2 vols. New York: S. J. Clarke Publishing Co., 1918.

*The History of Fond du Lac County, Wisconsin.* Chicago: Western Historical Company, 1880.

*History of La Salle County, Illinois, Together with Sketches of its Cities, Villages and Towns, Educational, Religious Civil, Military, and Political History, Portraits of Prominent Persons, and Biographies of Representative Citizens.* Vol. 1. Chicago: Inter-State Publishing Company, 1886.

*History of Milwaukee, Wisconsin: From Pre-Historic Times to the Present Date.* Chicago: Western Historical Company, 1881.

*The History of Sauk County, Containing an Account of Its Settlement, Growth, Development and Resources.* Chicago: Western Publishing Co., 1880.

Holberton, William B. *Homeward Bond: The Demobilization of Union and Confederate Armies, 1865–1866.* Mechanicsburg, Pa.: Stackpole Books 2001.

Holmes, David G. *Irish in Wisconsin.* Madison: Wisconsin Historical Society Press, 2004.

Howard, Michael. "War and Nations." In *Nationalism*, ed. John Hutchinson and Anthony Smith. New York: Oxford University Press, 1994.

Howe, Henry. *An Outline History of New Haven (Interspersed with Reminiscences).* New Haven: O. A. Dorman, 1884.

Hubbs, Ward G. *Guarding Greensboro: A Confederate Company in the Making of a Southern Community.* Athens: University of Georgia Press, 2003.

Hunt, Robert. *The Good Men Who Won the War: Army of the Cumberland Veterans and Emancipation Memory.* Tuscaloosa: University of Alabama Press, 2010.

Ignatiev, Noel. *How the Irish Became White.* New York: Routledge, 1995.

Jacobs, Meg. *Pocketbook Politics: Economic Citizenship in Twentieth-Century America.* Princeton: Princeton University Press, 2005.

Jacobson, Matthew Frye. *Barbarian Virtues: The United States Encounters Foreign People at Home and Abroad, 1876–1917.* New York: Hill and Wang, 2000.

———. *Special Sorrows: The Diasporic Immigration of Irish, Polish, and Jewish Immigrants in the United States.* Cambridge, Mass.: Harvard University Press, 1995.Jensen, Richard. "'No Irish Need Apply': A Myth of Victimization." *Journal of Social History* 36, no. 2 (Winter 2002).

Johnson, Paul E. *A Shopkeeper's Millennium: Society and Revivals in Rochester, New York, 1815–1937.* New York: Hill and Wang, 1978.

Johnson, Russell L. *Warriors into Workers: The Civil War and the Formation of Urban-Industrial Society in a Northern City.* New York: Fordham University Press, 2003.

Johnson, Tyler V. "Punishing the Lies on the Rio Grande: Catholic Immigrant Volunteers in Zachary Taylor's Army and the Fight against Nativism." *Journal of the Early Republic* 30, no. 1 (Spring 2010).

Jones, James Pickett. *Black Jack: John A. Logan and Southern Illinois in the Civil War Era.* Tallahassee: Florida State University Press, 1967.

Jones, Paul. *The Irish Brigade.* New York: Luce, 1969.

Jones, Terry. *Lee's Tigers: The Louisiana Infantry in the Army of Northern Virginia.* Baton Rouge: Louisiana State University Press, 1987.

Jordan, Brian Matthew. "'Living Monuments': Union Veteran Amputees and the Embodied Memory of the Civil War." *Civil War History* 57, no. 2 (June 2011).

———. *Marching Home: Union Veterans and Their Unending Civil War.* New York: Liveright, 2015.

Karamanski, Theodore J. *Rally Round the Flag: Chicago and the Civil War.* Chicago: Nelson-Hall, 1993.

Kautz, Craig L. "Fodder for Cannon: Immigrant Perceptions of the Civil War—The Old Northwest." Ph.D. diss., University of Nebraska, 1976.

Keating, Ryan. "Margaret Cahill and the 9th Regiment Connecticut Volunteer Infantry (Irish): A Middleclass Woman on the Urban Homefront and the Forced Changes of Domesticity." *Connecticut History* 50, no. 1 (Spring 2011).

Kee, Robert. *The Green Flag: A History of Irish Nationalism.* London: Penguin Books, 1972.

Keller, Christian. *Chancellorsville and the Germans.* New York: Fordham University Press, 2007.

———. "Flying Dutchmen and Drunken Irishmen: The Myths and Realities of Ethnic Civil War Soldiers." *Journal of Military History* 73, no. 1 (January 2009).

Keller, Patricia. "Class and Catholic Irish Masculinity in Antebellum America: Young Men on the Make in Chicago." *Journal of American Ethnic History* 28, no. 4 (Summer 2009).

Kellogg, Louis Phelps. "The Story of Wisconsin, 1634–1848: Foreign Immigration in Territorial Times." *Wisconsin Magazine of History* 3, no. 3 (March 1920).

Kenny, Kevin. *Making Sense of the Molly Maguires.* New York: Oxford University Press, 1998.

Kinealy, Christine. *This Great Calamity: The Irish Famine, 1845–52.* Dublin: Gill and Macmillan, 1994.

Klement, Frank L. "Catholics as Copperheads during the Civil War." *Catholic Historical Review* 80, no. 1 (January 1994).

———. *The Copperheads in the Middle West.* Chicago: University of Chicago Press, 1960.

———. *Lincoln's Critics: The Copperheads of the North*. Shippensburg, Penn.: White Mane Books, 1999.

———. *Wisconsin in the Civil War: The Home Front and the Battle Front, 1861–1865*. Madison: State Historical Society of Wisconsin, 2001.

Kleppner, Paul. *The Cross of Culture: A Social Analysis of Midwestern Politics, 1850–1900*. New York: Free Press, 1970.

Knobel, Dale. *"America for Americans": The Nativist Movement in the United States*. New York: Twayne, 1996.

Kohl, Lawrence, and Margaret Richard, eds. *Irish Green, Union Blue: The Civil War Letters of Peter Walsh*. New York: Fordham University Press, 1986.

Kohn, Richard H. "The Social History of the American Soldier: A Review and Prospectus for Research." *American Historical Review* 86, no. 3 (June 1981).

Kurtz, William B. *Excommunicated from the Union: How the Civil War Created a Separate Catholic America*. New York: Fordham University Press, 2015.

Larson, Lawrence H."Draft Riot in Wisconsin, 1862." *Civil War History* 7, no. 4 (December 1961).

Lawson, Melinda. *Patriot Fires: Forging a New American Nationalism in the Civil War*. Lawrence: University Press of Kansas, 2002.

Lee, John J., and Marion R. Casey, eds. *Making the Irish American*. New York: New York University Press, 2006.

Leed, Eric J. *No Man's Land: Combat and Identity in World War One*. New York: Cambridge University Press, 1979.

Lonn, Ella. *Desertion during the Civil War*. Gloucester, Mass.: Peter Smith, 1966.

———. *Foreigners in the Union Army*. Baton Rogue: Louisiana State University Press, 1951.

Lowry, Thomas P. *Don't Shoot that Boy! Abraham Lincoln and Military Justice*. Mason City, Iowa: Savas, 1999.

Lynch, Timothy G. "'Erin's Hope': The Fenian Brotherhood of New York City, 1858–1886." Ph.D. diss., City University of New York, 2004.

Macnamera, Daniel George. *The History of the Ninth Regiment, Massachusetts Volunteer Infantry, June, 1864–June, 1864*. 1899. Reprint, with an introduction by Christian G. Samito, New York: Fordham University Press, 2000.

Mahon, John. *New York's Fighting Sixty-Ninth: A Regimental History of Service in the Civil War's Irish Brigade and the Great War's Rainbow Division*. Jefferson, N.C. and London: McFarland and Co., 2004.

Man, Albon P., Jr. "The Irish in New York in the Early Eighteen-Sixties." *Irish Historical Studies* 7, no. 26 (September 1950).

Manning, Chandra. *What This Cruel War Was Over: Soldiers, Slavery, and the Civil War*. New York: Knopf, 2007.

Marszalek, John F. *Commander of All Lincoln's Armies: The Life of General Henry W. Halleck*. Cambridge, Mass.: Harvard University Press, 2004.

———. "Halleck Captures Corinth," *Civil War Times* 45, no. 1 (2006).

Marten, James. *Sing Not War: Civil War Veterans in Gilded Age America*. Chapel Hill: University of North Carolina Press, 2011.

Mattern, Carolyn J. *Soldiers When They Go: The Story of Camp Randall*. Madison: State Historical Society of Wisconsin, 1981.

McCaffrey, Lawrence J., Michael F. Funchion, Ellen Skerrett, and Charles Fanning, eds. *The Irish in Chicago*. Urbana and Chicago: University of Illinois Press, 1987.

McDonald, M. Justille. *History of the Irish in Wisconsin in the Nineteenth Century*. Washington, D.C.: Catholic University of America Press, 1954.

McGuire, Kathleen D. "The Transatlantic Paddy: The Making of a Transnational Identity in Nineteenth-Century America." Ph.D. diss., University of California, Riverside, 2009.

McKinney, Hannah J. *The Development of Local Public Services, 1650–1860: Lessons from Middletown, Connecticut*. Westport, Conn.: Greenwood Press, 1995.

McManus, Michael J. *Political Abolitionism in Wisconsin, 1840–1860*. Kent, Ohio: Kent State University Press, 1998.

McMurry, Richard. *Atlanta: Last Chance for the Confederacy*. Lincoln: University of Nebraska Press, 2000.

McPherson, James. *Battle Cry of Freedom: The Civil War Era*. New York: Oxford University Press, 2003.

———. *For Cause and Comrades: Why Men Fought in the Civil War*. New York: Oxford University Press, 1997.

Meagher, Timothy J. *Inventing Irish America: Generation, Class, and Ethnic Identity in a New England City*. Notre Dame, Ind.: University of Notre Dame Press, 2001.

Meier, Kathryn Shively. *Nature's Civil War: Common Soldiers and the Environment in 1862 Virginia*. Chapel Hill: University of North Carolina Press, 2013.

*The Metropolitan Catholic Almanac and Laity's Directory: For the United States, Canada, and the British Provinces*. Baltimore: John Murphy and Co., 1861.

Miller, Brian Craig. *Empty Sleeves: Amputation in the Civil War South*. Athens: University of Georgia Press, 2015.

Miller, Kerby. *Emigrants and Exiles: Ireland and the Irish Exodus to North America*. New York: Oxford University Press, 1985.

Mitchell, Reid. *The Vacant Chair: The Northern Soldier Leaves Home*. New York: Oxford University Press, 1993.

Moe, Richard. *The Last Full Measure: The Life and Death of the First Minnesota Volunteers*. St. Paul: Minnesota Historical Society Press, 1993.

Montgomery, David. "The Shuttle and the Cross: Weavers and Artisans in the Kensington Riots of 1844." *Journal of Social History* 5, no. 4 (Summer 1972).

Moore, Frank, ed. *The Rebellion Record: A Diary of American Events, with Documents, Narratives, Illustrative Incidents, Poetry, Etc.* New York: G. P. Putnam, 1862.

Moses, John, and Joseph Kirkland, eds. *History of Chicago, Illinois*. Vol. 2. Chicago: Munsell and Co., 1985.

Mulholland, St. Clair A. *The Story of the 116th Regiment, Pennsylvania Volunteers, in the War of the Rebellion*. 1903. Reprint, edited and with an introduction by Lawrence Frederick Kohl, New York: Fordham University Press, 1996.

Murdock, Eugene C. *One Million Men More: The Civil War Draft in the North*. Madison: State Historical Society of Wisconsin, 1971.

Murphy, Brian J. "The Secret War between Grant and Halleck." *Civil War Times* 45, no. 6 (2006).

Murray, Thomas Hamilton. *The History of the Ninth Regiment, Connecticut Volunteer Infantry, "The Irish Regiment," in the War of the Rebellion, 1861–65*. New Haven: Price, Lee and Adkins Co., 1903.

Neely, Mark E. *The Union Divided: Party Conflicts in the Civil War North*. Cambridge, Mass.: Harvard University Press, 2002.

Nesbit, Robert C. *Wisconsin: A History*. Madison: University of Wisconsin Press, 1930.

Niven, John. *Connecticut for the Union: The Role of the State in the Civil War*. New Haven: Yale University Press, 1965.

Noe, Kenneth. *Reluctant Rebels: The Confederates Who Joined the Army after 1861*. Chapel Hill: University of North Carolina Press, 2010.

O'Connor, Thomas H.. *The Boston Irish: A Political History*. Boston: Northeastern University Press, 1995.

Öfele, Martin W. *True Sons of the Republic: European Immigrants in the Union Army*. Westport, Conn. and London: Praeger, 2008.

*Official Records of the Union and Confederate Navies in the War of the Rebellion*. Series 1, vol. 17. Washington, D.C.: GPO, 1903.

Orcutt, Samuel. A History of the Old Town of Stratford and the City of Bridgeport. Vol. 2. Bridgeport, Conn.: Fairfield Historical Society, 1886.

Pierson, Michael D. *Mutiny at Fort Jackson: The Untold Story of the Fall of New Orleans*. Chapel Hill: University of North Carolina Press, 2008.

Pinheiro, John. "'Religion without Restriction': Anti-Catholicism, All Mexico, and the Treaty of Guadalupe Hidalgo." *Journal of the Early Republic* 3, no. 1 (Spring 2003).

Piston, William Garrett, and Richard W. Hatcher III. *Wilson's Creek: The Second Battle of the Civil War and the Men Who Fought It*. Chapel Hill: University of North Carolina Press, 2000.

Ramold, Steven J. *Across the Divide: Union Soldiers View the Northern Home Front*. New York: New York University Press, 2013.

Ramon, Marta. *A Provisional Dictator: James Stephens and the Fenian Movement*. Dublin: University College Dublin Press, 2007.

Rappaport, Armin. "The Replacement System during the Civil War." In Williams, *Military Analysis of the Civil War*.

Reid, Brian Holden. *America's Civil War: The Operational Battleground*. New York: Prometheus Books, 2008.

Reid, Richard M. *Freedom for Themselves: North Carolina's Black Soldiers in the Civil War Era*. Chapel Hill: University of North Carolina Press, 2008.

*Report of the Proceedings of the 42nd and 43rd Reunions of the Society of the Army of the Tennessee*. Cincinnati: Bacharach Press, 1915.

Richard, Patricia L. *Busy Hands: Images of the Family in the Northern Civil War Effort*. New York: Fordham University Press, 2003.

Richardson, Heather Cox. *The Greatest Nation of the Earth: Republican Economic Policies during the Civil War*. Cambridge, Mass.: Harvard University Press, 1997.

Rippley, La Vern J. *The Immigrant Experience in Wisconsin*. Boston: Twayne, 1985.

Robertson, John Gordon. "Rich Man's War, Poor Man's Opportunity? Civil War Re-Enlistment and the Right to Rise." Ph.D. diss., Carnegie Mellon University, 2009.

Rockey, John L., ed. *History of New Haven County, Connecticut*. Vol. 1. New York: W. W. Preston and Co., 1892.
Roediger, David W. *The Wages of Whiteness: Race and the Making of the American Working Class*. New York: Verso, 1991.
Rolfs, David. *No Peace for the Wicked: Northern Protestant Soldiers and the American Civil War*. Knoxville: University of Tennessee Press, 2009.
Romansky, Thaddeus. "Disunion in the Ranks: Soldiers, Citizenship, and Mutiny in the Union Army." Ph.D. diss., Texas A&M University, 2015.
Rossa, Jeremiah O'Donovan. *Rossa's Recollections, 1838–1898: Memoirs of an Irish Revolutionary*. 1898. Reprint, Guilford, Conn.: Lyons Press, 2004.
Rugh, Susan Sessions. *Our Common Country: Family Farming, Culture, and Community in the Nineteenth-Century Midwest*. Bloomington: Indiana University Press, 2001.
Ryan, Desmond. *The Fenian Chief: A Biography of James Stephens*. Dublin: Gill, 1967.
Ryan, Thomas J. "Out of Ireland and into the Union Army: The Battle over Irish Emigrants." *Irish Sword: Journal of the Military Society of Ireland* 23, no. 91 (2002).
Samito, Christian. *Becoming American under Fire: Irish Americans, African Americans, and the Politics of Citizenship during the Civil War Era*. Ithaca, N.Y.: Cornell University Press, 2009.
———. "The Intersection between Military Justice and Equal Rights: Mutinies, Courts-martial, and Black Civil War Soldiers." *Civil War History* 53, no. 2 (June 2007).
———, ed. *Commanding Boston's Irish Ninth: The Civil War Letters of Colonel Patrick R. Guiney, Ninth Massachusetts Volunteer Infantry*. New York: Fordham University Press, 1998.
Sandow, Robert M. *Deserter Country: Civil War Opposition in the Pennsylvania Appalachians*. New York: Fordham University Press, 2009.
Schafer, Joseph. "Know-Nothingism in Wisconsin." *Wisconsin Magazine of History* 8, no. 1 (September 1924).
Schaffer, Donald. *After the Glory: The Struggles of Black Civil War Veterans*. Lawrence: University Press of Kansas, 2004.
Schantz, Mark S. *Awaiting This Heavenly Country: The Civil War and America's Culture of Death*. Ithaca, N.Y.: Cornell University Press, 2008.
Schenker, Carl. L., Jr., "Ulysses in His Tent: Halleck, Grant, Sherman, and 'The Turning Point of the War.'" *Civil War History* 56, no. 2 (2012).
Schob, David E. *Hired Hands and Plowboys: Farm Labor in the Midwest, 1815–1860*. Chicago: University of Illinois Press, 1975.
Schrier, Arnold. *Ireland and the American Emigration, 1850–1900*. Minneapolis: University of Minnesota Press, 1958.
Seidman, Rachel Filene. "A Monstrous Doctrine? Northern Women on Dependency during the Civil War." In Cimbala and Miller, *An Uncommon Time: The Civil War and the Northern Home Front*.
Sellers, Charles. *The Market Revolution: Jacksonian America, 1815–1846*. New York: Oxford University Press, 1991.

Shannon, William H. *The American Irish: A Political and Social Portrait.* New York: Macmillan, 1963.

Sheffer, Debra J. "'No Sacrifice Is Too Great, Save that of Honor': Honor, Death, and Psychological Combat Trauma in the American Civil War." Ph.D. diss., University of Kansas, 2009.

Sheriff, Carol. *The Artificial River: The Erie Canal and the Paradox of Progress.* New York: Hill and Wang, 1996.

Silber, Nina. *Daughters of the Union: Northern Women Fight in the Civil War.* Cambridge, Mass.: Harvard University Press, 2005.

———. *Gender and the Sectional Conflict.* Chapel Hill: University of North Carolina Press, 2008.

Simon, John Y., ed. *The Papers of Ulysses S. Grant.* Vol. 6, *September 1–December 8, 1862.* Carbondale: University of Southern Illinois Press, 1977.

Slap, Andrew L. *The Doom of Reconstruction: Liberal Republicans in the Civil War Era.* New York: Fordham University Press, 2006.

Slap, Andrew L., and Michael Thomas Smith, eds. *This Distracted and Anarchical People: New Answers to Old Questions about the Civil War–Era North.* New York: Fordham University Press, 2013.

Sletcher, Michael. *New Haven: From Puritanism to the Age of Terrorism.* Chicago: Arcadia Publishing, 2004.

Smith, Hampton, ed. *Brother of Mine: The Civil War Letters of Thomas and William Christie.* St. Paul: Minnesota Historical Society Press, 2011.

Smith, Harold F. "Mulligan and the Irish Brigade." *Journal of the Illinois State Historical Society* 56, no. 2 (Summer 1963): 164–76.

Snay, Mitchell. *Fenians, Freedmen, and Southern Whites: Race and Nationality in the Era of Reconstruction.* Baton Rouge: Louisiana State University Press, 2007.

Stearns, J. W., ed. *The Columbia History of Education in Wisconsin.* Milwaukee: State Committee on Educational Exhibit for Wisconsin, 1893.Sterba, Christopher M. *Good Americans: Italian and Jewish Immigrants during the First World War.* New York: Oxford University Press, 2003.

Steward, Patrick John. "Erin's Hope: Fenianism in the North Atlantic World, 1858–1876." Ph.D. diss., University of Missouri–Columbia, 2003.

Stoker, Donald. *The Grand Design: Strategy and the U.S. Civil War.* New York: Oxford University Press, 2010.

Storey, Margaret. *Loyalty and Loss: Alabama's Unionists in the Civil War and Reconstruction.* Baton Rouge: Louisiana State University Press, 2004)

Strum, Harvey. "Famine Relief from the Garden City to the Green Isle." *Journal of the Illinois State Historical Society* 93, no. 4 (Winter 2000/2001).

Swan, James B. *Chicago's Irish Legion: The 90th Illinois Volunteers in the Civil War.* Carbondale: Southern Illinois University Press, 2009.

Symonds, Craig L. *Stonewall of the West: Patrick Cleburne and the Civil War.* Lawrence: University Press of Kansas, 1997.

Tanner, Robert G. *Retreat to Victory? Confederate Strategy Reconsidered.* Wilmington, Del.: Scholarly Resources Inc., 2001.

Trimble, Richard M., ed. *Brothers 'Til Death: The Civil War Letters of William, Thomas, and Maggie Jones, 1861–1865*. Macon, Ga.: Mercer University Press, 2000.

Truslow, Marian Archer. "Peasants into Patriots: The New York Irish Brigade Recruits and Their Families in the Civil War Era, 1850–1890." Ph.D. diss., New York University, 1994.

Tucker, Phillip Thomas. *Irish Confederates: The Civil War's Forgotten Soldiers*. Abilene, Tex.: McWhiney Foundation Press, 2006.

———. *"God Help the Irish": The History of the Irish Brigade*. Abilene, Tex.: McWhiney Foundation Press, 2007.

*United States Sanitary Commission Bulletin*. Vols. 1–3. New York: Sanitary Commission, 1866.

Walker, Daniel Howe. *What Hath God Wrought: The Transformation of America, 1815–1848*. New York: Oxford University Press, 2007.

Walker, Mabel Gregory. *The Fenian Movement*. Colorado Springs: Ralph Myles Publisher, 1969.

Wallace, Christopher. "The Opportunity to Grow: Springfield, Illinois during the 1850s." Ph.D. diss., Purdue University, 1963.

Waltrous, Jerome Anthony. *Memoirs of Milwaukee County: From the Earliest Historical Times*. Madison, Wis.: Western Historical Association, 1909.

*The War of the Rebellion: Official Records of the Union and Confederate Armies*. Washington, D.C.: GPO, 1899–1900.

Ward, David A. "Amidst a Tempest of Shot and Shell: A History of the Ninety-Sixth Pennsylvania Volunteers." Master's thesis, Southern Connecticut State University, 1988.

Warren, Craig. "'Oh, God, What a Pity!' The Irish Brigade at Fredericksburg and the Creation of a Myth." *Civil War History* 47, no. 3 (September 2001).

Warshauer, Matthew. *Connecticut in the American Civil War: Slavery, Sacrifice, and Survival*. Middletown, Conn.: Wesleyan University Press, 2011.

———. "Copperheads in Connecticut: A Peace Movement that Imperiled the Union." In Slap and Smith, *This Distracted and Anarchical People*.

Warshauer, Matthew, and Michael Sturges. "Difficult Hunting: Accessing Connecticut Patient Records about Post-Traumatic Stress Disorder during the Civil War." *Civil War History* 59, no. 4 (December 2013).

Webber, Jennifer L. *Copperheads: The Rise and Fall of Lincoln's Opponents in the North*. New York: Oxford University Press, 2006.

Welch, Richard. "The Green and the Blue." *Civil War Times* 45, no. 8 (October 2006).

Wescott, M. Ebenezer. *Civil War Letters, 1861 to 1865, Written by a Boy in Blue to His Mother*. 1909.

Wetherington, Mark V. *Plain Folk's Fight: The Civil War and Reconstruction in Piney Woods, Georgia*. Chapel Hill: University of North Carolina Press, 2005.

Wiley, Bell. *The Life of Billy Yank: The Common Soldier of the Union*. Indianapolis: Bobbs-Merrill, 1952.

———. *The Life of Johnny Reb: The Common Soldier of the Confederacy*. Indianapolis: Bobbs-Merrill, 1942.

Williams, David. *Bitterly Divided: The South's Inner Civil War.* New York: Oxford University Press, 2008.

Williams, David., Theresa C. Williams, and R. David Carlson. *Plain Folk in a Rich Man's War: Class and Dissent in Confederate Georgia.* Gainesville: University Press of Florida, 2002.

Williams, T. Harry, ed. *Military Analysis of the Civil War: An Anthology.* Millwood, N.Y.: KTO Press, 1977.

Wilson, David A. *United Irishmen, United States: Immigrant Radicals in the Early Republic.* Ithaca, N.Y.: Cornell University Press, 1998.

Wilson, Keith P. *Campfires of Freedom: The Camp Life of Black Soldiers during the Civil War.* Kent, Ohio: Kent State University Press, 2002.

Wilson, Mark. *The Business of the Civil War: Military Mobilization and the State, 1861–1865.* Baltimore: Johns Hopkins University Press, 2006.

Winters, John D. *The Civil War in Louisiana.* Baton Rouge: Louisiana State University Press, 1963.

Wood, Gordon. *The Radicalism of the American Revolution.* New York, Knopf, 1991.

Woodworth, Steven E. *Nothing but Victory: The Army of the Tennessee, 1861–1865.* New York: Knopf, 2005.

Wylie, Paul. *The Irish General: Thomas Francis Meagher.* Norman: University of Oklahoma Press, 2007.

Young, Warren L. *Minorities and the Military: A Cross-National Study in World Perspective.* Westport, Conn.: Greenwood Press, 1982.

Ziller, Carl. *History of Sheboygan County, Wisconsin, Past and Present.* Vol 2. Chicago: S. J. Clarke Publishing Co., 1912.

# Index

17th Wisconsin: and the Atlanta Campaign of 1864, 179–80; charges against Irish born soldiers in regiment, 122; conflict among officers, 116–17; Corinth, MS, at and around, 102, 106–7; court martial trials in, 120–21; demographics of recruits, 82–87; desertion, 126, 129–30; divisions within, 90–91; funds sent home by soldier, 159; geographic origins of, 81–86; initial organization, 78–80; Irish born volunteers in, 86–87; and the March to the Sea, 180; marital status of soldiers, 159; as a mounted infantry unit, 110; mutiny of, 88–90; optimism in state, 87; Pittsburg Landing, TN, arrival at, 92; reenlistment, 175; and the replacement system, 174–75; response to emancipation, 137; return home, 181; St. Louis, MO, reception in, 91; veteran furlough, 176–77; Vicksburg, MS, at, 109

23rd Illinois: charges against Irish born soldiers in regiment, 122; and conflict among officers, 117–18; Connecticut, views in, 59, 66; court martial trials in, 120–21; demographics of, 36–38; desertion, 126, 128, 130; Fenian movement, links to, 31; geographic origins, 32–34; initial organization, 30–32; at Lexington, MO, 40–42; marital status of soldiers, 159; memorialization, 204, 207–8; James Mulligan, death of, 178; national views in winter of 1861, 95–96; re-muster and demographics of second muster, 97–99; role in mutiny of 17th Wisconsin, 89; in the Shenandoah Valley, 105–6, 108, 186; reenlistment, 176, 178; Wisconsin, views in, 76

69th New York: Connecticut's response, 51, 53, 59, 66; early enlistment and service at Bull Run, 29, 40–42, 50–52; Fenianism, links to, 31; Irish Diaspora, and notion of the, 77; Irish service, accounts of, 77; memory of, 2, 29, 209–210; general courts martial: 120; Wisconsin's response, 76–80

abolition: Democratic Party concerns regarding war, 25, 135–37, 150, 270nn4,6; constitutionality of, 136; opposition to, 136; relationship between abolitionists and Northern riots, 144

Act of Union (Ireland), 8

African American Military Service, 136–38

African Americans: and competition in the work place, 135, 143–46; and population in Connecticut, Illinois, and Wisconsin, 146–47; and relationship with northerners, 272n24

aid societies, 162

alcohol: and discipline, 106, 116, 119, 121–24; and stereotypes, 4, 9

Algiers, LA, 108

Altamonte, VA, 108

American Party, 6. *See also* nativism

Americanization and military service, 41, 245n18, 273–74n1

Anbinder, Tyler, 181

antebellum militia and service in the Civil War, 54–55

Army of the Tennessee, 179

assimilation, 4–5; and debates surrounding military service, 12, 44; sacrifice on the battlefield, 41; and struggles with, 141
Atlanta Campaign, 179–80
Aurora, Illinois, 26–27

Battle of Antietam, 2, 60, 109, 135, 210
Battle of Baton Rouge, 106, 194
Battle of Cedar Creek, 177
Battle of Champion Hill, 109
Battle of Chancellorsville, 252n37
Battle of Corinth, 107–9
Battle of Decatur, 180
Battle of First Bull Run, 2, 29, 38, 40, 42 51, 52, 66, 76, 77, 84, 252n37
Battle of Fisher's Hill, 177
Battle of Fredericksburg, 2–3, 12, 60, 109, 134–35, 142, 210
Battle of Iuka, 107
Battle of Lexington, MO (1861), 39–42, 52, 77–78, 89, 95–97, 157, 171, 178, 189, 195, 209
Battle of New Creek, 178
Battle of Pass Christian, 99–100
Battle of Port Hudson, 137
Battle of Shiloh, 92, 102, 189, 262n15
Battle of Wilson's Creek, 39
Bayou Teche, LA, 110
Beauregard, Gen. PGT, 102
Beloit, WI: Settlement, 71; Irish Demographics, 71–72
Biloxi, MS: and expedition of the Ninth Connecticut, 99
Blight, David, 209
Boston, MA, 1, 4, 6, 9, 19, 47, 53, 62, 65, 74, 134, 142
bounties, 57, 58, 139; in Illinois, 98; and support for families, 161–62; in Wisconsin, 80, 87
Bragg, Gen. Braxton, 106
Brashear, LA, 110, 264n26
bravery, 26, 50, 52, 96, 105, 107, 108, 109, 119, 142, 149
Bremner, Robert, 163
Bridgeport, CT, 55; demographics of Irish residents, 49, 58
Bruce, Susannah Ural, 13, 141, 143, 181
Buckingham, Gov. William, 49, 59–60, 99
Burton, William, 12–13, 141
Butler, Gen. Benjamin, 59–62, 66, 99–100, 122, 216n11

Cahill, Daniel W., views on Irish in America, 5, 244n5, 244n6
Cahill, Thomas: background, 43, 49, 53 63; early war leadership, 49, 53; Fenian Movement, relationship with, 51; leadership, 99–100, 104–5, 264n26; slavery, views on, 64–65, 138; struggles with discipline, 59–61, 115–16, 118, 122–23, 187, 255n47; Vicksburg Campaign, views on, 103–4, 108
Camp Chase, MA, 60–61
Camp Douglas, 119, 187
Camp Parapet, 101–2
Camp Welch (New Haven, CT), 64
causality rates: and declining support for the war, 110; among Irish Brigade, 94
Catholic Church: in Connecticut, 46, 50–53; and expressions of patriotism, 27, 50–53, 74–75, 95, 148; in Illinois, 22, 28; and Irish immigrants, 4, 6–7, 9–10; Ireland, persecution in, 8; and loyalty, 11, 148–49; nativist views of, 21, 28, 50; and New York City Draft Riots, 142–43, 148–49; and priests in the field, 50, 65 255n50; and unionism, 74; and views of secession, 74; in Wisconsin, 74–75
Chicago: and the draft, 140; and Irish demographics, 22–23, 38; and Irish involvement in, 21; and nativism, 21–22; and support for the 23rd Illinois, 33; and urban growth, 19–20
citizen soldier, 55, 68, 84, 89–90, 113, 131, 266n8, 267n20
citizenship: and disorder, 141; and military service, 90, 138, 210; understanding of, 131, 153, 155

commutation fee, 135, 139, 141
competition in the workplace, 145–47, 271n18, 273n1
conflict: between officers, 114–19
Connecticut: demographics of, 49; and Irish organization in 1861, 49; responses to emancipation, 138, 146; responses to the draft; 140–41, 147–48; responses to New York City Draft Riots, 148, 150–54; settlement patterns, 43
conscription. *See* draft
Constitution (transport), 61–62
Copperhead Movement, 11, 139, 150–51, 153
Corcoran, Michael: 2, 11, 26, 50; memory of, 209; recruiting of the 69th New York, 29; view among Wisconsin's Irish, 76–80; visit of the Prince of Wales and subsequent court martial, 29, 249
Corinth, Mississippi, 102–3, 109, 118, 127, 169, 179, 183–84; Battle of, 106–7; on relationship between Gens. Grant and Halleck at Corinth, 262n15
courage: and representations on the home front, 94

Davies, Gen. Thomas, 107
death: economics of, 167; the good death, 167, 282n19; and impact on the family, 166–67, 276n19
democracy: and democratic ideals, 113; and protest, 113
Democratic Party: and accusations of disloyalty, 150–51; and belied in the republican process, 150; and early war support of the Lincoln administration, 26; and Irish support, 10; and Locofoco Movement, 248n2; and loyal dissent, 151–53; and loyal opposition, 151–52; and party principles, 151; and political opposition, 150; and protest of Lincoln, 152; and rejection of the New York City Draft Riots, 152; in Wisconsin, 72–74
demographics: of Irish immigrants, 274n6; and methodology, 248n5
desertion, 112, 119, 122,126–30, 268n25
Detroit, Michigan: and Irish Organization, 32; and links to 23rd Illinois, 34–35
diaspora, connection between, 100
disease: in the 17th Wisconsin, 184–85; and impact on soldiers, 188; in nineteenth-century cities, 187–88; in the Ninth Connecticut, 184–85
disloyalty, 59; accusations of, 133, 150; among Irish, 142; and racism, 143
disorder, 51, 59, 60, 112, 133
Doran, Col. John, 78–82, 84, 86–87; at Corinth, 106–7; and discord in the 17th Wisconsin, 92, 116–17, 118; and with sickness, 184
draft, 111, 126; and charitable aid, 166; and commutation fee, 135; and desertion, 126; impact on local communities, 147–48; reactions to, 139–41; and regimental strength, 175–76; resistance to, 126; and "rich man's war, poor man's fight," 135; and stereotypes, 113, 272n26; in Wisconsin in 1862, 166
Draft Riots, 11, 126, 132–33, 141–42; and the association with Democratic disloyalty, 150–51, 271n18; and the association with Irish Catholic disloyalty, 133–34, 141–43, 269n2, 271n18; and Democratic rejection of, 152; responses to, 146–50, 152–54, 156

Earlville, Illinois, 34, 97
Edward Albert, Prince of Wales, 244n5
Emancipation Proclamation: ideological shifts among soldiers, 138, 156, 272n24; of Gen. John W. Phelps, 64–65; New York City Draft Riots, influence on, 132–35; responses in Connecticut, Illinois, and Wisconsin, 66, 111, 135–37, 141, 156, 270n5
Emmet Guards (CT), 49, 51; and recruiting, 53–54

Emmet, Robert, 46, 81
enlistment: and bounties, 57, 161; and civic duty, 79; and ethnic ties, 80; geographic patterns, 34–35, 37, 55–57, 82–84; impact of draft upon, 139; of Irish in Wisconsin, 74–75; and loyalty, notions of, 79; and manhood, notions of, 75; motivations, 10, 12–14, 32, 35, 68, 74, 90, 278n3; trends among volunteers, 36–38, 57–58, 86–87, 211–12
Executive Committee of the Irish Brigade, 29–30

Fairmont, VA, 108
Farragut, Admrl. David, 100
Federal Pensions, 164, 167; and children, 168–69; and coaching on disability, 283n59; and the democratic tradition of, 171; and mothers, 170; for widows, 167
Fenian Movement, 5–6; 1867 uprising in Ireland, 207; on America as Political Refugee for Irish National Question, 243–44n5; Antebellum Militia Organization, 28–31, 249n20; in Connecticut, 53–55; in Illinois, 28–30, 249n15; invasions of Canada, 207; wartime and post-war organization and action, 180–81, 204–7, 279n15, 285n4, 286nn5–7
Five Points, 9
Fond du Lac, WI: Irish demographics, 71; 74; settlement, 71
Fort Jackson, 100
Fort St. Philip, 100
Fortress Monroe (VA), 62, 178
Frémont, Gen. John C., 38, 40, 65
Fugitive Slave Act, 75

gender,167–168, 247n22
general courts martial, by regiment, 120
Gleeson, David, 13
"good death," the, 113
Grand Army of the Republic, 207–9
Grand Gulf, MS: Grant's capture of, 108
Grant, Gen. Ulysses S., 2, 82, 117; and relationship with Gen. Henry Halleck, 262n15

Halleck, Gen. Henry, 102; and relationship with Gen. Ulysses S. Grant, 262n15
Hannibal Hamlin, 30
Hartford, CT: demographics, 58; demographics of Irish residents, 47–48; early Irish military organization, 49, 50, 51; and Irish recruiting, 53; early history of, 43–44
Harvey, Beauchamp, 81
Harvey, Gov. Louis P., 89; and belief in public assistance, 162
Herrera, Riccardo, 89
home front: and federal support, 163; and nationalism, 245n18; and relief efforts, 163; and stability, 163; and support networks, 158; and transfer of pay, 159–60
Hughes, Archbishop John: and the New York City Draft Riots, 153; and role in antebellum period, 7
Hunter, Gen. David, 65

Ignateiv, Noel, 181
Illinois: and the 23rd Illinois, 20; demographics of state population, 25; responses to the draft; 139–41, 147–48; responses to emancipation, 135–36, 138, 146; responses to New York City Draft Riots, 148, 150–54; settlement patterns, 19–21
industrialization, 243n4
*Irish American* (NY), 50
Irish Brigade (Army of the Potomac): antebellum relationship with Connecticut, 60; impact on Irish morale: 11, 110, 134–135, 142; casualty rates: 94; memory of, 2–3, 11–12, 201, 204, 209–210, 243; views of service at Antietam and Fredericksburg, 109, 134, 142

Irish immigrants: and tradition of military service, 50
Irish Penal Codes, 8

Jackson, William (United Irishmen), 36
Jacobson, Matthew Frye, 181, 249n15

Kee, Robert, 80
Keller, Christian, 92
Klement, Frank, 162
Know-Nothings. *See* nativism

*Lady Elgin* disaster, 75
LaSalle, Illinois: demographics of Irish residents, 24; history, 23–24; Irish enlistments, 37
Lincoln, Abraham: assassination of, 205; and call for troops, 1, 2, 25, 29, 38 51–52, 66; and opposition to, 148–49, 151–52; and war measures, 19, 26, 133–36, 141, 146
Lonn, Ella, 12
Lowell, MA, 60–61
loyal dissent, 134
loyalty: in battle, 106–7, 110; and combatting nativism, 181; in Connecticut, 49; in the context of ethnic organization, 28; and debates over, 132; differences across north, 14; and disorder, 59; Draft Riots, impact of on perceptions of, 11; among draftees, 140–41; dual loyalties, 3, 43; among ethnic soldiers, 95; fear of, 11; among Irish Americans, 209–11, 246n22, 269n2; among Irish in Wisconsin, 73–74; in the language of recruiting, 113; through military service, 155; and the New York City Draft Riots, 133–34, 146; perceptions of, 1, 2, 15, 28; through professions of support for the war, 155–56; questions of, 19, 50; and questions of Irish politics, 126; in response to secession, 25; and sacrifice on the battlefield, 40, 41
Lyon, Gen. Nathaniel, 38–39

Madison, WI: Irish demographics, 70–71; settlement, 70
manhood, 15, 130, 246n22
March to the Sea, 180
McArthur, Brig. Gen. John, 117
McClellan, Gen. George, 136; and 1864 election, 137
McDowell, Gen. Irwin, 77
Meagher, Thomas Francis, 2; and Irish symbolism, 11, 101; and motivation for ethnic organization, 53, 76, 78; and support of the Union war effort, 26, 51
memory: of ethnic service, 109; and generalizations of the Irish American experience, 17; of Irish service, 11–12; of military service, 203–4
Meriden, CT, and Irish recruiting, 53
Middletown, CT, 49
Mignault, Rev. Napoleon, 79
military hierarchy, responses to, 114
military service, notions of inclusion and, 172–73
militia: and antebellum organization, 245n18; and nativism, 45–46, 50, 245n18
Militia Act (1855), 45–46, 50
Miller, Kerby, 141, 143, 181
Milwaukee, WI: Irish demographics, 69–70, settlement, 69
Montgomery Guards (CT), 55
Montgomery, Gen. Richard, 36, 46
morale on the home front, 94
mothers, 170–73
Mullen, Rev. Daniel, 65
Mulholland, Col. St. Claire, 204, 209
Mulligan, James A.: background, 28–29; death, 178; defense of Lexington, 40–41; Fenian movement, involvement with, 30–32, 204, 206, 249n15; frustration with war effort, 106; growing fame, 41, 52, 77–78, 95–96, 252n35, 253n20, 260n2; memorialization, 204, 208–9, 285n2; role in putting down mutiny of 17th Wisconsin, 89;

Mulligan, James A. *(continued)*
struggle with command, 117–18; views on emancipation, 134
muster out of regiments, 180–81
mutiny: of the 17th Wisconsin, 87–91, 114; of Fort Jackson, 100

nationalism and activities on the home front, 277n28
nativism: 4, 6, 8–10, 66, 112, 244n6; in Connecticut, 44–46; in Illinois, 19, 21–22; impact on Irish place, 249n15, 273–74n1; and Irish stereotypes, 8–10, 19; in Lowell, MA, 61; and military service, 14, 43, 44, 66, 83, 95, 245n18, 252n37; and militia purges of 1855, 54; postwar revival of, 11; in postwar years, 181; response to, 45, 131; and the response to the Draft Riots, 133–34; responses to Irish volunteering, 50; and revised views of Irish service, 52; in Wisconsin, 72–73
Neely, Mark, 151
Neff, John, 209
New Creek, VA (1862), 186–87
New Haven, CT: and arrival of Irish immigrants, 44; early history of, 43–44; and nativism, 44–46; and demographics, 57–58; demographics of Irish residents, 46–47; and the draft, 140; early Irish military organization, 49–50; and Irish recruiting, 53; relationship to New York, 51
New Orleans, LA, 108, 169; and immigrant population, 261n11; and the reception of the Ninth Connecticut, 100
New York City: and Irish immigration, 9; and poverty, 9
Ninth Connecticut: at Battle of Baton Rouge, 104–5; at Battle of Pass Christian, 99–100; and Benjamin Butler, 59–62; at Camp Parapet, 102; charges against Irish born soldiers in regiment, 122; conflict among officers, 114–16; court martial trials in, 120–21; demographics, 57–58; desertion, 126, 129–30; disorderly behavior, 59–61; early organization, 50–51, 53; funds sent home by soldier, 159; geographic origins, 54–56; impact of disease, 185–85; and invasion of New Orleans, 100–1; issues with emancipation, 64–66; marital status of soldiers, 159; memorialization of service, 203, 209; motivations for volunteering, 56–57; move to Gulf of Mexico, 62–63; move to Lowell, MA, 60–62; reenlistment, 176; reception by Irish population in New Orleans, 100–2; recruiting in Louisiana, 101–2; in the Shenandoah Valley, 177–78; on Ship Island, 63–64; veteran furlough, 176–77; at Vicksburg (summer of 1862), 103–4
Niven, John, 162, 168
Northwestern Soldier's Fair, 156–57, 162, 166

O'Brien, William Smith, 249n15
O'Connell, Daniel, 273n1
O'Mahony, John, 31, 36, 244n5.
Öfele, Martin, 13, 142
order among ranks, 113
Ottawa, Illinois: and the 23rd Illinois, 32, 33; demographics of Irish residents, 25, 38; history, 24–25; Irish enlistments, 37; and patriotism, 34

Pass Manchac, LA, 108
patriotism, 1, 15, 158, 246n22; and combating nativism, 181; differences across the North, 14; and disorder, 59; in early enlistments, 10; and Irish Americans, 52, 76, 132; memory of, 11; in the responses to the New York City Draft Riots, 135, 146, 150; and sacrifice on the battlefield, 4, 107, 110; through act of volunteering, 61, 78
Peoria, IL, 30
Phelps, Maj. John, 64–65
Phillipi, VA, 108

*The Phoenix* (NY), 5, 14, 31, 244nn5,6
Pittsburg Landing, TN, 92
political machines, 4
Portland, ME, 62
post-traumatic stress disorder, 191–93
Potato Famine: charitable responses to famine immigrants, 164; condition of Ireland prior to famine, 7–8, 244n5; famine impact on Irish immigration to New York, 8; impact of famine on Irish-American memory, 3–4, 243n5; impact of famine on migration to Chicago, 19–22; response in Connecticut to famine immigrants, 44–45, 164
Prentiss, Gen. Benjamin, 116
Price, Gen. Sterling, 77, 95, 106; and Missouri Campaign of 1861, 38–40, 77; 95, 106
Proctorville, LA, 108
promotion and questions of merit, 117
provost duty and experiences, 110
public relief: in Connecticut, Illinois, and Wisconsin, 164; debates over, 160, 164; and the deserving poor, 164; and duty, 166; and growth of, 161–62; growth during the Famine, 164; and patriotism, 166; and religious charities, 164; as support for families, 164

racism among Irish Americans, 135
Randall, Gov. Alexander, 74
Ransom, Gen. Thomas, 109
recruiting: of African American regiments, 137; in Connecticut, 51–56; as ethnic competition, 42, 51; and ethnicity, 36–38, 55–56, 80–81, 86–87; and financial incentives, 58, 80; in Illinois, 26–28, 32–35, 97–98, 176, 178; and links to American nationalism, 10, 74–77; and links to the republic, 8, 27, 52, 74, 90; in Louisiana, 101–2; as a means of undercutting nativism, 27, 28, 35; and notions of patriotism, 26, 51–52, 79, 96; public enthusiasm for, 66; for the re-muster of the 23rd Illinois, 97–98; in response to Irish service 41–42; rhetoric in Wisconsin, 68, 78–84, 87, 179; and sacrifice, 10; and tradition of Irish military service, 26, 27, 76–78; trends among soldiers, 57; of veteran volunteers, 175–76
reenlistment: of 17th Wisconsin, 174–75; of 23rd Illinois, 176; and bounties, 175; of Ninth Connecticut, 176; and reception on the home front, 176–77; and veterans' furlough, 176–77
republicanism: ethos of, 267n20; and Fenian views of, 31; language of, 124; and transatlantic views, 14
"rich man's war, poor man's fight," 135, 141
riots: in Brooklyn, NY, 143; in Buffalo, NY, 143; in Chicago, 143; in Cincinnati, OH, 143; in Detroit, MI, 145; and ethnic stereotypes, 143; and issues of loyalty, 145; in Kensington, PA, 7; in Newburgh, NY, 145; in Toledo, OH, 143; and workplace competition, 143–47
Ripley, MS, 107
Rowlesburg, WV, 108

sacrifice: and growing animosity on the home front, 142; of Irish soldiers, 142; as patriotism, 157, 246n19
Samito, Christian, 13
Sanitary Commission, 156, 162–63
Savannah, GA, 178
Second Battle of Kernstown, 178
Sheridan, Gen. Philip, 178
Sherman, Gen. William T., 179
Shields, Gen. James B., 36
Ship Island, 62–64, 67, 99–100, 102, 115, and impact on soldier health, 184–85
slavery, 99, 136
Springfield, IL, 27, 30, 95, 137, 139, 147, 150, 164–65
St. Louis, MO, 88
state quotas during initial call for troops, 29, 30, 32
Stephens, James, 204–5, 285n4

stereotypes: of ethnic disorder, 106, 130; of Irish soldiers, 99; and military service, 113; surrounding ethnicity, 112–13
substitutes, 126, 139, 141, 148, 174–76
supply, frustration with, 59

Taylor, Gen. Richard, 110
Temperance Movement, 52, 123
Thibodaux, LA, 108
Third Battle of Winchester, 177
Thomas, Gen. Lorenzo, 137
Tyler, Gen. Richard, 108

Union Guards (WI), 75
Union War, 136, 137
United Irishmen, 36

Vallandigham, Clemet, 144
Van Dorn, Gen. Earl, 102, 104, 107
veterans: and debates over, 280n18; and memorialization, 182; and postwar life, 174, 182; and postwar mobility, 193–200, 284n42
veterans' homes, 193, 283n36
Vicksburg, MS: experiences of the Ninth Connecticut in the Canal Zone, 101, 103–5, 262n17; impact of Vicksburg on soldiers, 184, 189, 193; Ninth Connecticut's Vicksburg Memorial, 203, 285n1; Vicksburg Campaign, 108–9, 262n16, 264nn28,29
violence against African Americans, 143

Wade, Gen. Hampton, 180
war work, 155–57
Warren, Craig, 11–12, 201
Waterbury: demographics of Irish residents, 49; early Irish military organization, 49–50
Wheeler, Gen. Joseph, 180
Whig Party and nativism, 10
whiteness studies, 4, 273n1
widows, 158, 164, 167–68
Wiley, Bell, 12
Williams, Gen. Thomas, 103; death, 104
Winchester, VA (1862), 186
Winters, John, 104
Wisconsin: Irish immigration to, 68–69; demographics, 72; rise of Irish power, 72; responses to the draft; 139–41, 147–48; responses to emancipation, 135, 137, 146; responses to New York City Draft Riots, 148, 150–54
women, support on the home front, 155–58

Yates, Gov. Richard, 28–29, 117; and relief efforts in Illinois, 165
Yorktown Peninsula, 62
Young Ireland, 105, 249n15
Young, Warren, 90, 210

THE NORTH'S CIVIL WAR
Andrew L. Slap, series editor

Anita Palladino, ed., *Diary of a Yankee Engineer: The Civil War Story of John H. Westervelt, Engineer, 1st New York Volunteer Engineer Corps.*

Herman Belz, *Abraham Lincoln, Constitutionalism, and Equal Rights in the Civil War Era.*

Earl J. Hess, *Liberty, Virtue, and Progress: Northerners and Their War for the Union.* Second revised edition, with a new introduction by the author.

William L. Burton, *Melting Pot Soldiers: The Union's Ethnic Regiments.*

Hans L. Trefousse, *Carl Schurz: A Biography.*

Stephen W. Sears, ed., *Mr. Dunn Browne's Experiences in the Army: The Civil War Letters of Samuel W. Fiske.*

Jean H. Baker, *Affairs of Party: The Political Culture of Northern Democrats in the Mid-Nineteenth Century.*

Frank L. Klement, *The Limits of Dissent: Clement L. Vallandigham and the Civil War.* With a new introduction by Steven K. Rogstad.

Lawrence N. Powell, *New Masters: Northern Planters during the Civil War and Reconstruction.*

John A. Carpenter, *Sword and Olive Branch: Oliver Otis Howard.*

Thomas F. Schwartz, ed., *"For a Vast Future Also": Essays from the* Journal of the Abraham Lincoln Association.

Mark De Wolfe Howe, ed., *Touched with Fire: Civil War Letters and Diary of Oliver Wendell Holmes, Jr.* With a new introduction by David Burton.

Harold Adams Small, ed., *The Road to Richmond: The Civil War Letters of Major Abner R. Small of the 16th Maine Volunteers.* With a new introduction by Earl J. Hess.

Eric A. Campbell, ed., *"A Grand Terrible Dramma": From Gettysburg to Petersburg: The Civil War Letters of Charles Wellington Reed.* Illustrated by Reed's Civil War sketches.

Herbert Mitgang, ed., *Abraham Lincoln: A Press Portrait.*

Harold Holzer, ed., *Prang's Civil War Pictures: The Complete Battle Chromos of Louis Prang.*

Harold Holzer, ed., *State of the Union: New York and the Civil War.*

Paul A. Cimbala and Randall M. Miller, eds., *Union Soldiers and the Northern Home Front: Wartime Experiences, Postwar Adjustments.*

Mark A. Snell, *From First to Last: The Life of Major General William B. Franklin.*

Paul A. Cimbala and Randall M. Miller, eds., *An Uncommon Time: The Civil War and the Northern Home Front.*

John Y. Simon and Harold Holzer, eds., *The Lincoln Forum: Rediscovering Abraham Lincoln.*

Thomas F. Curran, *Soldiers of Peace: Civil War Pacifism and the Postwar Radical Peace Movement.*

Kyle S. Sinisi, *Sacred Debts: State Civil War Claims and American Federalism, 1861–1880.*

Russell L. Johnson, *Warriors into Workers: The Civil War and the Formation of Urban-Industrial Society in a Northern City.*

Peter J. Parish, *The North and the Nation in the Era of the Civil War.* Edited by Adam L. P. Smith and Susan-Mary Grant.

Patricia Richard, *Busy Hands: Images of the Family in the Northern Civil War Effort.*

Michael S. Green, *Freedom, Union, and Power: The Mind of the Republican Party During the Civil War.*

Christian G. Samito, ed., *Fear Was Not In Him: The Civil War Letters of Major General Francis S. Barlow, U.S.A.*

John S. Collier and Bonnie B. Collier, eds., *Yours for the Union: The Civil War Letters of John W. Chase, First Massachusetts Light Artillery.*

Grace Palladino, *Another Civil War: Labor, Capital, and the State in the Anthracite Regions of Pennsylvania, 1840–1868.*

Christian B. Keller, *Chancellorsville and the Germans: Nativism, Ethnicity, and Civil War Memory.*

Sidney George Fisher, *A Philadelphia Perspective: The Civil War Diary of Sidney George Fisher.* Edited and with a new Introduction by Jonathan W. White.

Robert M. Sandow, *Deserter Country: Civil War Opposition in the Pennsylvania Appalachians.*

Craig L. Symonds, ed., *Union Combined Operations in the Civil War.*

Harold Holzer, Craig L. Symonds, and Frank L. Williams, eds., *The Lincoln Assassination: Crime and Punishment, Myth and Memory.* A Lincoln Forum Book.

Earl F. Mulderink III, *New Bedford's Civil War.*

David G. Smith, *On the Edge of Freedom: The Fugitive Slave Issue in South Central Pennsylvania, 1820–1870.*

George Washington Williams, *A History of the Negro Troops in the War of the Rebellion, 1861–1865.* Introduction by John David Smith.

Randall M. Miller, ed., *Lincoln and Leadership: Military, Political, and Religious Decision Making.*

Andrew L. Slap and Michael Thomas Smith, eds., *This Distracted and Anarchical People: New Answers for Old Questions about the Civil War–Era North.*

Paul D. Moreno and Johnathan O'Neill, eds., *Constitutionalism in the Approach and Aftermath of the Civil War.*

Steve Longenecker, *Gettysburg Religion: Refinement, Diversity, and Race in the Antebellum and Civil War Border North.*

Harold Holzer, Craig L. Symonds, and Frank L. Williams, eds., *Exploring Lincoln: Great Historians Reappraise Our Greatest President.* A Lincoln Forum Book.

Lorien Foote and Kanisorn Wongsrichanalai, eds., *So Conceived and So Dedicated: Intellectual Life in the Civil War–Era North.*

William B. Kurtz, *Excommunicated from the Union: How the Civil War Created a Separate Catholic America.*

Kanisorn Wongsrichanalai, *Northern Character: College-Educated New Englanders, Honor, Nationalism, and Leadership in the Civil War Era.*

Ryan W. Keating, *Shades of Green: Irish Regiments, American Soldiers, and Local Communities in the Civil War Era.*